DESIGNING DATA-INTENSIVE
WEB APPLICATIONS

The Morgan Kaufmann Series in Data Management Systems

Management of Heterogeneous and Autonomous Database Systems
Edited by Ahmed Elmagarmid, Marek Rusinkiewicz, and Amit Sheth

Object-Relational DBMSs: Tracking the Next Great Wave, Second Edition
Michael Stonebraker and Paul Brown,with Dorothy Moore

A Complete Guide to DB2 Universal Database
Don Chamberlin

Universal Database Management: A Guide to Object/Relational Technology
Cynthia Maro Saracco

Readings in Database Systems, Third Edition
Edited by Michael Stonebraker and Joseph M. Hellerstein

Understanding SQL's Stored Procedures: A Complete Guide to SQL/PSM
Jim Melton

Principles of Multimedia Database Systems
V. S. Subrahmanian

Principles of Database Query Processing for Advanced Applications
Clement T. Yu and Weiyi Meng

Advanced Database Systems
Carlo Zaniolo, Stefano Ceri, Christos Faloutsos, Richard T. Snodgrass,
V. S. Subrahmanian, and Roberto Zicari

Principles of Transaction Processing
Philip A. Bernstein and Eric Newcomer

Using the New DB2: IBMs Object-Relational Database System
Don Chamberlin

Distributed Algorithms
Nancy A. Lynch

Active Database Systems: Triggers and Rules For Advanced Database Processing
Edited by Jennifer Widom and Stefano Ceri

Migrating Legacy Systems: Gateways, Interfaces, & the Incremental Approach
Michael L. Brodie and Michael Stonebraker

Atomic Transactions
Nancy Lynch, Michael Merritt, William Weihl, and Alan Fekete

Query Processing for Advanced Database Systems
Edited by Johann Christoph Freytag, David Maier, and Gottfried Vossen

Transaction Processing: Concepts and Techniques
Jim Gray and Andreas Reuter

Building an Object-Oriented Database System: The Story of O_2
Edited by François Bancilhon, Claude Delobel, and Paris Kanellakis

Database Transaction Models for Advanced Applications
Edited by Ahmed K. Elmagarmid

A Guide to Developing Client/Server SQL Applications
Setrag Khoshafian, Arvola Chan, Anna Wong, and Harry K. T. Wong

The Benchmark Handbook for Database and Transaction Processing Systems, Second Edition
Edited by Jim Gray

Camelot and Avalon: A Distributed Transaction Facility
Edited by Jeffrey L. Eppinger, Lily B. Mummert, and Alfred Z. Spector

Readings in Object-Oriented Database Systems
Edited by Stanley B. Zdonik and David Maier

DESIGNING DATA-INTENSIVE WEB APPLICATIONS

STEFANO CERI
Politecnico di Milano

PIERO FRATERNALI
Politecnico di Milano

ALDO BONGIO
Web Ratio

MARCO BRAMBILLA
Politecnico di Milano

SARA COMAI
Politecnico di Milano

MARISTELLA MATERA
Politecnico di Milano

MORGAN KAUFMANN PUBLISHERS

AN IMPRINT OF ELSEVIER SCIENCE

AMSTERDAM   BOSTON   LONDON   NEW YORK
OXFORD   PARIS   SAN DIEGO   SAN FRANCISCO
SINGAPORE   SYDNEY   TOKYO

Senior Editor	Lothlórien Homet
Publishing Services Manager	Edward Wade
Editorial Assistant	Corina Derman
Project Management	Matrix Productions, Inc.
Cover Design	Ross Carron Design
Cover Image	Getty Images
Text Design	Frances Baca Design
Composition	Omegatype Typography, Inc.
Copyeditor	Jennifer Ashley
Proofreader	Sean Tape
Indexer	Jeanne Busemeyer
Interior Printer	The Maple-Vail Book Manufacturing Group
Cover Printer	Phoenix Color Corporation

Designations used by companies to distinguish their products are often claimed as trademarks or registered trademarks. In all instances in which Morgan Kaufmann Publishers is aware of a claim, the product names appear in initial capital or all capital letters. Readers, however, should contact the appropriate companies for more complete information regarding trademarks and registration.

Morgan Kaufmann Publishers
An Imprint of Elsevier Science (USA)
340 Pine Street, Sixth Floor,
San Francisco, CA 94104–3205
www.mkp.com

Library of Congress Control Number: 2002114096
ISBN: 1–55860–843–5

This book is printed on acid-free paper.

Foreword

Adam Bosworth

Chief Architect and Senior Vice President of Engineering, BEA

I confess, at the start, to a sense of being inadequate to the job of writing the foreword to this book. I'm certainly not an academic. I developed my skills in industry and like to say I'm a simple country boy from Vermont. The authors of this book are dazzlingly bright, well-educated, and cosmopolitan, equally at home in Milano or at Stanford. I first met with the authors in 2000 while I was in the throes of building a startup, and they came and showed me a remarkably simple and elegant model for constructing data-centric applications. And as I watched it unfold in front of me, my entire working life flashed before my eyes. I've spent a third of that life helping build relational databases and tools for using them (OLAP, Reflex, Access, ODBC, SQL Server, Data Access Objects), another third helping build user interfaces and tools for constructing applications (VB, OLE controls, Form Designers, Quattro), and the final and most recent third on building plumbing and tools for using the Web and constructing applications on the Web (Internet Explorer's HTML engine, Active Server Pages, XML/XSLT/DOC/ XML Query, Web Services, and Web Logic Workshop). And there it was, built by a group of professors: a synthesis of all of these elements that reduced the problem to something very nearly as simple and elegant as the relational calculus. I was both delighted and in awe.

The authors took on a huge challenge in putting together WebML. They endeavored to create a formal language that could describe the entire range of user interfaces for traversing and viewing (and updating) data that might make sense. Some may be surprised that I don't limit the statement above to "make sense for the Web," but in point of fact, it is my belief that they wanted to have formalism for all data-centric user interfaces. This was, and is, an audacious goal. If successful, it can have the same effect on data-centric user interfaces that the relational calculus had on data access. In an age where the user interface will need to step up to its biggest challenge, namely being able to morph to fit different form factors and user interface paradigms, this is perhaps peculiarly apposite.

Furthermore, each chapter takes care to spell-out how the formalisms thus developed can be encoded in UML, which enables a wide range of compatible authoring tools to be built that can collaborate at a very high level. The potentials for productivity, if this holds true, are enormous. Add in the standardization that all "operations units" express themselves as Web Services and it suddenly becomes possible to have truly portable and interoperable Web sites where multiple sets of disparate developers can work seamlessly together in harmony and with great productivity. In short, I'm very excited by the potential.

So, how did they do?

Many of the problems we (industry) *never* solved particularly well in products heretofore (for example, building lists to select items for viewing), even with the richness of a GUI applications environment, are suddenly and elegantly resolved through the "Index Units." Access, PowerBuilder, and Delphi understood the idea of such building blocks (typically inelegantly called *forms* and known as *units* in WebML), but they never carefully formalized all the possible ways in which linkages between units could occur.

Another problem that has bedeviled the world of data-centric applications construction has been that of optional parameters. If the user selects a filtering value, such as cost range, then it should be used to filter the resulting set. But if not, then any price should be retrieved. Customers have gone through agony building the complex *if* logic into SQL to handle the case of the parameter either being null (in which case there should be no predicate test) or not null (in which case there should be, especially when there are several possible limiting values). WebML's concept of "optional predicates" using the "implied" keyword hides a remarkable amount of heavy lifting from the developer.

Probably the biggest problem never well-solved in the world of VB, Access, PowerBuilder, and Delphi was that of context. In the real world of applications, customers expect the applications to understand the context in which they are working. For example, traversing to a screen that lists employees from a departmental screen from a business unit screen will typically mean viewing the employees for that department for that business unit. On the other hand, traversing from a Key Performers Screen to a Titles Screen to an employee's screen would typically mean viewing the key performers for that title. Simple, right? Obvious? It is rather tricky to implement, in fact, in such a normalized world. In WebML this is solved simply and elegantly using parametric selectors, contextual links, global parameters, and, occasionally, optional or "implicit" predicates. The multi-valued idea of passing in a set of legal values is exquisitely elegant. The defaults make simple and intuitive sense, thus removing a huge amount of work. Look carefully at Section 3.4 and consider how much work you can save.

All this reminds those of us in industry of a basic truth. It behooves us to work closely and constantly with those in academia because the result will be a level of cleanliness, formalism, and elegance without which the solutions often feel like pastiches or Band-Aids that are ultimately unsatisfactory. As the "father" of Access, I was, and am, abashed.

Having made the point so trenchantly in the area of data-centric user interface in general with units and links, WebML doesn't rest on its laurels. It goes on to consider, in depth, the user interface paradigms that prevail specifically on the Web, and provides paradigms for higher-level components, pages (including home, default, and landmark ones), and areas. As with the formalism of their language for navigating through data, these formalisms both enable a huge range of possibilities and save a huge amount of developer work. The typical industry solution today, for example, for always including a link to the anchoring "home page" is to use a template for each page. But often the model is nested, and here the template model tends to break down because it is too static. WebML enables a graceful model for including these requisite navigation links without any painful plumbing on the programmer's part. The same is true for nested pages, which neatly shows the rich types of user interface that can be assembled as easily as I used to build buildings out of building blocks as a child. This is, of course, every developer's dream. One of the nicer points of this model is that the developer can always decide very cleanly how much should be done on one page (thus saving navigations) and how much should be cleanly separated across pages. The authors have thought extremely carefully about intra-page operations, not just inter-page ones and this is the stuff of good Web sites and good UI design.

What about actually getting work done? Does this model describe the actions that must be taken? Can real-world work be performed? Historically, our formalism for this has been code, or "built-in actions" in our user interface components. It has been very difficult to understand the actions in the overall context of choreography. What happens when the insertion of the customer fails versus when it succeeds? A nice pairing of two concepts, operations units with success links (OK) and failure links (KO)—proving either that the authors are boxing aficionados or have a sense of humor—has been used to cover an astonishing range of actions: Inserting, Deleting, Updating, invoking arbitrary code with the entire requisite context. My company, BEA, is particularly excited about this idea because it parallels some work we've been doing in page navigation to help our customers better handle site layout and management and the early indications are extremely promising. This model of interleaving operations with user interface elements is extremely powerful. Add in an applications model for accessing the inputs and publishing the outputs (for which I believe Web Services will turn out to be extremely well suited) and—*voilà!*—instant extensibility. At the same time, the basic predefined operations enable an enormous amount of standard work to be built with total interoperability and portability and, given suitable tools, built by the same sort of customers who use Access every day.

One way to think about WebML is as a spreadsheet for user interface. In essence, recalculation is used anytime an input is changed to "recompute" a page. Indeed, like spreadsheets, this process can be non-deterministic and even circular. Years ago I built a spreadsheet called Quattro. As with all spreadsheets, it had a complex calculation engine designed to resolve all expressions to their "correct values" wherever possible. The interaction between this declarative model of applications construction (so clearly understandable by tens or even hundreds of millions of customers) and that of procedural logic (so clearly required but understandable by only a million or so programmers) has always fascinated me. If, in fact, WebML enables the construction of data-centric user interfaces by the same volume of people who have been able to construct spreadsheets, this will be truly exciting.

Another, very different way to think about WebML is as a sort of super workflow. Conceptually, these "operations" and rich transacted sequences and workflows can be melded together to form overall sites and workflows. It is as though the world of Site Description, Page Layout, and BPM had been seamlessly unified and simplified in the process. A long time ago, a company called Metaphor started down this road with a product called capsules. What has been built here is a roadmap to complete that journey, at least in the context of constructing data-centric user interfaces.

There are some hard issues that remain to be resolved:

1 How do you model a UI to reflect history? If, for example, the tabs for navigation should only appear as the user navigates into them, as many wizards do today, how would one accomplish this in WebML? Much of this can be handled with the use of global parameters, but the conditional display of elements used for navigation doesn't seem to be covered.

2. How does the world of asynchrony interact with this model? There is a simple example of a credit card charge in Chapter 4 that assumes that it is OK to simply block and wait for approval/denial before returning the next page. Alas, we know that this is not always true.

3. How does the user interface gracefully morph to reflect the various roles that the user may hold? Chapter 7's methodology and Section 9.4.4 seem to assume that there can be different site maps for each possible class of user. In practice, this often turns out to be unworkable and pages must morph to reflect the rights of the user, meaning that in some cases data and links will or will not be visible and data will or will not be modifiable. To be clear, the model does support personalization, just not dynamic roles-based modification.

4. In a world where pages will be increasingly binding to applications data through Web services rather than directly to data through SQL, how does this model hold up? What changes are required?

5. As Google has so brilliantly shown, often the best way to create an index unit is through a simple text search ordered by linkages. This model cannot be expressed by relational databases in any reasonable manner. This isn't really a limitation of WebML, but as database designers wake up to the obvious and start to build this in as a core competence, the WebML predicates will need to extend to describe this model for populating a data set.

6. Will customers really use the formal design methodology carefully laid out in Chapters 7 through 10? It isn't clear. Customers in the real world have a greater fondness for bottom-up implementation rather than top-down design, much to the despair and frustration of IT professionals everywhere. Yet, in the end, customers have learned to do data design, and ER and UML diagrams have become a staple of most large-scale companies. It is entirely possible that we will see the same here.

Overall, WebML is an audacious and impressive achievement. It holds together elegantly and seems to be able to construct anything through suitable use of composition and the right building blocks. It is impressive that WEBML already has both a language and a visual design model worked out. The concerns above merely whet the appetite and suggest that this model will prove fruitful.

While I do suspect that the advent of Web services will alter this model in subtle but important ways, it is nevertheless one of the most promising directions I've seen. It may do for applications construction what SQL and ODBC/JDBC did for data access, or what Web services is now doing for applications-to-applications communication, namely providing a stable standards-based model that ultimately revolutionizes the industry and increases the number of people who can accomplish the goal by an order of magnitude or more. Bravo!

Contents

Preface

This book is about building data-intensive Web applications. By this term, we refer to Web sites for accessing and maintaining large amounts of structured data, typically stored as records in a database management system. Today, data-intensive Web applications are the predominant kind of application found on the Web; sites for online trading and e-commerce, institutional Web sites of private and public organizations, digital libraries, corporate portals, community sites are all examples of data-intensive Web applications.

The development of a data-intensive Web application is a multi-disciplinary activity, which requires a variety of skills, necessary to address very heterogeneous tasks, like the design of data structures for storing content, the conception of hypertext interfaces for information browsing and content management, the creation of effective presentation styles, the assembly of robust and high-performance architectures, and the integration with legacy applications and external services. The development and maintenance of data-intensive Web applications requires all the tools and techniques of software engineering, including a well-organized software development process, appropriate design concepts and notations, and guidelines on how to conduct the various activities.

By looking at the way in which data-intensive Web applications are built today and at the tools available to developers, one realizes soon that the software engineering principles and pragmatics are not exploited to their full potential. Designers often construct Web applications by applying the best practices and methods they have learned in developing other kinds of software systems, like enterprise information systems and object-oriented applications. Such practices work well for the "conventional" part of Web application development, for example, the design of the data structures and of the business logic at the back-end, but they do not address the specificity of a "Web" application, which is the delivery of content and services using an hypertextual front-end. This gap is particularly apparent in the design concepts and notations: when it comes to specifying the front-end of their Web application, development teams resort to rather rudimentary tools, like paper and pencil or HTML mock-ups. This situation, which we have frequently witnessed also in very large organizations well equipped with software engineering tools, demands for an adaptation of the software development process, capable of addressing the characterizing features of Web applications. The Web application lifecycle should be built around a solid nucleus of

Web-centric concepts and notations, and supported by specific guidelines on how to put such concepts to work.

The contribution of this book is the proposal of a mix of concepts, notations, and techniques for the construction of data-intensive Web applications, which can be used by Web development teams to support all the activities of the application lifecycle, from analysis to deployment and evolution.

The proposed mix blends traditional ingredients well known to developers, like conceptual data design with the Entity-Relationship model and Use Case specification with UML, with new concepts and methods for the design of hypertexts, which are central to Web development. However, the value of the proposed approach is not in the individual ingredients, but in the definition of a systematic framework in which the activities of Web applications development can be organized according to the fundamental principles of software engineering, and all tasks, including the more Web-centric ones, find the adequate support in appropriate concepts, notations, and techniques.

The distinguishing feature of this development framework is the emphasis on conceptual modeling. Conceptual modeling has proven successful in many software fields; in database design, where the Entity-Relationship model offers a high-level and intuitive notation for communicating data requirements between designers and non-technical people, and is the base for creating high quality database schemas; in object-oriented applications, where notations like the Unified Modeling Language have considerably raised the level at which developers document and reason about their applications. We advocate that these benefits should apply also to the design of data-intensive Web applications, which should be specified using a high-level, visual, and intuitive notation, easily communicable to non-technical users, and helpful to the application implementers.

Therefore, this book proposes a high-level modeling language for hypertext specification, called Web Modeling Language (WebML). In essence, WebML consists of simple visual concepts for expressing a hypertext as a set of pages made up of linked content units and operations, and for binding such content units and operations to the data they refer to.

WebML follows the style of well-known conceptual modeling languages like Entity-Relationship and UML: every concept has a graphical representation, and specifications are diagrams. Therefore, the reader should not worry about the need to learn yet another language. As for the Entity-Relationship constructs, also WebML diagrams could be represented using the UML syntax, possibly with some loss of conciseness, but not of expressive power.

However, we stress that concepts are more important than notations, and that the methods for applying concepts are even more important. Therefore, in the book we guide the reader both in learning the needed modeling concepts, Entity-Relationship and WebML, and in applying such concepts to the specification and design of a Web application, through such activities as requirements specification, data design, and hypertext design. Moreover, despite the slant toward conceptual modeling, we also focus upon the many problems of implementing and deploying a data-intensive Web application. The first chapter and the last part of the book are entirely devoted to technological matters, and show to the interested reader how to transform the conceptual design of a Web application into software components running on the current Web and database technologies, including HTTP, HTML, XML, XSL, relational databases and SQL, server side scripting languages and tag libraries, application servers, and caching architectures.

Last but not least, the book ends with a mention about CASE tools supporting the proposed lifecycle, because the benefits of applying conceptual modeling and a structured development process multiply, if adequate tools are available. All the proposed notations fit perfectly in the commercial tool suites popular among developers, like Entity-Relationship and UML editors and code generators. In particular, WebML can be easily supported, either by representing WebML diagrams using UML, or by exploiting WebML-aware tools, an example of which is presented in the last chapter of the book.

Book Organization and Chapter Summaries

The book is structured in four parts. The first part introduces the technological context in which development takes place; the second part presents the modeling languages used in the book, Entity-Relationship and WebML; the third part defines the software development process; the fourth part focuses on the implementation of data-intensive Web applications on top of modern Web-enabled architectures.

All chapters have a regular structure, with a motivational introduction that states the problem treated in the chapter, a central part that defines the proposed solution, and a conclusion, which summarizes the results. In the chapters devoted to the development process, the design steps are applied to a running case, which is progressively followed from requirements analysis to implementation.

Part I, including Chapter 1, summarizes the technologies relevant to data-intensive Web application development.

Chapter 1 contains a broad overview of the fundamental technologies employed in the construction of data-intensive Web applications. The chapter briefly illustrates the basic protocol and languages of the Web (HTTP, HTML, and client-side scripting and components); it focuses on XML, the new paradigm for content structuring and exchange, and on its collateral standards for document transformation (XSL and XQuery); then it discusses the second ingredient of data-intensive Web applications, relational databases, and the associated query language (SQL) and interoperability standards (ODBC and JDBC). Finally, it explains the architectures and languages for building dynamic Web pages, including Java servlets, server-side scripting languages such as ASP and JSP, tag libraries, and application server architectures. The chapter ends with the discussion of multi-device content publishing.

Part II, including Chapters 2–5, is dedicated to the presentation of the modeling languages used in the book.

Chapter 2 describes the primitives of the Entity-Relationship data modeling language. The fundamental elements of structure modeling are *entities,* defined as containers of data elements, and *relationships,* defined as semantic associations between entities. Entities have named properties, called attributes, with an associated type. Entities can be organized in generalization hierarchies, and relationships can be restricted by means of cardinality constraints. The chapter also shows how to specify attributes and relationships whose content can be determined from other data elements, by writing declarative expressions using the Object Constraint Language (OCL).

Chapter 3 describes the WebML hypertext modeling language, which is based on the notion of units, pages, and links. *Units* describe the elementary pieces of content to be displayed, *pages* indicate how units should be assembled together, and *links* describe the connections between units and/or pages. Multiple hypertexts, called *site views,* may be defined over the same content, to offer different viewpoints to different users. The modeling primitives are introduced gradually, using many examples inspired to frequently used hypertext configurations.

Chapter 4 describes the extension of the hypertext model for supporting content management functions, like the update of personal information, the filling of shopping carts, and so on. New constructs are introduced for representing operations, which are either predefined or generic. Predefined operations represent typical content management and utility functions normally found in Web sites, like the creation, deletion, and modification of objects, the user's login and logout, and the delivery of e-mail messages; generic operations represent black-box functions and enable the integration of WebML applications with external services.

Chapter 5 concentrates on clarifying the meaning of hypertexts with an arbitrary structure of pages, units, and links. The chapter also presents a simple but complete high-level procedure for computing the content of hypertext pages, which highlights the operational semantics of WebML and paves the way for the discussion on how to implement hypertext constructs, which is the subject of Part IV of the book.

Part III, including Chapters 6–9, presents the development process of data-intensive Web applications.

Chapter 6 is an overview of the application lifecycle. It discusses the specification, design, and implementation activities required to build a data-intensive Web application, by briefly describing the goals and tasks of each development phase.

Chapter 7 focuses on requirement analysis, an activity dedicated to the collection and specification of the application requirements, preliminary to the modeling and design phases. Requirements collection focuses on identifying users and groups, defining functional, data, and personalization requirements, as well as on nonfunctional requirements about presentation, usability, performance, availability, scalability, security, and maintainability. Functional requirements are formalized by means of UML use case diagrams; the core concepts and site views are expressed by means of a data dictionary and of site view maps; finally, visual style guidelines are expressed in the form of interface mock-ups.

Chapter 8 addresses the activity of data design and shows the particular flavor that this task assumes in the Web context. The data structure of Web applications often presents a regular organization, in which several interconnected sub-schemas can be recognized, each one centered on a "core entity" representing a fundamental business object. As a consequence, the design process assumes a regular shape too; it starts from the specification of the core concepts, which form the backbone of the data schema, and proceeds iteratively by adding four kinds of sub-schemas, which represent the internal components of core concepts, the interconnections for supporting navigation, the auxiliary objects for facilitating the access to the core content, and the concepts for supporting personalization.

Chapter 9 describes the hypertext design activities. Design proceeds in a top-down way: initially, a draft hypertext schema is obtained by partitioning each site view identified during requirements analysis into areas, and assigning a set of functions to each area, which support the browsing of core, access or interconnection objects, or content management operations. Then, the draft schema of each area is refined into a detailed schema, specified in WebML; in this phase, the designer establishes the actual units, links, operations, and pages of each site view. Hypertext design is facilitated by the usage of design patterns, which offer proved solutions to typical page configuration requirements.

Part IV, comprising Chapters 10–14, is dedicated to the implementation and deployment of data-intensive Web applications.

Chapter 10 concentrates on architecture design and is preliminary to the discussion of implementation. It reviews the reference architectures that can be used for building data-intensive Web applications and the criteria for choosing among the alternative options. The chapter specifically addresses the nonfunctional requirements of performance, security, availability, and scalability, and outlines the design decisions and trade-offs that must be faced to ensure the required level of service. The chapter ends with a section devoted to performance evaluation and caching, two important aspects of the design of Web architectures.

Chapter 11 deals with the mapping of conceptual data schemas onto the physical data sources. Various alternative scenarios are discussed, with a different degree of reuse of the existing schemas and content. The chapter starts by presenting the standard mapping rules for transforming a given Entity-Relationship schema into a relational database schema. Then it addresses the implementation of the relational schema in the context of the corporate data infrastructure, a task that presents several design choices and trade-offs, related to the problems of schema integration, data integration, and replication management.

Chapter 12 describes how to encode WebML pages into server-side programs. As a reference, the explanation adopts the Java Server Pages (JSP) scripting language and the JDBC database connection interface, but the discussion can be easily adapted to different platforms, such as the Microsoft's .NET architecture or the PHP scripting language. The explanation of the implementation techniques starts with simple page configurations, yielding relatively straightforward JSP page templates, and then progresses to cover a wide spectrum of features of dynamic hypertext pages.

Chapter 13 presents a more sophisticated implementation strategy, exploiting the Model View Controller (MVC) design pattern, which grants a well-balanced distribution of responsibility among the software components that collaborate to the page construction. In addition, the chapter illustrates other implementation techniques suited to large-scale applications, such as the definition of generic unit and operation services using XML descriptors, the development of distributed business objects with the Enterprise JavaBeans standard, and the centralized management of presentation with the help of CSS and XSL rules.

Finally, Chapter 14 describes an example of CASE tool, called WebRatio Site Development Studio, supporting the design of data-intensive Web applications and the automatic generation of code from Entity Relationship and WebML specifications. The chapter illustrates the architecture and functions of the tool, which covers the application lifecycle from data and hypertext design to their implementation. The annotated bibliography provides references to other tools supporting the specification and delivery of Web applications.

Several appendices complete the book; they summarize the elements of the WebML model, the syntax of WebML and of the Object Constraint Language, and the implementation techniques for transforming hypertext specifications into dynamic page templates and database queries.

Audience

This book has the ambitious objective of proposing a "paradigm shift" in the way Web applications are developed, rooted in the tradition of conceptual modeling and software engineering. It is directed not only to the IT specialists, but also to all the professionals involved in the construction of a Web application, an audience as broad as the spectrum of problems faced by Web application developers.

To address this target, we have made efforts to purge the book from any unnecessary formalism and academic discussion, and we have instead made intensive use of practical and motivating examples for explaining every new concept introduced to the reader. Therefore, the book should be approachable with limited effort by readers with a general background of database systems, software development, and Web technologies. Throughout the chapters, modeling concepts are shown at work, applied to the description of popular, real-life Web sites. In the same way, development tasks are exemplified with the help of a running case, taken from a real industrial project. In our intention, this book should emphasize "showing" things, with the help of progressive examples, rather than "telling" how things should be done.

The book could also be used in computer science courses dealing with data-driven design methods, especially now that computer science schools and universities are more and more orienting their curricula towards Web technologies and applications. Additional material for supporting professors in their lecturing and students in doing course work is available on the book's online Web site (see below).

Online Resources

The book is associated with several online resources. The Web site http://www.webml.org includes a variety of materials dedicated to model-driven Web development and to WebML, including examples of hypertext modeling, technical and research papers, teaching materials, and resources for developers (for instance, stencils for the popular Microsoft Visio diagram editor, which can be used to draw WebML diagrams quickly). In particular, the section http://www. webml.org/book is dedicated to this book. It contains the full text of the JSP programs discussed in Chapters 12 and 13, and a number of exercises, some of which accompanied by solutions. An entry form in the Web site permits qualified instructors to contact the authors, to obtain further high quality and up-to-date teaching materials.

The Web site http://www.webratio.com describes WebRatio Site Development Studio, the CASE tool presented in Chapter 14; an evaluation program is available for trying the software, and academic licenses are granted upon request to teachers willing to use the tool in their classrooms.

Background

The model-driven approach to Web application development at the base of this book is the result of more than five years of research at Politecnico di Milano, the largest Italian IT School, accompanied by an intense development activity in the industry. The first research prototype of a model-driven CASE tool for Web applications, called AutoWeb, was designed by Piero Fraternali and Paolo Paolini between 1996 and 1998. The tool, operational since 1997, has been used to develop several Web applications, and has demonstrated the possibility of automating the construction of data-intensive Web sites specified with a high level conceptual language.

WebML was conceived in the context of the Esprit project "Web-Based Intelligent Information Infrastructures" (W3I3, 1998–2000), supported by the European Community, with the participation of five partners (Politecnico di Milano and TXT e-solutions from Italy, KPN Research from Holland, Digia Inc. from Finland, Otto Versand from Germany); the project delivered a prototype development environment, called ToriiSoft. Since 1999, WebML has been used for the development of industrial Web applications, both inside research contracts with companies such as Microsoft and Cisco Systems, and in industrial projects with companies like TXT e-solutions and Acer Europe. In the fall 2001, a team of WebML designers and developers founded a start-up company with the goal of further developing, distributing, and marketing WebRatio Site Development Studio, a tool suite based on WebML.

Acknowledgments

We acknowledge the work and dedication of a huge number of developers, researchers, and students, who have contributed to the design of WebML and to the subsequent development of AutoWeb, Toriisoft, and WebRatio. We would like to thank, among others, Fabio Surini, Nicola Testa, Paolo Cucco, Roberto Acerbis, Stefano Butti, Claudio Greppi, Carlo Conserva, Fulvio Ciapessoni, Giovanni Toffetti, Marco Tagliasacchi, Andrea Rangone, Paolo Paolini, Stefano Paraboschi, Ioana Manolescu, Andrea Maurino, Marco Guida, Giorgio Tornielli, Alvise Braga Illa, Wim Timmerman, Pekka Sivonen, Stefan Liesem, Ingo Klapper, Daniel Schwabe, and Graham Robson.

Special thanks to Adam Bosworth, who was one of the first people to appreciate our effort to "change the way in which people think of the Web development." We owe to him many precious technical discussions, conducted on both sides of the Atlantic.

We thank Gianpiero Morbello, Massimo Manzari, and Emanuele Tosetti from Acer for permission to use the Acer-Euro application throughout Parts III and IV of the book.

Many thanks to the people of the CISCO IKF team, including Mike Kirkwood, Shirley Wong, Deepa Gopinat, Seema Yazdani, and Irene Sklyar. These people really know what a "large" Web application is!

We are also deeply indebted to Prahm Mehra and Paolo Atzeni, who assisted us with extremely careful comments and annotations, which greatly helped us in the revision of the manuscript.

1 CHAPTER Technologies for Web Applications

1.1 Introduction

Web applications are complex systems, based on a variety of hardware and software components, protocols, languages, interfaces, and standards. This chapter proposes a "guided tour" through the ingredients that characterize Web applications; the progression of arguments is such that every new development can be interpreted as the natural consequence of problems exhibited by previous technological solutions. This approach may help you in consolidating within a clear reference framework some background knowledge you might have already, but perhaps not systematically organized.

The review starts with the basic technologies for building Web applications: HTTP—the resource transfer protocol—and HTML—the language for writing hypertexts. The first section also describes client-side scripts and components that make a Web interface more interactive. HTTP and HTML alone enable the development of simple Web sites, but are insufficient for large and complex applications; in particular, HTML is limited in the number and expressive power of its tags, which embed presentation features inside pages. However, the latest version of HTML (HTML 4), and specifically the introduction of cascading style sheets, moves in the direction of separating content from presentation, which is essential for large scale applications.

The second section of this chapter presents the *eXtensible Markup Language* (XML) as an evolution of the concepts proposed by HTML 4; it shows that XML is totally independent of "look and feel" aspects, and that presentation can be superimposed on XML documents by means of the eXtensible Stylesheet Language (XSL), a technology comparable to cascading style sheets. We also explain the structure of XML documents, originally represented by *Document Type Definitions* (DTDs) and more recently by XML schema definitions (XSDs), and introduce the notion of an XML document being *well-formed* and valid with respect to a DTD or XML schema.

While Sections 1.2 and 1.3 illustrate technologies not specifically related to data-intensive applications, the subsequent sections drill down into the data-intensive aspects. Section 1.4 briefly addresses data management with relational databases and the SQL language, two very consolidated technologies in use for over 30 years. An interesting aspect of the integration of relational databases into Web applications is the existence of interoperability standards, such as Open Database Connectivity (ODBC) and Java Database Connectivity (JDBC), which simplify the access to data repositories produced by different vendors, by providing a uniform interface to developers.

Finally, Section 1.5 presents a broad spectrum of technologies specifically designed to support the dynamic construction of pages. We start by describing the Common Gateway Interface (CGI), as an extension of the HTTP protocol; then we discuss Java-based Web server extensions (the so-called servlet architecture) and server-side scripting (embodied in such languages as Java Server Pages [JSP] and Active Server Pages [ASP]); next, we present tag libraries as an evolution of server-side scripting; and finally we focus on complex, three-tier architectures, introducing the notion of Web Application Servers, and briefly comparing the two popular architectures Java 2 Enterprise Edition and Microsoft .NET. The chapter closes with a discussion of the next challenge of Web applications: the publishing of content for multiple devices with different rendition capabilities.

1.2 HTTP and HTML: The Foundation of Web Technology

We start the technology tour from the foundations, which lie in the HTTP protocol and in the HTML markup language.

1.2.1 Accessing Remote Resources: The Hypertext Transfer Protocol

The fundamental technology at the origin of Web applications is the well-known *HyperText Transfer Protocol* (HTTP), an application-level protocol for allowing users to make requests of resources to remote servers. HTTP is the invention of Tim Berners-Lee and Robert Cailliau, two researchers working at CERN, the European Nuclear Research Centre (formerly, Centre European pour la Recherche Nucleaire), located in Geneva, Switzerland. The origin of HTTP can be traced back to the World Wide Web (WWW) project, started in 1990 and aimed at building a distributed hypermedia system for accessing with a simple interface documents, reports, images, and online help stored in servers spread over a TCP/IP network.

Technically speaking, HTTP is a *client-server application protocol,* which defines the rules by which a client program, called a *browser* or user agent, and a server program, called a *Web server,* may interact in order to exchange requests and responses. In HTTP terminology, the user agent sends a request for a given resource to the Web server, which is a process running continuously and listening to requests coming from the network; upon receiving the request, the server locates or builds the resource and sends a response to the client (Figure 1.1). The basic resource requested by the client is an HTML page, which is a piece of text representing a multimedia hypertextual document. More generally, a request may address a file of any format stored in the Web server, or even the invocation of a program to be executed at the server side.

The HTTP protocol is conceived for exchanging resources distributed over the Internet and therefore exploits a standard resource addressing system. HTTP resources are identified by means of *Uniform Resource Locators* (URLs), which are structured strings of the format

```
http: // <host> [: <port>] [ <path> [? <query>]]
```

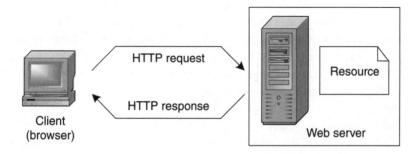

Figure 1.1 Request-response cycle of HTTP.

After the fixed prefix `http://`,[1] the URL contains the host name or IP address of the server, possibly followed by a port number (denoting the access to a specific server port), optionally followed by a pathname in the Web server file system pointing to the requested resource, optionally followed by a set of parameters, called the *query string*.

For example, the URL *http://www.theatlantic.com/unbound/flashbks/computer/bushf.htm* denotes the file named *bushf.htm,* stored in the directory named *unbound/flashbks/computer/,* in the file system managed by the Web server installed in the host named *www.theatlantic.com.*

HTTP requests are issued by the browser, either explicitly when the user types a URL in the "open page" command of the browser, or implicitly when the user clicks on an anchor within a page.

HTTP requests have a fixed format, which consists of three parts: a request line, some optional message headers, and the request body (also optional).

The request line is a formatted string, which consists of three parts; the HTTP method, the URL of the requested resource, and the protocol version. The most important HTTP methods are GET and POST, which respectively perform

- ■ The submission of a plain request for some resource to the Web server.

- ■ The submission of a request including sizeable user's input (e.g., a long text or a file) to be processed by the server. In such a case, the user's input is packaged as an attachment to the request, and constitutes the so-called request body.

For example, in order to display an HTML copy of the article "As You May Think," by Vannevar Bush published by the *Atlantic Monthly,* the browser may send the following GET request to the Web server installed in the host *www.theatlantic.com:*

```
GET /unbound/flashbks/computer/bushf.htm HTTP/1.1
```

The request includes the name of the method (GET), the URL of the requested resource, and the version of the HTTP protocol. Methods GET and POST will be further discussed in Section 1.5.1, in the context of the CGI protocol.

After receiving and interpreting a request message, a server responds with an HTTP response message, which is structured in three parts: a status line, a set of optional headers, and a message body.

---

[1]In a Web browser, the prefix may also refer to a different protocol (for instance, *ftp://*) supported by the browser.

The status line consists of the protocol version followed by a numeric status code and its associated message (for example: HTTP/1.1 404 Not found).

Because the HTTP protocol has only two very generic request methods and one kind of response, several optional fields (called headers) can be added to requests and responses to convey auxiliary information that the browser and the Web server must exchange. There are four kinds of headers: general, request-specific, response-specific, and entity headers, as follows:

- General headers are applicable both to requests and responses. For example, the Date header represents the date and time at which the request or response was originated.

- Request headers apply specifically to requests and not to responses. For example, the Accept-Language header establishes the set of languages that are preferred by the user as a response to the request.

- Response headers apply specifically to responses and not to requests. For instance, the WWW-Authenticate response-header field is used for access control; it is included in response messages having status code = 401 (which means "unauthorized"), emitted by the Web server when the user tries to access a resource stored in a password-protected domain.

- Finally, entity headers apply to the content transferred in the body of the request or response.[2] For example, the Content-Length header specifies the number of bytes associated with the body of the request or response.

Since its origin, HTTP has been subject to a deep revision process, which has produced two versions of the protocol: HTTP/1.0, the pioneering version, and HTTP/1.1, the stable version, approved as Draft Standard by the *Internet Engineering Task Force* (IETF) in July 1999.

Some important observations apply to HTTP, which are at the base of the evolution of Web application architectures:

- HTTP is *stateless:* Each HTTP request is treated by the Web server as an atomic and independent call. There is no difference between a sequence of two requests by different users or by the same user. As a consequence, HTTP is not capable of maintaining any information between two

---

[2]In the HTTP terminology, the word "entity" refers to the content transferred in the body of an HTTP request or response, which can be, for example, the HTML page returned to the browser, and the text submitted by the user in a form.

successive requests by the same user. In other words, there is not a notion of user session in HTTP. If the history of user interaction must be preserved, this feature must be implemented outside HTTP.

■ HTTP is *pull-based:* Interaction occurs only when the client calls the server. There is no way in which the server may call back the client. Therefore, notification of clients cannot be implemented using HTTP alone.

1.2.2   Writing Web Documents: The Hypertext Markup Language

The most popular resources requested on the Web are HTML pages. An HTML page is a textual file written in the *Hypertext Markup Language,* a language based on a document composition style known as "markup."

   Markup document processing is centered on the idea of inserting special tokens, called *tags,* in textual documents, in order to delimit selected portions of the text and express some properties of such text portions, like font color and size. With markup, the rendering of the document is separate from the creation of its content, and is delegated to a processor, which receives in input the marked-up text and transforms it into a rendered document, by interpreting the meaning of tags (Figure 1.2). In the Web context, the editing of HTML documents is done by the content producer using any text editor, and the processing is performed by the browser.

   Syntactically, HTML tags are symbols delimited by angle brackets, like <FONT> or <TABLE>. Most often tags are used in pairs, because they must delimit a portion of text. In this case the same tag has two variants, the start tag, positioned at the beginning of the text to delimit, and the end tag, positioned at the

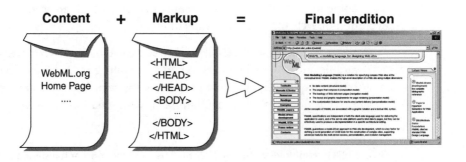

Figure 1.2   Processing of a marked-up text.

end; the end tag has the same name of the start tag, but is preceded by a "/" character.

The primary use of HTML tags is to give a general structure to the document. The entire document is delimited by the <HTML> tag, and contains two major sections: the header, delimited by the <HEAD> tag, and the body, delimited by the <BODY> tag, as shown in Figure 1.3.

The header section includes information about the document, for example the <TITLE> tag, which specifies the document title used by the browser to name the window where the document is rendered, or the <META> tag, which can be used to list keywords for document indexing by search engines. The body section is where the actual content is placed. In the example in Figure 1.3, the body

```
<HTML>
  <HEAD>
    <TITLE>A Simple Document</TITLE>
    <META name="keywords" content="HTML, tutorial">
  </HEAD>
  <BODY>
    <P align="center"><FONT size="+6">Hello world!</FONT></P>
  </BODY>
</HTML>
```

Figure 1.3   A simple HTML page and its rendition in the browser.

contains just the text "Hello world!", wrapped inside a paragraph and formatted with a larger font.

In the early versions of HTML, prior to HTML 4, the most common use of tags is to assign formatting properties to the text. The following example shows a portion of text delimited by the <B> (bold) tag, which sets the font style to bold:

```
The effect of inserting a bold tag pair <B> is to make the
included text bold.</B>
```

The effect of inserting a bold tag pair **is to make the included text bold.**

Sometimes a tag must be able to express a property having many possible values, like the size or the color of the font. To this end, tags may have attributes, which are label-value pairs. For example, the <FONT> tag has several attributes for setting the font properties, such as size and face:

```
The attributes of the FONT tag <FONT size="+1" face="Arial">
assign various properties to the font</FONT>
```

The attributes of the FONT tag assign various properties to the font.[3]

Table 1.1 summarizes some of the HTML tags for text formatting.

The most popular features of HTML are the two tags <A> and <IMG>, which are used to build multimedia hypertexts.

The anchor tag <A> delimits a portion of text, which is interpreted by the browser as the starting point (anchor, in the hypertext terminology) of a hypertext reference. The text is rendered in a special way (for example, underlined and in a different color) and clicking on it makes the browser issue an HTTP request for a resource to be displayed. The URL of the new resource, which is the target of the hypertext reference, is specified in the href attribute of the anchor tag, as highlighted in the example in Figure 1.4 on page 12.

A possible use of the anchor tag, besides expressing a hypertext link, is to open the default mailer with a click. To achieve such an effect, the href attribute specifies an e-mail address instead of an HTTP URL, as shown in Figure 1.5 on page 13.

---

[3]As will be explained later, the use of the <FONT> tag, and of similar tags that express graphic and formatting properties, is deprecated in HTML 4. The examples illustrate the original meaning of HTML primitives, not the most correct way of using HTML.

Table 1.1 HTML tags for text formatting.

Tag	Attributes	Meaning
`<BODY>`	`bgcolor, background, text, link`	Sets properties of the entire document, such as background color, background image, text, and link color.
`<B>`		Sets the font style to bold.
`<I>`		Sets the font style to italic.
`<U>`		Sets the font style to underlined.
`<PRE>`		Tells the browser to render the text in a fixed-pitch font, to preserve whitespace, and not to wrap long lines.
`<FONT>`	`size, color, face`	Assigns font properties.
`<P>`	`align`	Delimits a paragraph and sets text horizontal alignment (left, center, right, justify).
`<H1>`	`align`	Delimits a heading of level 1 (there are six levels of headings) and sets the horizontal alignment.

If the `<A>` tag introduces hypertext features into HTML, the `<IMG>` tag adds multimedia aspects. The `<IMG>` tag inserts an inline image into the document, the URL of which is specified using the `src` attribute, as shown in Figure 1.6 on page 14.

When the browser renders the HTML page and encounters the `<IMG>` tag, it sends an additional HTTP request to the Web server for the file mentioned in the `src` attribute, and displays the image received by the Web server inside the HTML document.

Table 1.2 (page 14) illustrates the most common attributes of the `<IMG>` tag. The image tag can be nested into the anchor tag, to produce clickable images, which act as anchors of a hypertext reference.

1.2.3 Client-Side Scripting for Enhancing Page Interactivity

HTML was originally conceived for writing hypertexts. However, the development of interactive applications, for example applications supporting form-based data entry, requires additional capabilities, like the possibility of defining events produced by the interaction of the user with the HTML page, and procedures for reacting to such events.

```
<HTML>
  <HEAD>
    <TITLE>A Simple Hypertext Anchor</TITLE>
    <META name="keywords" content="HTML, tutorial">
  </HEAD>
  <BODY bgcolor="#FFFFFF" text="#000000">
    <P align="left">
      <FONT size="+6"> Click
        <A href="http://www.webml.org">HERE</A> to open the WebML home page
      </FONT>
    </P>
  </BODY>
</HTML>
```

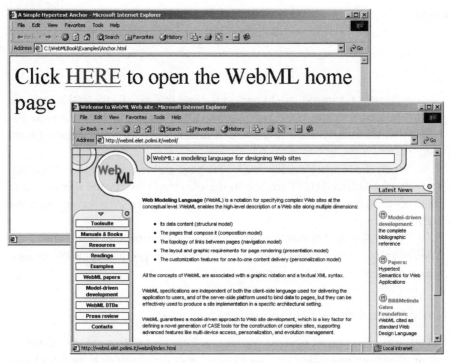

Figure 1.4   HTML page containing a hypertext anchor.

```
<HTML>
  <HEAD>
    <TITLE>A Simple Hypertext Anchor</TITLE>
    <META name="keywords" content="HTML, tutorial">
  </HEAD>
  <BODY bgcolor="#FFFFFF" text="#000000">
    <P align="left">
      <FONT size="+5"> Click <A href=
"mailto:piero.fraternali@polimi.it">HERE</A>to send me email</FONT>
    </P>
  </BODY>
</HTML>
```

Figure 1.5 HTML page containing a "mailto" anchor.

```
<HTML>
  <HEAD>
    <TITLE>A Simple Image</TITLE>
    <META name="keywords" content="HTML, tutorial">
  </HEAD>
  <BODY bgcolor="#FFFFFF" text="#000000">
    <P align="center">
      <IMG src="http://www.polimi.it/images2000/home/testata.gif">
    </P>
  </BODY>
</HTML>
```

Figure 1.6   HTML page containing an image tag.

Table 1.2   Essential attributes of the IMG tag.

Attributes of the image tag	Meaning
width, height	The screen space reserved to the image, in pixels.
align	The image alignment (top, middle, bottom, left, right).
border	Width of the image border in pixels.
alt	Alternative text, to be displayed when the image is not available, or in textual browsers.

HTML pages can be made more interactive by inserting into their code small programs, called *client-side scripts,* which are executed by the browser when the page is loaded or when the user produces some event.

The most popular languages for creating client-side scripts are JavaScript, by Netscape, and VisualBasic script, by Microsoft. Scripts are inserted inside a page using the <SCRIPT> tag, placed either in the head section of the HTML document, or in its body. Scripts in the head section are executed when they are explicitly called, or when an event is triggered; scripts in the body section are executed when the HTML page is loaded.

The example in Figure 1.7 uses JavaScript code to write the current date. The script is placed in the document body and is executed when the page is loaded in the browser. The instruction `document.write` in the <SCRIPT> tag makes the argument of the write function (for example, the current year calculated by the function call `d.getFullYear()`) to be output in the document, in the position where the <SCRIPT> tag appears. The result of loading the page in the browser appears in Figure 1.7 on page 16.

Client-side scripts can be activated after the occurrence of specific events. In this case, the scripts are placed in the head section of the document, and the event that triggers script execution is declared as an attribute of the appropriate HTML element. For example, the page in Figure 1.8 on page 17 contains the anchor text "Click here to enter my favorite Web site." The anchor tag includes the declaration of the `onClick` event, which is raised when the anchor text is clicked. The event triggers a JavaScript function named `dialog`, which opens a confirmation dialog box asking the user if he/she really wants to access the page linked to the anchor.

Client-side scripting is particularly useful in conjunction with the <FORM> tag, an HTML element for constructing data entry forms. In this case, events can be attached to the form fields and may trigger functions for validating the user input, for example, for controlling the validity of a date. Forms are treated in Section 1.5.1.

1.2.4   Client-Side Components for Enhancing Client Functionality

Client-side scripting is not the only way to add interactive functions to an HTML page. A more powerful feature is offered by client-side components, which are executable objects plugged into the page. Examples of pluggable components include Java applets, Microsoft ActiveX controls, Macromedia Flash movies, and more.

Similarly to scripts, client-side components are executed by the browser; unlike scripts, client-side components are full-fledged executable objects,

```
<HTML>
<BODY>
This is the date of today: <SCRIPT type="text/javascript">
var d = new Date()                  // create an object of type date
document.write(d.getMonth() + 1)    // get the month and print it
document.write("/")                 // print a separator
document.write(d.getDate())         // get the day and print it
document.write("/")                 // print a separator
document.write(d.getFullYear())     // get the year and print it
</SCRIPT>
</BODY>
</HTML>
```

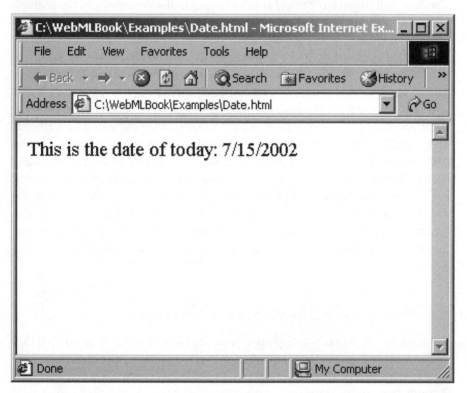

Figure 1.7 Example of client-side scripting in JavaScript.

```
<HTML>
<HEAD>
  <SCRIPT type="text/javascript">
    function dialog()
      {if (confirm('Are you sure you want to enter?'))
        window.location.href='http://home.netscape.com/'}
</SCRIPT>
</HEAD>
<BODY>
  <A href="http://home.netscape.com/" onClick="dialog()">
        Click here to enter my favorite Web site</A>
</BODY>
</HTML>
```

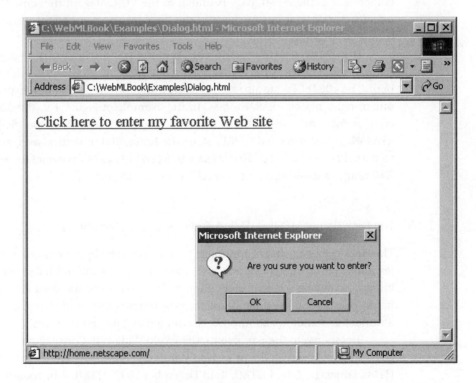

Figure 1.8 Example of client-side scripting with the script in the head section.

programmed by a technically skilled developer using a language like Visual Basic or Java and stored in a Web server, wherefrom they are downloaded by the browser. For example, client-side components written in Java, also known as *Java applets,* can be downloaded from the network and run inside the browser; they may implement complex functions, like showing in real time a graph of stock quotations, but are prevented for security reasons from executing potentially dangerous instructions, like reading and writing files on the file system, and making network connections to hosts different from the one from which they have been downloaded.

Client-side components are inserted into an HTML page using the <OBJECT> tag. For example, Figure 1.9 shows an HTML page containing an ActiveX component, a text rotator, which constructs an animation by taking an existing file and scrolling its content in a delimited portion of the screen. As shown in the code reported in Figure 1.9, the <OBJECT> tag used to insert the component in the HTML page is similar to the <IMG> tag, in the sense that it reserves a certain amount of space in the page for the component, using the attributes width and height.

The classid attribute is analogous to the src attribute of an image, in the sense that it references the actual object that implements the client-side component. The <OBJECT> tag also admits some initialization parameters, expressed by one or more nested <PARAM> tags. In the example of Figure 1.9, the client-side component scrolls the content of a Web page, whose URL is specified in the <PARAM> element named szURL, along the horizontal or vertical axis, according to the values of the ScrollPixelsX and ScrollPixelsY parameters. Y=10 and X=0 result in scrolling a text vertically from top to bottom.

1.2.5   The Evolution of HTML: HTML 4 and Cascading Style Sheets

The HTML language has been subject to some criticism by the community of professional graphic designers, due to its fixed set of tags and limited graphic capabilities. Achieving sophisticated graphic effects with the standard HTML tags is hardly possible; on the other hand, introducing new tags in the language requires a worldwide standardization process, which may take several years.

In response to these problems, the World Wide Web Consortium (W3C), the governing body devoted to the Web standards, issued the latest version of the HTML language, called HTML 4, in December 1997. HTML 4 introduces several enhancements over the previous versions, including a better separation of document structure and presentation, improved support for accessibility of documents and internationalization, and a better definition of complex constructs like

```
<HTML>
<HEAD>
  <TITLE>Marquee Control</TITLE>
</HEAD>
<BODY>
  <H1>The OBJECT Tag </H1>
  <P>
  <OBJECT id="Marquee1" width="500" height="300" align="top" border="1"
          classid="CLSID:1A4DA620-6217-11CF-BE62-0080C72EDD2D">
    <PARAM name="szURL" value="text.htm">
    <PARAM name="ScrollPixelsY" value="10">
    <PARAM name="ScrollPixelsX" value="0">
  </OBJECT>
</BODY>
</HTML>
```

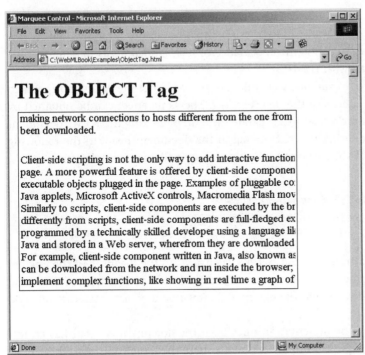

Figure 1.9 Example of ActiveX component: The text in the box rotates vertically.

frames and tables. However, the most innovative feature of HTML 4 is the introduction of *cascading style sheets* (CSS), a new technique for defining the presentation of HTML documents, separating the look and feel from markup and textual content.

A style sheet is a set of rules that tell a browser how to render a document. A rule is made of two parts: a selector, which specifies the HTML tag to which the style rule applies, and a style declaration, which expresses the style properties to be attached to the HTML tag mentioned in the selector. As an example, the following code fragment defines the `color` and `font-size` properties for the <H1> and <H2> tags:

```
<HEAD>
   <TITLE>CSS Example</TITLE>
   <STYLE type="text/css">
     H1 { font-size: 20pt; color: red }
     H2 { font-size: 18pt; color: blue }
   </STYLE>
</HEAD>
```

The CSS standard includes more than 60 rendition properties, which permit the designer to define the appearance of HTML documents in a much more precise way than with HTML 3.

In the above example, style rules are embedded in the document to which they apply, by means of the <STYLE> tag. The same effect can be obtained by storing the two style rules in a separate file, and by linking the HTML document to the style file, using the <LINK> tag in the document head. In the following example, the HTML document is linked to a style file named style.css:

```
<HEAD>
   <TITLE>CSS Example</TITLE>
   <LINK rel=StyleSheet href="style.css" type="text/css" >
</HEAD>
```

The `rel` attribute in the <LINK> tag expresses the meaning of the link between the document and the resource specified in the `href` attribute. The value `StyleSheet` declares that the external file must be used as a presentation style sheet.

Separating the presentation rules from the document content has an immediate advantage: if multiple documents share the same style rules, these rules can be placed in a single file and linked to all documents. As a consequence of this separation, updating the style rules requires modifying the single style file, instead of updating all documents.

1.3 XML: eXtensible Markup Language

Although HTML 4 is a great improvement over the preceding versions of HTML in the direction of better presentation, the imposition of a fixed tag set prevents developers from defining their own tags that could match the requirements of specific application domains. At the same time, the advent of cascading style sheets, and the consequent separation of the presentation rules from the HTML markup, makes HTML obsolete for content formatting.

A stronger position with respect to the separation of presentation, content, and markup is taken by the *eXtensible Markup Language (XML),* whose base specification (XML 1.0) became a W3C Recommendation in February 1998.

1.3.1 User-Defined Tags

XML is a standard syntax for defining custom tag collections. Unlike HTML, which consists of a fixed set of tags, XML is a meta-language (that is, "a language for defining languages"), which standardizes the syntactic rules whereby users can define their own sets of tags, suited to the needs of a specific application domain.

A *well-formed* XML document is a piece of marked-up content that obeys a few syntactic rules:

- The document must start with a standard line, declaring the language version, such as: `<?xml version="1.0"?>`

- All tags, called *elements* in XML terminology, can enclose some content, which can be text or other tags. XML elements have an opening tag and a closing tag. The latter is obtained by prefixing the opening tag by means of the symbol "/". Exception to this rules are the tags with no content, which may have no closing tag—but in such a case they must have the "/" symbol at the end of the tag name, as in `<emptytag/>`.

- The document must have one root element, and the nesting of elements must be well-formed, which means that any element containing an inner element must not be closed before the closing of the inner element.

- Elements may have attributes with given values, and attribute values must be delimited by quotes (" ").

The following example presents a short, but well-formed, XML document:

```
<?xml version="1.0"?>
  <root>
    <child>
      <subchild>..some content...</subchild>
```

```
    </child>
  </root>
```

The document starts with a standard line that declares the XML version, and then contains some custom tags. As another example, a fragment of the outline of this book could be represented in XML as shown in Figure 1.10. As illustrated in the example, XML elements may have different kinds of content:

- *Element content:* Contains other elements, like the <book> element.

- *Text content:* Contains character data, like the <chapter> element.

```
Designing Data-Intensive Web       <book>
Applications                       <publishing schedule="10-31-2002"/>
                                   <title> Designing Data-Intensive Web
Stefano Ceri, Piero Fraternali,    Applications </title>
Aldo Bongio, Marco Brambilla,      <author> Stefano Ceri </author>
Sara Comai, Maristella Matera      <author> Piero Fraternali </author>
                                   <author>Aldo Bongio </author>
Part I:     INTRODUCTION           <author> Marco Brambilla </author>
Chapter 1   Technologies for Web   <author> Sara Comai </author>
            Applications           <author> Maristella Matera </author>
                                   <part> Technology Overview
PART II:    CONCEPTUAL MODELING    <chapter> 1.Technologies for Web
Chapter 2   Data Model                        Applications </chapter>
Chapter 3   Hypertext Model        </part>
Chapter 4   Content Management     <part> Models for Designing Web
            Model                  Applications
Chapter 5   Advanced Hypertext     <chapter> 2.Data Model </chapter>
            Model                  <chapter> 3.Hypertext Model </chapter>
                                   <chapter> 4.Content Management
...                                            Model </chapter>
                                   <chapter> 5.Advanced Hypertext Model
                                   </chapter>
                                   </part>
                                   ..
                                   </book>
```

Figure 1.10   An example of XML tags for representing the outline of a book.

■ *Mixed content:* Contains other elements and/or character data, like the `<part>` element.

■ *Empty content:* No content, like the `<publishing>` element.

Besides content, XML elements may have attributes, like the `schedule` attribute in the `<publishing>` element.

An XML document may be associated with a *Document Type Definition (DTD)*, prescribing the common format of a class of XML documents. A DTD includes the description of the elements that can be used in the document, and for each element specifies the admissible content and attributes.

A DTD contains three categories of declarations: element, attribute, and entity declarations. An element declaration introduces an element and specifies its admissible content; an attribute declaration specifies which attributes can be put inside an element and expresses a few properties of such attributes; an entity declaration introduces a sort of "constant," which is a reference to some fixed piece of content. We do not further discuss entity declarations, although we next illustrate a few examples of element and attribute declarations.

A DTD for structuring documents about books may include *element declarations* like the ones in the following example:

```
<!ELEMENT book (publishing, title, editor?, author+,
                (chapter*|part*))>
<!ELEMENT publishing EMPTY>
<!ELEMENT title            (#PCDATA)>
<!ELEMENT editor           (#PCDATA)>
<!ELEMENT author           (#PCDATA)>
<!ELEMENT chapter          (#PCDATA)>
<!ELEMENT part             (#PCDATA|chapter)*>
```

The above rules declare seven elements: `book`, `publishing`, `title`, `editor`, `author`, `chapter`, and `part`. Element `book` has a complex content model: it may contain a sequence of subelements, denoted by the comma-separated list of element names. Specifically, the `book` element must contain one subelement of type `publishing`, one subelement of type `title`, zero or one (denoted by the "?" symbol) subelement of type `editor`, one or more (denoted by the "+" symbol) subelements of type `author`, and zero or more (denoted by the "*" symbol) chapters or parts. Chapters and parts are in *alternative* (denoted by the "|" symbol): either the book is organized in parts or in chapters. The `publishing` element has no content (EMPTY), the `title`, `editor`, `author`, and `chapter` elements have text data (PCDATA) as content. Finally, the part element contains zero or more chapters mixed with text data.

An *attribute declaration* lists all the attributes that an element may include, and poses some constraints on their values. For example, the attributes of the publishing element may be declared as follows:

```
<!ATTLIST publishing
    schedule    CDATA                   #REQUIRED
    editor      CDATA                   #IMPLIED
    format      (paperback|hardback)    "paperback"
>
```

The ATTLIST clause introduces three attributes for the publishing element: schedule, editor, and format. The schedule attribute consists of character data (CDATA) and is mandatory (#REQUIRED). The editor attribute has also character data as a value, but is optional (#IMPLIED). Finally, the format attribute is optional and may have a value chosen from a fixed set of options (paperback, hardback), with paperback as the default value assigned to the attribute when the user does not include the attribute in the publishing element.

A document that conforms to a given DTD is said to be *valid* with respect to that DTD. For example, the document of Figure 1.10 is valid with respect to the DTD expressed by the above clauses defining elements and attributes for describing books.

The DTD can be either placed inside the XML document, or stored in a separate file, as shown by the following example:

```
<?xml version="1.0"?>
<!DOCTYPE book SYSTEM "book.dtd">
<book>
..
</book>
```

The line: <!DOCTYPE book SYSTEM "book.dtd"> defines the type of the document by referring to the file book.dtd, where the DTD declarations are stored.

DTDs present several limitations in expressing the structure of documents: they do not allow you to specify data types for the content of elements and attributes other than character data, and are unable to express several useful constraints on the nesting of elements. To improve the document structure specification, DTDs can be replaced by *XML schema definitions (XSDs)*. An XML schema definition is an XML document, which dictates the structure of a family of XML documents, using a standard set of tags for element declaration, defined by the XML Schema specification. XML Schema became a recommendation of the World

Wide Web Consortium in May 2001 and is gradually replacing DTDs in those applications that require a more precise description of XML document structure.

Figure 1.11 shows an example of an XSD, corresponding to the structure of the XML document of Figure 1.10. Being an XML document, the XSD starts with the XML version declaration (line 1), followed by the <schema> element, which encloses all the element definitions. The xmlns attribute of the <schema> element also imports the definition of the XML Schema tags used to describe the

```
1    <?xml version="1.0"?>
2    <xs:schema xmlns:xs="http://www.w3.org/2001/XMLSchema">
3
4    <!-- definition of book element-->
5    <xs:element name="book">
6      <xs:complexType>
7        <xs:sequence>
8          <xs:element ref="publishing"/>
9          <xs:element ref="title"/>
10         <xs:element ref="editor" minOccurs="0"/>
11         <xs:element ref="author" maxOccurs="unbounded"/>
12         <xs:choice>
13           <xs:element ref="chapter" minOccurs="0" maxOccurs="unbounded"/>
14           <xs:element ref="part" minOccurs="0" maxOccurs="unbounded"/>
15         </xs:choice>
16       </xs:sequence>
17     </xs:complexType>
18   </xs:element>
19
20   <!-- definition of chapter, title, editor and author elements -->
21   <xs:element name="chapter" type="xs:string"/>
22   <xs:element name="title" type="xs:string"/>
23   <xs:element name="editor" type="xs:string"/>
24   <xs:element name="author" type="xs:string"/>
25
```

(continued)

Figure 1.11   XML Schema definition.

Figure 1.11   *(continued)*

```
26  <!-- definition of part element->
27  <xs:element name="part" mixed="true">
28    <xs:complexType>
29      <xs:element ref="chapter" minOccurs="0" maxOccurs="unbounded"/>
30    </xs:complexType>
31  </xs:element>
32
33  <!-- definition of publishing element -->
34  <xs:element name="publishing">
35    <xs:complexType>
36      <xs:attribute name="schedule" type="xs:date" use="required"/>
37      <xs:attribute name="editor" type="xs:string"/>
38      <xs:attribute name="format" default="paperback"/>
39        <xs:simpleType>
40        <xs:restriction base="xs:string">
41          <xs:enumeration value="paperback"/>
42          <xs:enumeration value="hardback"/>
43          </xs:restriction>
44        </xs:simpleType>
45      <xs:attribute/>
46    </xs:complexType>
47  </xs:element>
48  </xs:schema>
```

document structure. These tags are organized in a so-called XML *namespace,* specified in the document *http://www.w3.org/2001/XMLSchema.* All the tags belonging to the same namespace have a name starting with a common prefix; in the case of XML Schema tags, the prefix is xs.

The <schema> element encloses the definition of the element types for describing books. The root element <book> (lines 4–18) is declared as a complex type, because it contains several subelements (publishing, title, editor and so on). The <sequence> element inside the declaration of element <book> specifies the required order of the nested subelements (publishing, followed by title, and so on). The <choice> tag is used for specifying that an element can contain one of a set of subelements; in the example, element <book> may contain as subelement either chapter or part. For each element, occurrence indicators define how often an element can appear. In particular, the maxOccurs attribute specifies the maximum number of times an element can occur, whereas the minOccurs indicator specifies the minimum number of times an element can occur. The default values of the occurrence indicators are 1.

Elements chapter, title, editor, and author (declared at lines 21–24) are of type string, one of the basic types provided by XML schema, which also includes the decimal, integer, Boolean, date, and time types. Element part (lines 27–31) may contain both plain text and chapter elements: this feature is specified by setting the mixed attribute to true (line 27), and by defining the nontextual subelement of part (lines 28–30).

Finally, element publishing (lines 33–47) has empty content and three attributes. The three attributes are declared in the same way as elements; they are grouped into the definition of a complex type, which does not include the <sequence> element, to denote that the attributes can occur in any order. Attribute schedule is of type date and is required; editor is string-typed and optional (which needs not be explicitly specified); the type of attribute format is a string, whose content is restricted to a set of predefined values, enumerated inside the <restriction> tag (lines 40–43). The acceptable values are "paperback" and "hardback", with "paperback" as the default (line 38).

Like DTDs, XML schemas can be placed inside the XML document or in a separate file, referenced inside the document.

1.3.2 Presenting XML Documents Using XSL

XML is a platform-independent standard for describing and exchanging data, and not a markup language for presenting multimedia hypertext on the Web. The intended uses of XML cover a variety of applications, including electronic data exchange, document storage and transformation, document exchange in e-commerce and B2B transactions, and more. However, XML documents may also be presented to human readers, for example to Web users using a browser.

The best approach to displaying an XML document is to transform it into another document, encoded using a presentation-oriented markup language such as HTML. The transformation of XML documents is supported by the *eXtensible Stylesheet Language* (XSL).

XSL is a language for writing pattern-matching rules, similar to the rules of HTML 4 cascading style sheets. An XSL rule contains a matching part, for selecting the target XML elements, and an action part, to transform or format the matched elements.

XSL rules are much more powerful than CSS rules, both in matching primitives and in transformation capability. As a consequence, XSL is a much more complex language than CSS; actually, XSL is the union of three sub-languages:

- *XPath:* A language for writing expressions that define a portion of an XML document.

- *XSL Transformations* (XSLT): A language for defining transformations of XML documents.

- *XSL Formatting Objects* (XSL-FO): A language for defining the rendition of a document.

XSL is now a standard recommended by the W3C. The first two parts of the language became a W3C Recommendation in November 1999. The full XSL Recommendation including XSL Formatting Objects became a W3C Candidate Recommendation in November 2000.

The most common approach for presenting an XML document is to transform it into HTML; for this transformation, the XPath and XSLT sub-languages are sufficient. The transformation applies to an input document and produces an output HTML document. The processing is specified by writing an XSL style sheet, which consists of several rules written in XSLT. Each XSLT rule uses XPath to define parts of the source document that match one or more predefined templates. When a match is found, the XSLT rule transforms the matching part of the source document into some content in the resulting document.

The XSL style sheet in Figure 1.12 illustrates the XSLT rules that transform the XML document of Figure 1.10 into the HTML page shown in Figure 1.13 on page 30. We will show the flavor of XSL by walking through the example.

An XSL style sheet is a particular kind of XML document, containing pattern-matching rules called *templates*. The example in Figure 1.12 contains five templates. We will describe the first one completely (lines 5–18), and omit the detailed illustration of the other rules, for brevity.

The template starts with the `<xsl:template match="book">` clause (line 5), which introduces an XSL rule matching all the book elements of the input XML document. The meaning of such template is that if the match succeeds, then the document fragment contained inside the template (lines 6–17) is inserted into the output document. The document fragment inside the template may include plain tags in some document formatting language (HTML in Figure 1.12), and XSL tags denoting calls to other XSL rules. For example, the `<TITLE>` tag (line 8) contains a rule invocation (`<xsl:value-of select="title"/>`), which extracts

```
1   <?xml version="1.0"?>
2   <xsl:stylesheet xmlns:xsl="http://www.w3.org/1999/XSL/Transform"
3                   version="1.0">
4
5     <xsl:template match="book">
6       <HTML>
7         <HEAD>
8           <TITLE><xsl:value-of select="title"/></TITLE>
9         </HEAD>
10        <BODY>
11          <CENTER><H1><xsl:value-of select="title"/></H1></CENTER>
12          <CENTER><B><xsl:apply-templates select="author"/></B></CENTER>
13          <xsl:apply-templates select="publishing"/>
14          <HR/>
15          <xsl:apply-templates select="part"/>
16        </BODY>
17        </HTML>
18    </xsl:template>
19
20    <xsl:template match="author">
21      <xsl:if test="position() &gt; 1">, </xsl:if>
22      <xsl:value-of select="text()"/>
23    </xsl:template>
24
25    <xsl:template match="publishing">
26      <P align="right">
27        <I>Publishing date: <xsl:value-of select="@schedule"/></I>
28      </P>
29    </xsl:template>
30
31    <xsl:template match="part">
32      <P><H3><xsl:value-of select="text()"/></H3></P>
33      <xsl:apply-templates select="chapter"/>
34    </xsl:template>
35
36    <xsl:template match="chapter">
37      <P><H4>- <xsl:value-of select="text()"/></H4></P>
38    </xsl:template>
39  </xsl:stylesheet>
```

Figure 1.12   Document transformation in XSLT.

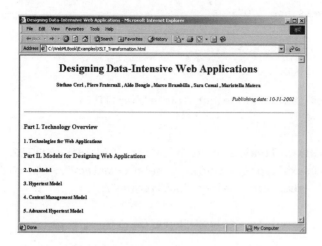

Figure 1.13   The HTML page resulting from applying an XSLT transformation
to the document in Figure 1.10.

the book's title from the input XML document. As an effect of such a call, the title
of the output HTML document will coincide with the book's title extracted from the
input XML document. The <BODY> elements contains four more rules calls. The first
rule invocation (line 11) extracts again the book's title and places it inside a pair of
<H1> tags, which produces the first line of the page shown in Figure 1.13. The rule
invocations at lines 12, 13, and 15, respectively, match authors, publishing information, and part elements, producing the HTML output shown in Figure 1.13.

Note that the XSL call for extracting the book title differs from those for extracting the publishing information, the authors, and the book parts. The former
extracts just an atomic piece of text from an XML element, which is achieved
using the basic XSL clause `xsl:value-of`; the latter require more elaborate
matching and output construction, which is delegated to another template, called
using the `xsl:apply-templates` clause.

The templates called for producing the output may be very simple, as the ones
for extracting the publishing information (lines 25–29) and the authors (lines
20–23), which just return either the textual content of XML elements or the value
of an attribute. Templates can be more complex and activate other templates, as the
rule for extracting the data of a book part (lines 31–34), which contains a nested rule
invocation (line 33) for finding the data of the various chapters that constitute a part.

Transformations of XML documents can be achieved also by means of the
XQuery language (also known, in conjunction with XPath, as *XML Query*), a W3C
standard proposal addressing the efficient querying of XML data. XQuery is still

```
1   <HTML>
2   <HEAD><TITLE>{//book/title/text()}</TITLE></HEAD>
3   <BODY>
4       <CENTER><H1>{//book/title/text()}</H1><CENTER>
5       <CENTER>
6         <B>
7           {//book/author[position()=1]/text()}
8           {FOR $a IN //book/author[position() > 1]
9             RETURN ", ", {$a/text()}
10           }
11         </B>
12       </CENTER>
13       <P align="right"><I>{//book/publishing/@schedule/text()}</I></P>
14       <HR/>
15         {FOR $p IN //book/part
16          RETURN
17           <P><H3>$p/text()</H3></P>
18           {FOR $c IN $p/chapter
19            RETURN <P><H4>$c/text()</H4></P>
20           }
21         }
22   </BODY>
23   </HTML>
```

Figure 1.14   Document transformation in XQuery.

a Working Draft, but several tools and databases already offer XQuery processing. The official XQuery recommendation is expected for early 2003.

Queries and document transformations are written as path expressions, specified in XPath, or as FLWR[4] expressions, a syntax for specifying iterations and for binding variables to intermediate results. To give the flavor of the language, the example in Figure 1.14 shows the XQuery version of the same transformation expressed by the XSL style sheet of Figure 1.12.

The transformation mixes HTML tags and XQuery expressions, which are replaced in the output document by the result of their evaluation. The result of

---

[4]FLWR stands for For-Let-Where-Return, pronounced as the word "flower."

the transformation shown in Figure 1.14 is an HTML document, wrapped inside the two HTML tags (lines 1 and 23). The HEAD tag includes the title of the book (line 2), which is determined by evaluating the XPath expression `//book/title/text()`. The BODY contains a heading where the title is repeated (line 4), and the list of authors (lines 5–12), centered and in bold face: the first author is obtained evaluating the expression `{//book/author[position()=1]/text()}` (line 7); then the subsequent authors are processed one at a time by means of the FOR clause, which iterates over the set of authors obtained by evaluating the expression `//book/author[position() > 1]`, which selects all the authors whose position is greater than 1. For each author retrieved in the loop (which is bound to variable `$a`), a comma is inserted, followed by the text of the AUTHOR element (lines 8–9). Then the value of the schedule attribute is enclosed in a paragraph (line 13), and, after a horizontal line (line 14), the parts and chapters of the book are inserted (lines 15–21): for each part of the book, bound to variable `$p` (line 15), the part name is displayed in a paragraph (line 17), and for each chapter of the part, bound to variable `$c` (line 18), the title of the chapter is displayed (line 19).

1.4 SQL: The Structured Query Language for Relational Databases

If HTTP and HTML/XML are the building blocks of the Web, SQL and relational databases are the cornerstones of information systems. Because relational databases are the leading products for building information systems, and over 80% of the pages found on the Web are actually built from database content, relational technology can be legitimately considered a key ingredient of data-intensive Web applications.

The main principle of the relational technology is extremely simple: data are formatted in tables (called relations) consisting of rows and columns. Each table stores the "facts" about a distinct concept of the application domain, like products or customers, organized as rows of elementary values. For example, the database in Figure 1.15 includes two tables: PRODUCT and CUSTOMER. The product table has three columns: CODE, NAME, and PRICE, which respectively store the code, name, and price of each distinct product.

To uniquely identify the facts stored in a table, it is a good practice to define that a group of columns form a *key* of the table. This definition implies that two rows cannot coexist in the table if they have coincident values of all the key columns. Therefore, the key of a table gives a unique "identity" to each one of the table rows. In the example of Figure 1.15, the key of table `product` is the CODE

PRODUCT

CODE	NAME	PRICE
100	Aladdin	35
101	Blue moon	67
102	Casper	40
104	Dundee	21

CUSTOMER

ID	NAME	ADDRESS
1	Acme Inc.	1 First St. Memphis TN
2	Gizmo Inc.	2 Second Av. New York NY
3	Widget Inc.	5 Third Av. S. Francisco CA
4	Supply Inc.	8 Fifth Rd. London UK

Figure 1.15　Tables in a relational database.

PURCHASE

PROD-CODE	CUST-ID	QUANTITY
100	1	30
102	1	15
104	4	43
101	3	30
101	4	30

Figure 1.16　Table storing purchases of products performed by customers.

column, and the key of table customer is the ID column. These columns are underlined in Figure 1.15 to denote that they are the key of the respective table.

The notion of *key* is central in relational databases, because it permits the expression of semantic relationships between the objects of the application domain. For example, the relationship between the customers and the products they have purchased, along with the information of the total quantity of each product purchased by each customer, can be represented using the table illustrated in Figure 1.16. Each row in the table specifies the product (PROD-CODE), the customer (CUST-ID), and the total purchased quantity (QUANTITY). The columns PROD-CODE and CUST-ID constitute the key of the PURCHASE table, because it does not make sense to allow multiple rows recording the total purchased quantity *for the same pair (product, customer)*.

The three tables shown in Figure 1.15 and Figure 1.16 constitute a small database. By combining the data stored in the three tables it is possible to extract complex information; for instance, which products were bought by "Acme Inc." or how many "Aladdin" lamps were bought by all the customers over time. The combination of information occurs by comparing values in the columns that constitute the keys of the three relations; such a "navigation" from one table to another one is expressed by means of query languages.

The *Structured Query Language* (SQL) is the most popular language for extracting and manipulating the information stored into relational tables. SQL offers the SELECT statement for querying data, and the INSERT, DELETE, and UPDATE statements for changing the database content.

A SELECT statement permits you to extract the desired information from one or more tables, formatted as a table of result rows. The basic form of a SELECT statement is:

```
SELECT column-list
FROM table-list
WHERE condition
```

The meaning of the statement is to build a table composed of the columns specified in the column list (SELECT clause), assembled from the values of the rows of the tables mentioned in the table list (FROM clause) that satisfy some condition (WHERE clause).

For example, to retrieve the name and price of all products costing less than $50, the following query can be formulated:

```
SELECT NAME, PRICE
FROM PRODUCT
WHERE PRICE < 50
```

Returning as result the table in Figure 1.17.

A more complex example is the query that retrieves the names of all the customers who have purchased products costing less than $50, together with the name of the purchased products. To fulfill this query, it is necessary to consider three tables: the PRODUCT, CUSTOMER, and PURCHASE tables. In the relational terminology, the PRODUCT table must be "joined" to the PURCHASE table to obtain a table that includes for every product the IDs of customers who have purchased

NAME	PRICE
Aladdin	35
Casper	40
Dundee	21

PRODUCT.NAME	CUSTOMER.NAME
Aladdin	Acme Inc.
Casper	Acme Inc.
Dundee	Supply Inc.

Figure 1.17   Result of a SQL query.

Figure 1.18   Result of a SQL query.

it, and then this intermediate table must be in turn joined to the CUSTOMER table, to add the information about the customer's name and address. The following query does the job:

```
SELECT PRODUCT.NAME, CUSTOMER.NAME
FROM PRODUCT,PURCHASE, CUSTOMER
WHERE PRODUCT.CODE = PURCHASE.PROD-CODE AND
      CUSTOMER.ID = PURCHASE.CUST-ID AND
      PRODUCT.PRICE < 50
```

The WHERE condition includes both "join conditions" (PRODUCT.CODE = PUR-CHASE.PROD-CODE and CUSTOMER.ID = PURCHASE.CUST-ID) and row selection condition (PRODUCT.PRICE < 50). The result of the query applied to the three tables shown in Figure 1.15 and Figure 1.16 is the table shown in Figure 1.18.

The SQL SELECT statement has more options than table joins and row selection; it includes primitives for applying aggregate functions to sets of rows, sorting and grouping query results, and building complex nested queries.

Figure 1.19 shows the various ways in which SQL queries can be submitted to the database. As a first option SQL queries can be posed directly by the user, using a dedicated graphical user interface. However, such an interface is rarely used, and queries are instead normally embedded inside programs, which interact with the database to extract or update its content according to the business logic of the application. The interaction between an external program and the database query processor takes place through the *Application Programming Interface* (API) of the database, which offers procedures for shipping queries to the database and for getting results back.

To ensure the portability of programs across databases of different vendors, which may have different APIs, special-purpose libraries are available that offer a standard set of functions masking the peculiarities of the specific database product. The most diffused interoperability libraries are the *Open Database Connectivity* (ODBC) library by Microsoft, and the *Java Database Connectivity* (JDBC) library,

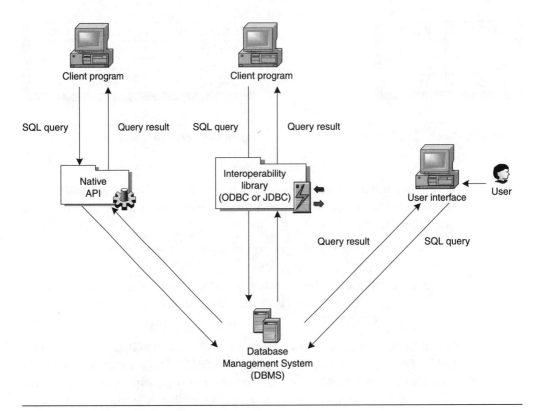

Figure 1.19 Interactions between clients and database management system.

by Javasoft, which is part of the Java 2 Enterprise Edition platform. These libraries expose a set of utility objects (for example, the "database connection" object, the "statement" object, the "result set" object), which hide the details of database interaction and facilitate the programming of database-aware applications. Programs that build dynamic Web pages from database content typically use the ODBC or JDBC libraries.

1.5 Beyond HTTP: Building Web Pages on the Fly

Real-life Web applications require the capability of serving to the users HTML pages that dynamically publish content coming from one or more data sources. For example, the content of the home page of a news magazine is refreshed daily, by extracting the latest news from the news repository. This requirement goes beyond the capabilities of the HTTP protocol, which is designed to ship requests for resources from the browser to the server, and not to govern the process by which the desired resource is located or built. This section reviews a progression of techniques for building Web pages on the fly, extending the capability of HTTP.

1.5.1 Common Gateway Interface

The simplest way to solve the problem of dynamically building a Web page in response to an HTTP request is to let the HTTP server delegate the construction of the page to an external program, using a standard interface called *Common Gateway Interface* (CGI), as illustrated in Figure 1.20.

The dynamic computation of the page introduces a "double" client server loop (Figure 1.20):

1. The browser issues an HTTP request to the HTTP server.

2. The HTTP server invokes an external program that constructs the page to be sent back to the user.

3. The external program sends the constructed page to the HTTP server.

4. The HTTP server uses the page constructed by the external program to assemble the HTTP response and sends this response back to the browser.

The invocation of an external program occurs when the HTTP request coming from the browser includes an URL pointing to an executable program called *CGI script* instead of pointing to a document or media file. The Web server must be properly configured to be able to distinguish URLs that point to resources that must be "executed" from URLs pointing to static resources to be served back as they are.

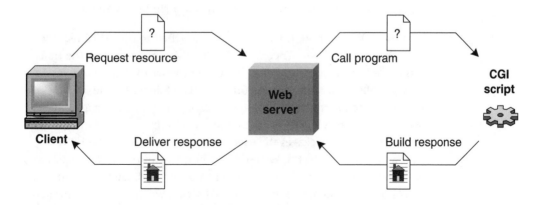

Figure 1.20 Dynamic construction of a Web page in response to an HTTP request.

When the HTTP request refers to an executable, the Web server launches it, typically by spawning a new process. The communication between the Web server and the CGI script is based upon a set of predefined system variables, which are initialized by the HTTP server upon receipt of the HTTP request. These variables describe the parameters of the HTTP request (such as the HTTP method used, the number of bytes attached to the request, and so on).

When the CGI script is launched, it reads the CGI variables and the request body (if there is one transmitted via the POST method), then it performs the elaboration required to compute the response page, and finally it outputs the page.

For an effective interaction, the user must be able to supply request parameters to the Web server, to be forwarded to the CGI script and used to elaborate the response. For example, the user must be able to supply the name of an artist to get a page listing all the music albums composed by him/her. User input coming from the browser must be transported by the HTTP request, which is the only means of interaction between the browser and the Web server. Transportation takes place by means of the two distinct HTTP methods already discussed in Section 1.2.1:

- With the *GET method,* the user input is appended to the requested URL. Parameters are encoded as label/value pairs appended to the URL, after a question mark symbol, as in the following example: *http://www.google.com/search?q=SQL&hl=it* When the GET method is used, the Web server initializes a CGI variable called "query string" with the value of the final part of the URL containing the label/value pairs, so that the CGI script can get the user input simply by fetching and decoding the content of this variable. Due to the limitations in the length of a URL (256 characters at maximum), the GET method is used when the client needs to communicate to the server only a few simple parameters.

- With the POST method, the user input is attached to the HTTP request using the message body. Therefore, the POST method supports the transmission of large amounts of data from the browser to the Web server. In order to collect user input in the browser, HTML includes the <FORM> element, which permits the designer to construct an HTML page to be used as a data entry mask. When the user clicks the submit button in the form, the browser packages the user's input in the body of the HTTP request and sends it to the Web server. Upon receipt of a POST request, the Web server extracts the user's input from the message body, and sends it to the standard input of the CGI script, which can use it for performing a business action and elaborating the response.

Figure 1.21 shows a simple example of HTML form for inputting the name of an artist and the desired recording medium. Syntactically, an HTML form is de-

```
<HTML>
<HEAD>
<TITLE>A simple HTML form</TITLE>
</HEAD>
<BODY>
<P align="center">An example of HTML form: please input the name of the
artist and your preferred recording medium</P>
<FORM action="html_form_action.exe" method="post">
  Artist's name: <INPUT type="text" name="name"> <BR>
  <INPUT type="radio" name="medium" value="CD" checked> CD
  <INPUT type="radio" name="medium" value="Vinyl"> Vinyl <BR>
  <INPUT type="submit" value="Submit">
</FORM>
  </BODY>
  </HTML>
```

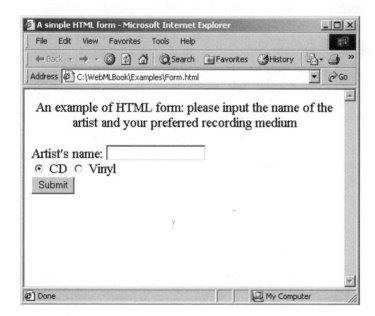

Figure 1.21   An example of an HTML form.

limited by the <FORM> element, which includes multiple <INPUT> elements for collecting input. The form of Figure 1.21 includes four inputs: a text input, for inserting a string; two radio buttons, for inputting the value of the recording medium; and a button, for confirming the data entry and submitting it to the Web server. The enclosing <FORM> element has two attributes:

- The `action` attribute specifies the URL of the server program to be called when the submit button is pressed.
- The `method` attribute specifies the HTTP method to use for sending the input.

A CGI program can exploit the user's input to assemble a SELECT query for retrieving data to be placed inside an HTML page, as well as to store the user's input into the database, issuing an INSERT or UPDATE query.

CGI is the simplest way of dynamically publishing or updating content on the Web, but its architecture has severe limitations, which make it unpractical in most situations:

- At each HTTP request for a CGI script the Web server spawns a new process, which is terminated at the end of execution. Process creation and termination is a very costly activity, which may quickly become the performance bottleneck.
- Terminating the process where the CGI script is executed after each request prevents information about the user interaction to be retained between consecutive user requests, unless such information is stored in a database, which again impacts performance. In addition, terminating the process also prevents the management of shared resources, like a database or network connection, used by multiple users across multiple HTTP requests.

For these reasons, more complex architectures have been developed to overcome the downsides of CGI and cope with applications that demand a high level of performance and the retention of user session data.

1.5.2   Web Server Extensions

The limitations of the CGI architecture, which are mostly due to the forced termination of the process where the CGI script is executed, can be eliminated by extending the capabilities of the Web server. The adopted solution is shown in Figure 1.22: the Web server is extended with an application execution engine, where the programs for computing the HTTP response can be processed in an efficient way.

The application execution engine can be implemented in several different ways, from a dynamically linked library directly integrated inside the Web server,

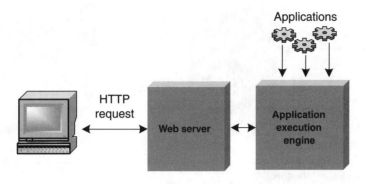

Figure 1.22 The extended Web server architecture.

to a distinct process running on the same or on a separate machine. Regardless of the technical details of its implementation, a Web server extension offers an efficient and persistent execution environment, where applications can be installed and executed in response to incoming HTTP requests, without being terminated after each request.

The extended Web server architecture offers several advantages with respect to the pure CGI approach:

- It eliminates the process creation and termination overhead.

- It permits the allocation of shared resources, associated with one or more applications and concurrently accessed by multiple users.

- It offers a main memory environment for storing session data, durable across multiple HTTP requests.

An example of extended Web server architecture is the Javasoft's Servlet API (illustrated in Figure 1.23), which associates the Web server with a *Java Virtual Machine* (JVM). The JVM supports the execution of a special Java program, called a *servlet container,* which in turn manages the execution of Java servlets and the maintenance of session data. A *Java servlet* is the counterpart in the Java world of a CGI program; it is a Java program that can be invoked to respond to an HTTP request for a dynamic page. The servlet container intermediates between the Web server and the various servlets: it is responsible for receiving the HTTP request from the Web server, creating a user session when needed, invoking the servlet associated to the HTTP request, and transmitting to the servlet the data of the HTTP request, wrapped in the form of a Java object.

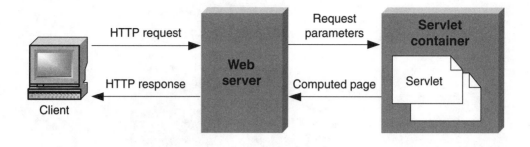

Figure 1.23   Java servlet architecture.

Each servlet is a Java class that extends the standard class `HttpServlet` included in the servlet API specification. The `HttpServlet` class offers the basic primitives for interacting with the servlet container, like the functions for inspecting the HTTP request and the session data, and for writing content to the HTTP response. The example in Figure 1.24 shows the flavor of servlet programming.

The servlet includes the declaration of class `RequestInfo`, which extends `HttpServlet` (line 5) and implements the standard function `doGet` (line 7), which is invoked by the servlet container when an HTTP request formulated with the GET method arrives. The `doGet` function has two input parameters, `request` and `response`, which are the Java objects wrapping the HTTP request and response.

By operating on these two objects, the servlet can inspect and manipulate the HTTP request and response, as shown in line 10, where the servlet sets the MIME type of the response to `text/html`, as necessary when the response is an HTML page. Then, the servlet calls the function `getWriter()` on the response object, which returns an output stream (represented by variable `out`) to write content to (line 11). Everything printed on this output stream ends up in the response sent to the user. After getting the output stream, the servlet starts the actual production of the HTML page, by printing content to the output stream. Lines 12–17 simply print some fixed HTML code and textual content. The lines 18, 20, and 22 extract information from the request object (namely, the request method, the URI[5] of the requested resource, and the version of the browser) and print it to the output stream. The result of invoking the servlet is shown in Figure 1.25 on page 44.

---

[5]The *Uniform Resource Identifier* (URI) is a generalization of the HTTP concept of Uniform Resource Locator (URL).

```
 1:  import java.io.*;
 2:  import javax.servlet.*;
 3:  import javax.servlet.http.*;
 4:
 5:  public class RequestInfo extends HttpServlet {
 6:
 7:    public void doGet(HttpServletRequest request,
 8:                      HttpServletResponse response)
 9:                      throws IOException, ServletException {
10:      response.setContentType("text/html");
11:      PrintWriter out = response.getWriter();
12:      out.println("<HTML>");
13:      out.println("<HEAD>");
14:      out.println("<TITLE>Request Information Example</TITLE>");
15:      out.println("</HEAD>");
16:      out.println("<BODY>");
17:      out.println("<H3>Request Information Example</H3>");
18:      out.println("Method: " + request.getMethod());
19:      out.println("<BR>");
20:      out.println("Request URI:  " + request.getRequestURI());
21:      out.println("<BR>");
22:      out.println("User Agent:" + request.getHeader("User-Agent"));
23:      out.println("</BODY>");
24:      out.println("</HTML>");
25:    }
26: }
```

Figure 1.24   Example of a Java Servlet.

1.5.3   Implementing Application State over HTTP

Web server extensions, like the Java servlet architecture, offer an efficient way of implementing *stateful* Web applications; that is, HTTP-based applications capable of retaining the state of the user interaction. State information can be stored at the server side, in the form of *session data,* and at the client side, in the form of *cookies*.

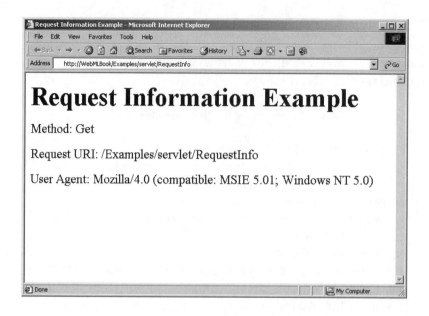

Figure 1.25   The result of executing the servlet program of Figure 1.24.

State maintenance at the server side requires the server to identify and distinguish the HTTP requests of the various clients, to associate each piece of state information to the user to which it belongs. This requirement is fulfilled by creating a *session identifier* upon arrival of the first HTTP request of a new client, and by making the browser communicate such identifier to the server in all the subsequent HTTP requests, so that the server can treat such requests as belonging to the same user's session. For example, in the servlet architecture, the servlet container creates a new session identifier for each HTTP request coming from a client not already associated to a valid session identifier and exploits the mechanisms of cookies and URL rewriting (explained later) to force the browser to communicate the session ID at each HTTP request. The server that originates the session decides when to terminate it, typically by setting a time out after the last user's request, or by offering suitable instructions whereby a server-side program can explicitly invalidate the session. When explicit invalidation or time out occurs, the next request from the client causes the server to create a new session identifier.

When a session is active, the server-side execution engine can associate to it state information. Typically, such information is temporary, and resides in some main-memory data structures, whose duration is the same as that of the user's session. In the servlet environment, session data are wrapped inside a Java object, called *session,* similar to the request and response objects: the servlet code can access the session object, which offers functions for retrieving and updating information pertaining to a user's session.

State information can also be mantained at the client side, using cookies. A cookie is an object created by a server-side program and stored in the client (typically, in the disk cache of the browser), which can be used by the server-side program to store and retrieve state information associated to the client. A cookie is set when the server includes in the HTTP response sent to the browser a `Set-Cookie` HTTP header, filled with the piece of information to store at the client. The cookie may include a description of the range of URLs for which an associated state information is valid. Any future HTTP requests made by the client that fall in that range of URLs will transmit the content of the cookie back to the server. The duration of the state information associated with a cookie is independent of the duration of a server-side session, and is decided by the client, who may explicitly delete his cookies. A typical usage of cookies in the context of e-commerce application is to store some user preferences that are transparently communicated to the server whenever the user accesses the application.

Cookies can also be used for communicating the session identifier from the server to the client and vice versa, as required for the proper management of session data. However, a disadvantage of cookies is that the user can disable their support in the browser. To overcome this problem, the same data that would be stored in the cookie, for instance, the session identifier, can be preserved for the duration of a session using a technique called *URL rewriting,* which appends the state information as extra parameters in the URLs embedded in the page sent to the client. In this way, the client communicates the needed information to the server even in absence of cookies, but the server-side application code must take care of appending to URLs embedded inside the dynamically generated pages the extra information to be maintained. In the servlet environment, URL rewriting for the communication of the session identifier is facilitated by a utility function, which automatically appends the session identifier to a dynamically produced URL. The following instructions inside a servlet produce an automatically encoded URL:

```
out.println("<A href=");
out.println(response.encodeURL("/appdir/myServlet"));
out.println(">Click here<A>");
```

Executing such instructions produces an HTML fragment similar to the one below:

```
<A href=/appdir/myServlet;jsessionid=XY56443HY3Y>Click here<A>
```

where the URL of the anchor tag contains an extra parameter called `jsessionid`, holding the value of the session identifier. When the user clicks on the anchor, the session identifier is communicated to the server.

1.5.4 Server-Side Scripting

As shown by the example in Figure 1.24, writing a servlet (but also a CGI script) is a technical task that requires programming skills. Analyzing the code of the example shows that programming is applied not only to calculate the dynamic portions of the page (in the example, the various parameters of the HTTP request), but also the fixed textual content and HTML markup. While the former task does require programming skills, the definition of the static content and markup of the result page requires only HTML skills, and could be delegated to the graphic designer.

This observation is at the base of a different linguistic approach to the construction of dynamic Web pages, called *server-side scripting*. Server-side scripting (not to be confused with client-side scripting, treated in Section 1.2.3) is a technique for inserting into an HTML page template some programming instructions that are executed by a server program to calculate the dynamic parts of the page.

With server-side scripting, the technical skills required for writing dynamic pages are reduced, because the programmer may add the necessary scripting instructions to an HTML *page template* prepared by the graphic designer. A page template must then be deployed in a Web server, extended with a script engine capable of interpreting the server-side scripting instructions, as shown in Figure 1.26.

When an incoming HTTP request refers to a page template, the Web server passes the page template to the script engine, which processes the embedded instructions, calculates the dynamic parts of the page, and inserts them in the page template. The output of this processing is a plain HTML page, where all the expressions in the server-side scripting language have been replaced by their

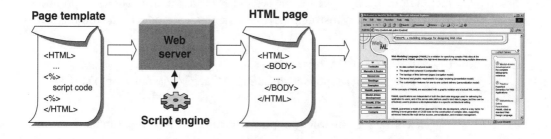

Figure 1.26   The execution of a server-side scripting page template.

calculated values. This page is handed back to the Web server, which forwards it to the client. For the browser receiving the result page, the server-side processing is completely invisible, and the HTML code received is perfectly identical to that of a manually produced, static page.

Various incarnations of the server-side scripting approach are available, among which the *Active Server Pages* (ASP) language by Microsoft, the *Java Server Pages* (JSP) language by Javasoft, and the PHP open language. Figure 1.27 shows the ASP code of a dynamic HTML page template, which displays the same information as the servlet listed in Figure 1.24. The code of Figure 1.27 can be stored in a textual file ending with the `.asp` extension, instead of the `.html` extension, and published under the Microsoft Internet Information Server Web server, for producing an HTML page similar to that shown in Figure 1.25.

The page template contains regular HTML tags and static content, and the elements that must be computed dynamically are coded as ASP statements, syntactically distinguished by special surrounding brackets (`<%..%>`). In the example in Figure 1.27, the ASP statements inside the brackets access the request object to fetch the desired information, and write it in the response. The effect of the `Response.Write` function invocation is to insert a piece of dynamic content in the output page, in the place where the instruction appears. For example, the server-side scripting instruction:

```
<%Response.Write(Request.ServerVariables("request_method"))%>
```

```
<HTML>
<HEAD>
<TITLE>Request Information Example</TITLE>
</HEAD>
<BODY>
<H3>Request Information Example</H3>
Method: <%Response.Write(Request.ServerVariables("request_method"))%>
<BR>
Request URI: <%Response.Write(Request.ServerVariables("URL"))%>
<BR>
User Agent: <%Response.Write(Request.ServerVariables("http_user_agent"))%>
</BODY>
</HTML>
```

Figure 1.27   Example of server-side scripting page template written in Microsoft ASP.

is equivalent to the instruction at line 18 of the servlet listed in Figure 1.24: it prints into the response output stream the value of variable `request_method`, which contains the HTTP method of the user's request.

Despite the similarity of the objective, the coding style of server-side scripting is completely different from the servlet style. A servlet contains programming instructions for printing the entire page, whereas a page template contains regular HTML, and programming instructions are limited to the computation of the variable part of the page. As a consequence, server-side scripting page templates are easier to write and maintain.

1.5.5   Server-Side Executable Tags

Although server-side scripting facilitates the development of dynamic Web applications, it does not eliminate the need of mixing programming with content and markup. The need remains for the programmer and the graphic designer to work jointly on the same source file, which prevents a full "separation of concerns" between the various aspects of Web development: the static content, the look and feel, and the programming logic.

The so-called *server-side tag libraries* take a further step in the direction of separating content and markup from the programming of a dynamic page template. The key idea of the tag library approach is to mask the code necessary for dynamic content production beneath "magic" tags, which can be inserted into the page as regular markup elements, but are executed by a runtime interpreter. With a tag library, the source code of the page template no longer mixes markup, content, and programming. Only content and markup remain, but the markup includes special XML tags that are executed by a server-side program to produce further content and/or HTML markup.

In this way, the roles of the programmer and of the graphic designer are cleanly separated: the programmer conceives a set of XML tags for producing the desired dynamic content, defines the tag properties to expose to the graphic designer, and writes the code for "executing" the tag; the graphic designer specifies the look and feel of the page, defines its static content, and inserts and edits the properties of the "magic" tags created by the programmer.

Tag libraries are available both in the Java world, starting with Version 1.1 of the JSP specification, and in the Microsoft .NET platform, as part of the ASP.NET language.

As an example, Figure 1.28 shows the use of a custom tag in the Microsoft ASP.NET language. In the first line of the HTML source code, an ASP.NET statement registers a custom tag library, named "Acme." Tags of this family can then

```
1:  <%@ Register TagPrefix="Acme" Namespace="Acme" Assembly="Acme" %>
2:  <HTML>
3:    <BODY>
4:      <H1>A user-defined tag for showing a calendar with the current
5:        date at the server highlighted</H1>
6:      <Acme:Calendar id="MyCal" runat=server/>
7:    </BODY>
8:  </HTML>
```

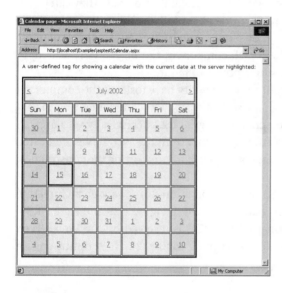

Figure 1.28 Example of server-side executable tag in Microsoft ASP.NET.

be introduced in the page, as XML tags, prefixed with the name of their family. One such tag, named `Calendar`, appears at line 6: it is a complex object, implemented by a server-side program, as declared by the `runat=server` attribute inside the tag. In this example, the behavior associated with the calendar is specified by a separate program, written in the latest version of Visual Basic, called VB.NET, or in C#, a new programming language designed by Microsoft.

The result of executing the ASP.NET template is also shown in Figure 1.28: the ASP.NET execution engine leaves the regular HTML tags intact, so that they are rendered by the browser in the usual way; conversely, the ASP.NET engine processes the `Calendar` tag, and replaces it with the content dynamically produced by the program. As shown in Figure 1.28, the output associated with such a tag is a table, listing the days of the current month, and permitting the user to scroll to the previous or next month.

A similar example could be recast in the context of the Java 2 platform: in this case, the program associated with the `Calendar` tag would be a Java class.

1.5.6   Increasing Scalability with Application Servers

Large-scale Web applications designed for supporting the electronic business must ensure a high level of availability, security, and scalability, because they can be exposed to millions of concurrent users in the potentially hostile Internet environment. To ensure the required level of service, enterprise Web applications must have a modular architecture, where each component can be easily replicated, to increase performance and avoid single points of failure.

The requirements of scalability and reliability have fostered the commercial success of *application servers,* which are software products complementing the extended Web server architecture described in Figure 1.22. Technically speaking, an application server is a software platform, distinct from the Web server, dedicated to the efficient execution of business components for supporting the construction of dynamic pages.

The typical organization and page computation flow of a Web architecture incorporating an application server are illustrated in Figure 1.29 and Figure 1.30.

The client request (1), formatted in HTTP, is received by the Web server, which transforms it into a request to the scripting engine (2). The scripting engine

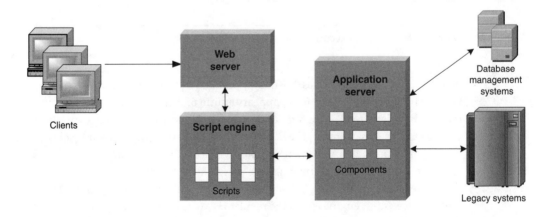

Figure 1.29   Architecture and components of an application server architecture.

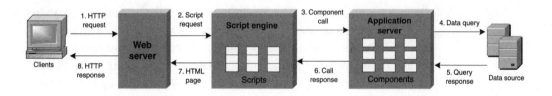

Figure 1.30   The flow of requests and responses in application server architectures.

executes the program associated with the requested URL, which may include calls to business components hosted in the application server (3). Typically, such calls involve the retrieval and elaboration of data from one or more data sources, like corporate databases or legacy systems. The components managed by the application server dispatch the query to the data source (4), collect the query result (5), possibly elaborate it and and hand it back to the scripting engine (6). Query results are integrated into the HTTP response by the scripts executed in the scripting engine, to obtain a result HTML page (7), routed by the HTTP server to the client (8).

The main purpose of the application server is to provide a feature-rich execution environment for the business components, which facilitates the construction of scalable and reliable applications. This execution environment, often called a "managed runtime environment" includes the following services:

- *Transparent component distribution, replication, and load balancing:* The business objects programmed by the user are installed into the managed runtime environment, which may be distributed on multiple processes and physical machines. The application server automatically manages the creation of processes, the replication of business objects and their allocation to the available processes, the allotment of client requests and of the calls issued by the scripting programs to the business objects, and the dynamic adaptation of the number of processes and business objects to the increase and decrease of the actual workload. The application server manages replication and load balancing in such a way that they are totally transparent to the calling client, which can behave as if interacting with a single instance of a business object.

- *Failure recovery:* The application server may monitor the active hosts, processes and business objects, detect hardware, software and network failures, and automatically avert client requests addressed to a failed component and route them to available replicas of the same business object.

■ *Transaction management:* The application server may provide the capability of defining units of work (called *transactions*), which are either executed successfully from start to end, or rolled back completely in case of failure of any of the included operations. Transactions are typically offered by database management systems for sequences of database update operations. In application servers, this important service is offered for generic sequences of calls to business objects.

■ *Resource pooling:* The application server may handle pools of expensive resources, like database connections, and share these resource among multiple business objects in an optimized way.

■ *Interoperability with legacy applications:* The application server may be equipped with predefined gateways or software developments kits for exchanging messages and data with applications developed on obsolete platforms or with surpassed technologies.

■ *Multi-protocol, multi-language application development support:* The application server may integrate multiple application distribution protocols and programming languages into a uniform development environment, and facilitate cross-platform application development and migration.

Factoring these services out of the individual applications greatly reduces their development complexity, which results in better software quality and easier maintenance. For this reason, application servers are at present the chief component of large-scale Web applications.

The application server architecture represented in Figure 1.29 has many commercial incarnations, which vary for the quality and quantity of services, and for the supported programming languages and communication protocols. The two most comprehensive solutions are Javasoft's Java 2 Enterprise Edition and Microsoft .NET.

Java 2 Enterprise Edition (J2EE) is a set of extension APIs of the Java 2 programming language, conceived to offer a portable environment for the development of enterprise-class Web applications. The core of the platform is the Enterprise JavaBeans API, which dictates the rules for defining object-oriented components managed in the application server.

The Microsoft .NET architecture is the new application development infrastructure designed by Microsoft that replaces several previous Web-related technologies, including Active Server Pages. The main innovation of the .NET architecture is the introduction of a managed runtime environment: applications written in VB.NET, C++, or C# are partially compiled into a byte code called *Microsoft Intermediate Language* (MSIL), executed by the *Common Language Runtime* (CLR).

The J2EE and .NET environments have many characteristics in common: both are software platforms conceived for multi-tier, object-oriented, distributed applications, running in a managed and feature-rich execution environment. The main difference between the two is not technical: J2EE privileges application portability with respect to operating systems, but restricts the programming language to Java; conversely, Microsoft .NET has a multi-language development environment, but it is limited to the Microsoft operating systems. Although a detailed comparison of the two approaches is outside the scope of this chapter, a parallel overview of the two platforms is given in Table 1.3.

Table 1.3 Overview of J2EE and .NET platforms.

Platform feature	J2EE	.NET
Operating systems	Any	Windows 2000, Windows XP
Browser	Any	Any (Internet Explorer, if ActiveX components are used)
Client-side components	Java applets	ActiveX components
Web server	Any	IIS
Server-side scripts	Servlet and JSP	ASP.NET and Web Forms
Server components	Enterprise Java Beans (EJB)	.NET Managed Components
Programming languages	Java	VB.NET, C++, C#
Communication protocol	Internet Inter Orb Protocol (IIOP)	Simple Object Access Protocol (SOAP)
Database access	JDBC, SQL/J	ADO.NET
Distributed transaction processing	Java Transaction Server (JTS)	Microsoft Distributed Transaction Coordinator (MS-DTC) COM+ Services
Security	Java Security Services	COM+ Security Call Context
Directory services	Java Naming and Directory Interface (JNDI)	Active Directory Services Interface (ADSI)

1.5.7   Three-tier Architectures

The application server architecture illustrated in Figure 1.29 is the "Web version" of a more general software architecture called *three-tier architecture*. The core principle of three-tier architectures is to provide an intermediate layer between the client and the data tier, which centralizes middleware services and the business logic of the application. Three-tier architectures were proposed in alternative to two-tier architectures (Figure 1.31), in which client programs interact directly with database management systems by posing queries, receiving the results, and processing them for presentation to the user.

Three-tier architectures offer a higher degree of scalability than two-tier configurations, thanks to better network utilization and to the virtually unlimited replication and load distribution capabilities of the middle tier.

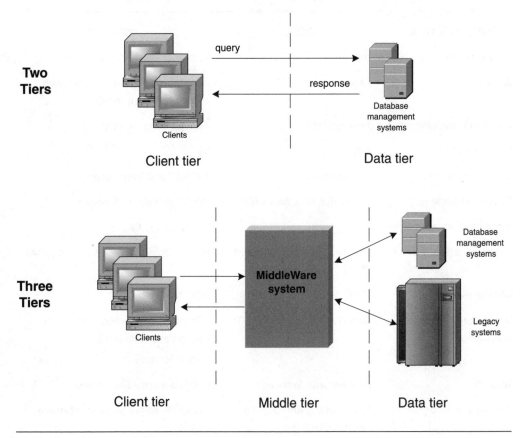

Figure 1.31   Two-tier architecture versus three-tier architecture.

Three-tier architectures existed prior to the advent of Web applications and were supported by a wide range of middleware products, including *Transaction Processing Monitors* (TP Monitors), message-based middleware systems, and distributed object request brokers. Such pre-Web middleware products have evolved into modern Web application servers by incorporating HTTP-specific features, like an HTTP server and a server-side scripting engine. Another distinctive feature of modern Web application servers with respect to their predecessors is the adoption of object-oriented components as the atomic elements of application programming and deployment, and the consequent adoption of object-based distribution protocols, like the Corba 2 Internet Inter-Orb Protocol, or SOAP (Simple Object Access Protocol).

1.5.8 Multi-Device Content Publishing with XML

We conclude this rather long technology overview with a last look at the technical challenges posed by the evolution of requirements to design and implement Web applications.

The advent of mobile terminals and their increasing popularity in the consumer market is shaping the scenario for a new generation of applications, characterised by the need for publishing the same content for a very large spectrum of access devices. A typical instance of this new scenario is mobile commerce, where users are expected to interact with the same application with such devices as their PC, mobile phone, and TV set.

Multi-device applications can be regarded as an extension of "traditional" Web applications, in the sense that content publishing must occur not only for regular Web users equipped with a normal PC screen, but also for other kinds of markup languages and access devices. Therefore, the need arises to reconsider the process of content publishing, to assess its adequacy to the broader scenario of multi-device Web applications.

As Figure 1.30 has shown, content publishing in conventional Web application architectures is characterised by a long flow of client-server request-response loops, in which data get progressively transformed from a native format to the format suitable for presentation to the user. This long chain of transformations is error-prone and difficult to maintain: any change in the requirements (such as changes in the database table format or in the page presentation) involves updating several programs, for example the SQL queries for data extraction and the servlets or JSP page templates for page assembly. The primary reason for this complexity is the mismatch between the format in which content is stored in the database, for example, as a set of relational rows, and the format in which it must be presented to the user, namely, as an HTML page. The inconvenience of the approach based on page construction programs, like servlets and JSP page templates, increases for multi-device applications; the same content must be rendered in different markup languages or with different presentations to meet the requirements of access devices with disparate rendition capabilities, from wide-screen monitors to the tiny screens of cellular phones. In such a scenario, a different set of programs must be implemented and maintained for each family of output devices with comparable content presentation features.

To alleviate these problems, *XML can be used as an intermediate data format*, exploited by the data extraction queries to encode their result, as illustrated in Figure 1.32. In this case, HTML-aware servlet programs and page templates can be replaced by XSL programs, which transform the XML results of data queries into pages, encoded in the markup language most suitable to the specific access device issuing the request.

The advantage of this alternative approach is granted by the nature of XML, which is a format usable for both structured data and semi-structured documents and thus alleviates the "format gap" between database and Web content. Database content can be transformed from the relational format to XML, using the SQL extensions for encoding query results into XML available in most com-

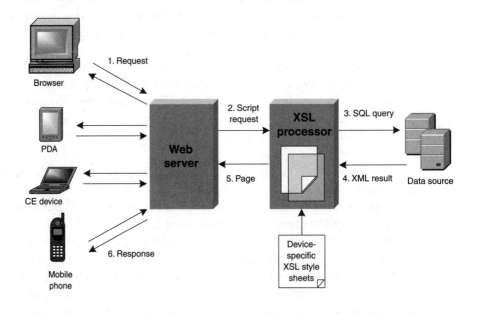

Figure 1.32 XML-based content publishing architecture.

mercial databases. Then, XML content can be converted into the desired markup language, exploiting declarative presentation rules written in XSL. This approach requires less programming and exploits better the power of such declarative languages as SQL and XSL; moreover, application evolution becomes easier, because adding yet another presentation format for a new device requires only the addition of the necessary XSL presentation rules, and not the coding of servlets or JSP templates.

Summary

This chapter has provided an overview of the technologies that constitute the foundations for building data-intensive Web applications. First, we surveyed the basic protocols and languages for the Web, such as HTTP, HTML, and client-side scripting.

Then, XML and the collateral XSL technology were introduced as the new paradigm for content definition and exchange. To cover also the "data" part of data-intensive Web applications, we have included in the chapter a brief compendium on relational databases, SQL, the most popular relational query language, and on the ODBC and JDBC database interoperability standards.

Next, the chapter discussed the architectures for constructing HTML pages on the fly, including CGI, Java servlets, server-side scripting, with a special mention of JSP and Microsoft .NET custom tag libraries, and application servers.

The concluding section addressed the challenging requirements of multi-device application development, and commented on the use of XML as an intermediate data format, and of SQL and XSL as the declarative languages for expressing the queries and transformations necessary to publish database content for multiple devices.

Bibliographic Notes

The bibliography of a survey chapter like the present one could easily become longer than the chapter itself, so many are the subjects touched to give the reader an overview of the technical issues involved. We will restrict our reading suggestions to the fundamental textbooks and publications, and to online resources where the reader may find useful materials and links for his/her personal study of the various matters.

An interesting starting point of the investigation of Web technologies is the specification of HTTP 1.0 [BLFF], which is the act of foundation of the Web. The original concept of HTTP is described by the actual words of its inventors. Other historical documents on the birth of the Web are available in the Web site of the World Wide Web Consortium (W3C) (*www.w3.org/History.html*) [W3Cf], for example, the source code of the first browser and Web server!

The Web site of the W3C contains a wealth of resources on Web standards [W3Ca, W3Cb, W3Cc, W3Cd, W3Ce] and should be continuously monitored by the reader interested in the technology evolution. The Consortium also organizes a yearly conference (called the WWW Conference), where the research and industrial communities meet to discuss the future of the Web.

HTML [BLC, Rugget] has been the subject of a huge number of textbooks and documents. A step-by-step tutorial on HTML is available on the Web site of the W3 Schools [W3S]. The site features tutorials on many other Web-related technologies, including CSS, JavaScript, Visual Basic Script, ASP, XML, XSL, and more. A complete and easy-to-use online reference manual of all HTML 4 tags can be found at [WDG].

XML is having an editorial success similar to that of HTML, and thus XML textbooks abound. We mention the books [Laurent01] and [Harold01], which offer an extended coverage of XML and of all the most important related standards, including XSL.

The fundamentals of database management systems and of the relational model are covered by many textbooks, among which [ACPT99], which covers both the classical aspects of database technology, and the more recent issues of Web-database integration. An in-depth treatment of the SQL query language can be found in [HV00], which guides the reader in the progressive familiarization with the subtleties of SQL programming.

For developers needing materials on dynamic page generation with Java servlets and server-side scripting with JSP, Sun's Web site offers the official reference guides and technical documentation [Suna, Sunb].

The reference source for the Java 2 Enterprise Edition platform is the Web site by Sun [Sun], which contains the platform specifications and a number of tutorials and developer's guides on the different extension APIs. An in-depth introduction to the development of Web application in the J2EE platform is contained in [Kassem01].

The official reference for application development in the Microsoft .NET architecture is the section of the Microsoft Developer Network devoted to this architecture, reachable from the home page at *http://msdn.microsoft.com*. Various books have appeared on the subject since Microsoft's first announcement of the .NET platform; among the available titles, [MS01] provides an effective tutorial on the integration of .NET server-side controls and databases. An online source of materials on everything related to the .NET world is [ASPNG], which contains tutorials, articles, and links on all aspects of .NET development.

PART

MODELS FOR DESIGNING WEB APPLICATIONS

2 CHAPTER

Data Model

2.1 Introduction

The goal of data modeling is enabling the specification of the data used by the application, in a formal yet intuitive way. The result of data modeling is a *conceptual schema,* which conveys in a simple and readable way the available knowledge about the application data. Designing such a schema is preliminary both to the design of the business functions that operate on the data, and to the implementation of the physical structures supporting data storage, update, and retrieval.

Data modeling is one of the most traditional and consolidated disciplines of Information Technology, for which well-established modeling languages and guidelines exist. For this reason, this book does not propose yet another data modeling language, but exploits the most successful and popular notation, namely the *Entity-Relationship* (E-R) model.

The essential ingredients of the Entity-Relationship model are *entities,* defined as containers of structured data, and *relationships,* representing semantic associations between entities. Entities are described by means of typed *attributes,* and can be organized in *generalization hierarchies,* which express the derivation of a specific concept from a more general one. Relationships are characterized by *cardinality constraints,* which impose restrictions on the number of relationship instances an object may take part in.

This chapter introduces the essential data modeling concepts, sufficient to specify the data schema of a Web application. The bibliographic notes at the end of the chapter mention several textbooks on data modeling, where the reader can find further examples and the discussion of advanced data modeling constructs. Data modeling will be reconsidered in Chapter 8, which illustrates how to model the schema of data-intensive Web applications, and in Chapter 11, which addresses the implementation of Entity-Relationship schemas on top of several data implementation architectures.

2.2   Entities

Entities are the central concept of the Entity-Relationship model. An *entity* represents a description of the common features of set of objects of the real world. Examples of entities are *Person, Car, Artist,* and *Album.* An entity has a *population,* which is the set of objects that are described by the entity. These objects are also called the *instances* of the entity. For example, the population of entity Person is a specific set of persons, and the population of entity Car is a specific set of cars, and so on.

As all the concepts of the Entity-Relationship model, entities are specified using a graphic notation. They are denoted by means of rectangles, with the entity name at the top. Figure 2.1 shows an Entity-Relationship schema consisting of two entities: Album and Artist.[1]

2.2.1   Attributes

Attributes represent the properties of real-world objects that are relevant for the application purposes. Examples of attributes are the name, address, and photo of

---

[1]Although the concepts of the Entity-Relationship model are very consolidated, the graphic notation has several variants. We adopt the essential style followed by OMT and UML, which lists attributes inside entities and represents relationships as simple lines connecting entity boxes.

Figure 2.1 Graphic notation for entities.

a person. Attributes are associated with entities, with the meaning that all the instances of the entity are characterized by the same set of attributes. In other words, the entity is a descriptor of the common properties of a set of objects, and such properties are expressed as attributes.

It is admissible that an entity instance may have a *null value* for one or more attributes. However, a null value may represent different modeling situations, and raises ambiguities in the interpretation of the properties of an instance:

- A null value may denote that a certain attribute does not apply to a specific entity instance (for example, the driver's license number for persons without a driver's license).

- A null value may denote that the value of a certain attribute is unknown for a specific entity instance (for example, the age or the marital status of a person).

Attributes are graphically represented inside the entity box, below the entity name, as shown in Figure 2.2. In the example, entity Album is characterized by attributes Title, Year, and Cover, and entity Artist by attributes FirstName, LastName, Biography, and Photo.

2.2.2 Identification and Primary Key

All the instances of an entity must be distinguishable, by means of a unique identity that permits their unambiguous identification. To express the unique identity of entity instances, one or more attributes can be defined as the *primary key*

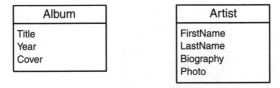

Figure 2.2 Graphic notation for entities and attributes.

of the entity. Primary key attributes must satisfy a few restrictions, not requested for regular attributes. Their value must be defined (that is, not null) for every instance of the entity, and unique, which means that there should not exist two entity instances with the same value of the key attributes.

It is good practice to define the primary key of entities using a single special purpose attribute, called *object identifier* (OID), whose sole purpose is to assign a distinct identifier to each instance of an entity. In the rest of this book, we will assume that the OID property is implicitly defined for all entities, and omit it from the Entity-Relationship diagrams.

If an entity admits alternative identification schemes, for example properties used in the application domain for naming entity instances, the identifying attributes can be defined as *keys* (also called *alternative keys*). Alternative keys must be not null and unique, just like primary keys.

Figure 2.3 shows the entities Album and Artist, completed with the specification of alternative keys. Attribute Title is chosen as a key of entity Album, while the pair of attributes <FirstName, LastName> is a key for entity Artist. Graphically, key attributes are distinguished by a small key icon placed at the right of the attribute's name.

2.2.3   Attribute Types

Attributes can be *typed,* which means that they assume values from well-defined domains, like for instance the set of integer or floating point numbers. The Entity-Relationship model does not prescribe any specific set of types for attributes, but it is good practice to express attribute types in the data model, both for making the specification more expressive, and for directing the data implementation.

In the sequel, we assume that entity attributes may be associated with the usual *data types,* supported by most programming languages and database products. Such data types may include *String, Text, Integer, Float, Date, Time, Boolean, Enumeration, Blob, URL,* whose meanings are summarized in Table 2.1.

All the data types listed in Table 2.1 are quite self-explanatory, with the exception of enumeration types, which deserve some explanation. An *enumeration*

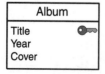
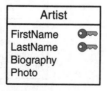

Figure 2.3   Graphic notation for primary keys.

type is a finite, ordered set of values, defined by the user. For example, an enumeration type may be defined to characterize the possible supports for a music album, and consist of the three values *CD, Tape,* and *Vinyl*; an enumeration type could also be defined for characterizing the working days of a week, taking as values the names of the weekdays from Monday to Friday.

Attribute types can be represented graphically, by means of a label positioned besides the attribute declaration in the entity box. Figure 2.4 shows the entities Album and Artist, with the attributes types specified.

Table 2.1   Typical built-in data types.

Data type	Description
String	A "short" sequence of characters
Text	A "long" sequence of characters. Text types can be further refined by expressing their MIME type (for example, text/html)
Integer	An integer numerical type
Float	A floating point numerical type
Date	A calendar date
Time	A temporal instant of time
Boolean	A true or false value
Enumeration	A sequence of user-defined values
BLOB	Binary Large OBject, for example an image or a video, which must be handled in a special way because of its size. BLOB types can be further refined by expressing their MIME type (for example image/gif)
URL	Uniform Resource Locator of a Web resource

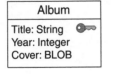

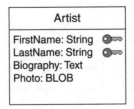

Figure 2.4   Graphic notation for attribute types.

2.2.4   Generalization Hierarchies

The Entity-Relationship model permits the designer to organize entities into a hierarchy, where they share some common features. The basic *generalization hierarchy* (also called *IS-A hierarchy*) has one super-entity and one or more sub-entities. Each sub-entity inherits all attributes and relationships defined in the super-entity and may add locally defined attributes and relationships. For example, Figure 2.5 specifies that JazzArtist and PopArtist are sub-entities of entity Artist, and JazzArtist has an extra attribute called Instrument, denoting the instrument played by a jazz artist. We say that Artist is specialized into PopArtist and JazzArtist, and conversely that PopArtist and JazzArtist are generalized into Artist.

A generalization hierarchy is not limited to two levels, but a sub-entity may in turn be specialized into one or more sub-entities, yielding an arbitrary-depth hierarchy.

Generalization is a well-known and much investigated concept, applied not only in the data modeling field, but also in artificial intelligence and object-oriented application design, with slightly different flavors. In the data modeling field, it is customary to assume a few restrictive hypotheses, which simplify the form of generalization hierarchies. The following assumptions ensure that the Entity-Relationship schema is easily implementable using conventional database technology:

1. Each entity is defined as the specialization of at most one super-entity. In technical terms, "multiple inheritance" is avoided.

2. Each instance of a super-entity is specialized exclusively into one sub-entity.

3. Each entity appears in at most one generalization hierarchy.

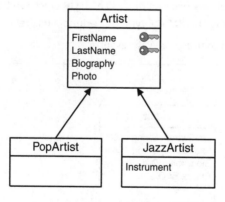

Figure 2.5   Graphic notation for IS-A hierarchies.

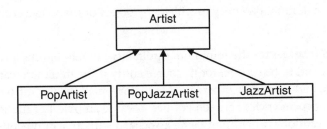

Figure 2.6 Generalization hierarchy approximating the use of multiple inheritance and non-exclusive specialization.

These restrictions reduce the expressive power of the Entity-Relationship schema: for example, due to the first two constraints, an instance of entity Artist cannot be a pop artist and a jazz artist at the same time. However, a similar meaning can be conveyed by the Entity-Relationship diagram of Figure 2.6, which specializes entity Artist into three sub-entities: pure jazz artists, pure pop artists, and jazz-pop artists. The locally defined attributes of entity PopArtist and JazzArtist must be repeated in entity PopJazzArtist.

2.3 Relationships

Relationships represent semantic connections between entities, like the association between an artist and his/her album, or between an artist and his/her reviews. The meaning of the association is conveyed by the relationship's name, which is established by the designer. For example, the relationship between an artist and the albums he/she has published could be named *Publication.* The simplest form of relationship is the *binary relationship,* which connects two entities. Relationships involving more than two entities, called *N-ary relationships,* are allowed; however, the use of N-ary relationships is discouraged, because they can be equivalently expressed by means of multiple binary relationships, as explained in Section 2.2.1.

Each binary relationship is characterized by two *relationship roles,* each one expressing the function that one of the participating entities plays in the relationship. For example, the relationship *Publication* between an artist and his/her album can be decomposed into two relationship roles, one from artist to album, named *Publishes,* and one from album to artist, named *Published_By.* Thus, a relationship role can be regarded as a sort of "oriented" association, connecting a *source* entity with a *destination* entity.

Relationship roles can be annotated with minimum and maximum *cardinality constraints,* respectively denoting the minimum and maximum number of objects of the destination entity to which any object of the source entity can be related.

- Relevant values for the minimum cardinality are zero or one; a relationship is said to be *optional* for its source entity if the minimum cardinality is zero, and *mandatory* otherwise. Mandatory relationships introduce existential dependencies between entities, because an object of the source entity cannot exist without being associated with at least one object of the destination entity.

- Relevant values for maximum cardinalities are one or many, the latter option being denoted as "N."

Based on their maximum cardinality constraints, relationships are called "one-to-one," if both relationship roles have maximum cardinality 1, "one-to-many," if one relationship role has maximum cardinality 1 and the other role has maximum cardinality N, or "many-to-many," if both relationship roles have maximum cardinality N.

Figure 2.7 shows the graphic notation for binary relationships, which are represented by labeled edges connecting entity boxes. In particular, the figure shows the relationship Publication, which is defined between entity Album and entity Artist. An album is associated with exactly one artist (cardinality 1:1), and each artist may be associated with several albums (cardinality 0:N); thus, the role from album to artist is mandatory, while the role from artist to album is optional. The relationship is "one-to-many," because it associates one artist to multiple albums.

Figure 2.8 shows the graphic notation for specifying the names of the relationship roles of the relationship Publication.

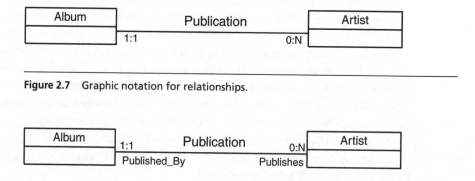

Figure 2.7   Graphic notation for relationships.

Figure 2.8   Graphic notation for relationship roles.

2.3.1   N-ary Relationships and Relationships with Attributes

The Entity-Relationship model admits the specification of relationships involving more than two entities, called N-ary relationships, and relationships with attributes. However, as is well known in the data modeling field, both these constructs can be represented using a combination of entities and binary relationships, as illustrated in Figure 2.9 and Figure 2.11.

A N-ary relationship is equivalent to one "central" entity and N binary relationships, connecting the central entity to the participant entities of the N-ary relationship (Figure 2.9). Cardinality constraints of the binary relationships have both minimum and maximum cardinality equal to 1 on the side of the central entity, to express the fact that an instance of the central entity must be connected to exactly one instance of each of the other entities, because it does not correspond to an object of the real world, but is a technical artifact denoting the connection of N real-world objects.

For example, the Entity-Relationship schema described in Figure 2.10 represents the supply of parts by suppliers to a company's departments, which is a ternary relationship representable by means of three binary relationships. Entity Supply is the central entity, which is connected to a part, a supplier, and a single department.

A (binary) relationship with attributes is equivalent to one "central" entity, connected by two binary relationships to the participant entities of the relationship with attributes (Figure 2.11). Also in this case, cardinality constraints of the binary relationships must have both minimum and maximum cardinality

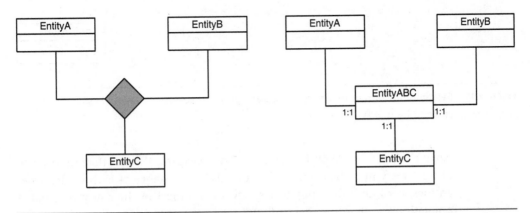

Figure 2.9   N-ary relationships expressed as a primitive construct (left) and using binary relationships and entities (right).

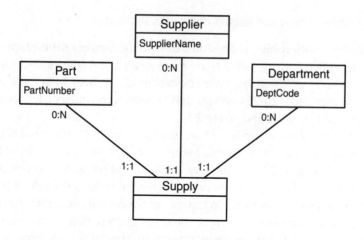

Figure 2.10   Data schema with a N-ary relationship, represented by the entity Supply.

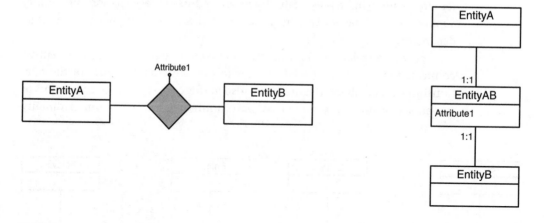

Figure 2.11   Relationships with attributes expressed as a primitive construct (left) and using binary relationships and entities (right).

equal to 1 on the side of the central entity, to express the fact that an instance of this entity must be connected to exactly one instance of each of the other entities, because it does not correspond to an object of the real world, but is a notation for denoting the attributes relevant to the connection of two real-world objects.

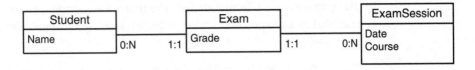

Figure 2.12 Data schema with a relationship with attribute, represented by the entity Exam.

For example, the grade given to a student in a given exam session could be represented using a relationship between the entities Student and ExamSession, with an attribute grade. The same situation can be equivalently modelled by replacing the relationship with attribute with an entity Exam, with an attribute grade. The Exam entity represents an individual exam performed by a student during an exam session. The resulting Entity-Relationship schema, consisting solely of entities and relationships without attributes, is represented in Figure 2.12.

N-ary relationships with attributes are treated similarly: one central entity is created, the relationship attributes are added to it, and then N binary relationships are drawn between the central entity and the other involved entities.

2.4 Derived Information

In data modeling, it may happen that the value of some attribute or relationship of an entity can be determined from the value of some other elements of the schema. For instance, the price after taxes of an article may be computed as the product of the price before taxes and the VAT, and the tracks published by an artist can be computed by "joining" all the albums published by the artist to the tracks contained in each album. Attributes and relationships that can be calculated are called *derived*.

The Entity-Relationship model does not include a standard notation for characterizing attributes and relationships as derived, nor a language for expressing their computation rule.

However, the specification of an attribute or of a relationship can be easily extended, to support the modeling of derived information:

■ An attribute or relationship is denoted as derived by adding a slash character (/) in front of the attribute or relationship name.[2]

---

[2]The notations used in this section are borrowed from UML, which permits the specification of derived attributes.

■ The computation rule that defines the derived attribute or relationship is specified as an expression added to the declaration of the attribute or relationship.

The language used for writing derivation rules may be any language supporting expressions built from the attributes of an entity and path expressions denoting the traversal of relationships. In the following examples, we use the *Object Constraint Language* (OCL) defined in the *Unified Modelling Language* (UML), a popular object-oriented notation briefly summarized in Section 2.5. The full syntax of OCL is reported in Appendix C.

Figure 2.13 shows two examples of derived attributes. Among its attributes, entity Article includes two regular attributes, Price and Discount, and one derived attribute /DiscountedPrice, which is computed as the value of the expression (Price* Discount).

Entity Artist contains one derived attribute, /NumberOfAlbums, which is computed as the value of the expression Count(Artist.ArtistToAlbum). This expression counts the number of albums associated with an artist according to the ArtistToAlbum relationship role. The sub-expression Artist.ArtistToAlbum is an example of *path-expression,* which is used for traversing a relationship role emanating from an entity.

Figure 2.14 shows an example of derived relationship: entity Artist is associated to entity Track by a derived relationship /ArtistToTrack, which is the concatenation of the two relationships between an artist and his albums and between an album and its tracks. The derivation rule is expressed on one of the two rela-

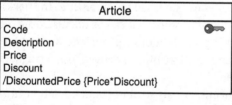

Figure 2.13   Derived attributes.

Figure 2.14 Derived relationship.

tionship roles by means of a path expression. In the example, the derivation rule is applied to the relationship role from entity Artist to entity Track, and is formally specified by adding to the role declaration the expression: Artist.Published-Tracks=Artist.ArtistToAlbum.AlbumToTrack.

2.5 Running Example

Figure 2.15 shows a simple data schema describing information about albums and artists. Artists publish albums composed of tracks and have reviews of their work. Artists have a name, a biography, a picture, date and place of birth, and, possibly, date and place of death. Artists are partitioned into jazz artists and pop artists, the former being characterized by an instrument. Albums have a title, year of publication, and a cover picture; each album track is characterized by its number, title, and duration. Each album is available on different supports, like CD, tape, and so on, and each support has a list price, a discount and an actual price, which is derived. For each review associated with an artist, the author, title, date, and text of the review are available. Relationships between entities are characterized by the following cardinality constraints: a review is associated with a single artist, an artist may have several reviews and several albums; an album belongs to a unique artist, may have different supports, and contains multiple tracks; finally, a track belongs only to an album.

The Album, Artist, and Review entities admit alternative keys, highlighted in Figure 2.15. Conversely, Support and Track are examples of entities for which no meaningful keys can be defined, because for both entities no "reasonable" combination of attributes is sufficient for identifying uniquely the entity's objects. For example, the attribute Title may appear a good candidate key for entity Track, but is discarded because there may be two tracks in different albums with the same title. In any case, the OID attribute is implicitly present as a primary key, and it uniquely identifies each instance of the Support and Track entities.

The Entity-Relationship schema of Figure 2.15 is inspired by the CDNOW Web site (*www.cdnow.com*), a Web site dedicated to the sale of music albums, which will be used throughout Part II as a running example.

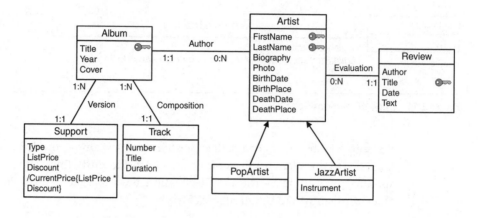

Figure 2.15   Entity-Relationship schema of the running example.

2.6   Modeling Data Using UML

Although the Entity-Relationship model is generally considered the de facto standard for data modeling, an alternative option is offered by the Unified Modeling Language (UML), an object-oriented design notation emerged from the fusion of the three most popular design methods for object-oriented applications analysis and design, namely OMT, OOSE, and the Booch's method (see the Bibliographic Notes for references about UML and the three mentioned object-oriented methods).

UML includes primitives for data modeling, which although originally conceived for representing the structure of the classes of an object-oriented application, can be used also for specifying the data model of an application domain. In particular, UML *class diagrams* can be used in alternative to Entity-Relationship diagrams.

The most prominent difference between a UML class diagram and an Entity-Relationship diagram is the difference between a class and an entity: a class is a generalization of the notion of entity, which permits the designer to specify not only the attributes, but also the functions (called methods) applicable to the instances of the class. However, this difference makes UML more general than the Entity-Relationship model, and thus the designer can exploit UML class diagrams to achieve the same specification as with the Entity-Relationship model.

UML class diagrams have more features than Entity-Relationship diagrams, like the already mentioned possibility of specifying derivation rules for attributes and relationships using the OCL language. Table 2.2 reviews the essential similarities and differences between the two notations. Since the Entity-Relationship notation used in this book is a strict subset of UML, designers already familiar with UML can continue using their favorite language for data modeling.

Table 2.2 Comparison of Entity-Relationship diagrams and UML class diagrams.

ER construct	Equivalent UML construct	Comments
Entity Artist FirstName: String LastName: String Biography: Text Photo: BLOB	**Class** Artist FirstName: String {unique} LastName: String {unique} Biography: Text Photo: BLOB BioUpdate()	UML classes can also include the specification of the methods applicable to their objects. UML attribute specification includes features not supported in ER: derived attributes, static attributes, visibility, multi-valued attributes, default values, and attribute constraints.
Generalization hierarchy Artist PopArtist JazzArtist	**Generalization hierarchy** Artist PopArtist JazzArtist	Generalization hierarchies have the same semantics. UML special notations (calledstereotypes) can be used todeclare that the IS-A relationshipis overlapping, disjoint, complete,or incomplete.
Relationship and role Album Published_By Publication Publishes Artist	**Association and role** Album Published_By Publication Publishes Artist	UML relationship specification includes features not supported in ER, like constraints, ordering, visibility, modifiability, and navigability. In UML relationships can be declared as part-of relationships, expressing a physical or logical containment.
Relationship cardinality Album Published_By 1:1 Publication Publishes 0:N Artist	**Association multiplicity** Album Published_By * Publication Publishes 1 Artist	In ER, the cardinality represents the minimum and maximum number of relationship instances an object may have. In UML, the multiplicity (either 1 or *) denotes the maximum number of objects connected to a source object; note that the multiplicity label * is placed at the opposite side with respect to the ER notation for "many" cardinality (N).

Summary

Data-intensive Web applications publish and manage information, typically stored within one or more data repositories. This chapter has presented the features of the Entity-Relationship model, used to represent the structure of information at the conceptual level.

The Entity-Relationship model exploits simple and expressive concepts, like entities, attributes, relationships, and IS-A hierarchies, and adopts a visual notation for expressing the specifications. The objects of the application domain are represented by entities, which abstract the common properties of similar instances. These properties are expressed as entity attributes, some of which can be specified as keys, meaning that they unambiguously identify entity instances. The semantic associations between objects are instead represented as relationships, characterized by cardinality constraints. A special kind of semantic association, the specialization of a general concept into a more specific one, is expressed using generalization hierarchies, which permit the designer to factor out the common aspects of entities and organize them in a taxonomy.

Although the primitives of the Entity-Relationship model can be used freely, we have suggested a few practices, which make an Entity-Relationship diagram simpler to implement using conventional relational technology.

Finally, we have briefly contrasted the Entity-Relationship notation to UML class diagrams, which can be used by designers already familiar with that notation, without any loss of expressive power.

Bibliographic Notes

The data model proposed in this book builds on the notation of the Entity-Relationship model introduced by Peter Chen [Chen76]. The original proposal did not include generalizations, which were added later [NFS79, SSW80]. Conceptual modeling is the core topic addressed by Batini et al. [BCN92]; further valuable sources are [ACPT99, Date95, EN94, MR92, Ullman88].

The proposed notation is also compatible with object-oriented models. A good introduction to the basic concepts of object-orientation is given by Bertrand Meyer, who illustrates the basic principles of object-oriented design in the context of the Eiffel programming language [Meyer88]. A presentation of object orientation from a databases perspective is provided in [KL88, Loomis95], while an in-depth view of this technology is given in [BM93]. All the books presenting object-oriented software engineering methods (including OMT [RBPEL91], Booch [Booch94], and OOSE [Jacobson94]) include an overview of the object-oriented paradigm and of the graphic formalisms adopted to represent it. In particular, Booch, Jacobson, and Rumbaugh provide an excellent guide to the Unified Modeling Language (UML), by means of an easy-to-understand example-driven approach [BJR98]. The Object Constraint Language is treated extensively in [CW02].

3 CHAPTER Hypertext Model

3.1 Introduction

The goal of hypertext modeling is to specify the organization of the front-end interfaces of a Web application. To be effective, such specification must be able to convey in a simple and intuitive way such aspects as the logical division of the application into top-level modules, each one embodying a set of coherent functions targeted to a specific class of users, the partition of the top-level modules into sub-modules, for a better organization of large applications, and the actual hypertext topology of each module, in terms of pages, made of content elements, and linked to support user's navigation and interaction.

The hypertext model should be at the right level of abstraction; the specification of the hypertext should be maintained at the conceptual level, which means that it should not commit too much to design and implementation details, such as the actual distribution of functionality between the various tiers of a Web application.

Unlike data modeling, which is a very consolidated activity, hypertext modeling is a younger discipline, still lacking a well-established base of concepts, notations, and design methods. WebML, the language used in this book, provides the primitives for hypertext modeling, borrowing from the Entity-Relationship model the idea of using simple and expressive specification concepts, supported by an intuitive graphic notation. Therefore, it should be perceived by the designer as a natural extension of the Entity-Relationship model, which permits the programmer to expand the data schema of the application with the specification of the hypertexts used for publishing and manipulating data.

The key ingredients of WebML are *pages, units,* and *links,* organized into modularization constructs called *areas* and *site views.*

Units are the atomic pieces of publishable content; they offer alternative ways of arranging the content dynamically extracted from the entities and relationships of the data schema, and also permit the specification of data entry forms for accepting user input. Units are the building blocks of pages, which are the actual interface elements delivered to the users. Pages are typically built by assembling several units of various kinds, to attain the desired communication effect. Page and units do not stand alone, but are linked to form a hypertext structure. Links represent a cornerstone of hypertext modeling: they express the possibility of navigating from one point to another one in the hypertext, and the passage of parameters from one unit to another unit, which is required for the proper computation of the content of a page.

A set of pages can be grouped into a site view, which represents a coherent hypertext serving a well-defined set of requirements, for instance, the needs of a specific group of users. In large applications, there may be multiple site views defined on top of the same data schema, and large site views can be hierarchically decomposed into areas, which are clusters of pages with a homogeneous purpose. Some properties of pages and areas, like the home, default, and landmark properties, permit the designer to fine-tune the visibility level of these constructs inside the hierarchical structure of a site view.

Finally, global parameters can be specified at the site view level, to denote small pieces of information, which can be "recorded" during the user navigation, to be later retrieved and exploited in the computation of the content of some page.

The described primitives are aimed at modeling hypertexts for the publication of content, which is the main subject of this chapter; in Chapter 4, we will present a few other constructs, which permit the designer to specify hypertexts for manipulating content and for interacting with arbitrary external services.

3.2 Units

Units are the atomic elements for specifying the content of a Web page. WebML supports five types of units:

- *Data units:* show information about a single object.
- *Multidata units:* present information about a set of objects.
- *Index units:* show a list of descriptive properties of some objects, without presenting their detailed information.
- *Scroller units:* enable the browsing of an ordered set of objects, by providing commands for accessing the first, last, previous, and next element of a sequence.
- *Entry units:* model entry forms, whose fields allow gathering input, needed to perform searches or to feed update operations.

The five basic types of content units can be combined to represent Web pages of arbitrary complexity. The first four units model the *publishing of information,* while entry units express the *acquisition of information* from users. Among the four units for information publishing, data and multidata units *present the actual content* of the objects they refer to, whereas indexes and scroller units facilitate the *selection of objects.* Data units refer to a *single object,* whereas multidata, index, and scroller units refer to a *set of objects.*

Data, multidata, index, and scroller units present content extracted from the data schema; therefore, it is necessary to specify where their content comes from. WebML uses two concepts for expressing the origin of a unit's content: the source and the selector.

- The source is the name of the entity from which the unit's content is extracted. Thus, the source entity tells the *type* of the objects used to compute the unit's content. A content unit can be associated with one source entity, which is the most common case, or with multiple source entities.
- The selector is a predicate, used for determining the *actual objects* of the source entity that contribute to the unit's content. Selectors are the conjunction of elementary conditions, built from the entity attributes and from the relationship roles in which the entity is involved, and from constant or variable terms. Variable terms are constructed using parameters associated with the input links of the unit. Selectors whose conditions use parameters are called *parametric selectors.*

All the concepts of WebML have a graphic representation, which conveys the essential features, and a textual representation, which may be used to specify additional detailed properties, not conveniently expressible by the graphic notation. Appendix A summarizes the graphical symbols and properties of WebML elements, and Appendix B contains the complete textual syntax.

Content units are graphically represented as rectangles enclosing a labeled icon, as shown in Figure 3.1, which illustrates an example of index unit. The unit name is placed inside the rectangle, above the unit icon. The source and selector are placed below the rectangle: in the example, the index unit has entity Album as its source, and includes a selector [Year = 2000], built from the entity attribute Year, from the equality predicate, and from the constant term 2000. The textual representation, also shown in Figure 3.1, adds further details, like, in the case of index units, the ordering of the objects shown in the index, and the attributes used to display each object.

3.2.1   Data Units

Data units publish a single object of a given entity. A data unit is characterized by the following properties:

- *Name:* the user-defined name for the data unit.
- *Source:* the entity providing the content to the unit.
- *Selector (optional):* a predicate identifying a unique object, which is displayed by the data unit. The selector of a data unit is optional, but it can be omitted only in the case in which the source entity has a single instance; otherwise, the object to be displayed in the data unit remains undefined.
- *Included attributes:* the set of attributes of the source entity to be visualized.

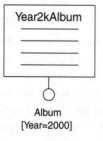

```
IndexUnit Year2kAlbum
(source Album;
 selector Year=2000;
 attributes Title;
 orderby Title)
```

Figure 3.1   Graphical and textual notation for a content unit.

Figure 3.2 shows the WebML graphic notation for representing a data unit called ShortArtist, with its source and selector highlighted below the icon. The unit is defined over entity Artist, and shows the specific object determined by evaluating its selector, which is the conjunction of two equality-based predicates on attributes FirstName and LastName. Because FirstName and LastName have been defined in Chapter 2 as key for entity Artist, the evaluation of the selector yields a single object, which is displayed in the data unit. Figure 3.2 also shows a possible rendition of the data unit, in an HTML-based implementation.

The ShortArtist unit contains only some of the attributes of the Artist entity, and thus publishes a sort of summary of the object's content. The included attributes are not specified in the graphic notation, but are visible in the textual definition:

```
DataUnit ShortArtist
(source Artist;
 selector FirstName="Celine", LastName="Dion";
 attributes FirstName, LastName, Photo)
```

The selector of Figure 3.2 includes a conjunction of two simple predicates. Besides conjunction, two forms of disjunction can be specified in a selector predicate:

- *Value disjunction:* a single attribute value is compared with a set of values using the expression [attribute operator value1 | value2 | ... | valueN]. This corresponds to the predicate ((attribute operator value1) OR (attribute operator value2) OR ... OR (attribute operator valueN)). An

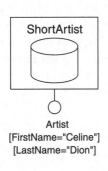

Figure 3.2 WebML graphic notation for data units, and rendition in HTML.

example of condition using value disjunction is: `BirthPlace contains "Italy" | "France"`.

▪ *Attribute disjunction:* a set of attributes is compared with a single value using the expression [attribute1 | attribute2 | . . . | attributeN operator value]. This notation corresponds to the predicate ((attribute1 operator value) OR (attribute2 operator value) OR . . . OR (attributeN operator value)). An example of attribute disjunction is: `BirthPlace | Biography contains "Italy"`.

3.2.2 Multidata Units

Multidata units present multiple objects of an entity together, by repeating the presentation of several data units. Therefore, a multidata unit is characterized by the following properties:

▪ *Name:* the user-defined name for the multidata unit.

▪ *Source:* the entity providing the content to the unit.

▪ *Selector (optional):* a selection predicate determining the objects displayed by the multidata unit. If the selector is missing, all objects are considered.

▪ *Included attributes:* the set of attributes of the source entity to be visualized for each object displayed by the multidata unit.

▪ *Order clause (optional):* the set of attributes used to sort the objects of the multidata unit and the sorting criterion to be applied, which can be ascending or descending. Ascending is assumed as default.

Figure 3.3 shows the WebML graphic notation for representing a multidata unit, with its source and no selector. The MultiArtist unit is defined over the Artist entity, and, because no selector is specified, displays all the existing objects.

Artists are sorted by last name and first name, and displayed using the last name, first name, and photo attributes, as specified in the following textual definition:

```
MultidataUnit MultiArtist
(source Artist;
 attributes FirstName, LastName, Photo;
 orderby LastName, FirstName)
```

Attributes used for ordering are considered in sequence: artists are sorted first by last name, and, if the same last name occurs for multiple artists, they are sorted by first name.

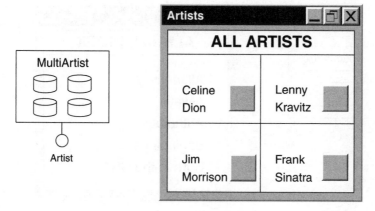

Figure 3.3   WebML graphic notation for multidata units, and rendition in HTML.

3.2.3   Index Units

Index units present multiple objects of an entity as a list. An index unit specification includes the following properties:

- *Name:* the user-defined name for the index unit.
- *Source:* the entity providing the content to the unit.
- *Selector (optional):* a selection predicate determining the objects displayed by the unit. If the selector is missing, all objects are considered.
- *Included attributes:* the set of attributes of the source entity used to display the index entries.
- *Order clause (optional):* the set of attributes used to sort the objects of the index unit and the sorting criterion to be applied, which can be ascending or descending. Ascending is assumed as default.

To better understand the difference between multidata and index units, we anticipate that an index unit is typically used to select *one particular object*. Conversely, multidata units can be used to process *all the objects* displayed by the unit. This distinction will become clearer in Section 3.4.1, when we introduce the outgoing links of units.

Figure 3.4 shows the WebML graphic notation for representing an index unit, with its source and no selector. The AlbumIndex unit is defined over entity Album and displays all the instances.

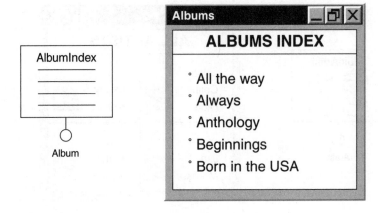

Figure 3.4   WebML graphic notation for index units, and rendition in HTML.

Albums are displayed using only the title attribute and presented in ascending order by title, as specified in the following textual definition:

```
IndexUnit AlbumIndex
(source Album;
 attributes Title;
 orderby Title)
```

Index units admit two variants, for choosing multiple objects, and for organizing the list of index entries hierarchically.

The first variant is represented by the *multi-choice index unit,* in which each element of the list of entries is associated with a checkbox, allowing the user to select multiple objects, instead of a single one.

The graphic notation for representing a multi-choice index unit and a possible rendition are depicted in Figure 3.5. The AlbumIndex unit is defined over entity Album and displays all the instances.

Album instances are denoted by the title and listed in ascending order by title, as specified in the following textual definition, where the keyword `multi-choice` is added to the declaration of the index unit:

```
IndexUnit AlbumIndex multi-choice
(source Album;
 attributes Title;
 orderby Title)
```

The second variant of index units is the concept of *hierarchical index,* in which the index entries are organized in a multi-level tree. The hierarchy is represented by a sequence of N source entities connected by N-1 relationship roles. The first source entity represents the instances at the top level of the hierarchy; the second source entity, introduced by the NEST clause, represents the instances at the second level of the hierarchy, and so on. Each relationship role denotes the father-child association between two entities at consecutive levels in the hierarchy.

Figure 3.6 shows the WebML graphic notation for a hierarchical index. The index displays a two-level hierarchy of albums and tracks. The top-level entries are all the instances of entity Album, and for each album instance, the tracks associated with it by the AlbumToTrack relationship role are listed.

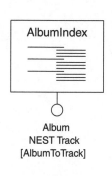
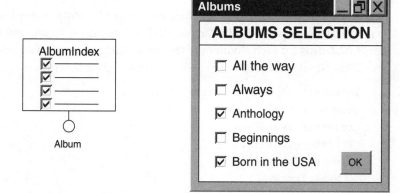

Figure 3.5 WebML graphic notation for multi-choice indexes, and rendition in HTML.

Figure 3.6 WebML graphic notation for hierarchical indexes, and rendition in HTML.

The textual notation includes as additional properties the order clause and included attributes, for each of the source entities in the hierarchy; moreover, the keyword `hierarchical` is added to the declaration of the index unit:

```
IndexUnit AlbumIndex hierarchical
(source Album;
 attributes Title;
 orderby Title
   NEST Track
   selector AlbumToTrack;
   attributes Title;
   orderby Title)
```

A selector condition can be specified for the source entities at any level of the hierarchy. Figure 3.7 defines a hierarchical index showing the albums published in year 2002, listing for each album only the tracks lasting less than two minutes.

The textual specification equivalent to the graphic notation is:

```
IndexUnit AlbumIndex hierarchical
(source Album;
 selector Year=2000;
 attributes Title;
 orderby Title
   NEST Track
   selector AlbumToTrack, Duration < 120;
   attributes Title;
   orderby Title)
```

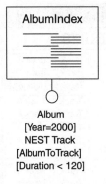

Figure 3.7   Hierarchical index with selectors on all the source entities.

A special case of hierarchical index exploits a recursive relationship defined over an entity, which expresses a part-of association. Assume that the Entity-Relationship schema contains an entity Part and a relationship PartToSubPart (from Part to Part) expressing recursively how each part is decomposed into sub-parts. In this case, the hierarchical index has a variable number of levels, depending on the actual part-of relationship instances in the data. Figure 3.8 shows a recursive hierarchical index representing the bill of materials for a PC.

The index is defined over the source entity Part, and exploits the recursive relationship role PartToSubPart, for determining the sub-parts that constitute a part. The textual definition includes the keyword RECURSIVE NEST to denote that the hierarchical index is recursive:

```
IndexUnit BillOfMaterials hierarchical
(source Part;
 attributes PartName;
 orderby PartNumber
   RECURSIVE NEST Part
   selector PartToSubPart;
   attributes PartName;
   orderby PartNumber)
```

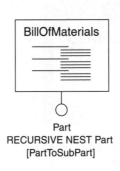

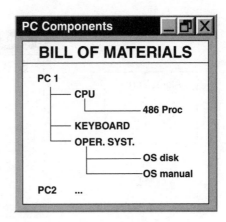

Figure 3.8 Recursive hierarchical index and a possible rendition in HTML.

3.2.4   Scroller Units

Scroller units provide commands to scroll through the objects in a set, for example to scroll over all the instances of an entity. A scroller unit specification is characterized by the properties:

- *Name:* the user-defined name for the scroller unit.
- *Source:* the entity providing the content to the unit.
- *Selector (optional):* a selection predicate determining the objects scrolled by the unit. If the selector is missing, all objects are considered.
- *Block factor:* the number of objects that are scrolled together. By default, the block factor is 1, which means that objects are scrolled one at a time.
- *Order clause (optional):* the set of attributes used to sort the objects of the scroller unit and the sorting criterion to be applied, which can be ascending or descending. Ascending is assumed as default.

Figure 3.9 shows the WebML graphic notation for representing a scroller unit and a possible rendition in an HTML-based implementation. The Album-Scroll unit is defined over entity Album and has no selector; thus, it can be used for moving along the set of all albums. In particular, it is possible to move to the first, previous, next, and last album, according to the sorting clause specified in the unit.

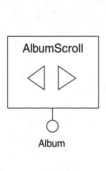

Figure 3.9   WebML graphic notation for scroller units, and rendition in HTML.

In the example in Figure 3.9 the block factor is set to 1, and the scroller is currently positioned on the thirty-fifth element of a list of 150 albums. The textual definition of the AlbumScroll unit expresses all the relevant properties:

```
ScrollerUnit AlbumScroll
(source Album;
 blockFactor 1;
 orderby Title)
```

3.2.5   Entry Units

Entry units support form-based data entry. They are used for gathering input, which is typically employed to do the following:

- Perform searches over the objects of an entity, for example to locate the instances of an entity whose attributes contain a given keyword.
- Supply parameters to operations like content updates, login, and external services.

Entry units are characterized by the following properties:

- *Name:* the user-defined name for the entry unit.
- *Fields:* the set of fields for inputting values.

  Figure 3.10 shows the graphic notation used for an entry unit (ArtistInput).

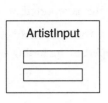

Figure 3.10   WebML entry unit, and rendition in HTML.

As shown in the rendition example, the entry unit in Figure 3.10 has four fields, for inputting the first name, last name, birth date, and death date of an artist. Fields are not shown in the graphical notation, but appear in the textual one:

```
EntryUnit ArtistInput
(fields
 FirstNameField String;
 LastNameField String;
 BirthDateField Date;
 DeathDateField Date)
```

Entry units fields correspond to the input fields normally found in the form constructs of mark-up languages. Input fields have a number of properties:

- *Name:* the name of the field.
- *Type:* the data type of the value input in the field (for example string, text, integer, date and so on).
- *Initial value (optional):* a default value to be initially proposed to the user.
- *Modifiability:* a flag which specifies if the user can modify the initial field value or not; by default all fields are modifiable.
- *Validity predicate:* a Boolean condition applicable to the value input by the user, to check its validity. The validity predicate can be any logical expression constructed using the field name, an operator applicable to the data type of the field, and a constant or variable term. The variable term can be the name of another field, which permits the comparison of values input by the user in different fields, for example, to ensure that the death date of an artist is greater than the birth date. The special keyword `notnull` can be used to require that the user specify some value for a field. The complete syntax for defining validity predicates is reported in Appendix B.

For example, the specification of the fields of the ArtistInput entry unit of Figure 3.10 can be enriched with all the relevant field properties, including validity predicates, as follows:

```
EntryUnit ArtistInput
(fields
 FirstNameField string, notnull;
 LastNameField string, notnull;
 BirthDateField date, notnull;
 DeathDateField date, DeathDateField > BirthDateField)
```

3.3 Pages

Pages are the actual interface elements delivered to the user, who browses the hypertext by accessing its pages in the desired sequence. A page typically consists of several units, grouped together to accomplish a well-defined communication purpose. In the rest of this chapter, we will show several examples of pages and will present frequently adopted page design patterns.

Figure 3.11 shows the graphic notation for pages, which is simply a labeled box surrounding the units that belong to the page. In the example, the page called AlbumPage contains two index units, one for displaying the list of all artists, and one for displaying the list of all albums. The figure also shows a possible rendition of the AlbumPage in HTML, which is simply the aggregation of the renditions of the two index units. Note that, although in Figure 3.11 the position of the index units in the HTML rendition is the same as that of the index unit icons in the WebML specification, this fact is purely coincidental. A WebML page specification is abstract, and has nothing to do with presentation aspects, like the relative position of content elements in the HTML rendition.

Like units, pages also admit a textual specification. The textual syntax for specifying page Album includes the page name and the list of its enclosed units:

```
Page AlbumPage
(units AlbumIndex, ArtistIndex)
```

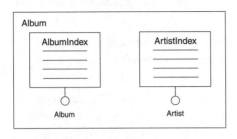

Figure 3.11 WebML graphic notation for pages.

3.4   Links

Neither pages nor units exist in isolation, because real-world hypertexts are made of connected pages, which contain several interrelated pieces of content and commands permitting the user to interact with the application. To express these features, pages and units can be linked, to specify the allowed navigation paths between pages, the selections offered to the user, and the effect of the user's interaction on the content of the units displayed in the page.

Navigation modeling is the part of hypertext modeling that deals with the specification of the links between units and pages, and of the properties of such links. The central notions of navigation modeling are the concepts of *link, link parameters,* and *parametric selectors:*

■ A link is an oriented connection between two units or pages.

■ A link parameter is the specification of a piece of information, which is transported from the source to the destination of the link.

■ A parametric selector is a unit selector whose predicates contain a reference to a link parameter.

These concepts and their applications are treated in detail in the rest of this section.

3.4.1   Specification of Links

Links abstract and generalize the fundamental notion of hypertexts: the concept of anchor. An *anchor* is an active device, whereby the user can interact with the hypertext.

The notion of anchor must be considered in a broad sense. The following practical cases, referred to an HTML-based hypertext, are all examples of what can be considered an anchor:

■ An HTML anchor tag with an `href` attribute *that refers to another page.* Clicking on the anchor replaces the currently visualized page with the page referred to by the tag anchor.

■ An HTML anchor tag with an `href` attribute *that refers to the same page.* Clicking on the anchor redisplays the currently visualized page, possibly with some new content; for example, due to a selection in some index, which causes the details of a new object to be displayed.

■ The confirmation button of an HTML form used for searching. Inserting input in the form and pressing the button causes a new page or the same page to be redisplayed with the search results.

■ The confirmation button of an HTML form used for sending input to an operation, for example for logging into a password-protected site.

As the previously mentioned examples suggest, the essence of links is twofold:

■ They enable the navigation of the hypertext, by letting the user move the focus from a source page to a destination page.

■ They transport information from one unit to another, for example the identifier of the object selected from an index to the data unit displaying the object details, or the input entered in a form to the index unit showing the result of the search, or to the operation performing password verification.

In the WebML terminology, links crossing the boundaries of pages are called *inter-page links,* whereas links with the source and destination inside the same page are called *intra-page;* links transporting information are called *contextual,* in contrast with *non-contextual* links, which do not transport information.

Graphically links are represented by oriented arcs, which connect the source unit or page to the destination unit or page.

The example in Figure 3.12 shows an *inter-page non-contextual* link. The link connects a source page (PopArtists), which includes a multidata unit showing pop artists, to a destination page (JazzArtists), which includes a multidata unit showing jazz artists. The content of page JazzArtists is independent from the content of page PopArtists, and thus the navigation of the link does not require any information to be passed from the source to the destination page.

The textual syntax for representing a link includes the user-defined name of the link, and its source and destination, as shown below:

```
link PopToJazz
(from PopArtists to JazzArtists)
```

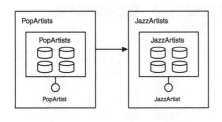  

Figure 3.12 Non-contextual link.

Figure 3.13 illustrates an example of *inter-page contextual link*. Page Artists contains an index unit, named AllArtists, which is defined over entity Artist; the index unit is linked to a data unit, named ArtistDetails, defined on entity Artist, and placed in a distinct page. The meaning of such hypertext is that the AllArtists index unit is rendered as a list of clickable entries, and selecting one entry opens page Artist where the ArtistDetails data unit shows the details of the artist chosen from the index. In this case, the content of the destination unit depends on information provided in the source unit, and the transfer of this context information is associated with the navigation of the link.

3.4.2 Link Parameters and Parametric Selectors

The binding between the source unit and the destination unit of the link is formally represented by a *link parameter* defined over the link, and by a *parametric selector,* defined in the destination unit.

A link parameter is a value associated with a link between units, which is transported, as an effect of the link navigation, from the source unit to the destination unit. A link may be associated with as many link parameters as required by the destination unit. A parametric selector is a unit selector whose condition mentions one or more parameters. An example of these concepts is visible in Figure 3.13, where the link includes a parameter (CurrArtist) representing the object identifier of the artist selected from the index, and the data unit has a selector [OID=CurrArtist], which uses the CurrArtist parameter to retrieve and display the details of the appropriate artist.

From a syntactic standpoint, a link parameter has a name and a label, separated by a semicolon. The name is a user-defined string (CurrArtist in Figure 3.13), which can be used to refer to the parameter in the selector of the destination unit. The label denotes the content of the parameter, which is either an attribute or a field of the source unit of the link; when the label refers to an

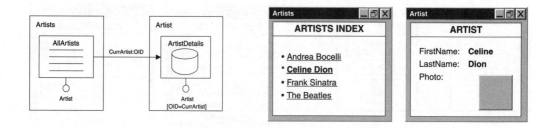

Figure 3.13   Inter-page contextual link with associated link parameter.

attribute, it consists of the concatenation of the entity and attribute names, separated by a dot. The entity name can be omitted, if clear from the context, like the label OID in Figure 3.13, which stands for Artist.OID. The output values produced by the various source units and the labels of the corresponding link parameters are summarized in Table 3.1.

The link parameter specification can be added both to the graphical and textual specification. The textual specification of the link graphically shown in Figure 3.13 is reported below:

```
link ToArtistsDetails
(from AllArtists to ArtistDetails;
 parameters CurrArtist:OID)
```

Figure 3.14 shows an *intra-page contextual link*. Now, the index unit and the data unit are placed in the same page and connected by a contextual link. This link

Table 3.1 Link parameters provided in output by content units.

Source unit	Link parameters (for outgoing links)	Labels of link parameters
Data unit	Any attribute (including the OID) of the object displayed by the unit	SourceEntity.attributeName
Multidata unit	The set of values of any attribute (including the OID) of the objects displayed by the unit	{SourceEntity.attributName}
Index unit	The value of any attribute (including the OID) of the object selected by the user clicking on an anchor of the index unit	SourceEntity.attributeName
Hierarchical index unit	The value of any attribute (including the OID) of the object selected by the user clicking on an anchor in the unit. All the objects displayed at all the levels of the hierarchy can be selected	SourceEntity.attributeName
Multi-choice index unit	The set of values of any attribute (including the OID) of the multiple objects selected using the check boxes of the unit	{SourceEntity.attributName}
Scroller unit	The set of values of any attribute (including the OID) of the block of objects selected by clicking on an anchor in the unit	{SourceEntity.attributName}
Entry unit	The value input by the user in each field	fieldName

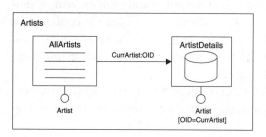
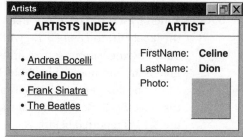

Figure 3.14   Intra-page contextual link with associated link parameter.

permits the user to select one object and redisplay the same page, with different content corresponding to the details of the newly selected instance. Also in this case, the link enables the passage of context information from the index unit to the data unit, and the binding between such units is represented by the CurrArtist link parameter and by the parametric selector of the data unit [OID=CurrArtist], which uses such a parameter.

The case of *intra-page non-contextual* links is also possible, although less frequently used, for connecting two alternative nested sub-pages of the same page. Nested sub-pages are treated in Section 3.6.3.

A link parameter can be *single-valued,* as the CurrArtist parameter in Figure 3.13 and Figure 3.14, which stores the OID of the single instance selected from an index unit, or *set-valued;* for example it may hold the set of OIDs of the objects selected from a multi-choice index unit.

Syntactically, set-valued link parameters are distinguished by enclosing their label in curly brackets, as shown in Table 3.1. Figure 3.15 gives an example of a set-valued link parameter: the ArtistMultichoice index unit allows the selection of a set of artists, whose details are displayed by the ArtistsMultidata unit. The passage of parameters from the source to the destination unit is denoted by the set-valued parameter SelArtists: {OID} associated with the link, which is used by the selector condition of the destination unit [OID IN SelArtists] for testing that the OIDs of the objects to display in the multidata unit belong to the set of OIDs denoted by parameter SelArtists.

The textual definition of the link graphically shown in Figure 3.15 is:

```
link ToArtistsDetails
(from ArtistMultichoice to ArtistsMultidata;
 parameters SelArtists:{OID})
```

Units may have multiple outgoing links, possibly associated with different parameters. Figure 3.16 shows a hierarchical index unit (ArtsitIndex), in which

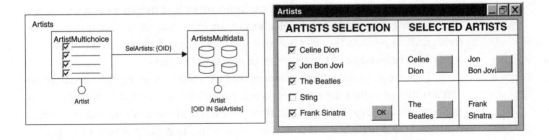

Figure 3.15 Multi-choice index and set-valued link parameter.

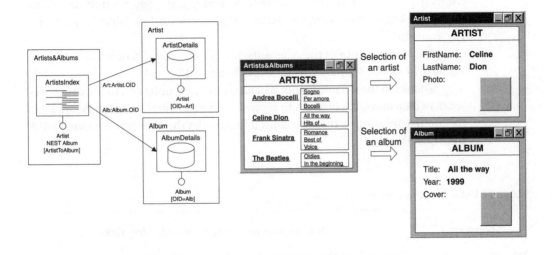

Figure 3.16 Hierarchical index with two outgoing links with different link parameters.

the top level of the hierarchy displays the instances of the Artist entity, and the second level of the hierarchy lists the albums connected to each artist by the relationship role ArtistToAlbum. Two links connect the hierarchical index unit and two data units placed in distinct pages: the link pointing to the ArtistDetails data unit is associated with a link parameter of type Artist.OID, which holds the OID of an artist selected from the top level of the hierarchy; the link pointing to the AlbumDetails data unit is associated with a link parameter of type Album.OID, which holds the OID of an album selected from the second level of the hierarchy. When the user selects an artist or an album, the appropriate page is displayed.

As Table 3.1 clearly indicates, multidata units, index units, hierarchical index units, and multi-choice index units differ in the meaning of the link parameter associated with their outgoing link: for index units and hierarchical index units, the outgoing link permits the selection of an *individual object,* for multi-choice index units it permits the selection of a *subset of objects,* for multidata units it permits only the passage of the *entire set* of visualized objects.

To make hypertext diagrams more readable, the link parameter specification can be omitted, when the parameters associated with the link are deducible from the context. To help this simplification, for each unit a default output parameter is defined, so that, when a link is associated with the default output of its source unit, the link parameter specification can be omitted without loss of information. Table 3.2 summarizes the default output of units.

A similar simplification can be done also for selector conditions. Table 3.3 shows the default selectors of units with incoming links; when a unit has an incoming link and no selector, the default selector specified in Table 3.3 is implicitly assumed.

As a consequence of these defaults, the graphic specification of the page in Figure 3.14 can be simplified as shown in Figure 3.17.

Thanks to the default output parameter of index units and to the default selector of data units, the diagram in Figure 3.17 is equivalent to that in Figure 3.14: its intuitive meaning is that the index unit supplies the OID of the selected artist to the data unit.

Table 3.2   Default link parameters of units.

Source unit	Default link parameters of outgoing links
Data unit	The OID of the object displayed by the unit
Multidata unit	The set OIDs of the objects displayed by the unit
Index unit	The OID of the single object selected from the unit
Hierarchical index unit	The OID of the single object selected from the unit. If the unit has multiple nested entities, the OID refers to an instance of the entity *at the top of the hierarchy.* Parameters associated with the objects of entities nested at inner levels must be specified explicitly
Multi-choice index unit	The set of OIDs of the multiple objects selected from the unit
Scroller unit	The set of OIDs of the selected block of objects, or a single OID if the block factor is 1

Table 3.3 Default selector conditions of units, when an input link is specified but no selector.

Destination unit	Default selector condition when an input link is specified and no explicit selector is mentioned
Data unit	OID = <link parameter of type OID of the input link>
Multidata, index, multi-choice index, scroller unit	OID IN <link parameter of the type {OID} of the input link>
Hierarchical index unit	The default selector is defined only for the entity at the top of the hierarchy and is: OID IN <link parameter of the type {OID} of the input link>

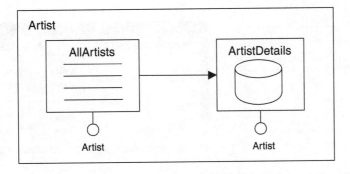

Figure 3.17 Simplified notation exploiting default link parameters and unit selectors.

Another example of the use of defaults is shown in Figure 3.18, which illustrates a WebML diagram equivalent to the one of Figure 3.15. In this case, defaults spare the explicit mention of the set-valued link parameter (SelArtists) and of the default selector condition of the multidata unit [OID IN SelArtists]. In the rest of the book, we will omit the specification of parameters and selector conditions that can be inferred by the defaults, unless the need arises for emphasizing their presence.

Link parameters are also used for transmitting the values input into an entry unit. Figure 3.19 shows an example of link having the value of a field as a parameter. The KeyWordEntry unit includes a single field called TitleKeyword, not shown in the graphic notation, for inputting a keyword. The value of such a field is assigned as a parameter, called Keyword, to the outgoing link of the entry unit,

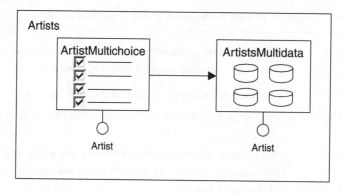

Figure 3.18   Example of use of a default link parameters and selectors.

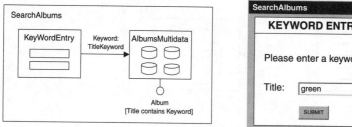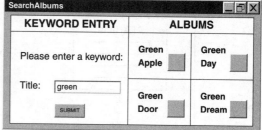

Figure 3.19   Contextual link with LINK parameter associated with an input field.

and is used in the selector condition of the multidata unit, to display only those albums whose title contains the keyword provided by the user.

The textual syntax for the entry unit and its outgoing link is the following:

```
EntryUnit KeyWordEntry
(fields TitleKeyword String)

link EntryToMultidata
(from KeyWordEntry to AlbumMultidata;
 parameters Keyword:TitleKeyword)
```

A very useful application of parametric selectors occurs when one unit must display *all the instances of an entity that are related to some instances of another entity.* In this case, a selector condition can be specified that retrieves the subset of the objects of the source entity that are connected by a specific relationship to the object(s) passed in input to the unit by an incoming link.

Figure 3.20 shows an example of selector condition built using a relationship role. The Artist page contains the ArtistDetails data unit, defined over entity Artist, and the PublishedAlbums index unit, defined over entity Album. The goal of the specification is to express that the index of albums displays exactly the albums published by the artist shown in the data unit. To achieve this effect, the index unit includes a selector built from the ArtistToAlbum relationship role [ArtistToAlbum(CurrArtist)]. This selector restricts the set of albums displayed in the index only to the albums connected by the ArtistToAlbum relationship role to the artist having OID equal to the CurrArtist parameter.

The textual definition of the PublishedAlbums index unit is as follows:

```
IndexUnit PublishedAlbums
(source Album;
 selector ArtistToAlbum(CurrArtist);
 attributes Title;
 orderby Title)
```

When the parameter associated with the link is a default parameter, it can be omitted from both the link and the selector, as shown in Figure 3.21, where the OID of the artist displayed in the data unit is implicitly assumed as the argument of the relationship role predicate ArtistToAlbum.

Links and selectors can be used to publish also more complex data configurations, based on N-ary relationships or relationships with attributes, which we discussed in Section 3.3.1. Consider the schema of Figure 3.22, already described

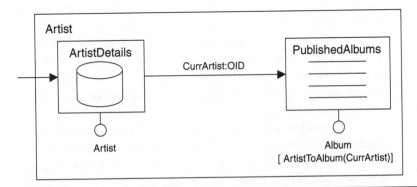

Figure 3.20 Contextual link, bringing context to a parametric role selector.

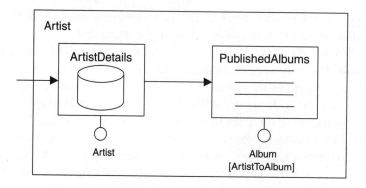

Figure 3.21   Short notation for relationship role selectors.

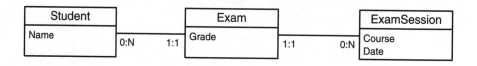

Figure 3.22   Schema describing exams taken by students.

in Chapter 2, in which each Exam object represents a binary relationship with at-tributes, and is connected exactly to one Student object and one ExamSession ob-ject, as indicated by the relationship cardinality constraints. For a given pair of objects *<Student, ExamSession>* it is possible to select exactly one exam and pub-lish the Grade earned by the student in a specific session.

In the hypertext of Figure 3.23 the user may select a student and an exam session by means of two distinct indexes. The OIDs of the selected Student and of the ExamSession are associated as default parameters with the two links in input to the Grade data unit, where they are used by the two selectors [Student-ToExam] and [ExamSessionToExam] to extract the grade of the student in the given exam session. When the user has clicked on both indexes, the OIDs neces-sary for computing the Grade data unit become available, and the content of the unit is displayed.

A parametric selector predicate can be tagged *implied,* to denote that the condition expressed by the predicate is optional. In this case, the absence of a value for the parameter used in the predicate can be tolerated, and the selector is evaluated as if the predicate were not specified. The value of a parameter may be absent in two cases: when the link carrying the parameter is not the one navi-gated for accessing or redisplaying the page that contains the unit, or when the link is navigated but the parameter value is void.

Graphically, optional predicates are represented by adding to them the tag `implied`, as shown in Figure 3.24. In this example, if the page is accessed via the contextual link entering the index unit and carrying the SelYear parameter, the optional selector predicate is evaluated, which means that only the albums of the year passed in input are listed. Instead, if the page is entered through the non-contextual link the value of the SelYear parameter is not available and the selector predicate [Year=SelYear] is ignored, which means that all the Album objects are shown.

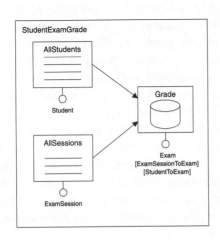

Figure 3.23   Complex selector for publishing the student's grade in a given exam session.

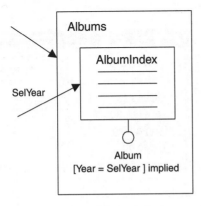

Figure 3.24   Implied selector predicate.

3.4.3   Automatic and Transport Links

Besides supporting user navigation, links can be used also to specify a particular kind of information flow between units, which takes place in absence of user intervention.

To illustrate this need, consider the page of Figure 3.25.

When the page is accessed only the index unit is displayed; then, if the user selects one of the entries of the index, the page is redisplayed and the data unit shows the details of the selected object. Prior to the user's click in the index, the data unit is not shown, because the OID of the selected object needed for computing the data unit is unavailable.

In some applications, it may be necessary to specify a different behavior, whereby the content of some unit is displayed as soon as the page is accessed, even if the user has not navigated its incoming link. This effect can be achieved by using automatic links. An *automatic link* is a link that is "navigated" in absence of user's interaction, when the page that contains the source unit of the link is accessed.

Figure 3.26 shows the same example of Figure 3.25, revised to exploit an automatic link. The meaning of such a specification is that, when the Albums page is accessed, not only the index unit is displayed, but also the data unit, which shows the details of one object selected from the index. The selection of the object from the index can be based on some heuristic criterion, for example choosing the first object according to the order clause of the index unit. In other words, the access to page Albums causes the "simulated" navigation of the automatic link, which propagates the automatically chosen context information from the source unit to the destination unit.

Note that the need of selecting heuristically context information to propagate along an automatic link occurs only for index units, hierarchical index units, multi-choice index units, and scroller units, which permit the user to select one

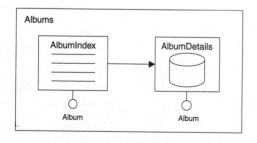

Figure 3.25   Example of page with two linked units and its HTML rendition at page access.

or more objects out of a set. Data units and multidata units do not allow the selection of objects out of a set, and thus do not require heuristic choices.

As Figure 3.26 illustrates, the graphic notation for automatic links is an uppercase "A" labelling the link arc. The same result can be achieved in the textual specification, by adding the keyword `automatic` to the declaration of the link.

All the links seen so far are rendered by means of anchors or confirmation buttons. However, there are cases in which a link is used only for passing context information from one unit to another one, and thus is not rendered as an anchor. This type of link is called *transport link,* to highlight the fact that the link enables only parameter passing, and not user navigation.

Figure 3.27 shows an example of transport link: page CelineDionAlbums contains the ArtistDetails data unit, which is filled with the details of the artist named Celine Dion, and the PublishedAlbums index unit, which lists the albums she has published.

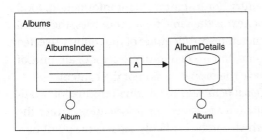

Figure 3.26 Example of automatic link and its HTML rendition at page access.

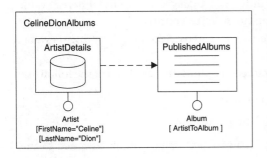

Figure 3.27 Example of transport link.

Because the link is defined as a transport link, when the page is accessed, both the data unit and the index unit are filled with content and displayed, and no anchor for the link is made available.

As illustrated in Figure 3.27, a transport link is represented in the graphic specification by means of a dashed arc; the same meaning can be expressed in the textual specification, by adding the keyword `transport` to the declaration of the link.

3.5   Global Parameters

In the previous examples, the context information needed to calculate units is associated to links, which go from one point of the hypertext to another one. However, there are situations in which context information is not transferred point-to-point during navigation, but must be available "globally" to all the pages of a site.

Consider, for example, the case of a multi-country Web site, where the user can select in the home page the country he/she is interested in and then browse the site's content relative to that country, for instance, album information, local artists, and so on. Although the hypertext is the same for all countries, the actual content varies country by country. Therefore, the identifier of the country selected by the user is a piece of context information needed in the selector of all units of all the pages of the site view, to retrieve the proper version of the content.

WebML offers the notion of *global parameter* for storing information available to multiple pages. A global parameter is a piece of information, either the OID of an object or a typed value, which can be explicitly set at some point during hypertext navigation, and then retrieved to compute the content of some unit, later during the navigation. The value of the global parameter is associated with the user's session, so that distinct users may have different values for the same global parameter; for instance, two users may browse the same multi-lingual application, but receive content in different languages, due to the different value of the global parameter representing the selected country.

Using a global parameter requires three steps: declaring it, setting its value, and then getting the value.

The declaration of a global parameter requires the definition of the following:

- A user-defined *name* for the parameter.

- The *type* of the value stored in the parameter.

- A possible *default value,* which is a constant value initially assigned to the parameter.

As an example, a global parameter for storing the country selected in a multi-language Web application may take as value the OID of an object of entity

Country, as illustrated by the declaration of the CountryOID parameter shown below; or it may simply contain a string value, for example the name of the country, as shown in the declaration of the CountryName parameter. In the latter case, the parameter can be given a default value, for example "Italy".

The textual definitions of the global parameters CountryOID and Country-Name are the following:

```
globalParameter CountryOID
(type OID;
 entity Country)
```

```
globalParameter CountryName
(type string;
 initialValue "Italy")
```

The value of a parameter is assigned by means of an ad hoc unit, called *set unit*. A set unit has only one input link, which is associated with a link parameter holding the value to be assigned to the global parameter. Because the assignment has a global side effect and becomes visible to all the pages of a site view, a set unit is graphically placed in the hypertext diagram outside pages. In the normal practice, links in input to a set unit are transport links, because the parameter setting occurs transparently to the user and no anchor is needed. Figure 3.28 shows an example of a set unit, which stores into the CurrentCountry global parameter a value received from a data unit via a transport link. The meaning of this hypertext is that, when the Country page is accessed and the CountryData unit is displayed, the OID of the country is also propagated to the set unit by the transport link, and thus saved in the CurrentCountry global parameter. Because the link to the set unit is a transport link, no clickable anchor is provided and the setting of the global parameter occurs without user's intervention.

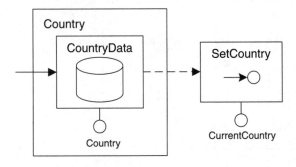

Figure 3.28 WebML graphic notation for set units.

The textual definition of the set unit and of its input link is:

```
link CountryDataToSetCountry transport
(from CountryData to SetCountry)

setUnit SetCountry
(parameter CurrentCountry)
```

The same unit configuration of Figure 3.28 can be used to store into a global parameter the name of the country instead of its OID: to do so, the input link of the set unit should have a custom link parameter (say Name: Country.Name).

A global parameter is retrieved by means of the *get unit,* which can be considered the dual operation with respect to the set unit. A get unit has no incoming links, and has only one outgoing link, transporting the value of the retrieved parameter; the unit is placed inside the page where the global parameter value is used, to show the fact that the parameter is retrieved to help the computation of some unit local to the page.

In the example of Figure 3.29, the global parameter CurrentCountry stores the OID of a particular country, previously set by the user. The CountryData unit receives from its input link such an OID and uses the implicit selector [OID=<linkparameter>] to display the data of the current country.

The textual definition of the get unit and of its output link is as follows:

```
getUnit GetCountry
(parameter CurrentCountry)

link GetCountryToCountryData transport
(from GetCountry to CountryData)
```

Figure 3.30 shows a complete example of use of global parameters. The Home page comprises an index for selecting the current country (CountryIndex),

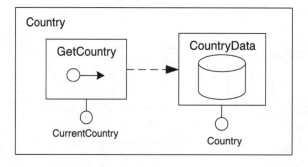

Figure 3.29 WebML graphic notation for get units.

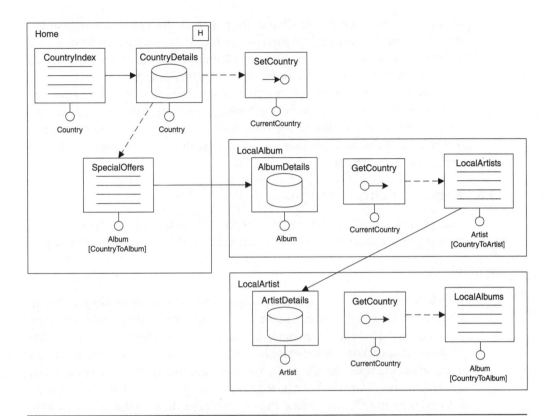

Figure 3.30 Sample schema containing set and get units.

a data unit showing the details of the selected country (CountryDetails), and a list of special album offers available locally (SpecialOffers), built using a selector over the relationship role CountryToAlbum, which connects each country to the locally offered albums. As a side effect of selecting a country, the transport link from the CountryDetails data unit to the SetCountry set unit saves the OID of the chosen country into the global parameter associated with the set unit, which is used in two further pages, LocalAlbum and LocalArtist. Page LocalAlbum contains a data unit (AlbumDetails), reached by selecting a special offer album from the Home page. The page also contains an index (LocalArtists), displaying selected artists promoted especially in the country the user is browsing. To determine such artists, the page includes a get unit (GetCountry), which retrieves the OID of the country set in the Home page, which is used in the selector of the LocalArtists index unit. Selecting an artist from the LocalArtists index unit leads to page LocalArtist, which contains a data unit (ArtistDetails), with the details of the selected artist, and an index unit (LocalAlbums), which presents the list of locally promoted albums. To retrieve the proper albums, the page includes a get unit (GetCountry) over the CurrentCountry global parameter, which is used in the selector of the LocalAlbums index unit, for retrieving the albums connected by the relationship role CountryToAlbum to the country chosen in the Home page.

As this example demonstrates, global parameters and set and get units permit the specification of hypertext exhibiting a sort of "navigation memory," whereby past user's selections, like the choice of the country in the home page, are made available in other pages, reached later during the navigation, for enabling the computation of some units.

3.6 Hypertext Organization

The specification of large and complex hypertexts can be organized hierarchically, by using modularization constructs, such as site views, areas, and nested pages.

3.6.1 Site Views

A WebML hypertext is packaged into an application to be delivered to users by enclosing its linked pages and units into a modularization construct called *site view*.

Figure 3.31 shows an example of the graphic notation for site views. Site views are characterized by a user-defined name and contain a set of pages and/or areas. In the example, the Album site view contains four pages. Artists page shows a list of artists (AllArtists). Artist page presents the details (ArtistData) of the artist selected from the AllArtists index. Page AlbumIndex displays the data of an artist (ArtistShortData) and the list of his/her albums (AlbumIndex). Finally, page Album

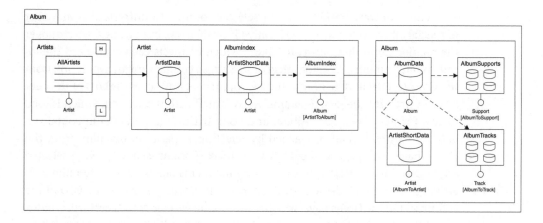

Figure 3.31   Site view in WebML.

provides some information about a single album (AlbumData), like the name of its artist (ArtistShortData), the available supports (AlbumSupports) and the list of its tracks (AlbumTracks).

The textual representation of the site view contains the site view name and the list of its pages and/or areas:

```
siteview Album
   (pages Artists, AlbumIndex, Album, Artist)
```

3.6.2   Areas, Landmarks, and Home Pages

Many real-world Web applications exhibit a hierarchical structure, whereby the pages of the site are clustered into sections dealing with an homogeneous subject. WebML provides primitives for improving the organization of site views and pages: areas, landmarks, and homes.

Areas are containers of pages or, recursively, other sub-areas, which can be used to give a hierarchical organization to a site view. Most real-life Web sites are partitioned into areas; for example, Figure 3.32 shows two HTML fragments taken from Web sites whose pages include a navigation bar with anchors pointing to the various areas of the site.

The most typical structure of a site view, illustrated in Figure 3.33, is a two-level hierarchy: the site view is sub-structured into a number of areas, and each area contains one or more pages, which deal with some related topic, such as Corporate News or Customer Information.

Links can be drawn between pages and units in the usual way, and can cross the borders of areas. Following an inter-area link simply implies that the focus moves from a page of one area to a page of another area.

If a site view encloses both areas and pages, then its textual specification lists the areas as well as those top-level pages that are directly enclosed within the site view; each area is then defined separately, by listing its pages and sub-areas. The hypertext conforming to the site view structure depicted in Figure 3.33 is specified as follows:

```
siteview Company
(areas CorporateNews, CustomerInformation;
 pages Home)

area CorporateNews
   (pages NewBrands, InvestorInfo, EcologyPolicy)

area CustomerInformation
   (pages ContactUs, TechSupport)
```

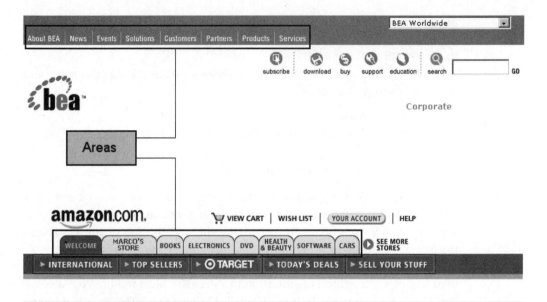

Figure 3.32   HTML portions of popular Web sites.

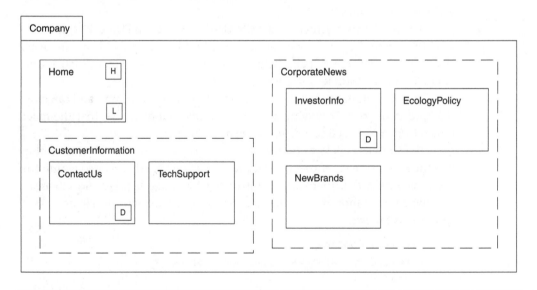

Figure 3.33   Two-level decomposition of site views into areas.

Pages and areas are characterized by some distinguishing properties, which highlight their "importance" in the Web site. In particular, pages inside an area or site view may have the following three properties (Figure 3.33):

■ The home page is the page at the default address of the site or presented after the user logs in to the application. The home page must be unique across the site view. In the graphic specification, an "H" inside the page icon denotes the home property of a page; in the textual declaration, the keyword home is added to the page specification.

■ The default page is the one presented by default when its enclosing area is accessed. The default page inside an area must be unique. In the graphic specification, a "D" inside the page icon denotes the default property of a page; in the textual declaration, the *default* keyword is added.

■ A landmark page is reachable from all the other pages or areas within its enclosing module (the site view or a super-area). In the graphic specification, an "L" inside the page icon denotes the landmark property; in the textual declaration, the *landmark* keyword is added.

Areas can be associated with the landmark and default properties (Figure 3.33):

■ The default area is the sub-area accessed by default when its enclosing super-area is accessed. If the user navigates a link pointing to the super-area, he/she is redirected to the default page of the sub-area. The default page of the sub-area is defined recursively: it is either the default page defined locally inside the sub-area, or a default page recursively nested inside an arbitrary number of default sub-sub-areas.

■ A landmark area is an area implicitly reachable from all other pages or areas of the enclosing site view or super-area.

Properties of being default and landmark are added to the textual and graphical definition of areas, using the same notations illustrated for pages.

As an example of the usefulness of the concept of landmark, Figure 3.34 shows two equivalent WebML diagrams. In the diagram on the left, the Home page is also a landmark page; the meaning is that every page enclosed in the site view is the source of an implicit non-contextual link pointing to the landmark page. The diagram on the right shows these non-contextual links explicitly. The meaning conveyed by the diagram on the left is therefore that the Home page can be reached from any other page of the enclosing module. If a site view contains many pages, the landmark property reduces significantly the number of non-contextual links to be drawn, and makes the diagram much more readable.

The same benefit occurs with the sub-areas contained in a site view. The diagram in the left side of Figure 3.35 represents an example of landmark area, which is equivalent to the diagram on the right side, where the implicit non-contextual links are made explicit. In practice, the pages called Home, Trolley,

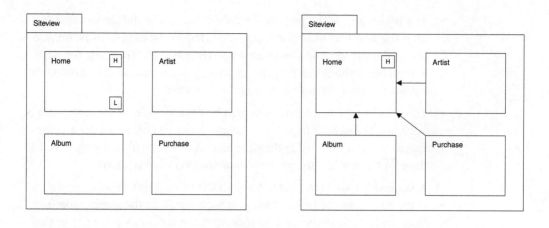

Figure 3.34 Home and landmark pages (left) and equivalent diagram with explicit links (right).

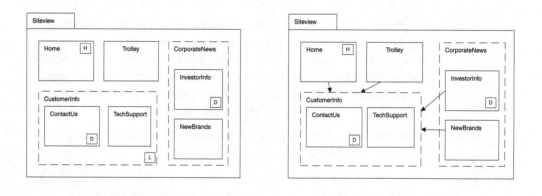

Figure 3.35 Landmark area (left) and equivalent diagram with explicit links (right).

InvestorInfo, and NewBrands are linked to the default page ContactUs of the CustomerInfo area.

3.6.3 Nested Pages

The hypertext pages seen so far are organized as collections of one or more units. This page structure covers the requirements of most Web applications, but not all. WebML offers the notion of *nested pages,* for modeling the physical organization of some complex pages. Nested pages permit the designer to give a hierarchical structure also to pages, by dividing them in sub-pages.

Nested sub-pages may be in conjunctive form, which means that they are displayed together, or in disjunctive form, which means that the display of one sub-page replaces the display of another sub-page.

Conjunctive nested pages (also called AND sub-pages) are used to divide the page contained in a screen into portions, so that one portion is kept fixed and the others display variable information based on user commands, like with frames in HTML, where the information in some variable frames may be replaced by different data after a user's click on a link in a fixed frame.

The page of Figure 3.36 contains two AND sub-pages: the sub-page named Leftmost contains two indexes of past and recent issues, and the sub-page named Rightmost displays album information. The Rightmost sub-page is reloaded at each click on the Leftmost sub-page, which is kept fixed.

The textual representation of the outermost page contains the list of its pages, which are defined separately, as follows:

```
page Outermost
(and-pages Leftmost, Rightmost)

page Leftmost
(units RecentIndex, PastIndex)

page Rightmost
(units AlbumInfo)
```

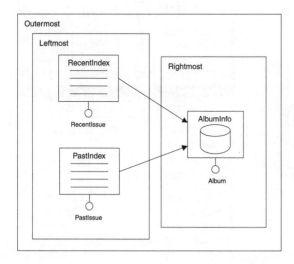

Figure 3.36 WebML notation for nested AND pages and rendition in HTML.

Disjunctive nested pages (also called OR sub-pages) are used to specify that certain portions of the screen may contain *alternative* configurations of units, each one modeled as a distinct page. At runtime, one of the pages is selected and rendered based on the user's choice. Figure 3.37 shows a page including the index of albums and artists, together with the information of *either* the album *or* the artist. The composition of the page, and not only the object to display, changes if the user selects an artist or an album from the indexes, which requires the use of two OR sub-pages, one for displaying the artist details and one for the album information. One of the OR sub-pages can be marked as the *default OR sub-page* to specify that it is the one to show before the user makes a choice, when the enclosing page is accessed.

In Figure 3.37 the outermost page contains two AND pages, named Leftmost and Rightmost. The latter encloses two OR sub-pages, one of which is marked as the default sub-page. Graphically, pages enclosing OR sub-pages, like the Rightmost

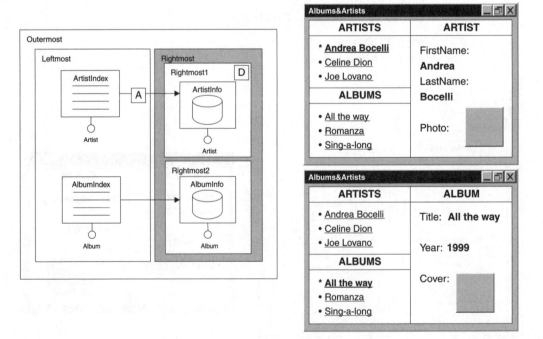

Figure 3.37   WebML notation for nested OR pages and rendition in HTML.

page, have a different filling color. The textual definition of the Rightmost page and of its OR sub-pages is:

```
page Rightmost
(or-pages Rightmost1 default, Rightmost2)

page Rightmost1(units ArtistInfo)
page Rightmost2(units AlbumInfo)
```

3.7 Patterns for Content Publishing

The organization of content in Web pages typically follows some predefined patterns, which are frequently recurrent in real-life applications. The typical configuration of a structured hypertext alternates data or multidata units, showing information about objects, with units that support the navigation from one object to another related one. In this section, we briefly present a selection of representative patterns, which demonstrate how WebML concepts can be composed in many ways to obtain a wide variety of effects.

3.7.1 Cascaded Index

A *cascaded index* is a sequence of index units defined over *distinct* entities, such that each index unit specifies a change of focus from one object, selected from the index, to the set of objects related to it via a relationship role. In the end, a single object is shown in a data unit, or several objects are shown in a multidata unit.

Figure 3.38 shows a cascaded index for navigating from a set of artists to a given album of a specific artist. The first index (ArtistsIndex) shows all the objects

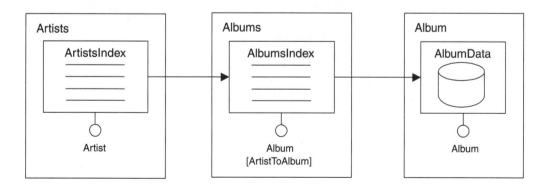

Figure 3.38 Cascaded index pattern.

of the entity Artist; the second one (AlbumsIndex) shows the Album objects associated with the Artist object selected in the ArtistsIndex. Finally, the AlbumData unit displays the details of the album chosen in the AlbumsIndex unit.

Figure 3.39 shows a variant of the basic cascaded index pattern, where index units are interleaved with data units. This variation allows showing some features about the object selected at each step.

3.7.2   Filtered Index

A *filtered index* is a sequence formed by an entry unit followed by an index unit, both defined over the same entity; the set of instances of the index unit is restricted by a selector based on the values entered by the user in the form fields. The meaning of this pattern is a two-step selection. First, the user provides input values to use as search keywords and the objects matching such keywords are presented in the index; next, the user may choose the desired object from the smaller set shown in the index, and have it displayed in a data unit.

Figure 3.40 shows an example of filtered index; the entry unit allows you to enter the title and year of publication of albums in a form. The output link of the entry unit transports the input values as link parameters (AlbumTitle and PublYear) to the index unit, where the two parameters are used in the selector, to retrieve only albums matching the given title and year. In this example, the selector requires that the title contain the keyword entered in the first field and stored in the AlbumTitle parameter *and* the year of publication of the album be equal to the value entered in the second field and stored in the PublYear parameter. Both conditions are defined as implied, to point out that if a parameter value is void, then the predicate is ignored. In the example of the rendition shown in Figure 3.40, the user enters a value for the year and leaves the title field un-

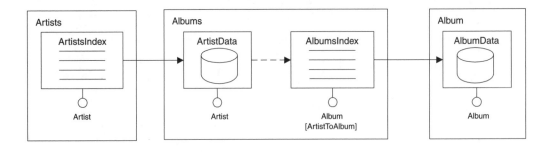

Figure 3.39   Cascaded index pattern with interleaving of index units and data units.

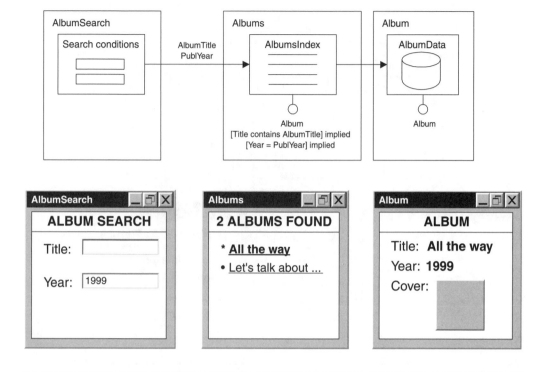

Figure 3.40   Filtered index pattern and rendition in HTML.

specified. The condition about the title is therefore ignored and all the albums published in 1999 are displayed.

3.7.3   Filtered Scrolled Index

The *filtered scrolled index* pattern is typically used by search engines, which accept sequences of keywords, and then present the result of the keyword search divided into pages, with scrolling commands for accessing one result block at a time. The effect of paging the search results into blocks is modeled in WebML by using scroller units and by setting their block factor.

Figure 3.41 shows an example of a filtered scrolled index on entity Album. In the example, the user enters keywords in a form for matching the title and year of albums. The link in output from the entry unit transports this information as link parameters (AlbumTitle and PublYear) to the scroller unit, which retrieves all

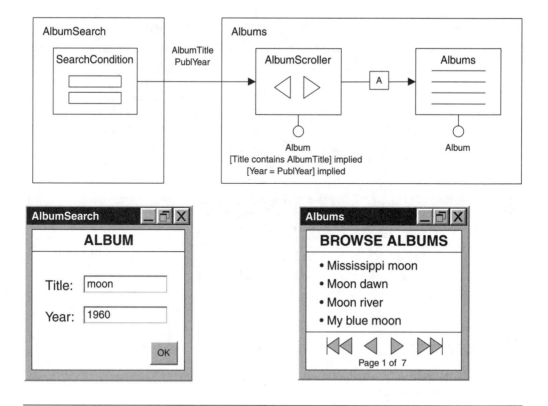

Figure 3.41   Filtered scrolled index pattern and rendition in HTML.

the matching albums. Then, an index unit displays one block of retrieved albums, and the user may access the first, last, previous, or next block in the sequence using the scrolling commands. The link between the scroller unit and the index unit is automatic, to make a heuristically selected block (for instance, the first) appear in the index as soon as the user submits the search keywords.

3.7.4   Guided Tour

A *guided tour* is a pattern for browsing the objects of a sequence one by one. The pattern consists of a scroller unit with block factor equal to 1, linked via an automatic link to a data unit. On the first access to the page enclosing the scroller unit, due to automatic navigation of the intra-page link, the first object of the scroller unit is shown in the data unit. Then the user can exploit the first, last, previous, and next commands to scroll through the sequence.

Figure 3.42 shows an example of guided tour through the albums of a given artist. In this example, all albums of the artist are included in the tour. Notice that the selector on the scroller unit could express more complex conditions, for example to scroll over the albums published by an artist in a given period of time.

3.7.5   Indexed Guided Tour

An *indexed guided tour* supports browsing a sequence of objects in a way similar to a guided tour; the difference is that the first object being accessed is selected via an index, and such first access permits the user to "jump in the middle" of the sequence to scroll. The pattern includes an index unit and a scroller unit, both linked to the same data unit.

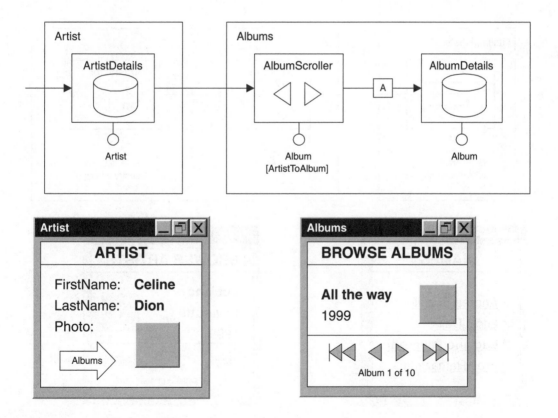

Figure 3.42   Guided tour pattern and rendition in HTML.

Figure 3.43 shows an example of indexed guided tour. When the user performs a selection in the index, the selected object determines the context of the scroller unit, where the commands to access the first, last, previous, and next in the sequence become active.

3.7.6 Object Viewpoints

An *object viewpoint* pattern is a chain of two or more linked data units, so that each data unit gives a different viewpoint on an object; typically, one data unit displays essential information, and one adds more details.

Figure 3.44 presents two data units on the same artist, in which the essential data are shown in the ArtistIntro page, from which a second page can be

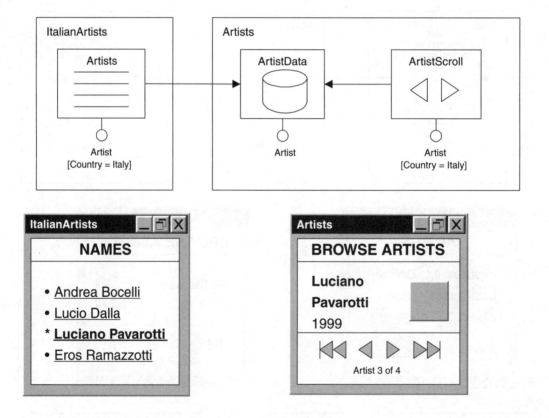

Figure 3.43   Indexed guided tour pattern and rendition in HTML.

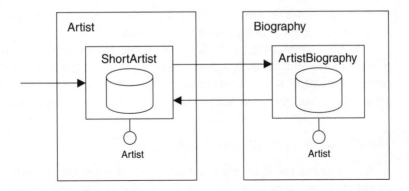

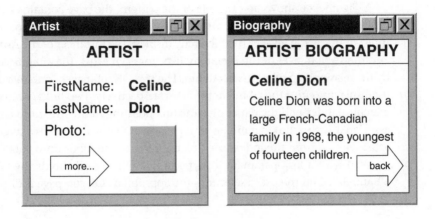

Figure 3.44 Data units on the same object pattern and rendition in HTML.

reached showing the biography data of the same artist in more detail. From the detailed page it is possible to move back to the ArtistIntro page.

3.7.7 Nested Data

A *nested data* pattern is a hierarchical index composed of two entities, such that the entity used at the top level of the hierarchy is connected by a one-to-one or many-to-one relationship to the entity at the second level of the hierarchy; its purpose is to show content related to, but not directly included in, each object of the index. This pattern illustrates the role of hierarchical indexes as "repeaters," which show several objects of the same entity, extended with content "imported" from other entities reached by following a chain of relationship roles departing from the source entity at the top of the hierarchy.

In the example of Figure 3.45, the hierarchical index unit shows the titles of all the albums and, for each album, the first name and last name of the single artist associated with it. The artist's first name and last name are not part of the album object, but can be reached by following the relationship role AlbumToArtist.

3.7.8   Hierarchical Index with Alternative Sub-Pages

A *hierarchical index with alternative sub-pages* pattern is used to present a hierarchy of objects of different types, permitting the user to select any object from the index and display its details.

Figure 3.46 shows an example of the pattern: the page contains a hierarchical index defined on the Artist and Album entities, and two OR sub-pages. In the index unit, the top level of the hierarchy displays the instances of the Artist entity, and the second level of the hierarchy lists, for each artist, the albums connected by the relationship role ArtistToAlbum. The two OR sub-pages contain a data unit, for displaying *either* the album *or* the artist, respectively. Two links connect the hierarchical index and the data units: the link pointing to the ArtistInfo data unit is associated with a link parameter of type Artist.OID, which holds the OID of an artist selected from the index; the link pointing to the AlbumInfo data unit is associated with a link parameter of type Album.OID, which holds the OID of an album. Based on the user's selection, the appropriate OR sub-page is displayed.

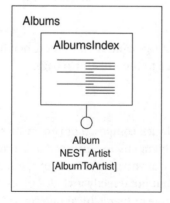

Figure 3.45   Nested data pattern and rendition in HTML.

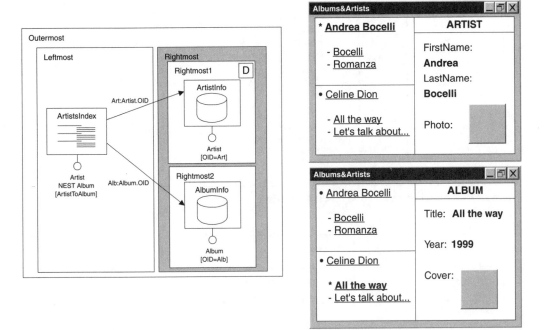

Figure 3.46 Hierarchical index with alternative sub-pages and rendition in HTML.

3.7.9 Reusable Units

Sometimes the same page must be accessed with different navigation paths, possibly carrying different types of parameters to the same unit of the page. A unit receiving different types of parameters must include multiple implied selectors, one for each different way in which it can be accessed.

The typical configuration consists of a data unit in a page, which is accessed from several sources. In the example in Figure 3.47, the ArtistDetails data unit is an example of reusable unit, because it is accessed by two different links, providing different inputs and requiring different selectors. The link from the ArtistIndex unit is associated with the SelArtist parameter, holding the OID of an artist: when this link is navigated, the data unit uses the selector [OID=SelArtist] to display the data of the selected artist, and ignores the implied selector [AlbumToArtist(AlbumOID)]. The link from the ShortAlbum unit is associated with the AlbumOID parameter, holding the OID of an album, which is used by the implied selector [AlbumToArtist(AlbumOID)] to retrieve the artist object connected to such an album; in this case the implied selector [OID=SelArtist] is ignored.

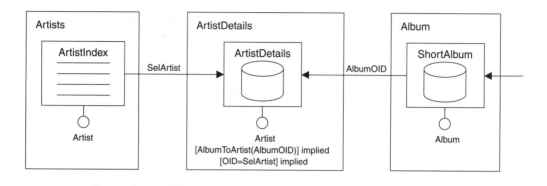

Figure 3.47   Reusable data unit and rendition in HTML.

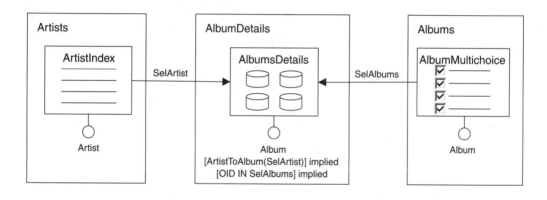

Figure 3.48   Reusable multidata unit and rendition in HTML.

This pattern applies also to multidata units. In the example in Figure 3.48 the ArtistIndex unit permits the user to select a particular artist, whose OID is associated as a parameter (SelArtist) with the input link of the AlbumsDetails unit, which uses the implied selector [ArtistToAlbum(SelArtist)] to retrieve and display the set of albums of the selected artist. The AlbumsDetails unit can also be accessed in a second way: the AlbumMultichoice index unit allows the user to select *a set* of albums, whose OIDs are associated as a link parameter (SelAlbums) with the second input link of the AlbumsDetails multidata unit; when this link is navigated, the implied selector [OID IN SelAlbums] is used to display the details of the albums selected in the multi-choice index.

3.8 Running Example

Figure 3.49 reexamines the simple site view fragment inspired by the CDNOW Web site already illustrated in Figure 3.31. The site view models the browsing of an artist and of its albums.

We now show how the WebML model compares to the real pages from which the running example has been taken. For each page, we consider only the most relevant content elements and links.

The first page (Artist) shows the data of a particular artist (ArtistData): the artist's first and last name, his/her photo, his/her dates and places of birth and death, and biographic information. Figure 3.50 represents a snapshot of the CDNOW Web site, which demonstrates how such a page may look like in a real Web site.

Starting from the artist page a link leads to a second page (AlbumIndex) containing the artist's first and last name (ArtistShortData) and the list of all his/her albums (AlbumIndex). For each album, the cover picture, the title and year of publication are presented. The rendition of such a page in the CDNOW Web site appears in Figure 3.51.

By selecting one of the albums, the Album page is reached, showing the data of the album (AlbumData), the name of the artist (ArtistShortData), all the available supports for the album together with their discounted and list prices (AlbumSupports), and the list of the tracks (AlbumTracks). Figure 3.52 shows the album page in CDNOW.

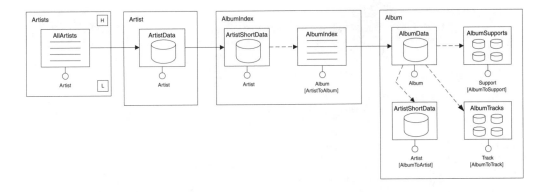

Figure 3.49   Fragment of site view of the CDNOW site.

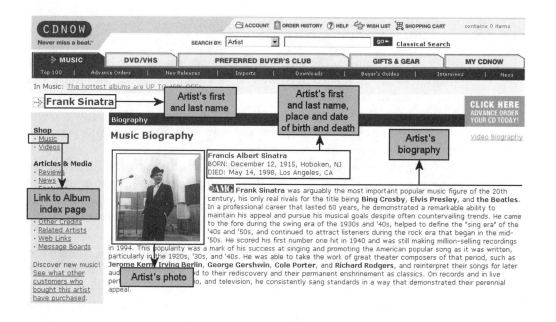

Figure 3.50 Artist page in CDNOW.

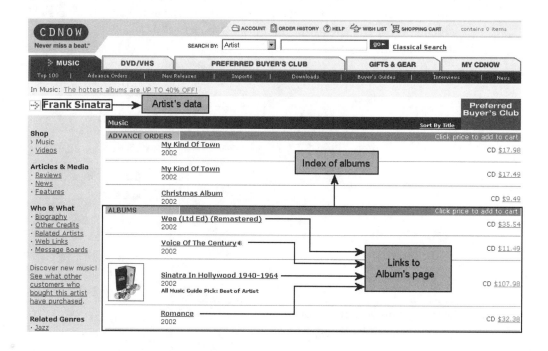

Figure 3.51 Page in CDNOW, showing the albums of an artist.

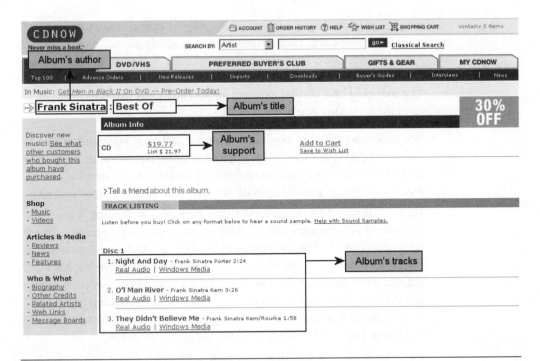

Figure 3.52 The album page in CDNOW.

3.9 Representing WebML Hypertexts Using UML

Similarly to what we have done for the Entity Relationship model in Chapter 2, in this section we briefly sketch the way in which hypertext-modeling concepts can be represented in UML, so that users familiar with this notation can perform the conceptual modeling of hypertexts using their favorite representation.

A WebML diagram essentially conveys structural information: the organization of the application into sub-systems, expressed by site views and areas, the decomposition of site views into areas and pages, the components that constitute a page, and the linking associations between pages and units.

This information is represented at an abstract level, corresponding, in the object-oriented terminology of UML, to the analysis-level description of the system. Indeed, a WebML diagram purposely ignores how the functions of the hypertext are partitioned between server-side components and client-side objects executed in the browser, but concentrates on the logical view of the application.

These considerations suggest the use of UML class diagrams as the most appropriate tool for representing the information of a WebML diagram. As is customary in UML modeling, a WebML class diagram may contain standard UML elements, like classes and associations, and custom elements, represented by stereotypes, tagged values (that is, custom properties of modeling elements) and constraints, useful for denoting modeling primitives specific to hypertexts.

The mapping of a WebML schema into a UML class diagram proceeds according to the following guidelines:

- Site views and areas are expressed as nested packages, representing the top-down decomposition of the application. The tagged values {default} and {landmark} can be used to convey the respective properties of areas. Figure 3.53 shows the UML notation for representing site views and areas.

- Pages are denoted by classifiers with the <<page>> stereotype. A page is considered as a complex object, made of sub-components and associated with other objects. The tagged values {home}, {default}, and {landmark} can be used to convey the respective properties of pages. Nested AND pages are simply denoted by nesting one page inside another page. Nested OR pages are represented by a nested page, with the <<alternative>> stereotype, comprising further sub-pages corresponding to the WebML OR sub-pages. Figure 3.53 shows the UML notations for pages.

- Units are represented as classes associated by a part-of association with the page enclosing them, represented by nesting units inside the page. The stereotypes <<data>>, <<multidata>>, <<index>>, <<multi-choice index>>, <<hierarchical index>>, <<scroller>>, and <<entry>> are used to distinguish the different kinds of WebML units. As customary in UML, textual stereotype labels can be replaced by graphic icons, to improve diagram readability. The attributes displayed by the data, index, and multidata units are listed as class attributes of the unit element. The fields displayed by the entry units are listed as class attributes of the entry unit element, with the stereotype <<input>>. Specific properties of units (like the sorting criterion of index and multidata units, or the block factor of scroller units) are represented by suitable tagged values. Figure 3.54 summarizes the representation of the different kinds of WebML units.

- The source entity and selector of a unit are represented as an association between the unit class and the entity class, labeled with an OCL constraint expressing the selector conditions. Figure 3.54 shows units with selectors expressed in UML.

- A link between pages or units is represented as an oriented association, with stereotype <<link>>. The parameters of links are expressed by one or more tagged values associated with the link. The stereotypes <<automatic>> and <<transport>> can be used to convey the respective type of links. Figure 3.55 summarizes the notations for WebML links and link parameters.

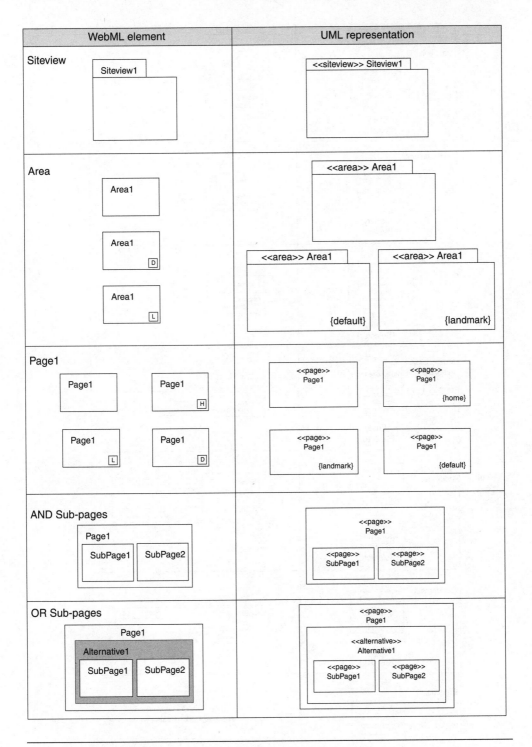

Figure 3.53 WebML site views, areas, and pages represented in UML.

[1]In UML, nesting of pages within their areas or site views is represented by graphically nesting page classifiers within the package of the enclosing module. Nesting of graphical elements is also adopted for representing the inclusion of areas within site views (or other areas).

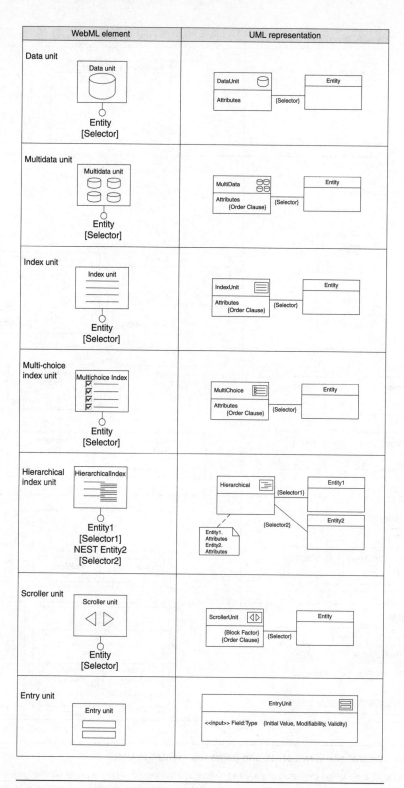

Figure 3.54 WebML units represented in UML.

Figure 3.56 shows the UML representation of a simple hypertext (whose WebML specification was shown in Figure 3.13), including a link between an index unit and a data unit.

Figure 3.57 shows the WebML Filtered Scrolled Index pattern already introduced in Section 3.7.3, reformulated in UML.

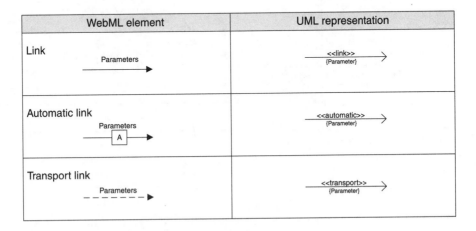

Figure 3.55 WebML links represented in UML.

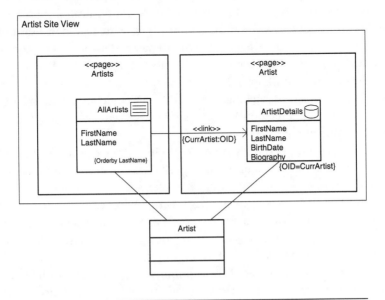

Figure 3.56 A simple hypertext expressed in UML.

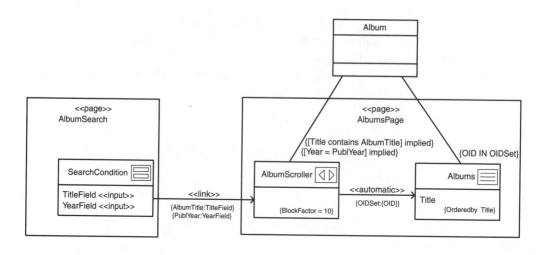

Figure 3.57   Filtered Scrolled Index.

Summary

This chapter has presented the primitives for hypertext modeling, focusing on the Web applications for publishing content in read-only mode. The illustrated hypertext model is centered on the notions of units, pages, and links. Units describe the elementary pieces of content to be displayed; pages are combinations of units delivered to the user to fulfill a well-defined communication purpose; links denote connections between units and/or pages, which support user's navigation and interaction, and enable the passage of parameters needed for computing the content of units. The specification of units builds upon the Entity Relationship model described in Chapter 2: a unit is defined on top of one or more entities of the data schema, and can be associated with selector conditions exploiting the entity attributes and relationships, for specifying the objects actually contributing to the unit content.

Pages, units, and links are packaged into site views, which represent cohesive hypertexts, aimed at fulfilling a specific set of requirements, like the delivery of content to a specific user group. Complex site views can be partitioned into a hierarchy of areas, which cluster pages with a homogeneous purpose. Inter-page and inter-area navigation may exploit global parameters, which are atomic pieces of information, recorded at some point during the user's navigation, and later exploited to compute the content of some unit.

The modeling power of these primitives lays in the possibility of combining them in many ways, obtaining a high variety of communication effects. We have shown several examples of useful page and unit configurations, which represent frequently used Web design patterns.

Finally, we have shown how to represent the WebML primitives in UML, to let designers familiar with this notation reuse their skills for modeling the hypertextual front-end of their Web applications.

Bibliographic Notes

The hypertext model presented in this chapter draws upon a number of design models proposed in the past for hypermedia applications, such as Hypermedia Design Model (HDM) [GPS93], Object Oriented HDM (OOHDM) [SR95], and Relationship Management Methodologies (RMM) [ISB95]. The first hypermedia model to gain acceptance was the Dexter Model [HBR94], a model providing a uniform terminology for representing the different primitives offered by hypertext construction systems. In the Dexter Model components describe the pieces of information that constitute the hypertext and links represent navigable paths. Many subsequent proposals in the hypermedia field started from the Dexter Model and added more sophisticated modeling primitives, formal semantics, and structured development processes. For example, HDM adds more complex forms of hypertext organization and more powerful navigation primitives to capture the semantics of hypermedia applications. RMM proposes a modeling language built upon the Entity-Relationship model and goes further in the definition of a structured methodology for hypermedia design. OOHDM takes inspiration from object-oriented modeling, by adding specific classes for modeling advanced navigation features, and exploits classical object-oriented concepts and notations in the design process.

The development of Web sites with a model-driven approach has been specifically addressed by two important research projects, namely Araneus [AMM98] and Strudel [FFKLS98]. Both these methods allow the designer to separately define the site's structure and content. In the former, the Entity-Relationship model is used to describe the data structure, whereas a logical model called Araneus Data Model (ADM) is proposed to describe the site structure. ADM is based on the nested relational model, where the concept of *page scheme* is introduced to represent the structure of a page. A page scheme may include both atomic attributes (a text, an image, and so on) of a single object and complex nested attributes representing sets of objects, similar to the WebML concept of index. A site is defined as a set of linked page schemes.

In Strudel, both the schema and the content of a site are described by means of queries over a data model for semi-structured information. Content is represented using the Uniform Graph Model, a graph-based data model capable of describing objects with partial or missing schema. Web sites are defined in a declarative way, by writing one or more queries over the internal representation of data, using the Strudel query language (StruQL): such queries identify the data to be included in the site, and the links and collections of objects to be provided for navigation.

The UML representation of the hypertext-modeling primitives is indebted to the Web extension of UML proposed by James Conallen [Conallen00]. Unlike our approach, the Web extension of UML uses class diagrams to represent the hypertext in the design phase, and thus the hypertext specification takes into account such design issues as the allocation of the various functions to the different tiers of the Web architecture. For example, pages are split into a client-side component, which represent the HTML and client-side scripting code, and a server-side component, which represents the server-side scripting code. In WebML, the hypertext model is more abstract, and does not consider the architectural aspects of hypertext implementation.

Among the commercial tools only very few products [HIM98, Oraclea, Oracleb] provide a hypertext conceptual model, typically based on an extension of the Entity-Relationship model.

4 CHAPTER Content Management Model

4.1 Introduction

Web applications often perform operations on data. Examples are the filled-in forms of personal profile information, the addition of items into a shopping cart, or the update of content published on the Web by means of Web-enabled content management applications. In all these cases, actions performed via the Web interface have side effects, for example they change the content of some data sources connected to the Web site. In addition to updating data, Web applications may invoke externally defined programs, providing them with input, which depends on the content of the current page and on the user's selections or inputs. Examples of such general-purpose operations are the login of a user, the sending of messages such as e-mails, and so on.

Introducing operations in WebML does not affect the data model, and requires two quite simple and intuitive extensions of the hypertext model presented in Chapter 3. The first extension is the notion of *operation units,* which are used to express some processing executed as the result of navigating a link; an operation unit may denote either a data manipulation or the execution of a generic external service. The second extension applies to the outgoing links of operation units, which are distinguished into *OK-links* and *KO-links.* OK and KO-links capture the concept of operation success and failure, respectively, and permit the designer to take alternative courses of action after the execution of an operation, depending on the outcome of execution.

WebML includes several *predefined operation units,* which offer the most commonly used primitives for updating the instances of the entities and relationships of the application, by creating, modifying, and deleting objects, and connecting and disconnecting them through relationships, plus a few other utility operations, like the login, logout, and send mail operations. The predefined content management operations can be clustered into *transactions,* which are sequences of updates executed atomically; when a transaction is specified, either all the individual operations that constitute it execute successfully, or the entire sequence is undone.

Besides the above-mentioned built-in operations, arbitrary application-dependent services and business components, like e-payment services, can be represented using the general concept of *generic operation.* A generic operation is a "black box," whose internal details are not specified in WebML, which can be linked to WebML units or pages. As for the normal units and operations, links pointing to and coming from generic operations may transport context information, which flows between the WebML units and the external operations. This feature permits the integration of arbitrary external business logic into a WebML hypertext specification.

4.2 Operations

WebML operation units (*operations,* for short) are a new kind of units, which can be placed outside of pages and linked to other operations, or to content units defined inside pages. Unlike content units, operations do not display content, which justifies the fact that they are placed outside pages; rather, they perform an action. Like content units, operations may have a source object (either an entity or a relationship) and selectors, may receive parameters from their input links, and may provide values to be used as parameters of their output links.

Operations can be either predefined or generic. The former, illustrated in Section 4.3, model content management functions, like the creation, deletion and modification of objects, and the creation and deletion of relationships. The latter, discussed in Section 4.7, allow the integration of external procedures of arbitrary complexity. Regardless of their type, WebML operations obey the following design principles:

- An operation may have multiple incoming links, providing values for its input parameters.

- Operations can be linked to form a sequence. Firing the first operation of the sequence implies executing also the remaining operations. One of the incoming links must be a regular link, and all the remaining links should be transport links. The operation is executed by navigating the regular link and uses the parameters associated with all the input links.

- Each operation has one OK link and one KO link; the former is followed when the operation succeeds; the latter when the operation fails. The selection of the link to follow (OK or KO) is based on the outcome of operation execution and is under the responsibility of the operation implementation.

- An operation may have any number of outgoing transport links, which are used to specify link parameters needed by content units or other operation units. The specification of transport links does not alter the execution sequence of operations, which is based only on the OK and KO links, but permits the designer to use the various outputs of operations as input in other units.

Operations do not display content, but execute some processing as a side effect of the navigation of a link. However, the result of executing an operation can be displayed in a page, by linking an operation to an appropriate content unit, which accepts input parameters from the operation and uses such parameters to retrieve and display the relevant information.

4.3 Predefined Operations

WebML provides a number of built-in operations, whose meaning is predefined in the language. Due to the orientation toward data-intensive Web applications, most predefined operations address data-management tasks; a few other built-in operations are provided, which offer services of general utility, frequently used in Web applications; they are the login and logout operations and the send-mail operation. The following sections describe the syntax and usage patterns of each predefined operation.

4.3.1   Object Creation

The first built-in operation is the *create unit,* which performs the creation of a new entity instance. Each create unit is characterized by the following:

- A user-defined *name.*
- The *source entity* to which the operation applies.
- A set of *assignments,* binding the attributes of the object to be created to the parameters values coming from the input link, or to some constant values.

The input of a create unit is a set of attribute values, typically coming from one input link exiting from an entry unit. These values are used by the create operation to construct the new object; if some attributes have no associated input value, they are set to null, with the exception of the OID, which is treated differently: if no value is supplied, a new value, unique with respect to the entity instances, is generated by the operation. The output produced by the create operation is the set of attribute values, including the OID, of the newly created object. This output is defined only when the operation succeeds, and thus can be meaningfully associated as a link parameter only to the OK link, and not to the KO link. The default output of the create unit is the value of the OID attribute, which is assumed as the implicit link parameter of the OK link, if no parameter is specified explicitly.

The example in Figure 4.1 shows the typical usage pattern for create operations, which consists of the combination of an entry unit (ArtistEntry) providing input to a create unit (CreateArtist), creating a new instance of an entity (Artist). In the example, the entry unit has two fields (FirstName, LastName), for entering the first name and the last name of an artist. The values inserted by the user are associated as explicit parameters with the link from the entry unit to the create operation. These parameters are bound to the attributes of the artist object to be created by means of two assignments, represented below the source entity of the create unit. In the rendition, shown in Figure 4.1, the link exiting the entry unit is displayed as a submit button, permitting the activation of the operation. The CreateArtist operation has two output links: the OK link points to the ArtistDetails data unit and is associated with the default link parameter (the OID of the new object). The KO link points back to the ArtistCreation page, to let the user retry the operation.

The complete textual description of the example of Figure 4.1 is shown on page 141. In particular, the create unit and its OK and KO links are exemplified.

```
EntryUnit ArtistEntry
(FirstName String, LastName String)
```

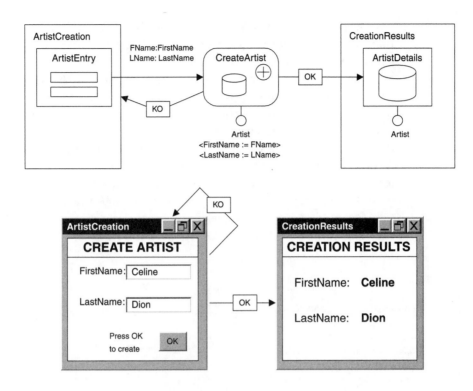

Figure 4.1 WebML graphic notation for create units, and a possible rendition in HTML.

```
link toCreateUnit
(from ArtistEntry to CreateArtist;
 parameters FName:FirstName, LName:LastName)

CreateUnit CreateArtist
(source Artist;
 FirstName:=FName, LastName:=LName)

OKLink createOKlink
(from CreateArtist to ArtistDetails;)

KOLink createKOlink
(from CreateArtist to ArtistCreation;)

DataUnit Artist details
(Source Artist;
 attribute FirstName, LastName)
```

A special case of object creation is represented by the *specialization of an existing object* to make it belong to a sub-entity of a generalization hierarchy. For example, an existing artist could be specialized as a jazz artist or as a pop artist, by extending him/her with the suitable attributes required by the sub-entity. However, some care must be adopted in the creation of the specialized object, because the object of a sub-entity is also an object of the super-entity, and thus it must have the same OID as its corresponding super-entity object. In other words, for a JazzArtist object to be a specialization of an Artist object, the Artist and the JazzArtist objects must have the same OID. Therefore, a create unit for specializing objects must receive as input also the OID of the super-entity object, which is needed to correctly create the new instance of the sub-entity.

Figure 4.2 shows an example of creation of a specialized object. First the user selects an existing artist, then he/she specializes the artist as a jazz artist by filling

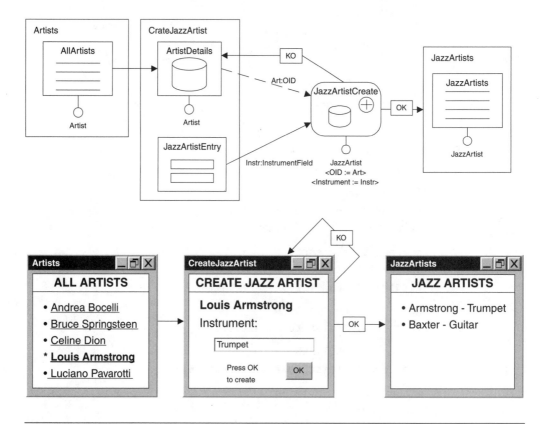

Figure 4.2   Specialization of an object, and a possible rendition in HTML.

a form with its characteristic instrument. The OID of the selected artist is defined as a parameter of the transport link between the ArtistDetails data unit and the create unit, whereas the artist's instrument is defined as a parameter of the link between the entry unit and the create unit. The create operation is fired by the navigation of the outgoing link of the entry unit, which is rendered as the submit button of the form, and creates a JazzArtist object using the OID of the artist visualised in the ArtistDetails data unit.

4.3.2   Object Deletion

The *delete unit* is used to delete one or more objects of a given entity. Each delete unit is characterized by the following:

- A user-defined *name*.

- The *source entity and the selector,* which determine the object or set of objects to which the operation applies. The objects to delete are those that satisfy the selector condition.

The user typically chooses at runtime either a single object, displayed by a data unit or selected by an index or scroller unit, or a set of objects, displayed by a multidata unit or selected by a multi-choice index unit; the corresponding OID or set of OIDs is associated as a link parameter to the incoming link of the delete unit, which actually deletes the objects.

The delete unit has a default selector, based upon the cardinality of the set of OIDs received in input: it is [OID=<link parameter>] if the input link parameter is single-valued, or [OID IN <link parameter>] if the input link parameter is multi-valued. As usual, the default selector can be inferred and need not be expressed in the graphical and textual notation.

The OK link is followed when all the objects determined by the selector have been deleted, and has no link parameters. The KO link is followed when at least one of the objects has not been deleted, and is associated with a link parameter holding the OID or set of OIDs of the objects that could not be deleted.

The example in Figure 4.3 illustrates the graphic notation for the delete operation and represents an example of the deletion of a single object. The Albums page includes the AlbumIndex unit, linked to the delete unit. The link has a default parameter, holding the OID of the selected album, which is used in the implicit selector of the delete unit. The navigation of the link fires the deletion of the selected object. If the operation succeeds the Albums page is redisplayed, but the deleted album no longer appears in the index; in case of failure, the Albums page is redisplayed and the album that has not be deleted still appears.

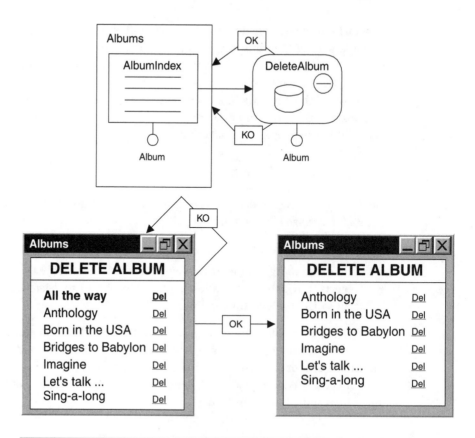

Figure 4.3   WebML graphic notation for delete unit, and rendition in HTML.

The textual specification of the delete unit of Figure 4.3 is simply:

```
DeleteUnit DeleteAlbum
(source Album;)
```

The example in Figure 4.4 shows a multi-choice index unit used to display the titles of several albums: the user checks a set of titles, and fires the deletion of the selected albums. In this case, the default parameter of the input link of the delete unit holds a set of OIDs and the implicit selector has the form [OID IN <link parameter>], which identifies the objects to delete. If the operation succeeds and all the objects have been correctly deleted, the OK link is followed and the Albums page is reloaded. If the operation fails, an error page is displayed, showing the details of the albums that have not been deleted.

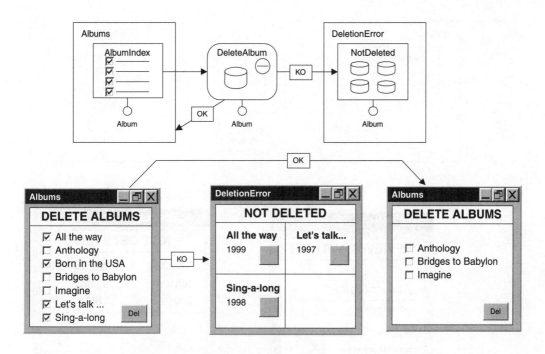

Figure 4.4 WebML graphic notation for object selection and deletion, and rendition in HTML.

The set of objects to be deleted can also be determined by means of an attribute-based selector. A simple example is represented by the hypertext of Figure 4.5: an entry form allows the user to enter the name of a review author, in order to select and delete all his reviews. The link outgoing from the entry unit has a parameter containing the name of the review author, which is used in the selector of the delete unit to retrieve and delete all the reviews written by such author. The OK link points back to the Name page, for entering the name of another reviewer, and the KO links points to an error page.

The textual description of the delete unit in Figure 4.5 and of its input link is the following:

```
link toDeleteUnit
(from NameEntry to DeleteReview;
 parameters N:Name)

DeleteUnit DeleteReview
(source Review;
 selectorAuthor=N)
```

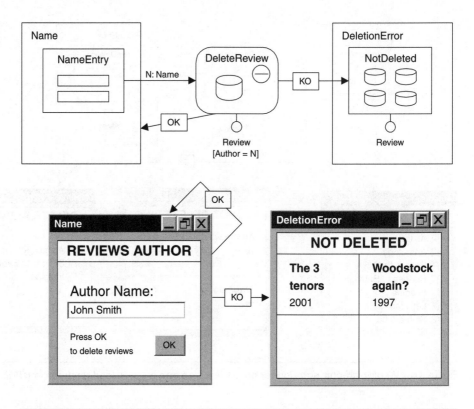

Figure 4.5   WebML graphic notation for attribute-based deletion, and rendition in HTML.

The implementation of the delete unit must preserve the *referential integrity constraint* of relationships. This means that, when an object is deleted, which participates to some relationships, also *all its relationships instances with other objects are deleted*. In the example in Figure 4.5, when a review is deleted, also the relationship instance between that review and the corresponding artist is deleted. Similarly, a delete operation applied to an instance of a super-entity eliminates also all the sub-entities instances related to the cancelled object. Referring to the example of specialization illustrated in Figure 4.2, the deletion of the instance of the Artist entity named "Louis Armstrong" implies the elimination of the related JazzArtist object, which holds the played instrument.

4.3.3   Object Modification

The *modify unit* is used to update one or more objects of a given entity. Each modify unit is characterized by the following:

▓ A user-defined *name*.

▓ The *source entity and the selector,* which identify the object or set of objects to which the operation applies; the objects to modify are the set of objects that satisfy the selector.

▓ A set of *assignments,* binding the new values to the attributes of the objects to be modified.

The user typically chooses at runtime either a single object or a set of objects to be modified; in the latter case, the same modification applies to all the selected objects.

A modify unit must be properly linked to other units, to obtain the needed inputs:

▓ *The new attribute values:* these are typically defined as parameters of an input link coming from an entry unit.

▓ *The objects to modify:* these are usually specified as a parameter of an input link, holding one OID or a set of OIDs, which is used in the selector of the modify unit. The modify unit has a default selector of the form [OID=<link parameter>], if the OID parameter is single-valued, and [OID IN <link parameter>], if the link parameter is multi-valued.

▓ Alternatively to the usage of link parameters of type OID, the objects to modify can be identified by means of attribute-based or relationship-based selectors inside the modify unit, possibly exploiting parameters associated with input links.

The OK link of a modify unit is followed when all the objects have been successfully modified: in this case the OK link has a default parameter holding the set of modified objects. The KO link is followed when at least one of the objects could not be modified, and has as a default parameter the set of OIDs of the objects that were not modified.

The example in Figure 4.6 shows an entry unit used to supply values to a modify unit. Page ModifyArtist comprises a data unit (BioData), which shows the name of the artist to modify, and an entry unit (BioEntry), whereby the user can modify the existing biography. A transport link from the data unit to the modify unit has a default parameter holding the OID of the artist to modify, which is used by the default selector of the modify unit. The modify unit is activated by a second link, exiting the entry unit; such a link has an explicit parameter (called Bio), which holds the value of the input field of the entry unit, used in the assignment <BiographicInfo:=Bio> of the operation. The OK link leads to the Result page, which shows the current value of the BiographicInfo attribute; the KO link points

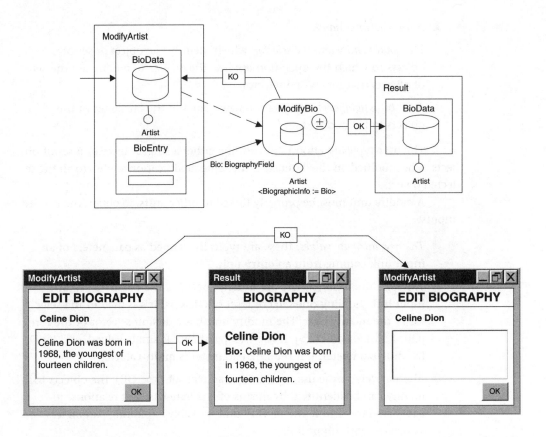

Figure 4.6 Modify unit, and rendition in HTML.

"back" to the BioData unit. Note that in case of success the new value of the bi-ography is presented in the BioData data unit.

The textual specification of the modify unit, with the default selector omit-ted, is the following:

```
ModifyUnit ModifyBio
(source Artist;
 BiographicInfo:=Bio)
```

The example in Figure 4.7 illustrates the modification of a set of objects. An entry unit allows the user to specify a type of support, like tape or CD, and a dis-count percentage to be applied to the selected type of support. The outgoing link of the entry units is associated with two parameters (S and D), containing, re-spectively, the type of support and the value of the discount. The former para-

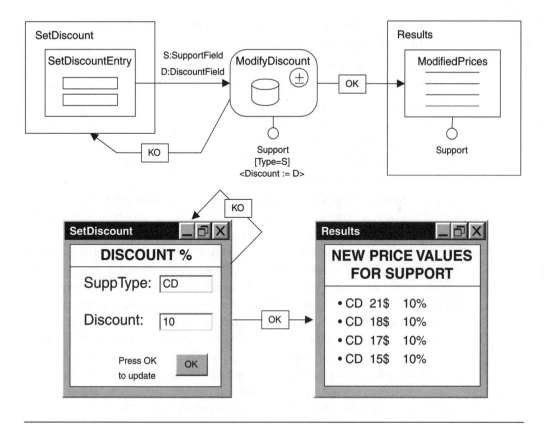

Figure 4.7   Modification of a set of objects, and rendition in HTML.

meter is used in the selector condition of the modify unit to extract all the objects involved in the operation; the latter parameter is the new value assigned to the discount attribute of all the extracted objects. As a result, the operation is applied to an arbitrary number of objects, possibly zero, if the support chosen by the user is not available. The operation succeeds if the modification can be applied to all the objects identified by the selector, in which case the OK link is followed; the operation fails if the modification cannot be applied to some of the selected objects, which causes the KO link to be followed.

4.3.4   Relationship Creation

A *connect unit* is used to create new instances of a relationship. More precisely, a connect unit applies to one of the two possible roles of a relationship, and creates one or more instances of the relationship role connecting some objects of the source entity to some objects of the destination entity. The properties of the connect unit are the following:

- A user-defined *name*.
- The *source relationship role,* that is, the role to which the operation applies.
- Two *selectors,* one for locating the objects of the source entity and one for the objects of the destination entity. To distinguish the conditions applied to the source and destination entity, the attributes and relationship roles used in the selector predicates can be prefixed with the name of the entity to which they refer.

The connect operation creates one instance of the source relationship role for each pair of objects of the source and destination entities retrieved by evaluating the two selectors; it provides in output two values, respectively holding the OIDs of the objects of the source and of the destination entity retrieved by the selector. These values can be used to define parameters in the OK, KO, and transport links of the operation. The KO link is followed if the creation of at least one relationship instance fails, whereas the OK link is followed if all the connections can be created. If the connect operation attempts at connecting two objects for which a relationship instance already exists in the database, then the operation execution does not introduce a duplicate relationship instance, but is still considered successful.

Figure 4.8 shows an example of connect unit for attaching a review to an artist. For clarity, the specification shows all the link parameters and selectors, even if they could be inferred thanks to the default rules. The Review page includes a data unit over the Review entity (NewReview) and an index on the Artist entity (AllArtists). The connect operation has two input links: a transport link from the NewReview data unit, with a parameter holding the OID of the current review; and a link from the AllArtists index unit, with a parameter holding the OID of the selected artist. The user fires the operation by clicking on one of the anchors of the AllArtists index unit. The effect produced by the operation is to connect the selected artist to the current review, using the ArtistToReview relationship role. On success, the OK link is followed, which points to page Artist, where the current review and the selected artist are displayed. Note that the ArtistDetails unit receives input from the OK link, whereas the ReviewDetails data unit takes input from a transport link exiting the AssignReview connect unit. On failure, the KO link is followed and page Review is presented again.

The textual description of the connect unit and of its input links is the following:

```
link toConnectDestination transport
(from NewReview to AssignReview;
 parameters Rev:OID)
```

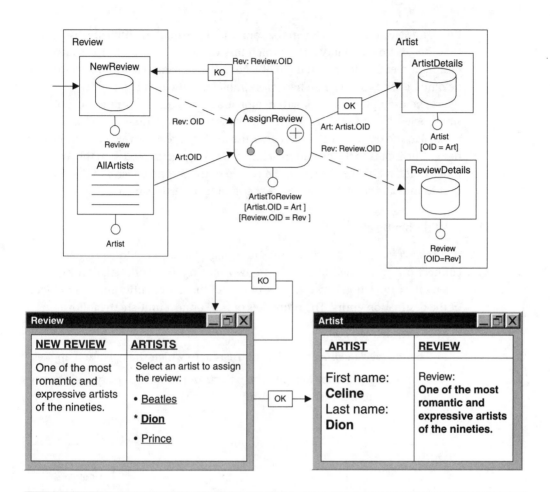

Figure 4.8   Connect unit, and rendition in HTML.

```
link toConnectSource
(from AllArtists to AssignReview;
 parameters Art:OID)
ConnectUnit AssignReview
(source ArtistToReview;
 [Artist.OID = Art];
 [Review.OID = Rev])
```

As usual a short notation can be used to simplify the diagrams. When the parameters of links and the selectors of units can be inferred from the context, they are omitted from the specification. For connects unit, the simplification of links and selectors applies when the source and destination entity are distinct, so that there is no ambiguity about which link carries the objects of the source and destination entity. In the example of Figure 4.8, all parameters and selectors can be omitted, and the diagram becomes simpler as shown in Figure 4.9.

The example in Figure 4.10 demonstrates a connect operation coupling a single object to a set of objects, selected by means of an attribute-based selector. In particular, the operation connects an artist to all the reviews that contain his/her name. The inputs to the operation are the OID of the artist selected in the AllArtists index unit, and his/her name, which is used in the second selector of the connect unit to find all the reviews whose text contains the artist's name.

4.3.5   Relationship Deletion

A *disconnect unit* is used to delete instances of a relationship. More precisely, a disconnect unit is applied to one of the two possible roles of a relationship, and deletes the connection between some objects of the source entity and some objects of the destination entity. The properties of the connect unit are the following:

- A user-defined *name*.

- The *source relationship role*, that is, the role to which the operation applies.

- Two *selectors*, one for locating the objects of the source entity and one for the object of the destination entity.

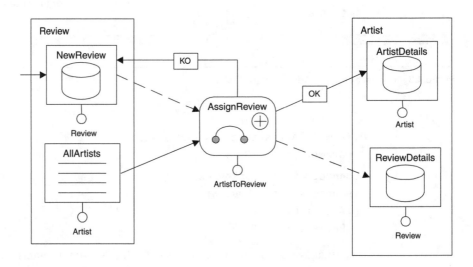

Figure 4.9   Diagram exploiting defaults for parameters and selectors.

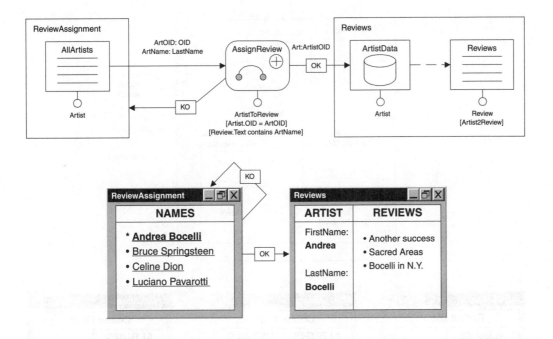

Figure 4.10   Connection of a set of objects, and possible rendition in HTML.

The operation deletes one instance of the source relationship role for each pair of objects of the source and destination entities identified by the two selectors.

As for the connect unit, the disconnect operation provides in output two values respectively holding the OIDs of the objects of the source and of the destination entity retrieved by the selector. These values can be used to define parameters in the OK, KO, and transport links. The KO link is followed if the deletion of at least one relationship instance fails, whereas the OK link is followed if all the connections can be deleted. If two objects to be disconnected are not linked by a relationship instance, then no disconnection occurs but the operation is still considered successful. Also for disconnect units, when parameters and selectors are implied from the context, they can be omitted from the diagram.

Figure 4.11 shows an example where a disconnect unit is used to "detach" one album from an artist. Page Artist&Albums contains a data unit over the Artist entity (ArtistDetails), connected by a link to an index unit (PublishedAlbums), defined over entity Album and including a selector condition built using the relationship role ArtistToAlbum. An album selected from the PublishedAlbums index unit is displayed by the AlbumDetails data unit. The disconnect unit has two input links: a transport link from the data unit, with a parameter holding the OID of the artist, and a link from the index unit, with a parameter holding the OID of

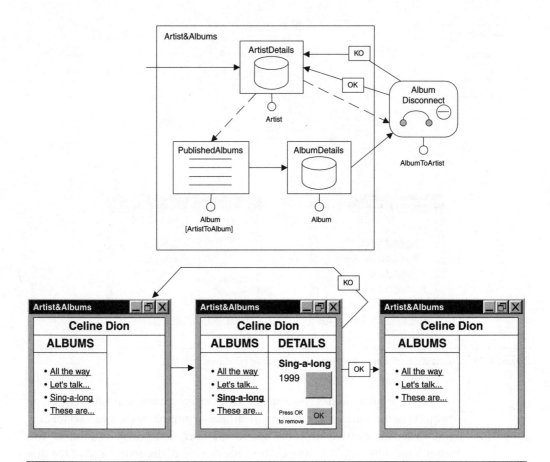

Figure 4.11   Disconnect unit, and rendition in HTML.

the currently selected album. When the user navigates the output link of the Al-bumDetails data unit, the disconnect operation is fired and detaches the selected album and the current artist. Both the OK and KO links lead back to the Artist-Details data unit and cause the redisplay of the page.

Note that in Figure 4.11 the "Sing-a-long" album has disappeared from the rendition of the destination page of the OK link, because it has been disconnected from object "Celine Dion."

The textual description of the disconnect unit of Figure 4.11 and of its input links, with default parameters and selectors omitted, is the following:

```
link ArtisDetailsToDisconnect transport
(from ArtistDetails to AlbumDisconnect;)
```

```
link AlbumDetailsToDisconnect
(from AlbumDetails to AlbumDisconnect;)

DisconnectUnit AlbumDisconnect
(source AlbumToArtist;)
```

The example in Figure 4.12 disconnects an artist object from a set of review objects. The disconnect operation has two input links: a transport link from the

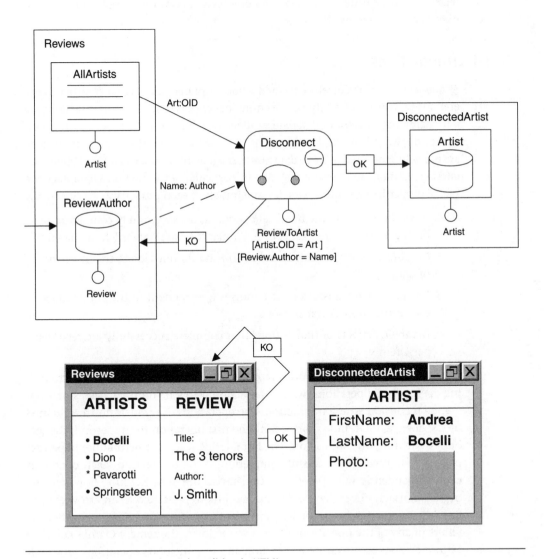

Figure 4.12 Disconnect unit, and rendition in HTML.

ReviewAuthor data unit, with a parameter holding the name of the author of the current review; and a link from the AllArtists index unit, with a parameter holding the OID of the selected artist. The user fires the operation by clicking on one of the anchors of the AllArtists index unit. The effect produced by the operation is to disconnect the selected artist from all the review authored by the person with the name passed in input to the disconnect unit.

Note that the deletion of a relationship does not cause the deletion of objects: if an artist is disconnected from one review, both the review and the artist objects continue to exist.

4.4 Transactions

A *transaction* is an atomically executed sequence of operations; that is, either all operations execute successfully, or the entire sequence is rolled back. Transactions are a fundamental concept of database systems, which grant the correct synchronization of the work of multiple concurrent users operating on the same content; they are natively supported in most database management products, and also offered by latest-generation middleware systems. In particular, a transaction guarantees the "acid" properties (so-called by taking the initials of each property as an acronym):

- *Atomicity:* either all the involved operations are successfully completed, producing a new database state, or the initial database state is left unchanged.

- *Consistency:* carrying out a transaction should not violate the integrity of data.

- *Isolation:* each transaction execution is independent of the simultaneous execution of other transactions.

- *Durability:* effects of transactions that complete successfully are recorded persistently.

Graphically, a transaction is represented as a named dashed box surrounding the involved operations; when transaction boxes are omitted, each single operation is considered as a transaction. The operations of a transaction are chained by a sequence of OK links, connecting the first operation to the second, the second to the third one, and so on. The last OK link leads to the (unique) hypertext page shown after the successful completion of the transaction. Each operation can independently fail, therefore it can have a different KO link; however, the overall transaction can have a unique KO link, represented as an arrow exiting from the transaction box, which means that the destination page shown after the failure of any of the operations of the transaction is the same. KO links could be associated both to the entire transaction and to some of its operations, in which case the locally defined KO link associated with the individual operation prevails over the KO link specified for the whole transaction. Transactions are exemplified in the next section, dedicated to content management patterns.

4.5 Content Management Patterns

The hypertexts for content management, perhaps even more than those for content publishing, follow very regular patterns. Indeed, the examples presented in Section 4.3 illustrating the five WebML basic operations already exemplify operation patterns, as they present the typical ways in which content creation, deletion, or modification are specified. In this section we present two further frequently used patterns, which involve multiple operations, organized in transactions.

4.5.1 Create-Connect Pattern

The *create-connect* pattern is a sequence formed by a create operation followed by an arbitrary number of connect operations, which associate the newly created object to one or more related objects, typically supplied by one or more transport links.

The example in Figure 4.13 illustrates a simple create-connect pattern for creating a new review and attaching it to an artist. The Review page includes the

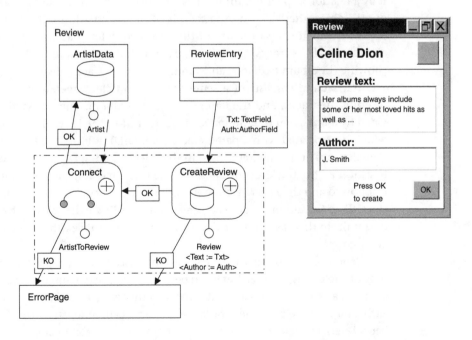

Figure 4.13 Create-connect pattern for adding a review to an artist.

artist's data, and an entry unit to input the review author and text. When the review data have been introduced, a new review object is created and, subsequently, connected to the artist object. Note that the link exiting the CreateReview unit transports the new object, which is then used by the Connect unit. Because the two operations are part of the same transaction, they are executed atomically: if any of the two fails, the whole transaction fails and no effect is produced on the data.

In Figure 4.13, the KO links exiting from both operations point to the same error page. In this case, an equivalent notation can be obtained by representing one only KO link, going from the transaction box to the error page, meaning that the failure of either one of the two operations leads to the same page.

4.5.2   Cascaded Delete

The *cascaded delete* pattern allows you to remove a particular object and all the objects associated with it via one or more relationships. It is a sequence formed by two or more delete operations, one for removing the main object and the others for removing the related objects. In particular, cascaded deletion is used to propagate the deletion of an object to other objects, which are connected to it by a relationship with minimum cardinality 1, and thus could not exist without the object they refer to. An example of such a situation is illustrated in Figure 4.14, which shows the use of the cascaded delete pattern for deleting an album and all its tracks. The Album page includes a data unit (AlbumDetails) showing the album to delete, and a multidata unit (Tracks) displaying its tracks. The transaction consists of a sequence of two delete operations, the former deleting the tracks, and the latter deleting the album. The transaction is activated by a link from the AlbumDetails data unit to the DeleteTracks operation, which is associated with a parameter (AlbumOID) holding the OID of the current album. This parameter is used in the selector of the DeleteTracks operation to cancel all the tracks of the album; if the track deletion succeeds, the OK link is followed and the DeleteAlbum operation is executed. This operation receives the OID of the album to delete from a transport link exiting the AlbumDetails data unit. In this case, the pattern uses a single KO link, exiting from the transaction box.

The example in Figure 4.14 shows the cascaded delete pattern applied to only one relationship level, but it can be extended to two or more relationship levels; for example, an artist can be deleted, together with all his/her albums, and for each album all the contained tracks can be cancelled. Independently of the number of levels, the deletion always starts from the deepest relationship level, and pro-

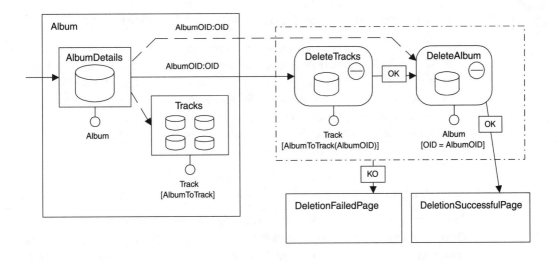

Figure 4.14 Cascaded delete pattern for deleting an album and all its tracks.

ceeds by deleting objects backwards along relationships, until the main object is deleted. In the above example, first the tracks are deleted, then the albums.

As will be discussed in Chapter 11, cascaded deletion is a primitive capability of SQL-based relational databases, which offers suitable table definition statements ensuring the propagation of deletions from a "master" object to its sub-components. However, in absence of such a mechanism, the application of the cascaded delete pattern ensures that the state of the data remains consistent after the deletion of an object associated with dependent components. Note that, according to the standard behavior of the delete operation, the relationship instances between the deleted album and its tracks need not be explicitly cancelled, but they are implicitly erased: for each deleted track, all the relationship instances in which the track object is involved are automatically removed.[1]

---

[1]The behavior of the delete operation is consistent with the usual meaning of the Entity-Relationship model, in which an instance of a binary relationship is considered as a pair of key values referencing objects actually existing in the database. If an object is deleted, any relationship instance referencing it becomes invalid and is no longer considered. This "conceptual" characteristic of the Entity-Relationship model can be easily supported in relational databases, as described in Chapter 11.

4.6 Operations for Access Control and for Sending E-mail

In addition to content management operations, many Web applications need to invoke externally defined programs, supplying them with some input that depends on the current Web page and on the user's interaction. This section presents a few examples, such as user login and logout, and e-mail sending. Login and logout operations allow the designer to specify the controlled access to the site, while e-mail sending is useful, for instance, for delivering purchase notifications, or for sending text or documents to particular recipients.

4.6.1   Login Operation

To implement access control and to verify the identity of a user accessing the site, WebML provides a predefined operation called *login*. The operation has two fixed parameters (username and password), whose values must be passed in input by a link, typically exiting from an entry unit, as shown in Figure 4.15.

The textual description of the login operation of Figure 4.15 is the following:

```
login LoginOperation
(parameters UserName :=UName, Password :=Pwd)
```

The login operation checks the validity of the identity of the user, and if the verification succeeds, forwards him/her to a default page. If the credentials are invalid, the login operation forwards the user to the error page pointed by the KO link.

A very useful application of global parameters in conjunction with login units is the storage of the OID of a user who has successfully logged into the application. For this purpose, a predefined global parameter, called CurrentUser, is automatically set with the OID of the user who has successfully completed the

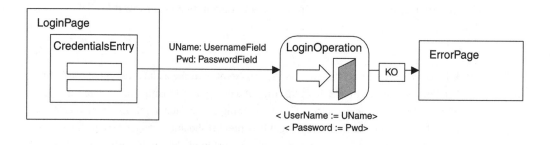

Figure 4.15   WebML login unit, preceded by an entry unit for credential input.

login. This OID can then be retrieved by means of a get unit, whenever it is necessary to publish data about the current user or retrieve objects related to the current user. Section 4.7 and the running example at the end of this chapter will demonstrate the application of the CurrentUser global parameter.

4.6.2 Logout Operation

The *logout* operation is used to "forget" the session of a logged user, and forward him to a default page with no access control. The logout operation has no input and output, and can be invoked by a simple non-contextual link, as shown in Figure 4.16.
 The textual description of a logout operation is as follows:

```
logout LogoutOperation
```

4.6.3 Sendmail Operation

Another WebML predefined operation is the *sendmail* unit, which provides the capability of sending e-mail messages. The operation has five parameters: the text of the e-mail, the set of addresses of the receivers, the address of the sender, the subject of the message, and a (possibly empty) set of attachments. A typical usage pattern is represented in Figure 4.17. The operation is activated from the page MailSending, which permits the user to choose all the parameters of the mail message. The addresses of the recipients and the attachments are selected from two multi-choice index units (RecipientsSelection and AttachmentsSelection), connected to two multidata units showing the details of the selected objects (Recipients and Attachments); these multidata units are connected by transport links to the SendMailOperation, which ensures that the operation is fed with the set of recipients and attachments. An entry unit (MailData) permits the user to fill in the subject, body, and sender of the message, and is connected by an activating link to the operation, which is fired by pressing the submit button of the entry unit. A possible rendition in HTML of this page is shown in Figure 4.18.

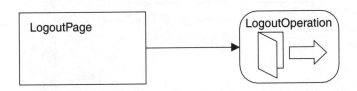

Figure 4.16 WebML logout operation unit, invoked via a non-contextual activating link.

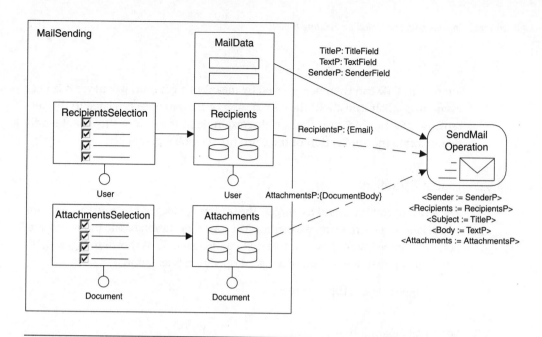

Figure 4.17 WebML sendmail operation unit, fed by an entry unit and a data unit.

MailSending

RECIPIENTS SELECTION	SELECTED RECIPIENTS
☐ John Brown ☑ James Green ☑ Janet Russell ☐ Jack Smith [Select]	James Green jgreen@webml.org Janet Russell jrussel@webml.org

ATTACHMENTS SELECTION	SELECTED ATTACHMENTS
☑ brochure.pdf ☑ industrial_case.doc ☑ logo.jpg ☐ application.zip [Select]	brochure.pdf industrial_case.doc logo.jpg

MAIL DATA

Sender:
Subject:
Text:

[Send]

Figure 4.18 Rendition of page MailSendingPage.

The textual description of a sendmail operation is:

```
sendMail SendMailOperation
(parameters Sender:=SenderP, Recipients:=RecipientsP,
Subject:=TitleP,
Body:=TextP, Attachments:=AttachmentsP)
```

4.7 Generic Operations

WebML allows the designer to define generic operations, whose specification is just the operation name. The *generic operation* unit has a graphic symbol shown in Figure 4.19.

A generic operation executes outside the WebML context; users may interact with it by supplying input using an arbitrary hypertext pattern, and possibly no longer "come back" to the WebML application. Thus, it is perfectly legal to model an external operation with no output links.

Alternatively, an external operation may have OK and KO links. In this case, upon completion of the execution, the operation is expected to autonomously decide the link to follow, for example based on some result code or exception encountered during processing. In this case, the interaction with the WebML application restarts from the destination page of the followed link.

4.7.1 Credit Card Charge

Charging a credit card by means of an external service is a typical situation occurring in many e-commerce applications. A commercial organization building an e-commerce site in many cases does not want the responsibility of managing credit cards, and uses the secure services developed by third parties, for example by a bank. To model this scenario, an external operation is defined, which wraps the e-payment service. The operation receives as input the purchase details, like the sale total and the code of the merchant, so that the merchant's accounts can be credited. All the details about credit cards data entry and user billing are instead dealt with by the external operation.

Figure 4.19   Symbol of the WebML generic operation unit.

An example of use of such an external operation is shown in Figure 4.20. Page ShoppingCart contains two data units holding the purchase details. The ShopDetails data unit displays the details of the shop the user is browsing, and the CartDetails data unit displays the user's shopping cart, which is retrieved by evaluating the role-based selector [UserToShoppingCart(UserOID)]; such a selector uses the parameter (UserOID), supplied by the GetUser unit defined over the CurrentUser global parameter. In this way, the OID of the user currently logged into the site is exploited to retrieve the data of his/her personal shopping cart.

Navigating the link from the CartDetails data unit to the ChargeCreditCard unit fires the external generic operation; when its execution is completed, the control is returned to the WebML application, by following the OK and KO links.

The textual description of the external operation is the following:

```
external ChargeCreditCard
(parameters TotAmount:=TotPrice, Shop:=ShopID)
```

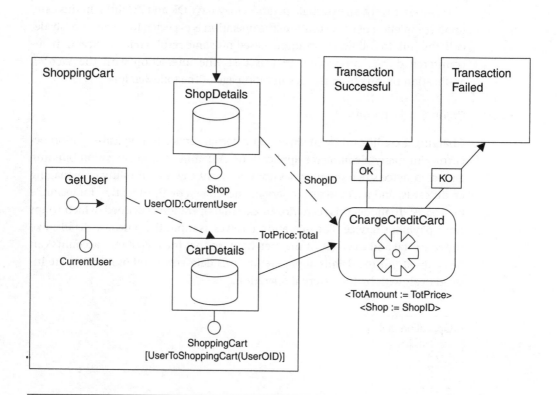

Figure 4.20 Invocation of the external operation "credit card charge."

4.8 Running Example

Figure 4.21 extends the data schema of the running example by adding the entities and relationships necessary to model the *shopping cart* of a user, as found in the CDNOW Web site and in many other e-commerce applications. Each user is associated with a shopping cart entity, containing several order lines. Each order line includes two regular attributes (Quantity and UnitPrice) and one derived attribute (/Price), defined as the product of the UnitPrice and the Quantity. Entity ShoppingCart includes a derived attribute (/Total), defined as the sum of the prices of the order lines associated with the cart. Each order line is also connected to a particular support of a given album.

In CDNOW, in order to purchase an album, the user must subscribe and provide his/her details, so that a shopping cart is created and connected to the user. Afterward, he/she can add to his cart the items offered online, like the albums available on tapes or CDs, and see the articles currently placed in the cart.

Figure 4.22 shows the Album page, which displays the details of an album and can be used for adding one of its supports to the shopping cart. Figure 4.24 shows a second page (ShoppingCart), for displaying the current content of the shopping cart and for updating it.

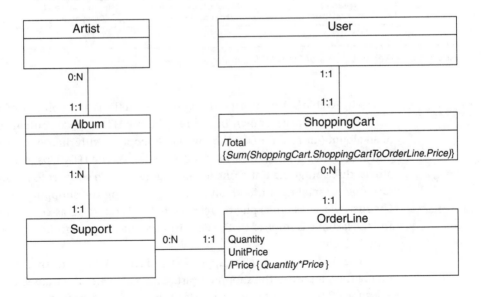

Figure 4.21   Data schema modeling a user shopping cart.

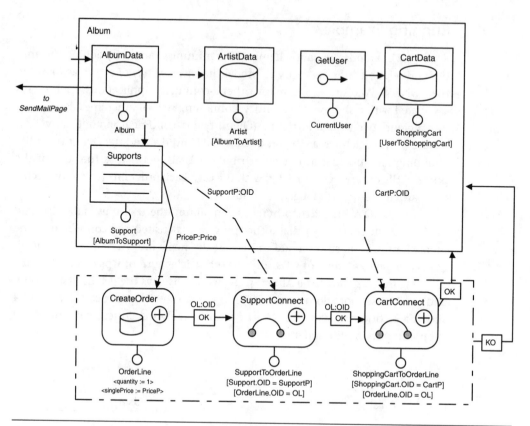

Figure 4.22   WebML schema of CDNOW AlbumPage.

The WebML Album page in Figure 4.22 reflects the content of the real CDNOW album page, shown in Figure 4.23; the HTML page contains the data of an album (unit AlbumData), its available supports with their prices (unitSupports), and the name of the artist (unit ArtistData). The HTML page has, among others, three outgoing links: one for adding the chosen support to the shopping cart, one for mailing a friend, and one for accessing the shopping cart details. The first two links are explicitly represented in Figure 4.22 as contextual links, and the last one is implied by the definition of the ShoppingCart page as a landmark in Figure 4.24.

The Add to Cart anchor appearing in Figure 4.23 represents the link for adding the support to the shopping cart, which activates the transaction shown in Figure 4.22. The transaction consists of three operations: first a new order line is created, using the support price defined as a parameter of the input link; then the new order line is connected to the support object, using the support OID

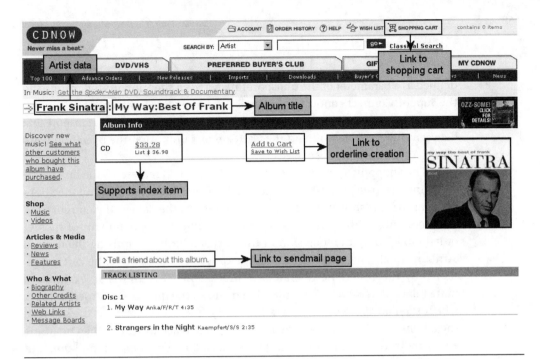

Figure 4.23 CDNOW page showing the data of an album, equivalent to the WebML AlbumPage.

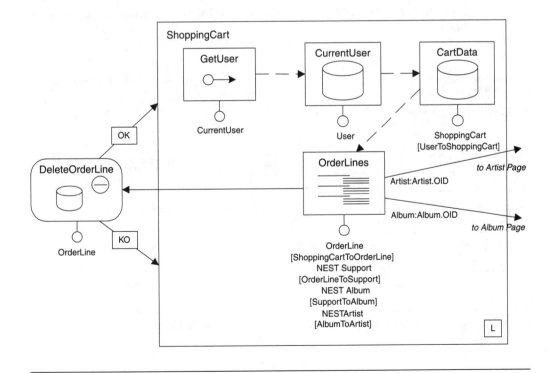

Figure 4.24 WebML hypertext schema of the CDNOW ShoppingCart page.

defined as a parameter of the transport link between the Supports index unit and the SupportConnect connect unit. Finally, the order line is attached to the user's cart, using the OID of the order line defined as a parameter of the transport link between the CartData unit and the CartConnect unit. After the operation completes, Album page is redisplayed.

The Shopping Cart anchor shown in Figure 4.23 represents the link to the shopping cart page, specified in Figure 4.24. The HTML equivalent of the ShoppingCart page is shown in Figure 4.25: it contains the data of the current user, corresponding to the CurrentUser data unit, and the total amount of his/her order, modeled by the inclusion in the CartData unit, comprising the derived attribute Total. The page also shows the order lines present in the cart, represented by the OrderLines hierarchical index unit. This unit is an example of nested data pattern: for each order line it shows the quantity of ordered items, which is an attribute of the OrderLine entity, and also data about the support, the album and the artist, which are transitively reachable from the OrderLine entity by traversing relationships OrderLineToSupport, SupportToAlbum, and AlbumToArtist. Several links depart from the ShoppingCart page: among them, one allows the deletion of the selected order line. When fired, the order line is cancelled, as modeled by the WebML DeleteOrderLine operation unit, and the

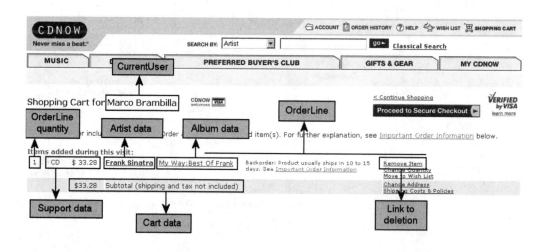

Figure 4.25 CDNOW page showing the shopping cart of a user, equivalent to the WebML ShoppingCart page.

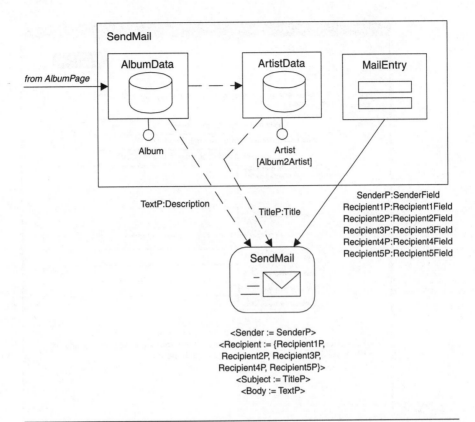

Figure 4.26 Hypertext schema of the CDNOW page for mailing the details of an album.

updated ShoppingCart page is redisplayed, as represented by the OK link of the delete operation.

The anchor "Tell a friend about the album," shown in Figure 4.23, represents a link leading to page SendMail, whose WebML schema is shown in Figure 4.26, and whose HTML rendition appears in Figure 4.27. The SendMail page includes a form, whereby the user can input the e-mail address of several recipients; one of the recipient fields is tagged as not null, to specify that it must be filled, whereas the remaining four fields are optional. The mail title and body are composed using the AlbumData and ArtistData units, connected to the SendMail operation via transport links, equipped with the suitable link parameters. The SendMail operation is launched by navigating the link exiting the entry unit, which corresponds to pressing the send button in the CDNOW page.

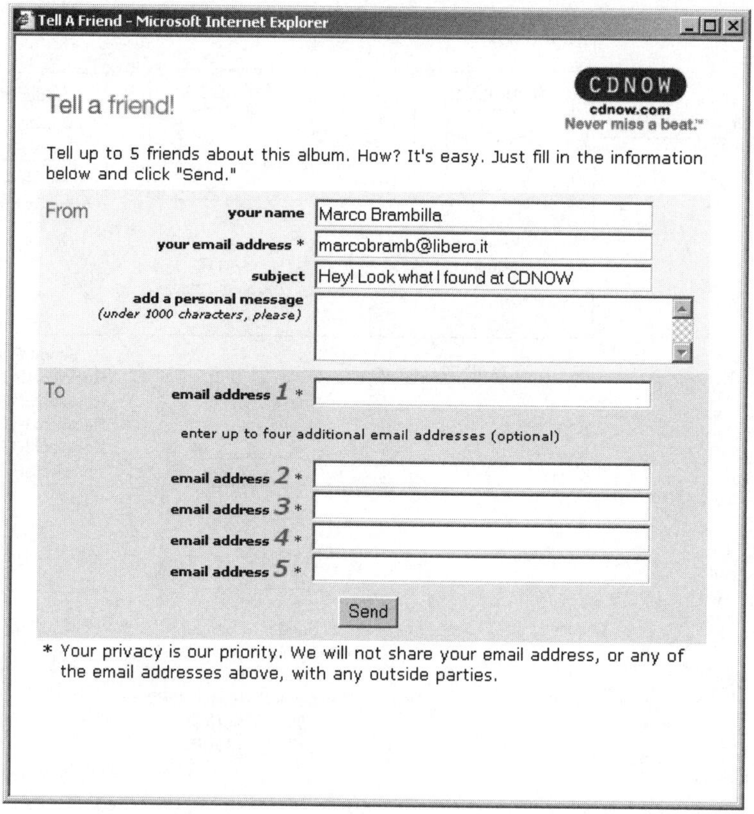

Figure 4.27   CDNOW page equivalent to the WebML SendMail page.

4.9 Representing WebML Operations Using UML

The extensions of the hypertext model presented in this chapter easily fit in the UML representation of the WebML primitives discussed in Chapter 3.

WebML hypertext diagrams aim at giving a high-level view of the operations that can be triggered by the user's navigation of the hypertext, and of the precedence relationships between the various operations that constitute a complex transaction; they are not conceived for expressing the internal behavior of transactions characterized by a complex business logic, requiring the collaboration of multiple objects, conditional branching, looping, iteration, and so on. If these aspects are relevant, they can be encapsulated into a WebML generic operation, whose internal details can be specified using the most appropriate notations.

Therefore, the integration of WebML operations into the UML hypertext diagrams illustrated in Chapter 3 requires only a few minor extensions, pictorially summarized in Figure 4.28:

- A built-in content management operation can be represented as a class, which interfaces the unit from which the operation is called to the entity or entities on which the operation works. The stereotypes <<create>>, <<delete>>, <<modify>>, <<connect>> <<disconnect>> (or the corresponding user-defined icons) can be used to distinguish the different types of operation classes. Each operation class exposes a single method to the calling unit and wraps the procedural details of executing the operation. Entities expose methods for content manipulation: one method for each of the three operations create, delete, and modify, plus a pair of connect/disconnect methods for each relationship role to which the entity participates.

- The login, logout, and sendmail operations are represented by classes with a single method, corresponding to the WebML operation.

- Links pointing to operations are represented as usual, using oriented associations with the <<link>> stereotype, possibly enriched with tagged values representing the parameters associated with the link.

- Transactions are treated as composite operations; they are represented as classes with the start(), commit(), and abort() methods, connected by part-of associations to the operations they contain.

- Two link stereotypes (<<OK>> and <<KO>>) are added, to represent the outgoing links of operations and transactions.

Figure 4.29 shows the create-connect content management patterns illustrated in Section 4.5, reformulated in UML.

The reader familiar with UML should notice that WebML, being primarily a hypertext modelling notation, is less concerned with the representation of the procedural logic of applications than UML; however, the approach for integrating operations into hypertext diagrams described in this section can be extended, by using other UML diagrams more suited to the description of the operational aspects, like sequence and collaboration diagrams. In this way, the expressive power of WebML in representing the features of hypertexts adds up to the expressive power of UML in representing the dynamics of applications, resulting in a very comprehensive set of concepts for modeling Web applications that are intensive both in the data and in the business logic.

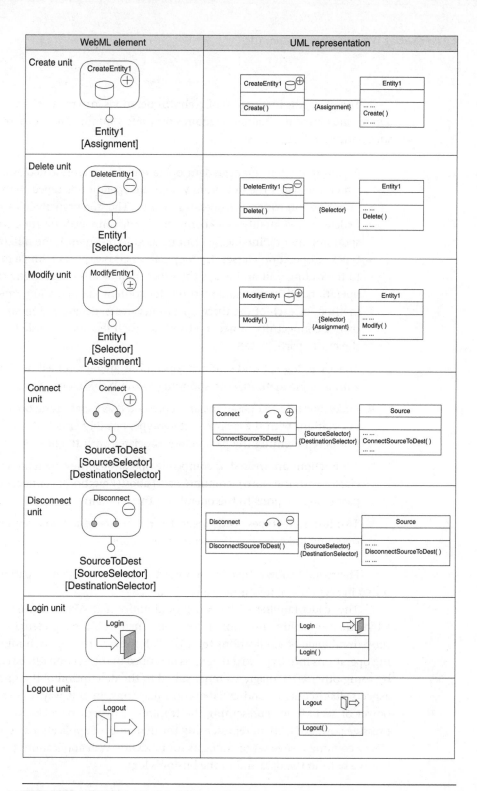

Figure 4.28 WebML operational features represented in UML.

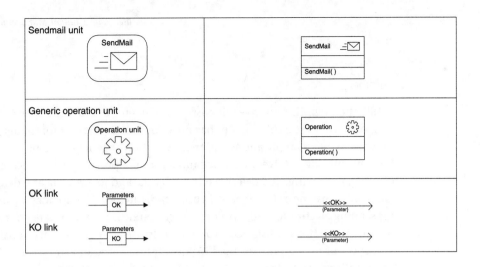

Figure 4.28 (continued)

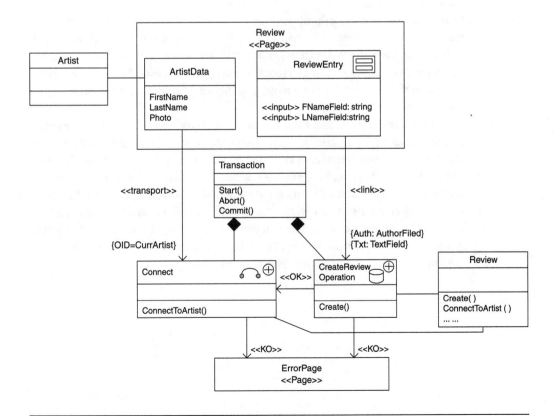

Figure 4.29 WebML content management patterns in UML.

Summary

While the WebML primitives discussed in Chapter 3 allow the specification of read-only Web sites, this chapter has introduced the concepts for modeling content management applications and the invocation of generic external operations. We have introduced five predefined units for manipulating data, specifically, for creating, modifying, and deleting entity objects, and for creating and deleting relationships instances. Other built-in operations are provided for logging users and for sending electronic mails. We next discussed how operations are encapsulated within transactions, illustrated two frequently used design patterns, consisting of sequences of operations executed inside a transaction, and shown how WebML specifications can be integrated with externally defined operations. To conclude, we have shown the UML equivalent of the WebML notations for operation units, transactions, and OK and KO links.

Bibliographic Notes

Currently, the only model proposed for the specification of Web sites that allows the integrated description of hypertexts and content management and other arbitrary operations is the Web extension of UML proposed by Conallen [Conallen00], in which UML sequence and collaboration diagrams are used to show the flow of control in the computation of a page, possibly including the invocation of operations of objects.

In the research community, several works have appeared on the semantics of conceptual models, among which there are contributions describing the semantics of database operations and the behavioral aspects of advanced database applications, such as [CPB80, MBW80, Brodie81, BR82, GBM86], just to name a few. Several other articles focus on transactional aspects [BVGM92, ELMB92, WR92, WS92], giving an overview of extended transactional models both for relational and object systems. The integration of conceptual models with workflows, discussed in [GVBA99] and [RS95], has several aspects in common with the integration of operations within Web applications.

CHAPTER

Advanced Hypertext Model

5.1   Introduction

In the previous chapters, we have gradually introduced the primitives for content publishing and management. We have on purpose adopted a high level and informal style, as appropriate in the illustration of a conceptual model. In particular, we have avoided showing intricate hypertexts, with several units linked in complex ways, whose meaning may be difficult to understand. In most situations, there is no need to build very complex schemas: the page configurations of existing sites are usually simple, and even if they include many units, they are relatively easy to understand. However, discussing the meaning of hypertexts with arbitrary arrangements of pages, units, and links is not a waste of time, but permits one to identify cases where computing the content of a page is impossible, because the hypertext specification contains subtle modeling errors, or is non-deterministic, which means that the same user's action may produce different results in an unpredictable way.

The essential point of this section is the algorithm of page computation, which describes how the content of the page is determined after a navigation event produced by the user. Page computation amounts to the progressive evaluation of the various units of a page, starting from input parameters associated with the navigation of a link. This process implies the orderly propagation of the value of link parameters, from an initial set of units, whose content is computable when the page is accessed, to other units, which expect input from automatic or transport links exiting from the already computed units of the page.

The discussion of the operational semantics of hypertexts of this chapter will also be helpful in the last part of the book, where we introduce the techniques for implementing the hypertext-modeling primitives. In Chapters 12 and 13 we will show how to transform a WebML site view into a set of page templates and server-side components, and the understanding of the page computation algorithm gained in this chapter will serve as a baseline for the implementation.

5.2 Computation of a Page

In WebML, pages are the fundamental unit of computation. A WebML page may contain multiple units linked to each other to form a complex graph, and may be accessed by means of several different links, originating from other pages, from a unit inside the page itself, or from an operation activated from the same page or from another page. In this section we explain how the content of a page is computed, which information is received in input by the page after the navigation of a link, in which order units are instantiated, and how the context produced by units is propagated along automatic and transports links to other units inside a page.

The content of a page must be computed or recomputed in the following cases:

1. When the page is entered through a link (contextual or non-contextual) originating in another page; in this case the content of all units of the page is calculated afresh, based on the possible parameter values carried by the link.

2. When the user navigates an intra-page link and thus supplies some new input to the destination unit of the link; in this case, part of the content of the page is calculated based on the parameter values associated with the intra-page link, but part of the content of the page is computed based

on the values of parameters existing prior to the navigation of the intra-page link, so that past user's choices are not lost when navigating the link.

3. When an operation is invoked, which ends with a link pointing back to the same page: this case is similar to the navigation of an intra-page link, but in addition the operation may have side effects on the content visualized in the page, which may change the content displayed by the page.

The example in Figure 5.1 illustrates the three cases: 1) when the ArtistIndex page is accessed through the non-contextual link labeled *Link1* or the Artist page is accessed through the contextual link labeled *Link2,* the content of the entire destination page is computed afresh, taking into account the possible input values transported by the link. 2) When the user selects a new album from the AlbumIndex unit, new context information flows along the link labeled *Link3* and determines the album to be displayed in the AlbumData unit; at the same time, the Artist displayed in the ArtistData data unit must be "remembered" and redisplayed, because the input of the ArtistData unit is not directly affected by the navigation of the intra-page link. 3) When the delete operation is performed successfully and the page is re-entered through *Link4,* the content of the ArtistData unit is preserved, so to remember the past user's choice, whereas the content of the AlbumIndex unit

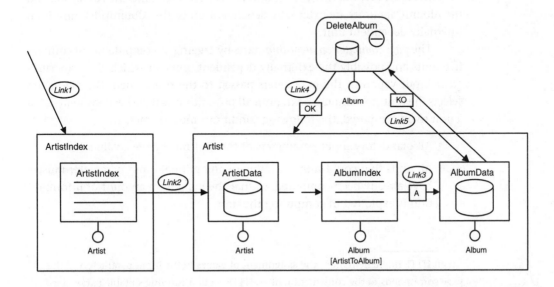

Figure 5.1   Page that can be accessed by three methods.

and of the AlbumData unit is refreshed, so that the deleted album no longer appears in the AlbumIndex unit and in the AlbumData unit. When the delete operation fails and the contextual *Link5* is followed, the content of the AlbumData unit is refreshed using the OID of the object that could not be deleted, and the content of the other units is restored. This ensures that the previously selected artist, his/her albums, and the details of the album tentatively deleted continue to be displayed when the page is re-accessed after the failed operation.

The page computation process is triggered by any of the previously discussed navigational events (inter-page link navigation, intra-page link navigation, operation activation). Based on the navigated link, a set of parameter values is collected and passed in input to the page, which determines the initial value of the input for some of the page units.[1] Then, computation proceeds by evaluating the units one after another, in a way that depends on the initial parameter values, on the topology of the intra-page links, and, in some cases, on the past user selections affecting the units in the page. The computation process exploits the propagation of context along automatic and transport links, and a rule telling which alternative input should be considered when multiple choices are available for evaluating the same unit.

In order to better describe the page computation process, units of a page can be statically classified based on their input links, as shown in Table 5.1.

In Figure 5.1, the ArtistIndex unit is a context-free unit; the ArtistData and the AlbumData units are externally dependent units; the AlbumIndex unit is an internally dependent unit.

The *page computation algorithm* starts by tagging as computable all context-free units and possibly the externally dependent units for which there are sufficient input values in the parameters passed to the page. Then, the algorithm selects the units to compute next, until all possible units have been evaluated. For a unit to be computed, the following conditions must be met:

- All mandatory input parameters of the unit must have a value.
- All units that could supply a value to an optional input parameter must have already been computed, so that the maximum amount of information is exploited in computing the unit.

---

[1]In an HTTP implementation, the assignment of values to the input parameters of the page corresponds to the construction of an HTTP request carrying suitable parameter-value pairs. Each parameter-value pair is associated with one unit, and is extracted from the request and used for computing the respective unit.

Table 5.1 Classification of units for context propagation purposes.

Context-free unit	A unit having no incoming links. These units are always computable, irrespective of the way in which the page is accessed.
Externally dependent unit	A unit requiring mandatory input from at least one incoming contextual link originating in a different page or exiting from an operation.
Internally dependent unit	A unit requiring input only from links originating from units inside the same page.

If at some step there are multiple computable units, the algorithm does not prescribe a specific order and thus, as illustrated in Section 5.2.3, the semantics of WebML is nondeterministic. As units are computed, further internally dependent units become computable, due to context propagation along automatic and transport links; the process continues until a point where no additional units can be computed. At the end of the process, some units may remain non-computable, due to the lack of their input context; this happens, for instance, to externally dependent units lacking input, or to internally dependent units receiving input from a link, when the link is not explicitly navigated. Units that remain non-computable have no content, and thus are not displayed in the page.

The page computation process can be summarized by the following pseudocode:

```
INPUT: initial set of computable units
OUTPUT: all computable units
PROCEDURE:
WHILE (there are units to compute) DO
IF a unit U exists such that
   (All mandatory input parameters of U have an input value
   AND
   All units potentially providing input to U have been
   computed)
THEN
   Assign to each parameter of U the most specific value
   available
   Compute U using the chosen input values
ELSE HALT
   END DO
```

The page computation algorithm assumes that there is some mechanism for computing the content and output of a unit from the values of its input parameters, and a criterion for deciding which input parameter to use, when multiple values for the same input parameter are available.

The *input parameters* of a unit are the parameters appearing in the unit selector. For example, in Figure 5.1, the input of the AlbumIndex unit is the OID of an artist, which (implicitly) is used in the relationship-based selector [ArtistToAlbum].

The *output parameters* of a unit are the values that the units makes available to its automatic and transport outgoing links. For example, the output parameter of the AlbumIndex unit of Figure 5.1 is the OID of the first album displayed in the index, which is associated with the outgoing link of the unit.

Unit computation is the process of using the input parameters of the unit for performing some data retrieval query, which determines both the content to be visualized by the unit and the values of the output parameters. For the purpose of the explanation of this chapter, we will disregard the technical details of how the content and output parameters of units are computed from the input parameters, because this topics concerns implementation and will be addressed in Chapter 12.

Therefore, in the sequel we will treat unit computation as a "black box," which consumes input parameters and produces output parameters. Note that the conversion of input values into output values is relevant only for automatic and transport links: links that are neither automatic nor transport do not automatically propagate parameters, because they require an explicit navigation performed by the user, which starts a distinct page computation cycle.

In some page configurations it may happen that a unit has multiple incoming links assigning values to the same parameter; in this case, the computation of the unit is ambiguous and a *specificity rule* is necessary for deciding which value to use. The specificity of input parameters is assessed according to the following principles:

1. Values which are directly or indirectly derived from the current user's choice, expressed by the last navigation event, are the most specific.

2. Values that depend on past user's choices, or from global parameters accessed through get units, are the second most specific.

3. Values heuristically chosen from the content of other units are the less specific.

The page computation process and specificity rule apply to arbitrary WebML pages, possibly containing nested pages. In the case of OR sub-pages, only one sub-page at a time is computed: when the page enclosing the OR sub-page is accessed, the default sub-page (if it exists) is computed; conversely, when a specific OR sub-page is accessed, only that sub-page is computed using the page computation algorithm, and all the other sub-pages at the same level are not considered.

5.2.1 Examples of Page Computation

We show the page computation process at work on the page illustrated in Figure 5.2, which can be computed in several ways, depending on the actual navigation performed by the user. Each navigation provides to the page computation procedure a set of parameters values, which are either "fresh," that is, produced by the user's navigation action, or "preserved," that is, passed in input to the page in order to remember past user's selections.

Page access along Link1

Page Artist is accessed via a non-contextual inter-page link, and thus no initial values are passed in input to the page. Therefore, unit computation starts from either one of the ArtistIndex and the NewAlbumIndex units, which are context-free. Their content is the entire population of the underlying entities, and their output is, by default, a heuristically chosen object appearing in the index, for instance, the first

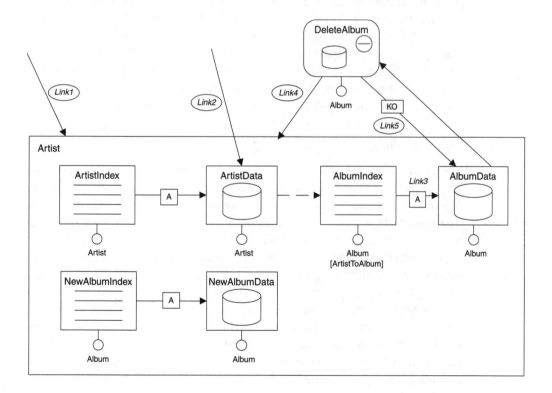

Figure 5.2   Examples of page computation.

object; after the computation of the units, both the ArtistData and NewAlbumData units have their mandatory input parameter available and thus become computable. When the ArtistData unit is computed, it provides an artist OID as output to the AlbumIndex unit, which becomes computable; after the AlbumIndex unit has been computed, the first album listed in the AlbumIndex unit is available in output and can be used as input for the AlbumData unit, which becomes computable.

Page access along Link2

The navigated link (Link2) points to the ArtistData unit and thus the initial assignment of the input parameters includes the value of the OID to be shown in the data unit, which is a "fresh" value. Computation can start from the context-free units or from the externally dependent ArtistData unit, for which the mandatory input parameter is available. Supposing that computation starts from the context-free units, everything proceeds as in the previous case; the only difference occurs in the computation of the ArtistData unit, which has two possible values for its input parameter: the fresh OID value coming from the link navigation, and the OID of the object heuristically chosen from the ArtistIndex unit. For the specificity rule, the value passed in input to the ArtistData unit through Link2 prevails over the one supplied by the ArtistIndex unit. Then, the units depending from the ArtistData unit are computed as before: the AlbumIndex unit will contain the albums of the artist shown in the ArtistData unit, and the AlbumData unit will display the first album appearing in the AlbumIndex unit.

Page access along Link3

The page is computed after the user selects a new album in the AlbumIndex unit. The parameters passed in input to the page comprise the input parameter of the AlbumData unit, as a fresh value, plus the input parameters of unit ArtistData and NewAlbumData, as values to be preserved. Computation starts from the context-free units (ArtistIndex and NewAlbumIndex), and proceeds to their dependent units; due to the specificity rule, preserved values prevail over defaults taken from index units, and thus the ArtistData, AlbumIndex, and NewAlbumData units continue to show the same content they displayed before the navigation; fresh values prevail over defaults, and thus the AlbumData unit shows the album selected by the user and not the default album extracted from the AlbumIndex unit. In summary, after the navigation of Link3, the Artist page shows content that depends on new input (the object shown in the AlbumData unit) and on "old" input (all the remaining units). The new input affects the units directly or indirectly depending on the user's navigation, whereas the old input is preserved for all the units not affected by such navigation, to maximize the "stability" of the page.

Note that "old input" does not mean "old content," as the following example demonstrates.

Page access along Link4

Page Artist is accessed through Link4 after the successful deletion of an album. The parameters in input to the page comprise the input parameters of unit ArtistData and NewArtistData, as preserved values. Conversely, no input is preserved for the AlbumData, because such input would correspond to an object no longer existing after the deletion. Computation starts from the context-free units, and proceeds to their dependent units, whose input parameters are set to the preserved values. In particular, the AlbumIndex unit has the same input as before, because the OID of the artist shown in the ArtisData unit has been restored, but different content, because the deleted object no longer appears in the index. Then, the default value of the AlbumIndex unit is used as the input of the AlbumData unit, replacing the OID of the deleted album.

Page access along Link5

Page Artist is accessed through Link5 after the deletion of the currently displayed album has failed. The parameters in input to the page comprise the output of the operation unit, which is the OID of the Album object that could not be deleted, plus the input values of units ArtistData and NewAlbumData, which are preserved. The computation starts from the context-free units (ArtistIndex and NewAlbumIndex), and proceeds to their dependent units, which are instantiated according to the parameters passed in input to the page, which leads to restoring all units to their previous content.

As a final remark, in the explanation of the page computation algorithm, we assumed that the content of units is calculated from scratch, even if the page is reaccessed with the same input parameters for the various unit; this is done both for simplicity of illustration and because in this way the content of units always reflects the most recent database state. In a practical implementation, caching mechanisms can be used to improve the performance of page computation, by saving the result of a unit query and using the cached data instead of recalculating the same query. Caching will be discussed in Chapter 10.

5.2.2   Preserving Input of Units Across Pages

As discussed in Chapter 4, global parameters, set units, and get units enable the recording of context information during the navigation, which can be used at a later time to retrieve the content of a unit. This mechanism blends smoothly in the page computation process described in the previous section. Before showing how page computation copes with global parameters and get units, we introduce an example, which recalls the motivations of these primitives.

The hypertext in Figure 5.3 contains two pages: page CountryAndNews shows the list of the available countries and allows the user to access the local news of a selected country; page News shows in a separate page the details of the piece of news selected from the LocalNewsIndex unit. From the News page it is possible to go back to the CountryAndNews page, navigating the non-contextual link; but this action causes the previously selected country to be "forgotten," and forces the user to choose the desired country again, for accessing another piece of news.

Set and get units circumvent the loss of input values of units during inter-page navigation, because they permit saving the input values of selected units into global parameters accessible by all pages of a site view.

The hypertext of Figure 5.4 extends the previous example with set and get units: the CountryData unit is now equipped with a get and a set unit. The set unit saves into a global parameter the OID of the country displayed in the data unit, and the get unit retrieves this value, if necessary. Thus, the input parameter of the CountryData unit can be determined in three ways:

1. From the value of the CurrentCountry global parameter retrieved with the get unit.

2. From the choice performed by the user when navigating the output link of the CountryIndex unit.

3. From a default value supplied by the CountryIndex unit.

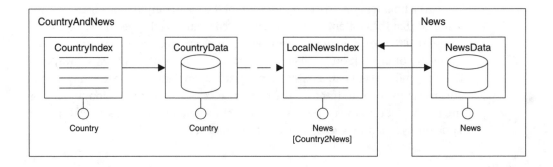

Figure 5.3   History-less hypertext.

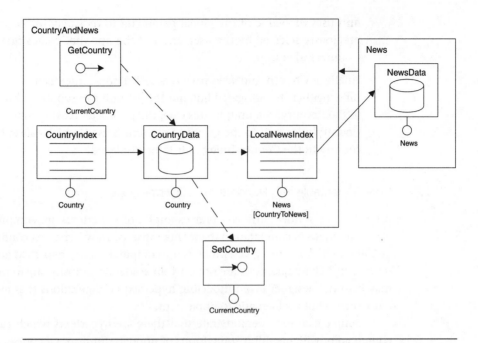

Figure 5.4   Use of set and get units for reconstructing the history of a page.

The parameter specificity rule makes the calculation of the content of the CountryData unit unambiguous in all the possible cases in which the Country-AndNews page is accessed.

- When the user explicitly selects a country from the CountryIndex unit, the link transports a fresh value for the input OID of the CountryData unit; for the specificity rule, this value prevails over the possible value supplied by the GetCountry unit. Therefore, the country selected by the user is displayed, and its OID is also transferred to the set unit and stored into the CurrentCountry global parameter.

- When the page is accessed navigating the inter-page link from the News page, the navigated link no longer transports a value for the input OID of the CountryData unit; in this case propagation starts from the context free units GetCountry and CountryIndex, which can both supply a value for the same parameter to the CountryData unit. Thanks to the specificity rule, the global parameter prevails over the default value coming from CountryIndex unit. Therefore, the CountryData unit uses the value of the global parameter to redisplay the country previously selected by the user, and not the one that comes first in the CountryIndex unit.

▪ Finally, if CountryAndNews page is accessed non-contextually for the first time, neither the navigated link nor the get unit can supply an input value to the CountryData unit; in this case, the parameter-passing rule from the CountryIndex unit to the CountryData unit is used, which causes the first country in the CountryIndex unit to be displayed.

5.2.3   Non-Computable and Nondeterministic Hypertexts

After discussing how fairly complex examples of hypertexts are computed, the classic questions of computation theory may arise: can any hypertext configuration be computed? And, for a given input, is the computation of a hypertext always deterministic? These questions are not only an academic curiosity; answering them may help the designer avoid modeling hypertext configurations that are apparently correct but problematic to implement.

Simple examples demonstrate that there are hypertexts which cannot be computed or which exhibit some forms of nondeterminism. Of course, a hypertext containing syntactically wrong units cannot be computed. For instance, Figure 5.5 shows a unit that needs an input parameter for its selector but has no incoming links. Similar modeling errors are easily spotted, by means of syntactic

Figure 5.5   Wrong unit.

checks analyzing the match between link and selector parameters, which may uncover ambiguities, lack of information, type errors, and so on.

More subtle cases occur when units are individually correct and yet form a hypertext that cannot be computed. Consider the case in Figure 5.6, relative to a "cyclic" data schema in which News are related to Products, Products to Countries, and Countries to News. In the example, the News page is syntactically correct but cannot be computed. The page contains three index units with mandatory selectors. Taken individually, the three units have all the input links needed for instantiating the parameters in their selectors, so they seem perfectly OK. However, the computation of the News page after the navigation of the link coming from the Product page cannot take place: the NewsIndex unit receives from the ProductDetails data unit the OID of a product, but lacks the (mandatory) OID of a Country, which should come from the CountryIndex unit. Unfortunately, the CountryIndex unit needs the (mandatory) OID of a product from the ProductIndex unit, which needs the OID of a News from the NewsIndex unit. Thus, there is a

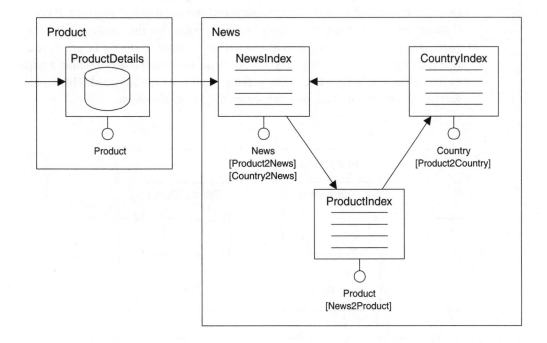

Figure 5.6 Non-computable hypertext.

circular dependency and no unit can be computed. This case can be generalized to the following observation: whenever a unit requires, in order to be computed, some mandatory parameter that indirectly depends upon the computation of the unit itself, the unit cannot be computed.

The example of Figure 5.7 is even simpler, but subtler. The user can access the News&Product page using Link1, which points to the NewsData unit, or via Link2, which points to the ProductData unit. Even if the page is syntactically correct, because all units have the needed incoming links and parameters, accessing it along any of the two contextual links supplies the parameter of only one of the two data units, leaving the other unit without a required input.

Finally, we address the issue of nondeterminism, which occurs when the same user action can produce different content for the same page. This situation arises because the specificity rule for the input parameters of units defines a partial order, and not a total order. As a consequence, the choice of the value to take for a parameter, among those at same level of specificity, may be nondeterministic.

The example in Figure 5.8 shows a page containing an index of jazz artists, an index of pop artists, and a data unit for showing an artist's data. One artist can be selected from either of the two indexes, and displayed in the data unit. If both links are automatic, when the page is accessed for the first time, either one of the two index units can be used to pass the OID of an artist to the data unit. In this case the hypertext schema is ambiguous, because it does not clarify whether a pop or jazz artist should be displayed by default when the page is loaded. This ambiguity is resolved by making one of the two links non-automatic.

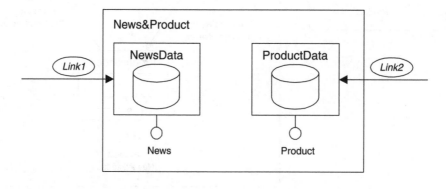

Figure 5.7   Unit may be non-computable depending on the navigated link.

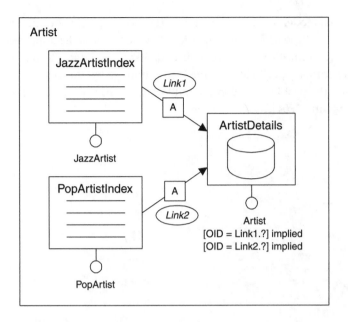

Figure 5.8 Non-deterministic hypertext.

Summary

This chapter has addressed the computation of a WebML page, which may take place after inter-page link navigation, intra-page link navigation, and content update operations. Understanding the page computation process helps in the subsequent development phases, in which WebML constructs must be translated into executable code, and also unveils subtle modeling errors, corresponding to page and unit configurations, which can be syntactically correct, but semantically problematic.

Bibliographic Notes

Very few authors have investigated the issues of the behavior and computation of dynamic hypertext at a conceptual level. Among the early works, [SF89] used Petri Nets to describe the navigation semantics of static hypertexts, where pages do not access content dynamically. Also [ZP92] addresses the navigation semantics of static hypertexts, using Statecharts instead of Petri Nets. [FTM01] introduces

Hypermedia Model Based on Statecharts (HMBS), to specify both the structural organization and the browsing semantics of static hypermedia applications, focusing on synchronization of multimedia data (like video, audio, animations, and so on). The formal specification languages adopted by these authors allow approaching the problems of computability and determinism, as it has been done for WebML in [CF01].

PART

DESIGN OF WEB APPLICATIONS

6 CHAPTER

Overview of the Development Process

6.1 Introduction

Developing a Web application, as with any other kind of software system, is a complex achievement that requires the ability to master a broad spectrum of tasks, jointly performed by a number of persons with different skills. Following a well-organized development process, centered on the appropriate modeling concepts, is essential to overcome the complexity inherent to such kind of development.

The goal of this chapter is not to invent yet another software development lifecycle, but to examine how the classic incremental and iterative development process advocated by the modern software engineering methodologies can be adapted to the specificity of data-intensive Web applications. To this end, this chapter provides a breakdown of the development activity, which matches the requirements of data-intensive Web applications, builds upon appropriate notations and concepts for data and hypertext modeling, enforces the separation between the different aspects of structure, navigation, and presentation, and lends itself to be automated by C.A.S.E. (Computer Aided Software Engineering) tools. In this introductory chapter the development process is observed from several viewpoints: the expected inputs and outputs, the involved actors, and the development phases that compose the application lifecycle. The next chapters will zoom into the most relevant activities, and will show the proposed development process at work.

6.2   Inputs and Outputs

Figure 6.1 shows the fundamental inputs and outputs of the development process of a data intensive Web application.

The most important input is the set of *business requirements* that drive application development. These requirements are mostly non-technical and express the long-term goals of building the application, by stating the value that the application is expected to produce to its users and to the organization who builds it. Business requirements also identify the business actors (human beings or orga-

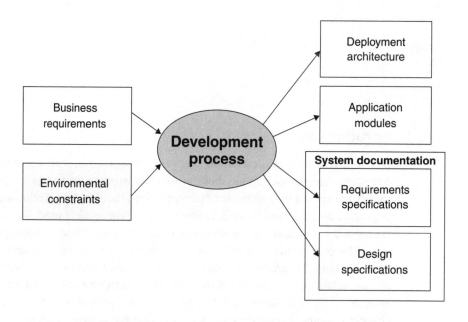

Figure 6.1   Inputs and outputs of the Web application development process.

nization's functions) taking advantage of the application, the processes affected by the application, the boundaries between the application and the preexisting systems, and the quality factors that the application must pursue, such as the quality of content, services and interfaces, response times, availability, security, privacy, and so on.

The second input is the set of *environmental constraints* that affect the construction of the application. Constraints are the limitations imposed by the real world's conditions to the achievement of the application goals. Such constraints include architectural restrictions, compatibility with existing systems and applications, available technical skills, and time and resource limitations. The deployed application is the result of a careful tradeoff between the business requirements and the environmental constraints.

The output of the development process is the implemented system, consisting of the deployment architecture, the application modules installed on this architecture, and the system documentation:

- The *deployment architecture* is the hardware, software, and network infrastructure that ensures the required level of service and the respect of the project's technical constraints.

- The *application modules* are the developed pieces of software, including data repositories, dynamic page templates, and business components, that deliver the functions demanded by the business requirements.

- The *system documentation* is the set of non-software products developed during the application lifecycle that specify the important design choices and milestones in the development of the application. The prominent pieces of documentation produced are the Requirement Specifications and the Design Specifications. The *Requirements Specifications* express what the application should do, by recasting the business requirements into a more concrete and operational set of functional and nonfunctional requirements. The *Design Specifications* document how the application is designed to meet the requirements; their fundamental components are the data design, the hypertext design, and the architecture design specifications.

6.3 Development Roles

Web application development involves different actors with complementary skills and goals as follows:

- The *application analyst* collects the business requirements and turns them into a specification of the application requirements. In doing this, he/she interprets the long-term strategic business goals and constraints and transforms them into short-term, concrete, application requirements.

- The *data architect* focuses on the part of the application requirements that deals with the data, and produces the conceptual data model.

- The *application architect* focuses on the part of the application requirements dealing with the services to be delivered, and designs the application hypertexts by specifying site views built on top of the data schema produced by the data architect.

- The *graphic designer* conceives the presentation styles of pages, based on the business requirements that deal with the visual identity and communication standards of the organization.

- The *developer and site administrator* is responsible for site implementation, architecture design and tuning, and site view deployment and evolution. In particular, he/she focuses on the nonfunctional requirements of performance, availability, security, scalability, and manageability, and is responsible for ensuring the appropriate level of service.

Other specialists are devoted to the independent testing and evaluation of the application, and have the responsibility of verifying the consistency of the application with respect to the functional and nonfunctional requirements.

The described roles are not necessarily played by different figures; in simple applications, it may happen that several roles converge in the same person.

6.4 Development Lifecycle

The phases of the development process of a data-intensive Web application are shown in Figure 6.2. In line with the classic Boehm's Spiral model, and in line with modern methods for Web and software engineering, the development phases must be applied in an iterative and incremental manner, in which the various tasks are repeated and refined until results meet the business requirements.

Application development undergoes several cycles of problem discovery/ design refinement/implementation, and each iteration produces a prototype or partial version of the system. At each iteration, the current version of the system is tested and evaluated, and then extended or modified. Such an iterative and incremental approach is not exclusive of Web application development, but appears particularly appropriate for this class of systems, because Web applications must be deployed quickly (in "Internet time"), and their requirements are often subject to changes.

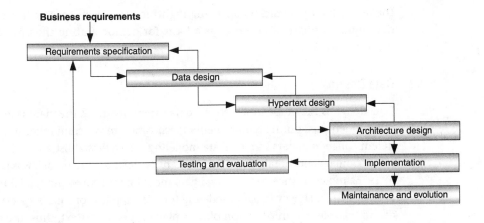

Figure 6.2   Phases in the development process of data-intensive Web applications.

Of the entire process illustrated in Figure 6.2, the "upper" phases of analysis and design are those most influenced by the adoption of a conceptual model. They constitute the subject of this part of the book, which comprises Chapters 7, 8, and 9. The "lower" phases of the development process are closer to the physical aspects of a Web application and are the subjects of the final part of the book, Chapters 10 through 13.

6.4.1   Requirements Specification

Requirements specification is the activity in which the application analyst collects and formalizes the essential information about the application domain and expected functions. The input to requirements specification is the set of business requirements that motivate the application development, and all the available information on the technical, organizational, and managerial context where the application must operate. The output of the requirements specification activity is a user-oriented, easy-to-understand, yet precise, specification, which is addressed both to the designers, who use it to understand what the application must do, and to the stakeholders, who use it to validate the adherence of the specifications to the business requirements, before proceeding with development.

Requirements specification is the subject of Chapter 7, which drills down in the activities of requirements collection and analysis. The chapter also introduces a running case, called the Acer-Euro application, to which the tasks of requirement specification are applied. Such a running example is followed throughout the rest of the book, each chapter highlighting the aspects specific to a different development phase, and serves as a basis for demonstrating the development process at work.

6.4.2   Data Design

Data design is the phase in which the data expert organizes the main information objects identified during requirements specification into a comprehensive and coherent conceptual data model. Data modeling is a well-established discipline: the most popular conceptual data model, the Entity-Relationship model, was proposed in 1976, and ever since consolidated data modeling practices and guidelines have been available. However, data modeling for Web applications has a special flavor, due to the role that information objects play in such a context; thus, the data design method discussed in Chapter 8 is tailored to Web applications. It focuses on the design of typical sub-schemas describing the core application objects, the categorization data required to access them, the interconnection between core objects necessary for navigation, and personalization data.

An important aspect of data design for a Web application concerns its relationship with the past design choices embodied in the existing data sources. A Web application typically publishes already existing content, stored in the corporate database, possibly "enriched" by means of other less structured content, like multimedia files or documents, necessary to address the Web audience. Data design and implementation in such a scenario must balance two possibly competing goals: meeting the requirements of the new application, and adhering to the past data design and implementation constraints.

Even when the content managed by the Web application already exists (either in a database or a legacy system) conceptual data design remains relevant, and should be performed independently of the existing data sources, with the aim of designing the "best" data schema for the Web application. Then, the implementation phase will face the challenge of mapping onto existing data sources the conceptual data schema of the Web application. The mapping task is a technical one, for which a number of effective methods, tools, and technologies exist.

Data design is the subject of Chapter 8, where the various steps involved in assembling the application data schema using the Entity-Relationship (E-R) model are discussed in detail, and also applied to the Acer-Euro running example.

6.4.3   Hypertext Design

Hypertext design is the activity that transforms the functional requirements identified during requirements specification into one or more site views embodying the needed information delivery and data manipulation services. Hypertext design operates at the conceptual level, exploiting the WebML model, which lets the hypertext architect specify how units, defined over data objects, are composed within pages, and how units and pages are connected by links to form hypertexts. Unlike data design, hypertext conceptual modeling is a novel discipline, with little methodological support.

Hypertext design is the phase of the entire lifecycle that mostly benefits from a conceptual and model-driven approach. Reasoning about the functions to be delivered by site views and pages is much easier at the conceptual level and with a visual model than at the source code level, and results into a more consistent and qualitative design. The availability of design patterns further facilitates the task of the hypertext architect and enforces a coherent design style over a possibly very large application, augmenting hypertext regularity and usability. In addition, the WebML detailed specifications of site views, which are the output of hypertext design, document the structure of the designed hypertext in a formal, yet implementation-independent, way; they are fundamental for managing the changes required for maintenance and evolution. Hypertext design is the subject of Chapter 9, which presents the coarse design notations for drafting the site view schema, and the guidelines for obtaining a detailed WebML schema from a draft site view schema. These notations and procedures are concretely illustrated using the running example.

6.4.4 Deployment of the Web Application

Although the main focus of this book is conceptual modeling, applications must eventually be delivered to their users, and therefore need to be implemented, tested, deployed, and maintained on top of a given architecture, which must also be designed and put in place. These activities are covered in the last part of the book.

Architecture design is the definition of the hardware, network, and software components that make up the architecture on which the application delivers its services to users. The goal of architecture design is to find the mix of these components that best meets the application requirements in terms of performance, security, availability, and scalability, and at the same time respects the technical and economic constraints of the application project. The inputs of architecture design are the nonfunctional requirements and the constraints identified during business requirements collection and formalized in the requirement specifications. The output may be any specification that addresses the topology of the architecture in terms of processors, processes, and connections. Architecture design is the theme of Chapter 10.

Implementation is the activity of producing the software modules necessary to transform the data and hypertext design into an application running on the selected architecture.

Data implementation addresses the mapping of the E-R data schema onto one or more data sources. This task aims at associating the conceptual-level entities, attributes and relationships to some physical data structures in the data sources, where the actual data will be stored. As explained for the data design phase, data implementation may occur in one of two scenarios: when the data source is designed and implemented together with the Web application, or when the data sources preexist to the Web application and must be integrated with it. In the former case, data mapping amounts to the classic activity of transforming a conceptual data schema into the schema of the "online" database, where the content is stored and managed. In the latter case, a more complex problem of data and legacy system integration must be faced, for which several alternative solutions are possible. These topics are discussed in Chapter 11.

Hypertext implementation deals with the production of dynamic page templates or scripting programs, translating the conceptual-level pages and units specified in a WebML site view into the selected mark-up and server-side scripting language. Page templates may interoperate with business objects, deployed either in the presentation layer or in the business layer, which provide the procedural logic required to compute the pages and fulfill the client's requests. Hypertext implementation is treated in Chapter 12, where Java Server Pages, relational databases, and the JDBC data access API are used to exemplify the fundamental page coding techniques; the subject is expanded in Chapter 13, where we show advanced solutions for scaling hypertext implementation to very large applications. These solutions include software architectures based on the Model-View-Controller design pattern, the use of enterprise Java Beans for implementing the application business objects, and the separation of presentation style from application code by means of XSL and CSS.

The remaining phases of the development lifecycle are not specifically covered in the book, but only hinted at, for highlighting interesting aspects, specific to Web application development.

Testing and evaluation is the activity of verifying the conformance of the implemented application to the functional and nonfunctional requirements. The most relevant concerns in testing and evaluating Web applications are the following:

- Functional testing: the application behavior is verified with respect to the functional requirements. Functional testing can be broken down into the classical activities of module testing, integration testing, and system testing.

■ Usability testing: the nonfunctional requirements of ease of use, communication effectiveness, and adherence to consolidated usage standards must be verified against the produced site views. Evaluation criteria may change from site view to site view, because different site views may be directed to user groups with different usability requirements, for example customers and internal personnel. Chapter 9 includes a section summarizing the criteria for designing usable hypertexts.

■ Performance testing: the throughput and response time of the application must be evaluated in average and peak workload conditions. In case of inadequate level of service, the deployment architecture must be monitored and analyzed for identifying and removing bottlenecks. Methods for assessing and enhancing performance of Web applications are briefly discussed in Chapter 10.

Deployment is the activity of installing the developed modules on top of the selected architecture. Deployment involves both the data layer, where the new databases must be made operational, or the software gateways to the legacy data sources and applications must be activated, and the business and presentation layer, where the page templates and business objects must be installed. Deployment is a technical task that requires the skills of the site administrator.

Maintenance and evolution encompass all the modifications effected after the application has been deployed in the production environment. Differently from the other phases of development, maintenance and evolution are applied to an existing system, which includes both the running application and its related documentation. In the model-driven process, change management benefits from the existence of a conceptual model of the application. Requests for changes are analyzed and turned into changes at the design level, either to the data model or to the hypertext model. Then, changes at the conceptual level are propagated to the implementation. This approach smoothly incorporates change management into the mainstream production lifecycle, and greatly reduces the risk of breaking the software engineering process due to the application of changes solely at the implementation level.

Bibliographic Notes

Software development processes are the subjects of many textbooks of software engineering, and of many books devoted to specific software development methodologies. The spiral lifecycle, first introduced by Boehm [Boehm88], gives the foundation to most last-generation software development methods. Ever since, the debate on the software development lifecycle has revolved around the notion of incremental and iterative development, which seems the most appropriate paradigm to capture the reality of building large software systems.

One of the most influential discussions of the software lifecycle is introduced by Grady Booch [Booch94]. The arguments expressed by the author in favor of a round-trip design process for object-oriented development are of general validity for building any kind of complex systems.

In recent years, the approach of Grady Booch was integrated with the contribution of Ivar Jacobson's and James Rambaugh's object-oriented methodologies, to lay the base of the Unified Modeling Language (UML), the standard notation for modeling systems according to the object-oriented model. The development of systems with UML is supported by the Rational Unified Process [JBR99], which puts together the best practices in applying object-oriented analysis and design, and organizes them into a coherent development workflow. The Rational Unified Process advocates six principles as the foundation of effective software development: an iterative and incremental approach to development, the proper management of requirements, the use of components and design patterns, the visual modeling of software, the continuous assessment of software quality, and the management of change. These principles apply to all software applications, and most notably to Web applications, and are at the basis of the process described in this part of the book.

James Conallen has adapted UML and the Rational Unified Process to the specific context of Web application development [Conallen99, Conallen00]. The resulting method includes a comprehensive Web application development process, which prescribes a workflow inspired to the principles and phases of the Rational Unified Process. This workflow includes the activities of requirements gathering, analysis, design, implementation, testing, deployment, configuration, and change management. The most innovative contribution is in the design phase, where ad hoc UML stereotypes can be used to describe the components of pages. In this way, page design is made visual, according to one of the basic principles of the Rational Unified Process.

7 Requirements Specifications

7.2 Requirements Collection

7.3 Requirements Analysis

7.4 The Acer-Euro Running Case

Summary

Bibliographic Notes

7.1 Introduction

Requirements specification is the activity in which the application analyst elaborates the business requirements that motivate the application development, and all the available information on the technical, organizational, and managerial context where the application must operate, and turns these inputs into the specifications of what the application should do.

As highlighted in Figure 7.1, requirements specification consists of two subphases: requirements collection and analysis.

Requirements collection aims at identifying a general picture of the application domain and of the solution to be developed, by interviewing the relevant "players" and reviewing the available documentation. At the end of this activity, the

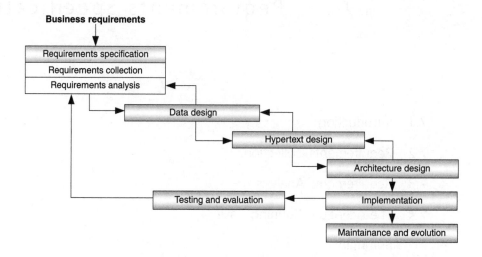

Figure 7.1   Activities of the requirements specification phase.

main business actors that will use the application, the functions to be supported, and the main nonfunctional requirements and constraints must be known.

   Requirements analysis focuses on reviewing and formalizing the elicited requirements, producing in output a set of semi-formal specifications, including:

- The list of the user groups that will access the Web application, together with preliminary assignment of their access rights over the information content.

- The most significant application use cases, which show the interactions between the identified user groups and the application.

- A data dictionary collecting the most relevant information objects in the application domain.

- The informal specification of the site views that will allow users to accomplish the functions expressed by the identified use cases.

- The nonfunctional requirements to be fulfilled by the application.

- A set of presentation guidelines, which give indications about the look and feel of the interfaces to be developed.

7.2 Requirements Collection

Requirements collection consists of reviewing the business requirements that drive the development of the application, identifying and interviewing the relevant business actors, and examining all the documentation that may shed light on the application to be developed. Requirements collection is a fairly unstructured activity, in which the experience and the receptivity of the analyst are the fundamental success factors. Aware of this fact, we will restrain from distilling prescriptive checklists of the "things to do"; every experienced analyst has his/her own checklist, and updates it every time he/she faces a new application. Therefore, the examples of requirements reviewed in the rest of this chapter should not be taken literally as prescriptions.

7.2.1 Identification of Users

The first objective of requirements collection is to establish who are the users, and cluster them into groups characterized by homogeneous goals and behaviors. Typically, each group is associated to a distinct site view, which embodies the content and functions necessary for fulfilling the requirements of the users of the group.

As a first criterion, users should be classified as internal or external; *internal users* are the members of the organization that supplies the content or services, while *external users* are the customers or the members of the organization that receives the content or services.

Another useful distinction is between *business users* (such as registered users, customers, partners), and *non-business users* (casual visitors, members of interest groups, and so on). Generally, business users are granted with different services than non-business users; for example, registered users see more information than casual visitors. For business users, more refined clustering criteria can be deduced from their role in the company or from the organization function they belong to. Conversely, the clustering of non-business users is mostly based on their service and content requirements.

Once a first list of user groups is established, it is possible to examine if there are hierarchical relationships among the identified user groups. For example, the "marketing" user group may specialize into the "national marketing," "European marketing," and "worldwide marketing" sub-groups.

Finally, the need for an *administrative role* must be considered because all the applications need to be administered. Administrators have very different functions and requirements with respect to "regular" users. For example, they may create and register new application users, or update restricted-access content. Therefore, application administrators normally deserve the introduction of a separate user group.

7.2.2 Functional Requirements

Functional requirements address the essential functions that the application should deliver to its users. The objective of functional requirements collection is *to identify the processes* that are supported by the application. A process is a cohesive set of activities, which must be performed by the users interacting with the Web application. For example, a typical process found in most data-intensive Web applications is content management, which consists of the editing and verification of the content to be published within the application.

A practical way of gathering functional requirements is to identify and examine a number of representative usage scenarios (or *use cases*, in the UML terminology). A use case is a "unit of interaction" between the application and one or more users that describes the execution of a well-defined business process, finalized to the accomplishment of a specific goal. The identification of groups is preliminary to the study of functional requirements, because it is more natural to examine the application usage scenarios by considering the requirements of each group separately.

For each process identified in the business requirements, a use case can be defined. If the process is complex, it is convenient to break it into sub-processes, and define a use case for each sub-process. Each identified use case may have variants or special cases, which can be described by further use cases. For instance, in a multi-device application the same user's activity may be supported in different ways, each one specialized to the characteristics of a specific access device.

7.2.3 Data Requirements

Data requirements describe the information assets that the application should manage to accomplish its goals. The objective of data requirement collection is to *identify the data* managed by the application. The starting point of data requirement collection is the investigation of the "where, when, and by whom" content is produced and consumed. The entities to investigate are the organizations that supply data to the application, and the organizations or non-business users that use the data. The business processes behind the application represent another fundamental source of knowledge, because their investigation permits the analyst to discover the data items exchanged by the business actors, and produced or consumed by their activities. At the level of requirements collection, the analyst should focus on the definition of the main data elements, which will become the core concepts of the data schema elaborated during data design.

7.2.4 Personalization Requirements

Personalization requirements refer to the need of delivering content and services in different modalities to different individuals, based on their preferences and access rights.

The personalization of a Web application involves three aspects:

- The collection and storage of data about the users.

- The analysis of the user data to infer those features that can drive the delivery of personalized content or services.

- The actual construction of a hypertext embodying content and services personalized with respect to the user's features.

User data collection addresses the definition, population, and maintenance of data about users, called *user profile data*. User profile data can be collected *explicitly* or *implicitly*. In the former case, users provide information about themselves, for instance by registering into the Web application and filling in their personal profile. In the latter case, no data is requested to the user, but the profile needed for personalization is inferred from some data source, for instance, from data about the user behavior during the interaction with the application. This inference can be done online, by proactively monitoring the clicking behavior of users, or offline, by processing log data about past user interaction.

Data analysis entails the elaboration of the raw data about the users, to infer further properties of their profile, which can be exploited for personalization purposes. A typical example of data analysis is the clustering of individual users into homogeneous groups, which can be the target of special content or services. Data analysis typically applies to external users, who may have unknown goals and behavior, whereas internal users are usually clustered into groups a priori by the designers, based on their application usage requirements, which can be precisely estimated before the application deployment.

The construction of a personalized application exploits the available knowledge about the users to customize content, navigation, and presentation. The goal of such a customization can be the delivery of a more attractive experience to the user, or the enforcement of access rights over the data objects, whereby each user is enabled to access only the portion of data and hypertext pages he/she is entitled to.

Personalization requirements may range from the simplest case of a Web application serving the same content in the same way to all users, in which case no user profile data or content customization policies are needed, to the case of an application designed for different categories of internal and external users, with sophisticated policies for delivering customized content and services to each user, based on personal profile data and on the user's group. In this case, requirements collection must identify the relevant user groups, the content of their profile data, and the parts of the hypertext that must be customized based on the user's profile.

7.2.5   Device-Specific Customization Requirements

A special case of customization occurs in the case of multi-device or mobile applications, where the interaction context of the user may influence the application usage requirements. In this scenario, it is important to identify the devices that can be used to access the application, cluster them into families with homogeneous rendition capabilities, and establish the presentation constraints that the application interfaces should respect for each device class. The investigation of access device requirements can be further refined, by identifying, for a given class of devices, the families of user agents that can be used to access the application. For example, considering PC-based access, it is possible to cluster the versions of Web browsers installed on the user's PCs based on their support of the various Web standards (HTML, client-side scripting languages, cascading style sheets, XML and XSL, and so on). Such a clustering can be used to express the presentation constraints of the application more precisely.

Other environmental factors may be relevant to the delivery of content and services to the user, like the network connection speed, the geographical position of the user, the time of the day in which access occurs, and so on. Appropriate content delivery policies could be established for each influential factor.

7.2.6   Nonfunctional Requirements

Nonfunctional requirements include "all the other requirements" that are relevant for accomplishing the business goals, but not specifically related to one of the system functions. Nonfunctional requirements span a variety of aspects, and affect both technical and communication issues. The most relevant nonfunctional requirements for the Web application scenario are the following:

- ■ *Usability:* addresses the ease of use of the application, which is determined by multiple factors, such as the ease of learning the user interfaces, the adherence of the interaction objects (menus, links, buttons) to well-known standards, the coherent use of the interaction objects across all the application interfaces, the availability of mechanisms for orienting and assisting the user, and the completeness and quality of documentation.

- ■ *Performance:* refers to the efficiency with which the application exploits the available resources. In the Web context, the most critical resource is time, and performance is measured in terms of throughput (the number of requests that can be served per unit of time) and response time (the time employed to serve a request). Performance must be evaluated both in average and peak conditions. Average refers to the normal operational conditions in which the application is used, whereas peaks are special situations in which high volumes of requests concentrate in a short interval.

- *Availability:* refers to the tolerated frequency of errors and failures, which affects the percentage of time in which the application is available to users. The achievement of a high level of availability requires the introduction of redundant resources in the application architecture, and the implementation of failure detection and management procedures capable of masking the occurrence of faults. In the ideal scenario, the application architecture should be designed in such a way that no single point of failure exists, to ensure total availability. However, budget and resource constraints may prevent from attaining the ideal architecture design, and in this case availability requirements for the different application functions should be carefully gathered and examined to reach a reasonable tradeoff between the costs of redundancy and the risks of failures.

- *Scalability:* is the ability of increasing the performance of the application in response to the increase of the volume of requests. Scalability is achieved by cloning elements of the architecture so that more resources (servers, network connections, and network appliances) can accommodate more traffic. The key factors for achieving scalability are an adequate architecture topology, grouping resources with homogeneous capabilities into clusters, and the presence of load-balancing procedures for flexibly sharing the workload among the clusters. Multi-tier architectures are inherently conceived for scalability, because the different tiers can be effectively organized as clusters, managed by flexible load balancing systems. However, clustered architectures are more complex to manage than simple, non-clustered ones. The requirements for scalability should be carefully pinned down in terms of workload growth rates, to let the architecture designer establish the correct tradeoff between complexity and scalability.

- *Security:* is a multifaceted requirement that spans several topics, including the protection of integrity, confidentiality, and privacy of information, the availability of services, the authentication of the users, and the protection of the information flowing between the users and the application. In the case of Web applications offered to the general public over the Internet, content protection is a major concern and is attained by dividing the application architecture into separate domains with different levels of security: the public network accessible by the external users, the secure network where corporate content is stored, and a middle domain, often called *demilitarized zone* (DMZ), separating the secure and the public networks. User authentication and information flow protection are especially relevant in the domain of electronic commerce applications, which require a trust infrastructure for the user to perform e-commerce transactions in a secure way. *Private Key Infrastructure* (PKI) cryptography and *digital signature* must be considered, when secure transactions are part of the application requirements.

■ *Maintainability:* refers to the ease of repairing application errors, and adapting the Web application to changed or new requirements. Although maintainability is a factor mainly associated with the quality of the final application, it also relates to the development process, which must be organized and conducted so as to accommodate errors repairing and application evolution. The achievement of maintainability is facilitated by simplicity of the design, software modularity, and completeness and clarity of the documentation. A model-based design of the application can greatly enhance maintainability, because it helps specify, communicate, and document the application, which in turn helps change management. Maintainability can be also improved by adopting modular software architectures, which permit developers to intervene on the different components of the application separately.

Performance, availability, scalability, and security concerns are technical subjects. They will be revisited in Chapter 10, which examines architecture design, showing how different architecture topologies meet the abovementioned nonfunctional requirements. Maintainability will be discussed in Chapter 13, which presents software architectures able to improve the separation of concerns and modularity of Web applications.

7.3 Requirements Analysis

Requirements analysis formalizes the collected knowledge about what the application should do into semi-formal documents, which serve as the input to application design. The following pieces of information should be clarified before starting the design phase:

■ The relevant user groups and their hierarchical relationships.

■ The main use cases resulting from the functional requirement collection and the groups involved in them.

■ The data dictionary, including the data objects and their semantic associations.

■ The required site views and the assignment of site views to the user groups entitled to use them.

■ The essential usability and presentation guidelines.

▓ The specification of acceptance tests for the evaluation of nonfunctional requirements, for instance, performance acceptance tests.

Personalization requirements are transversal, as they span all the aspects of requirements analysis:

▓ Profile data and access rights are defined in the specification of user groups.

▓ Customization policies related to content and navigation are expressed in the use cases and site view specifications.

▓ Customization policies related to presentation are expressed in the presentation guidelines.

7.3.1 Group Specification

In many cases, a Web application is directed to different user categories, which can be identified a priori during design, and formalized into a set of user groups. Groups may be organized hierarchically, to denote that a certain set of users with homogeneous requirements specializes into sub-groups, which add further properties to the super-group. The hierarchy of subgroups can be expressed in a diagrammatic form, using the notation of Figure 7.2.

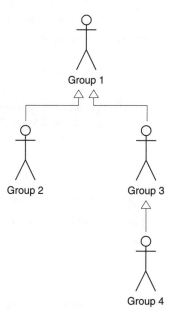

Figure 7.2 Example of group hierarchy diagram.

For each identified user group, a specification sheet is filled-in, which consists of the following elements:

- *Name:* the group name.

- *Description:* a concise description of the clustering criteria that define the members of the group.

- *Profile data:* a set of attributes characterizing the members of the group, and the indication of the way in which profile data are created (by explicitly asking the user, or by implicitly calculating them).

- *Super-group:* the group that generalizes the features common to various sub-groups (optional).

- *Sub-groups:* the list of sub-groups expressing special properties of selected members of the group (optional).

- *Relevant use cases:* the list of the uses cases in which users of the group take part.

- *Access rights:* the essential data accessed or managed by the users of a group. It is divided into two sub-fields: *objects accessed in read-only mode,* and *objects accessed in content management mode.*

Figure 7.3 shows an example of specification sheet for a user group clustering the marketing and communication personnel of a company.

7.3.2   Use Case Specification

A use case expresses a unit of interaction with the application by users of a given group. Each use case is described with a specification sheet, which includes the following elements:

- *Name:* the name of the use case.

- *Purpose:* a brief description of the function represented by the use case.

- *Pre-condition:* the condition that must be satisfied before performing the use case.

- *Post-condition:* the condition that becomes true after performing the use case.

- *Workflow:* the steps to be performed for successfully executing the use case.

Group name	**Mar-Com manager**
Description	Marketing and communication personnel in charge of inserting, modifying, and deleting product-marketing materials.
Profile data	First name, last name, email, office address. Profile data are provided explicitly by the user.
Super-group	Corporate.
Sub-groups	None.
Relevant use cases	"Login," "Add a news item," "Modify a news item," "Remove a news item," "Add a news category," "Modify a news category," "Remove a news category," "Modify profile data."
Objects accessed in read mode	Product and product news.
Objects accessed in content management mode	Product news.

Figure 7.3 Example of group specification sheet.

Figure 7.4 shows an example of use case specification sheet, for a use case entitled "Login of user belonging to multiple groups."

If a use case is complex, UML *activity diagrams* can be used to visually express its workflow. These diagrams define a process as a sequence of steps, and for each step identify the involved actor, which can be a human or a software system. If necessary, the objects produced by a step can be represented.

In the UML notation, actors are mapped to areas of the activity diagram (the so-called *swim lanes*), steps are enclosed within circular shapes, precedence relations among steps are represented as arrows connecting the steps, and products are enclosed within rectangles. Figure 7.5 shows a UML activity diagram, which represents the activity flow of the use case "Login of user belonging to multiple groups."

The interaction between user groups and use cases can be described by means of UML *use case diagrams*. In these diagrams, users are represented with a graphic symbol and connected to the relevant use cases denoted by circles. Figure 7.6 shows a UML use case diagram expressing the processes in which the members of the Mar-Com Manager group are involved.

Title	**Login of user belonging to multiple groups**
Purpose	To express how users with more than one role access the functions of the applications.
Pre-condition	A user that belongs to multiple groups is registered. For each group, the site view serving the requirements of the group members is defined.
Post-condition	The user successfully logs into the application and accesses the site view corresponding to one of his/her groups.
Workflow	The following steps must be performed:

1. The user receives an input form asking for username and password.

2. The user inputs his credentials.

3. If the credentials are correct, the user is authenticated, the list of groups the user belongs to is determined, and the list of names and URLs of the home pages of the site views of such groups is displayed.

4. The user chooses one entry from the list, and enters into the selected site view.

Figure 7.4 Example of use case specification sheet.

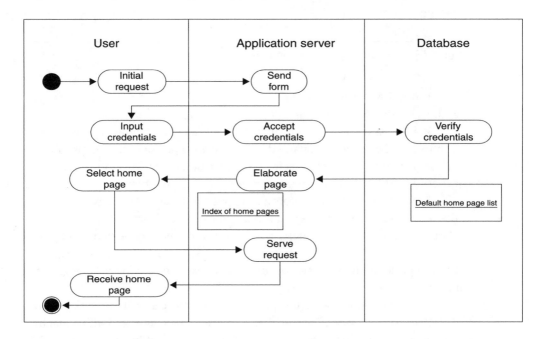

Figure 7.5 UML activity diagram corresponding to the "Login of user belonging to multiple groups" use case.

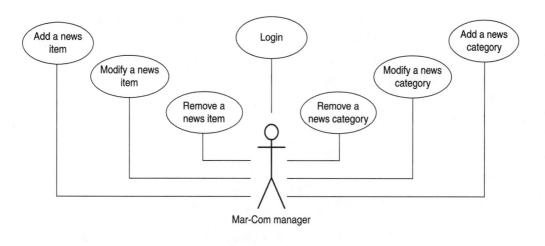

Figure 7.6 UML use case diagram of a user group.

7.3.3 Data Dictionary Specification

Data dictionary specification produces the list of the main information objects identified during data requirements collection. Each entry of the data dictionary can be qualified by means of the following properties:

- *Name:* the main descriptive name with which the concept is identified.

- *Synonyms:* alternative names used in the application domain to denote the same concept.

- *Description:* a short description of the meaning of the object in the application domain.

- *Sample instances:* some representative instances that may help understanding the concept.

- *Properties:* a list of essential attributes of the object, with the name and a short description.

- *Relationships:* a list of the most significant relationships with other objects.

- *Components:* a list of the most significant internal components of the object. Components correspond to complex and possibly multi-valued properties, described by means of further information objects.

■ *Super-concept:* the concept that generalizes the features of the information objects (optional).

■ *Sub-concepts:* the list of concepts that specialize the information object (optional).

Figure 7.7 shows an example of data dictionary entry, which specifies the News Item concept.

Name	**News Item**
Synonyms	None.
Description	A piece of news about a product or corporate activity.
Sample instances	**Acer Launches TravelMate 610**
	20th June, 2001
	Acer UK announces the launch of the TravelMate 610, its newest series of thin and light, high performance mobile PCs. Offering superb portability, the TravelMate 610 boasts a large display, the latest connectivity and storage options . . .
Properties	
Title	The headline of the news item.
Body	The text of the news item.
Image	An image illustrating the news item (optional).
Date	The date of the news item.
. . .	
Relationships	
NewsToProduct	Optionally relates a news item to the product or products it is related to.
. . .	
Components	None.
Super-Concepts	None.
Sub-Concepts	Highlighted news.

Figure 7.7   Example of data dictionary specification.

7.3.4   Site View Specification

Site view specification pins down the list of site views needed for accomplishing the requirements of the identified groups. The input to site view specification is the list of user groups, the list of use cases, and the data dictionary: a site view serves the use cases associated to one or more user groups, and offers access or content management functions over selected data elements.

For each site view, a specification sheet is filled, which includes the following items:

- *Name:* the name of the site view.
- *Description:* a short explanation of the purpose of the site view.
- *User groups:* the list of user groups entitled to access the site view.
- *Use cases:* the list of use cases covered by the site view.
- *Site view map:* a table illustrating the different areas that compose the site view. It includes the following items:
  - *Area name:* the name of the area.
  - *Area description:* a short description about the contents and services provided by the area.
  - *Accessed/managed objects:* the list of the information objects specified in the data dictionary that will be accessed or managed through the area.
  - *Priority level:* a numeric or symbolic value, which reflects the area importance. The designer will use this priority to establish the order in which areas must be considered in the design and implementation iterations. In principle, an area should be given high priority if it addresses "important" requirements, it can be designed and implemented independently of other areas, and its availability affects the design, implementation, or testing of other areas or site views.

Figure 7.8 shows an example of specification sheet for a site view through which the users of the Mar-Com manager group can administer the news.

7.3.5   Style Guidelines Specification

Style guidelines establish rules for the presentation of pages, to be used in the production of the application interfaces. Style guideline specification covers the following issues:

- *Specification of standard page grids:* a page grid is a table containing a specific arrangement of rows, columns, and cells, which represents the

Site view name	**News content management**
Description	Includes the pages through which the Mar-Com managers will access content management functions, for inserting or updating content about news categories and news items.
User groups	Mar-Com managers
Use cases	"Login," "Add a news category," "Edit a news category," "Remove a news category," "Add a news item," "Edit a news item," "Remove a news item."

Site view map

Area name	Area description	Managed/Accessed objects	Priority
News content management	In the area default page, the user accesses the list of countries for which he/she is content manager and selects a country to administer.	NewsCategory NewsItem	High
	In the NewsCategory page, the user accesses the list of news categories for the selected country. Here, the user can perform content management functions over news categories, according to the use cases "Add a news category," "Edit a news category," "Remove a news category." Otherwise, he/she can select one category, and access the list of the available news items in the selected category.		
	In the News page, the user can perform content management functions over a selected news item according to the use cases "Add a news item," "Edit a news item," "Remove a news item."		

Figure 7.8   Site view specification sheet

layout in which static and dynamic content can be organized. The specification of a page grid dictates the number of rows and columns, and the absolute or relative size of the various grid elements. Several alternative page grids can be specified, for presenting pages with different contents. Figure 7.9 shows an example of page grid specification.

▪ *Content positioning specification:* addresses the rules for assigning standard content elements, like banners, menus and sub-menus, and login and search fields, to selected positions in the page grid. Well thought out positioning guidelines help reduce the cognitive overhead of the user during the application learning phase, because they force elements with similar semantics to be placed in the same position across different pages, with the effect of reducing user's disorientation. Figure 7.10 shows an example of content positioning specification.

▪ *Graphical guidelines:* refer to formatting rules for graphic items, like fonts, colors, borders, and margins. The rules apply to such recurrent page elements as normal text, headings, headers and footers, anchors, tables, lists, menus, and so on. Formatting rules can be expressed by means of *Cascading Style Sheet* (CSS) rules or an equivalent specification. Graphical guidelines may also include sample graphic resources, such as bullets,

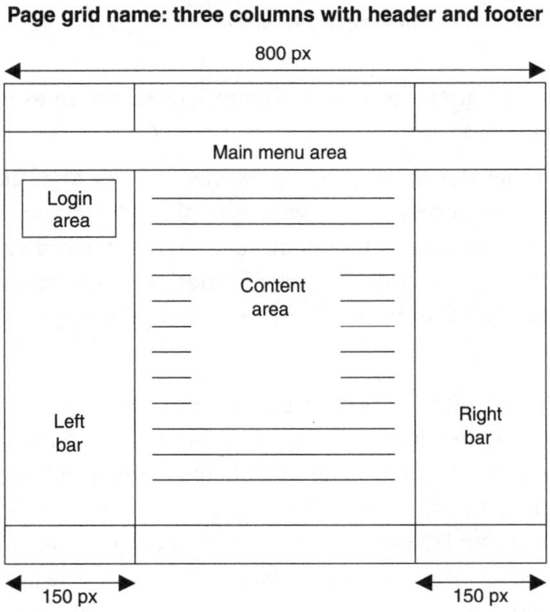

Page grid name: three columns with header and footer

Figure 7.9 Example of page grid.

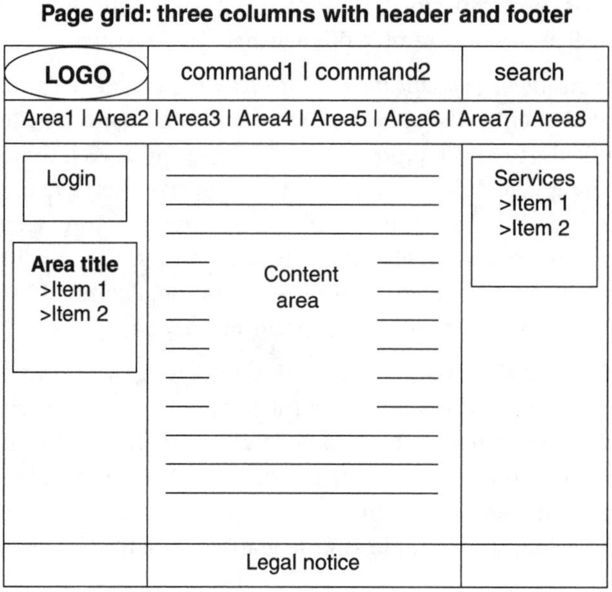

Page grid: three columns with header and footer

LOGO	command1 I command2	search
Area1 I Area2 I Area3 I Area4 I Area5 I Area6 I Area7 I Area8		

Login

Area title
>Item 1
>Item 2

Content
area

Services
>Item 1
>Item 2

Legal notice

Figure 7.10   Example of content positioning specification.

button icons, delimiters, and so on. Figure 7.11 shows an example of graphical guidelines.

■ *Device-specific and user agent-specific guidelines:* specific style guidelines may be needed for access devices with special rendition requirements, for example, limited size or monochromatic screens. Extra guidelines may be needed also for addressing the limitations of older versions of the user agents, for example, browsers not supporting HTML 4 and CSS.

Style guidelines are often embodied into *page mock-ups*. Mock-ups are sample representations for a specific device and rendition language of a few typical application pages, for example the home page and the most important pages reachable from it. Mock-ups are particularly effective, because they supply self-evident indications about how static and dynamic content should be organized. Moreover, they have the benefit of being immediately understandable also by the non-graphic experts, thus permitting early usability testing on a sample of real users. An example of mock-up of the Acer-Euro application is shown in Figure 7.17.

CSS rules for site view X	Graphical resources for site view X

`.main-menu {`
`FONT-WEIGHT: bold; FONT-SIZE: 12px;`
`COLOR: #ffffff; FONT-FAMILY: Arial;`
`}`
 	
`A.main-menu {`
`FONT-WEIGHT: bold; FONT-SIZE: 12px;`
`COLOR: #ffffff; FONT-FAMILY: Arial;`
`}`
 	
`A.main-menu:visited {`
`FONT-WEIGHT: bold; FONT-SIZE: 12px;`
`COLOR: #ffffff; FONT-FAMILY: Arial;`
`}`
	■ `Normal bullet`
	
	▢ `Selected item bullet`
	
	◤ `Box corner (upper left)`
	
	── `Ruler (light)`
	
	━━ `Ruler (strong)`

Figure 7.11 Example of graphical guidelines.

7.3.6 Acceptance Tests Specification

Nonfunctional requirements about performance, availability, scalability, security, and maintainability can be formalized into a plan of acceptance tests, which are conducted on the implemented application to assess if the required level of service is met.

Acceptance tests typically focus on performance, for which the acceptable response times in different workload conditions are defined, and on availability, for which the response to different kinds of failures is established. The definition of acceptance tests is a technical matter, related to the design of the application architecture. We devote Chapter 10 to this important subject, and in particular we discuss the parameters for measuring performance and the techniques for testing and improving it.

7.4 The Acer-Euro Running Case

This section presents the requirements collection and analysis of the Acer-Euro Web application, a simplified version of a real application, developed in early 2000 by the European branch of Acer Corporation. For reasons of simplicity and confidentiality, some aspects of the application have been omitted or altered, but the nature of the Acer-Euro application described in the book is still faithful to the "real" application.

7.4.1   Business Requirements

Acer Corporation is a well-known multinational company in the business of computers and peripherals manufacturing. The goal of the Acer-Euro application is to serve the needs of the customers and internal personnel of the Acer European branch by organizing, collecting, managing, and publishing on the Web content about the Acer products. The application development is planned inside a wider corporate project, aimed at reorganizing the structure of the European branch, which consists of 21 national subsidiaries and one headquarter site. The essential mission of the Acer-Euro project is to replace a set of locally managed, independent national Web sites with a centrally managed Web application, which is used to gather content from the headquarters and from the national subsidiaries, and for delivering such content to Acer customers throughout Europe.

The Acer-Euro application will serve three categories of users:

- Customers will be provided with richer and up-to-date information about the company's products and services. The published information will have the same organization and look and feel throughout Europe, but content will be a mix of centrally administered data, for example product specifications and list prices, and locally produced data, for example country-specific news and events.

- Product managers will use a Web-based environment for verifying and updating data about the products they manage. The data management functions will be customized to take into account the personal profile of each manager, for example the European countries and product lines for which each manager is entitled to update product data.

- Marketing and communication managers will use the Acer-Euro application to administer marketing materials, like news and event lists. Also the marketing and communication personnel will be offered customized functions based on their profile data.

The centralized, Web-based architecture of Acer-Euro will also facilitate application management, because all administration functions will be incorporated into a dedicated Web site, accessible only to supervisors.

7.4.2   User Groups

Figure 7.12 shows the Acer-Euro user groups, organized into a specialization hierarchy. A first distinction is made between *external users* and *internal users*. The former represent customers, who will access the front-end Web site with the aim

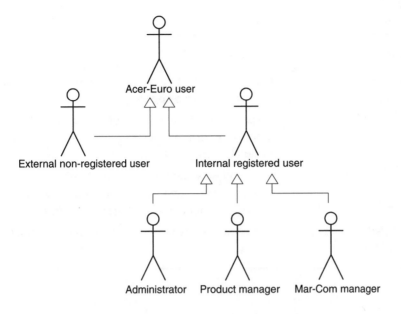

Figure 7.12 Specialization hierarchy of the Acer-Euro user groups.

of gaining a better understanding of the company's profile and of the available products. The latter are selected employees of the company, who are in charge of inserting and updating the content published for the customers.

In the present version of the application, external users are not identified, do not need authentication, and no personalized content is addressed to them. Conversely, internal users are identified and registered by the administrator, who creates the first version of their profile data, and are partitioned into sub-groups based on the content they manage:

■ *Administrators* are in charge of managing user profiles and user groups, and of maintaining information about the European countries served by the Acer-Euro application.

■ *Product managers* are in charge of managing data about products, like descriptions, prices, technical specifications, awards, and so on.

■ *Marketing and Communication (Mar-Com) managers* are in charge of managing marketing materials such as press releases, corporate news, events, product announcements, and so on.

The roles and the access rights for each group in Figure 7.12 are summarized in the group description sheets reported in Tables 7.1 through 7.4.

Table 7.1 Group sheet of External users.

Group name	External user
Description	Generic visitors interested in accessing content published in the Acer-Euro Web application.
Profile data	No profile required—they do not need credentials for authentication and no personalization is addressed to external users.
Objects accessed in read mode	News and News Categories. Product categories (Product Groups and Product Brands), and product technical features (tech specs, configurations, logos, benefits, awards).
Objects accessed in content management mode	None. Content management operations are not allowed.

Table 7.2 Group sheet of Administrators.

Group name	Administrator
Description	Technical personnel in charge of managing application users and user groups, setting up new countries, when new European Web sites must be deployed, and managing data about the existing countries.
Profile data	First Name, Last Name, Email, Login, Password.
Objects accessed in read mode	News and News Categories, Product categories (Product Groups and Product Brands), and product technical features (tech specs, configurations, logos, benefits, awards), which are accessible from the public Acer-Euro Web site.
Objects accessed in content management mode	User, User Group, Country.

Table 7.3 Group sheet of Product managers.

Group name	Product manager
Description	Business personnel in charge of managing the creation and update of product technical descriptions.
Profile data	First Name, Last Name, Managed country, E-mail, Login, Password.
Objects accessed in read mode	News and News Categories, Product categories (Product Groups and Product Brands), and product technical features (tech specs, configurations, logos, benefits, awards), which are accessible from the public Acer-Euro Web site.
Objects accessed in content management mode	Products and their categories (Product Groups and Product Brands), product tech specs, product configurations, awards, and logos. News about products.

Table 7.4 Group sheet of Mar-Com managers.

Group name	Mar-Com manager
Description	Business personnel in charge of managing the creation and maintenance of marketing materials.
Profile data	First Name, Last Name, Managed country, E-mail, Login, Password.
Objects accessed in read mode	News and News Categories, Product categories (Product Groups and Product Brands), and product technical features (tech specs, configurations, logos, benefits, awards), which are accessible from the public Acer-Euro Web site.
Objects accessed in content management mode	News Items and News Categories.

7.4.3   Functional Requirements

For each user group, functional requirements are visually represented by means of use case diagrams. For brevity, only the use cases identified for external non-registered users and for Mar-Com managers are detailed through specification sheets. Activity diagrams describing the use case workflow are reported only for a few relevant Mar-Com managers use cases.

External non-registered users functional requirements. External non-registered users access the application in a read-only mode, and look for company information, product technical descriptions, company announcements, news, and press releases. The use case diagram reported in Figure 7.13 shows the use cases associated with external users. A few use case specification sheets are reported in Tables 7.5 through 7.8.

Mar-Com managers functional requirements. As illustrated by the use case diagram of Figure 7.14, Mar-Com managers are in charge of inserting, updating, and deleting content about news items and news categories. Since these operations are restricted, Mar-Com managers must first log into the application by providing their credentials.

The specification of the login use case has already been shown in Figure 7.4 and Figure 7.5, and is not repeated here. The specification sheets of the remaining Mar-Com manager use cases are reported in Tables 7.9 through 7.12; these include the use cases "Add a news category," "Edit a news category," "Remove a news category," and "Add a news item." The "Edit a news item" and "Remove a news item" use cases are similar to the "Edit a news category" and "Remove a news category" scenarios, and are omitted for brevity.

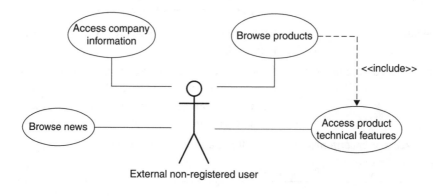

Figure 7.13   Use case diagram for external non-registered users.

Table 7.5 "Browse products" specification sheet.

Title	**Browse products**
Purpose	To express how external users browse product groups and product brands, in order to access a specific product.
Pre-condition	None.
Post-condition	The user can browse all the online resources related to a selected product.
Workflow	1. The user enters the product section of a national Web site.
	2. The user receives the list of product groups available in that country and selects a group.
	3. The user receives the list of product brands for the selected product group, and selects one brand.
	4. The user receives the list of products for the selected brand and selects a product.
	5. The user accesses an overview of the most important product features.

Table 7.6 "Browse news" specification sheet.

Title	**Browse news**
Purpose	To express how external users browse news categories and highlighted news for accessing a specific news item.
Pre-condition	None.
Post-condition	The user can access the online resources related to a selected piece of news.
Workflow	1. The user enters the news section of a national Web site.
	2. The user receives the list of news categories and may select one; he/she also receives the list of highlighted news and may select one, jumping to point 4.
	3. The user receives the list of news items for the selected category, and selects one.
	4. The user accesses the details of the selected news item.

Table 7.7   "Access product technical features" specification sheet.

Title	**Access product technical features**
Purpose	To express how external users, once they access a product (through the "Browse products" use case), may access additional technical specifications, available configurations, awards, and benefits.
Pre-condition	The user has accessed the main page of a product.
Post-condition	None.
Workflow	1. The user enters a subsection about one technical feature.
	2. The user receives the relevant information about the selected technical feature.
	3. The user can go back to the product page and select another technical feature.

Table 7.8   "Access company info" specification sheet.

Title	**Access company info**
Purpose	To express how external users can have access to information about the company.
Pre-condition	None.
Post-condition	None.
Workflow	1. The user selects an appropriate link from the home page of a national site.
	2. A short company overview is displayed.
	3. Links to other related information, for example to job opportunities, are provided.

Product managers functional requirements. As shown in the use case diagram of Figure 7.15, *product managers* insert or revise content about product groups, product brands, and products. All these functions are password-protected, and can be performed only after a successful login into the Product manager site view.

Administrators functional requirements. Administrators manage user accounts by creating or revising user profiles, and associate each user to one or more

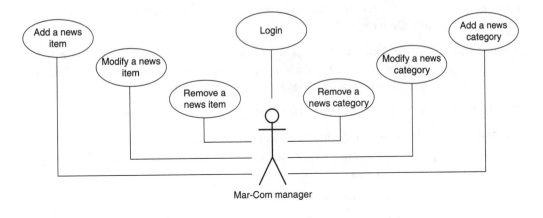

Figure 7.14   Use case diagram for Mar-Com managers.

Table 7.9   "Add a news category" specification sheet.

Title	**Add a news category**
Purpose	To express how Mar-Com managers add news categories for a given country.
Pre-condition	The Mar-Com Manager logs into the application and accesses the site view corresponding to the Mar-Com manager group. He/she selects a country from a personalized list of those ones for which he/she is responsible.
Post-condition	The created News Category is available, and News Items can be added to it.
Workflow	1. The user receives the list of existing news categories and an input form for inserting data for a novel category.
	2. The user inputs data.
	3. All the necessary validity checks on the submitted data are performed.
	4. If submitted data are incorrect, the user is given an error message, and sent back to the input form, where data can be corrected and re-submitted.
	5. If submitted data are correct, a novel news category is created.
	6. If the creation operation succeeds, the user is presented the updated list of categories available for the current country, including the newly created one.

Table 7.10 "Edit a news category" specification sheet.

Title	**Edit a news category**
Purpose	To express how Mar-Com managers modify content about news categories for a given country.
Pre-condition	The Mar-Com manager logs into the application and accesses the site view associated with the Mar-Com manager group. He/she selects a country from a personalized list of countries for which he/she is responsible.
Post-condition	The content of a selected News Category has been modified.
Workflow	1. The user receives the list of existing news categories and selects one.
	2. The data of the selected news category and a form for inserting new data are presented.
	3. The user inserts the new data.
	4. All the necessary validity checks on the submitted data are performed.
	5. If submitted data is incorrect, the user is given an error message, and sent back to the input form, where data can be corrected and submitted again.
	6. If submitted data is correct, the category instance is modified.
	7. If the operation succeeds, the data of the updated news category is displayed, together with a form for further modifying it.

Table 7.11 "Remove a news category" specification sheet.

Title	**Remove a news category**
Purpose	To express how Mar-Com managers delete existing news categories for a given country.
Pre-condition	The Mar-Com manager logs into the application and accesses the site view corresponding to the Mar-Com manager group. He/she selects a country from a personalized list of countries for which he/she is responsible.
Post-condition	A selected News Category has been eliminated.
Workflow	1. The user receives the list of existing news categories.
	2. The user selects one news category for deletion.
	3. The news category instance is removed.
	4. If the operation fails, an error page is displayed.
	5. If the operation succeeds, the list of news categories is re-displayed.
	6. If the user wants to delete other news categories, he/she goes back to point 2.

Table 7.12 "Add a news item" specification sheet

Title	**Add a news item**
Purpose	To express how Mar-Com managers can add news items for a given country in a given news category.
Pre-condition	The Mar-Com manager logs into the application and accesses the site view corresponding to the Mar-Com manager group. He/she selects a country from a personalized list of countries for which he/she is responsible. The user also selects the news category in which the news item must be included.
Post-condition	The created news item is now visible to end-users on the Web site under its category.
Workflow	1. The user receives the list of existing news items in the selected category, and an input form for entering the data of a news item.
	2. The user inputs the news item data.
	3. All the necessary validity checks on the submitted data are performed (for example, date format checks).
	4. If submitted data are incorrect, the user is given an error message and sent back to the initial page, where data can be corrected and submitted again.
	5. If submitted data are correct, the news item is created and associated to the previously selected news category.
	6. If any of the creation and connection operations fails, the user receives an error page and is taken back to step one.
	7. If the creation and connection operations succeed, the updated list of news items in the selected category is redisplayed, including the news item just created.

groups. They are also responsible for the content related to each country. The Administrator use case diagram is represented in Figure 7.16.

7.4.4 Data Dictionary

As clearly visible from the use case diagrams of the previous section, two main information objects are managed in the Acer-Euro application: *Product* and *News*. Products include several components representing complex and possibly multivalued properties, like technical specifications, configurations, awards, and logos.

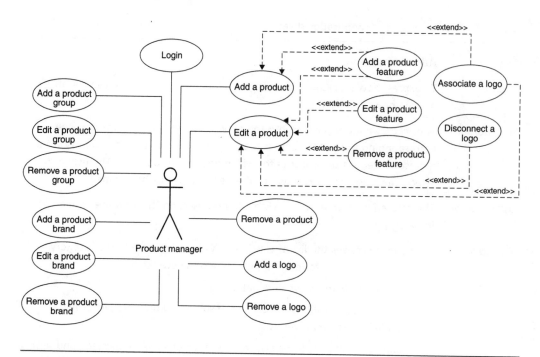

Figure 7.15 Use case diagram for Product managers.

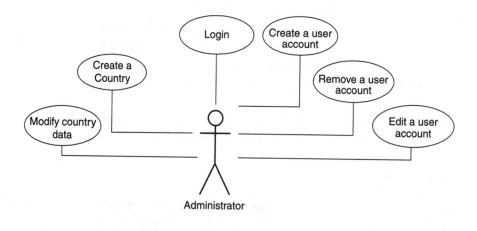

Figure 7.16 Use case diagram for Administrators.

Other objects are required for grouping news and products into categories, helping the user to access the desired content. Product instances are organized according to a two-level hierarchy, including *Product Groups* and *Product Brands*. News items are categorized by an ad hoc concept: *News Category*.

Country is another object to be managed: it stores information about the different European countries served by the Acer-Euro application, like the country name in the original language, a list of search engine keywords in the native language, and the URL of the national Web site of the country.

Personalization requirements also prompt for the introduction of two further objects, *User* and *Group*, which represent the user profile data and the identified groups. These objects host the data for access rights verification required for authorizing internal users to access their content management functions, as well as profile data of Acer's employees.

The properties of the identified objects are detailed in the data dictionary reported in Table 7.13.

Table 7.13 Acer-Euro data dictionary.

Name	**Product**
Synonyms	ProductFamily
Description	The commercial definition of a product line.
Sample instances	**TravelMate α-550**
	The TravelMate α-550 has been designed for employees in small and medium businesses, as well as for those self-employed professionals who need a fully fledged workplace wherever they stay, and who also want to use it occasionally for leisure and entertainment.
Properties	
Name	The product name.
Description	Short text describing the product.
Image	Product picture.
PDFBrochure	Downloadable PDF brochure of product.
PDFCertificate	A document about the certification of product quality properties.

(continued)

Table 7.13 *(continued)*

Components

  TechSpec Items

The set of technical specifications.

Properties: Name (the tech spec name), Description (a short textual description).

  ProductConfiguration (synonym: SKUs)

The set of available product configurations (e.g., "128 MB RAM, HD 9 GB, . . ."; "256 MB RAM, HD 20 GB, . . .").

Properties: Name (the configuration name), Description (a short textual description).

  Award

The set of awards won by the product.

Properties: Name (the award name), Logo (an image depicting the award logo).

  Logo

The set of commercial logos used site-wide and Europe-wide, highlighting the brand of some hardware components (e.g., "Intel Inside" logo), or the adherence to standards (e.g., "CE" logo).

Properties: Name (the logo name), Image (the logo shown in the product page).

Relationships

  ProductToProductBrand

Relates a product instance with its brand.

  ProductToNews

Optionally relates the product to the news items mentioning the product.

  AwardToNews

Optionally relates a product award to the news items mentioning the award.

Name	**ProductGroup**
Synonyms	None.
Description	Main product categorization (e.g., Notebooks, Desktops, and so on).
Sample instances	Notebook, Personal Computer, Server, etc.

Properties

  Name

The product group name.

Relationships

  ProductGroupToCountry

Relates a ProductGroup with all the countries whose Web site publishes the ProductGroup content within the product catalogue.

  ProductGroupToProductBrand

Relates a product group with all the available product brands for that group.

Table 7.13   *(continued)*

Name	**ProductBrand**
Synonyms	None.
Description	Sub-categorization of products by commercial brand.
Sample instances	Travelmate for the Notebook group; Acer Veriton, Acer Power, and PC Aspyre for the Personal Computer group, etc.
Properties	
Name	The product brand name.
Relationships	
ProductBrandToProductGroup	Relates a ProductBrand to the ProductGroup it belongs to.
ProductBrandToProduct	Relates a product brand to all the available products for that brand.

Name	**NewsItem**
Synonyms	None.
Description	A piece of news about a product or a corporate activity.
Sample instances	**Acer Launches TravelMate 610** *20th June, 2001* Acer UK announces the launch of the TravelMate 610, its newest series of thin and light, high performance mobile PCs. Offering superb portability, the TravelMate 610 boasts a large display, the latest connectivity and storage options . . .
Properties	
Title	The headline of the news item.
Body	The text of the news item.
Image	An image illustrating the news item (optional).
Date	The date of the news item.
Relationships	
NewsToNewsCategory	Relates a news item to the category it belongs to.
NewsToProduct	Optionally relates a news item to the product or products it is related to.
NewsToAward	Optionally relates a news item to the awards announced by it.
Sub-Concepts	Highlighted news.

(continued)

Table 7.13   *(continued)*

Name	**NewsCategory**
Synonyms	None.
Description	Identifies the news category.
Sample instances	Press Releases.
Properties	
Name	The category name.
Relationships	
NewsCategoryToCountry	Relates a news category to the countries publishing it in the Web site.
NewsCategoryToNews	Relates a news category to the news available for that category.
Sub-Concepts	Highlighted news category.
Name	**Country**
Synonyms	None.
Description	Identifies the currently selected country.
Sample instances	Germany, Italy, France, UK, etc.
Properties	
Name	Autochthonous name of the country.
EnglishName	Standard English name of the country.
URL	URL of the national Web site for the country.
Relationships	
CountryToProductGroup	Relates a country to the product groups available for that country.
CountryToNewsCategory	Relates a country to the news category available for that country.
CountryToUser	Relates a country to internal users that are allowed to manage content for that country.

Table 7.13 *(continued)*

Name	User
Synonyms	None.
Description	Identifies the user currently logged into the application.
Sample instances	
Properties	
Login	User name, for user authentication.
Password	Authentication password.
Email	E-mail address.
Relationships	
UserToGroup	Relates a user to one or more groups he/she belongs to.
UserToCountry	Relates a user to the country for which he/she is a registered user.
Name	Group
Synonyms	None.
Description	Identifies clusters of users. Each group corresponds to a specific user role.
Sample instances	External Customer, Product Manager, Mar-Com Manager, Administrator.
Properties	
GroupName	Name of the group.
Relationships	
GroupToUser	Relates a group to the users who belong to it.
GroupToSiteView	Records the default site view associated to the group.

7.4.5 Site View Identification

Four main site views compose the Acer-Euro application, each one supporting the use cases associated to one of the identified user groups:

■ *External non-registered users site view,* represents a national Web site and includes the pages through which the external customers of a country gather information about the local subsidiary, its products, and its latest news and events.

- *Product managers site view,* includes the content management pages for entering or updating content about products.

- *Mar-Com managers site view,* contains the content management pages for creating or updating content about news.

- *Administrators site view,* addresses the management of user accounts and the update of some properties of countries.

Tables 7.14 through 7.17 show the specifications of the four identified site views.

7.4.6   Style Guidelines and Page Mock-ups

The visual style adopted for the identified site views follows the guidelines dictated by the company worldwide headquarters, which ensure a uniform look and feel across all the national and central Web sites. Users are expected to access the Acer-Euro Web sites by means of desktop computers. The standard mark-up language is HTML 4.0. All pages are designed for use with a Netscape or Explorer browser, version 4.*x* or higher, for a resolution of 800×600 pixels. Page content should be lightweight, so that loading a page should take no longer than 10 seconds when using a 28.8 modem.

Figure 7.17 shows a *page mock-up* summarizing the guidelines for page organization and content positioning. The basic page contains a two-column grid, in which three main areas and five standard elements can be recognized.

A *title banner* area, displayed in the upper part of the page, shows the page title, the Acer logo, and includes the main menu, which contains the links to the top-level areas of the Web site (Home, Product, News, etc.), and the function menu, including links to landmark pages (Home, Contact us, etc.). Graphical and layout properties of the title banner area are shown in Figure 7.18.

The *sub-menu area,* positioned in the left side of the page, includes categories and subcategories used to classify content, organized in a two-level menu. The bottom part of the area may also include the company legal references. Graphic and layout properties of the sub menu area elements are illustrated in Figure 7.19.

The *content area,* positioned in the center of the page, displays descriptive information about one of the topics selected in the top main menu or in the lateral sub-menu. As shown in Figure 7.20, the area can be organized as a one-column or a two-column grid. Some required layout properties are depicted in Figure 7.21.

Table 7.14 Specification of the External non-registered users site view.

Site view name	**External non-registered users site view**
Description	Represents a national Web site and includes the pages through which the external customers of a country gather information about the local subsidiary, its products, and its latest news and events.
User groups	External non-registered users.
Use cases	"Browse products," "Browse News," "Access product technical features," "Access company information."

Site view map

Area name	Area description	Accessed/Managed objects	Priority
Home	Consists of a single page, corresponding to the Web site Home Page. This page shows titles and abstracts of the latest local news, and links to the local news categories, and links to the local product groups. The user can change country, and the page content changes consequently.	Static Content, Country, Highlighted News, News Categories, Product Groups.	Low
What's New	The News category page includes links to the news items in the category. The news item page displays the detailed piece of news/announcement. When the news item refers to a product, a link to the product page is provided.	News, News Category.	High
Products	The Product groups page shows the list of product groups and the list of product brands for a selected group. Each brand page includes the list of all the products in the brand. Each product page presents the product description, configurations, technical specifications, etc.	Product Group, Product Brand, Product.	High
About Us	The area contains a set of linked documents on the company mission, job opportunities, and so on.	Static content	Low

Table 7.15 Specification of the Product managers site view.

Site view name	**Product managers site view**
Description	Includes the pages through which the Product manager accesses content management functions, for inserting or updating content about product groups, brands, products, and product technical features, like tech specs, configurations, benefits, awards, and logos.
	In order to access this site view, the Product manager needs to log in, according to the Login use case. He/She accesses page including the index of countries for which he/she is responsible. He/she selects one country to work on.
User groups	Product managers.
Use cases	"Login," "Add a product group," "Edit a product group," "Remove a product group," "Add a product brand," "Edit a product brand," "Remove a product brand," "Add a product," "Edit a product," "Remove a product," "Add a product feature," "Edit a product feature," "Remove a product feature," "Add a logo," "Remove a logo," "Associate a logo," "Disconnect a logo."

Site view map

Area name	Area description	Accessed/Managed objects	Priority
Product Content Management	The area default page includes the index of the user roles, according to the Login use case. If the user selects the Product manager role, he/she is taken to the Product group page, for managing content about product groups, according to the use cases "Add a product group," "Edit a product group," "Remove a product group." From this page the user can also select a product brand. In the Product brand page the user can perform content management functions over product brands, according to the use cases "Add a product brand," "Edit a product brand," "Remove a product brand," or he/she can select one brand.	Product Group, Product Brand, Product.	High

Table 7.15   *(continued)*

Area name	Area description	Accessed/Managed objects	Priority
	The Product page includes the index of the available products for the selected brand. In this page, the user can start content management functions over products (according to the use cases "Add a product," "Modify a product," "Remove a product"), or update a specific product feature (tech specs, award, benefits, configurations), as prescribed by the use cases "Add a product feature," "Edit a product feature," "Remove a product feature." From the product page, the user can also invoke the function for managing logos, according to the use cases "Add logo" and "Remove Logo", or can associate and disconnect a logo from a product ("Associate a logo," and "Disconnect a logo" use cases).		

Finally, Table 7.18 shows a sample of the standard icons adopted for representing links, indexes, and text boxes.

7.4.7   Acceptance Tests

In the first version of the Acer-Euro application, the site view for the external users is published in the different countries as a set of static HTML pages, materialized from the dynamic pages of the application, which is hosted within the company intranet and not directly accessed by Internet users. For each country, a snapshot of the local content is automatically produced at the end of each day from the database content, and is uploaded by night to the local ISP of the country.

Conversely, the content management and administration site views are available online in the company Virtual Private Network, and are accessible by the entitled European managers and administrators 24 hours a day, seven days a week.

Table 7.16 Specification of the Mar-Com managers site view.

Site view name	Mar-Com managers site view
Description	Includes the pages through which the Mar-Com managers access content management functions for inserting or updating news categories and news items.
	In order to access this site view, the Mar-Com manager needs to log in, according to the Login use case. He/She accesses page including the index of countries for which he/she is responsible. He/she selects one country to work on.
User groups	Mar-Com managers.
Use cases	"Login," "Add a news category," "Edit a news category," "Remove a news category," "Add a news item," "Edit a news item," "Remove a news item."

Site view map

Area name	Area description	Accessed/Managed objects	Priority
News Content Management	The area default page includes the index of news categories for the selected country.	News Category, News Item.	High
	The news category page provides access to content management functions over news categories, according to the use cases "Add a news category," "Edit a news category," "Remove a news category."		
	The selection of a category leads to the news management page, including the index of the available news items for the selected category. Each news item can be selected.		
	In the news management page, content management functions over news items can be performed, according to the use cases "Add a news item," "Edit a news item," and "Remove a news item."		

Table 7.17 Specification of the Administrators site view.

Site view name	**Administrators site view**
Description	Includes the pages through which the Administrator access content management functions for inserting or updating content about user accounts and for modifying some country attributes.
	In order to access this site view, the Administrator needs to log in, according to the Login use case. The administrator receives the site view Home Page, which includes the index of countries for which he/she is responsible. He/she selects a country to work on.
User groups	Administrator.
Use cases	"Login," "Create a user account," "Edit a user account," "Remove a user account," "Modify a country."

Site view map

Area name	Area description	Managed/Accessed objects	Priority
User Management	The site view home page contains a link to the User Management area.	User Group	High
	A user page contains the index of already created users. Here the Administrator can perform content management functions over users according to the use cases "Create a user account," "Edit a user account," "Remove a user account."		
Country Management	The site view home page contains a link to the Country Management area.	Country	Low
	The Manage Country page contains a form for modifying the country local name, Web site URL, and keyword list, according to the "Modify a country" use case.		

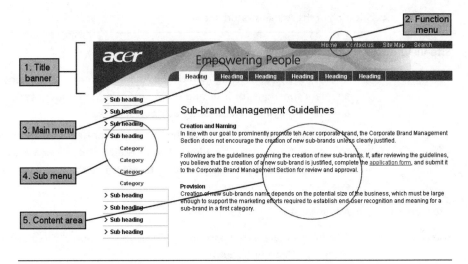

Figure 7.17   Mock-up for Acer-Euro pages.

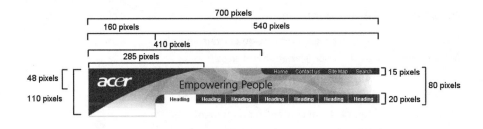

Figure 7.18   Properties of the title banner and its menus.

Performance acceptance tests refer to the average speed of the page materialization process, which must ensure that the complete snapshot of a European country is produced in less than 20 minutes; they also address the response time of the content management functions offered to the content owners, which must ensure that each content management function executes on average in less than five seconds.

Availability requirements for the customer pages are granted by the contracts with the ISP and do not affect the application architecture, whereas the intranet site views must be deployed in a replicated architecture, ensuring that the failure of the Web server, of the application server, or of the database does not stop the operations of the internal users.

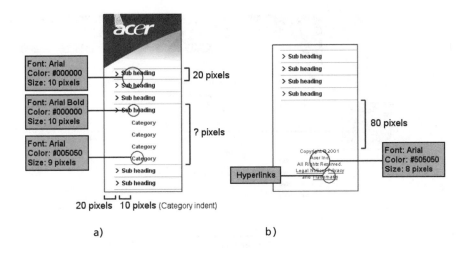

Figure 7.19   Properties of the sub-menu area.

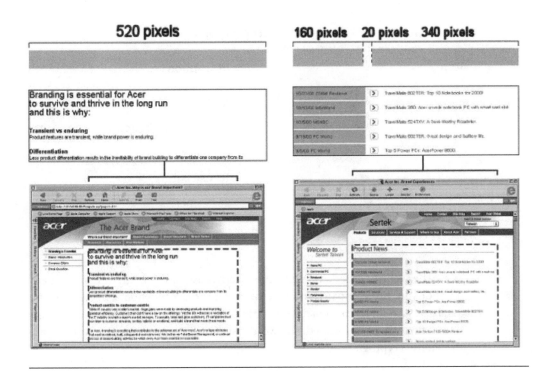

Figure 7.20   Content area grids (one and two columns).

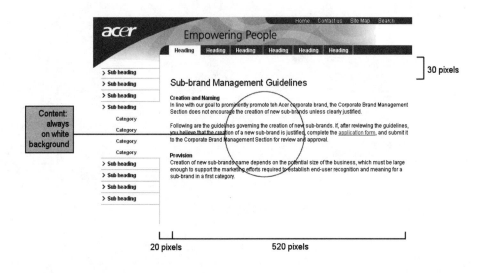

Figure 7.21   Content area style properties.

Table 7.18   Graphical resources of the Acer-Euro pages.

Icon	Description
>	Next button
∧	"Top of page" button
>	List bullet
■	Textual bullet
◢	Box corner

The security criteria relate to the internal use of the content management functions by the company employees. User profile data should be kept in the database, and login to the administration and content management functions should be password protected. Password transmission and storage in the database should use cryptography.

Summary

This chapter has addressed the specification of requirements for a data-intensive Web application, which involves two tasks: requirements collection, in which the business requirements driving the application development are established, and requirements analysis, in which the collected requirements are formalized. Application requirements focus on a variety of subjects, including users and groups, data elements, functional and non-functional requirements, personalization, and presentation. These aspects are specified using a lightweight documentation, which includes group specification sheets, UML use case and activity diagrams, data dictionaries, site view maps, mock-ups sketching the presentation guidelines, and acceptance test plans. The final part of the chapter exemplified the requirements analysis activities, applied to the Acer-Euro running case, which serves the needs of four different user groups, accessing localized content about the company products and activities in different ways.

Bibliographic Notes

Requirement collection and specification is a classic software engineering topic, discussed in all the textbooks on this discipline. As a recent example, Kruchten's book on the Rational Unified Process [Kruchten99] devotes a chapter to the collection and management of requirements, which is considered a central element of the development lifecycle.

The popularity of the use case approach to requirement analysis is mostly due to the influential work of Ivar Jacobson on the object-oriented software development methodology. His book [Jacobson94] includes a wealth of guidelines and examples on how to put use cases to work in the development of industrial applications. Shneider et al. in their popular book [SWJ98] provide additional examples and practical hints for the application of use cases in the context of the UML notation.

Core object identification is a fundamental activity, for which guidelines have been proposed by almost all software development methodologies. An extensive treatment of the subject can be found in [Booch94], which contains a review of the various techniques for identifying the relevant concepts of the application domain. Additional materials can be found in other books on object-oriented analysis and design, like the works of James Rambaugh's on OMT. A particular attention to data requirements specification is present in data-driven software development methods, like the data analysis and design method of [BCN92].

Web design and application usability textbooks, like [Sano96] and [Nielsen00], also address requirement collection for Web site development, and emphasize the techniques for achieving an effective communication.

Business requirements specification, the activity preliminary to requirements collection and analysis, is treated in [EP00], where the authors show how to use UML for the specification of the business architecture, highlight recurrent business patterns, and describe how business requirements can be translated into software requirements.

8 CHAPTER Data Design

8.1 Introduction

Design is the activity in which the knowledge about the application, collected and formalized during requirements specification, is turned into the description of the software components. This chapter concentrates on data design and shows how the dictionary of core concepts, obtained after requirements analysis, is transformed into an Entity-Relationship schema.

As highlighted in Figure 8.1, the input to data design is the entire set of requirements, because the list of core objects identified during requirements analysis is preliminary, and may be extended during data design. For example, further concepts may be discovered from the requirements about the access mechanisms for reaching the application objects, or from functional and personalization requirements, as well as from the maps of the site views.

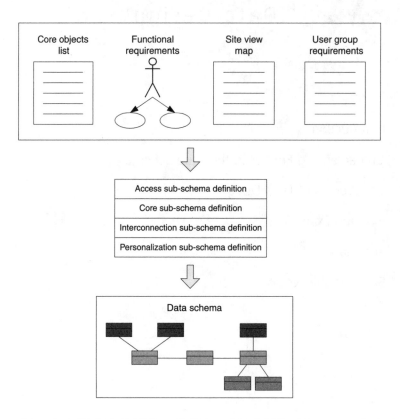

Figure 8.1   Data design input, output, and activities.

Data design is a consolidated discipline, treated in many textbooks, which discuss alternative modeling strategies. Our approach to data design does not aim at replacing the general-purpose guidelines for conceptual data modeling, but simply extends them with a few specific rules of thumb, which may help designing data "for the Web." Indeed, data publishing and content management applications have some regularities and peculiarities, which can be exploited in the design of data. Recognizing them may help the data designer organize his/her work in a systematic way, which normally results into more consistent data schemas. Therefore, in the sequel we will stress the distinct roles played by objects, and use this distinction to propose a sequence of steps for assembling the data schema of a Web application. These steps, shown in Figure 8.1 are illustrated in the remainder of this chapter.

Before entering the discussion on data modeling, it is important to understand its positioning with respect to the design of the corporate data sources, from which the content of the site may be drawn. The development of a data-intensive Web application may take place in two different scenarios:

- The data store for the content of the application *does not exist* and must be designed together with the Web application. This is the simplest scenario, in which the data design phase aims at producing a dedicated data schema for the Web application, which is directly used to construct the physical database storing the application's content.

- The content managed by the Web application *already exists* (totally or in part) and is stored in some data repository, either a database or a legacy system. In this case, the Web application extracts the content from the existing data sources, and publishes it in the Web application pages.

Also in the latter scenario, conceptual data design remains relevant, and should not be influenced too much by the existence of already designed and implemented data sources.

The motivations for this approach are manifold:

- Data design is an essential means for clarifying application requirements. Building a Web application without reconsidering the structure of its underlying data may lead to requirements misinterpretation and design errors.

- Data design feedbacks hypertext design. The two activities benefit from each other and performing them in parallel allows the designer to perform a lot of useful crosschecks.

- The existing data schemas, typically designed for a non-hypertextual application, can hardly serve the needs of a Web application, especially with respect to navigation requirements.

As we will see more precisely in the next sections, the data underlying a Web application is used for Web-specific purposes, like classifying other objects for easier access, interconnecting objects for navigation, or enabling personalization. These Web-specific data structures are normally not present in the schema of a database conceived for a traditional information system, and should be designed from scratch based on the requirements of the Web application. Thus, even if content is totally or partially reused from existing data sources, data design must still be conducted, to produce an Entity-Relationship schema conforming to the requirements of the Web application. Adapting such a schema to the existing data sources requires the appropriate data integration techniques and tools, which are explained in Chapter 11.

8.2 Characterizing Entities in the Data Schema

An important help for the definition of the data schema of a Web application comes from understanding the role that information objects play in the application. We distinguish four classes of objects, which participate to four types of sub-schemas in the Entity-Relationship schema of a typical Web application:

- *Core objects:* are the essential assets managed by the application, identified during requirements analysis. In a Web application they are either presented to the external users, or managed by internal users with administrative or content management privileges. Core objects form the backbone of the Entity-Relationship schema, around which the rest of the data schema is progressively built. Each core concept may require more than a single entity to be represented, due to the presence of complex properties and internal components. For this reason, core concepts become *core sub-schemas,* which are sets of entities correlated by relationships, collectively representing one core concept.

- *Interconnection objects:* stem from the semantic associations between core concepts mentioned in the data dictionary. In a Web application they are used to construct links and indexes for navigating from one object to a related one. From the Entity-Relationship point of view, interconnection objects are denoted by relationships between core entities, which express the desired semantic associations.

- *Access objects:* are auxiliary objects used to classify or specialize the core objects, with the purpose of facilitating access to the application content in various ways:

  - By superimposing a categorization over the core objects, which can be exploited to build index hierarchies, progressively leading the user to the desired core objects.

  - By providing more precise keyword-based search mechanisms, focused on well-defined categories of core objects.

  - By clustering representative core objects into collections, like the "picks of the day" or the "site's best choices" collections, which can be exploited to offer a preview of the most attractive core objects.

  Access objects are normally mapped into entities, connected to the core entities by relationships or specialization links. Also in the case of access objects, it is more appropriate to speak of *access sub-schemas,* because the same core object may be categorized or specialized in different ways, using multiple categorizing entities, relationships, and specialized sub-entities.

■ *Personalization objects:* are used to incorporate into the data model the relevant properties of the user, needed for personalization purposes. For example, entities may be used to model user profile data and the groups in which users are clustered, and relationships may be exploited to connect the user and group entities to the applicative entities, to represent aspects like object ownership or personal preferences.

The distinction between the different roles played by the entities and relationships must not be taken dogmatically, but must consider the application domain and the mission of the specific Web application. For instance, in an e-commerce Web site for selling books, the author concept associated with the book concept could be considered either as a piece of core content, or as a complex internal property of books, not deserving the status of a core concept. A concept is core if it independently contributes to the achievement of the site mission. In the bookselling example, authors may qualify as core concepts if the site offers also information about authors, regardless of books; in this case, the designer should treat authors as first-class objects, and, for example, publish their biography, interviews, and so on. As another example, the profile data about users are auxiliary content used for personalization in most e-commerce applications. Conversely, in a marriage agency or matchmaking Web site, data about people are the main asset, and profile data are the core content of the application.

8.3 The Process of Data Design

The data design process can be naturally structured as an incremental and iterative activity, consisting of the tasks shown in Figure 8.1. Starting from an initial nucleus, typically consisting of the most important core concepts, the data designer can progressively extend the Entity-Relationship diagram by applying refinements operations, such as the following:

1. Adding a new core sub-schema, or enriching an existing core sub-schema by detailing the internal properties and components of a core concept.

2. Adding an interconnection sub-schema, by drawing relationships between core entities, which makes explicit the semantic association between core concepts.

3. Adding an access sub-schema, by introducing a categorization entity and connecting it to a core entity, or by specializing a core entity using a sub-entity that denotes a special collection.

4. Adding a personalization sub-schema, by introducing the user and group entity, defining their properties, and connecting them to the core objects, for expressing user or group-related preferences and personal objects.

The order in which the above extensions are listed is the suggested order. However, the designer may proceed according to his/her personal experience.

Following the above data design process produces an Entity-Relationship diagram structured into well-identified layers and centered on the core entities, as shown in Figure 8.2:

■ The *core sub-schema* includes the entities and relationships denoting core concepts.

■ The *access sub-schema* comprises the entities and relationships playing the role of access facilitators.

■ The *interconnection sub-schema* includes the relationships that connect core entities.

■ The *personalization sub-schema* incorporates the user and group entities and their relationships to core entities.

The decomposition into layers of the data schema not only facilitates building, understanding, and maintaining the data model, but also benefits the

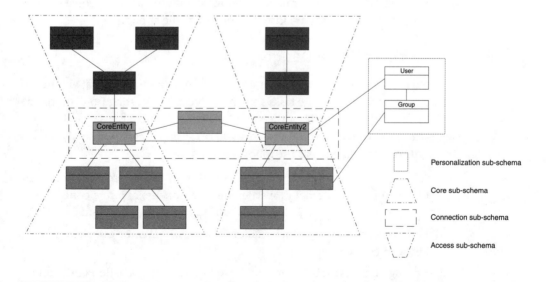

Figure 8.2   Data schema composed of access, core, interconnection, and personalization sub-schemas.

hypertext design phase. Designing the data schema while keeping in mind the intended use of concepts in the Web application helps in designing the front-end for serving data to users. In Chapter 9, we will show how typical data sub-schemas can be coupled to typical configurations of units and pages. Pairs of data and hypertext patterns may constitute the reusable building blocks for constructing applications starting from customizable components, rather than from scratch. As in other engineering disciplines, the availability of components, which can easily be assembled into a working application, makes development faster and results more reliable.

8.3.1 Designing the Core Sub-schema

The process of defining a core sub-schema from the description of a core concept in the data dictionary is quite straightforward:

1. The core concept is represented by an entity (called *core entity*).

2. Properties with a single, atomic value become *attributes* of the core entity. The identifying properties become *keys* of the core entity.

3. Properties with multiple or structured values become internal *components* of the core entity.

Internal components are represented as entities connected to the core entity via a relationship. Two cases are possible, which differ in the cardinality constraints of the relationship connecting the component to the core entity:

1. If the connecting relationship has a 1:1 constraint for the component (Figure 8.3), the component is a proper sub-part of the core concept. In this case, no instance of the internal component can exist in absence of the core entity instance it belongs to, and multiple core objects cannot share the same instance of the internal component. Internal components of this kind are sometimes called *weak entities* in the Entity-Relationship terminology, or *part-of components* in the object-oriented terminology.

2. If the relationship between the component and the core entity has 0:N cardinality for the internal component, the notion of "component" is interpreted in a broader sense. The internal component is considered a part of the core concept, even if an instance of it may exist independently of the connection to a core entity instance, and can be shared among different core objects. Nonetheless, the internal component is not deemed an essential data asset of the application and thus is not elevated to the status of a core concept.

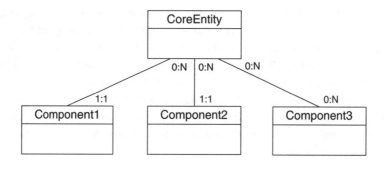

Figure 8.3   Typical core sub-schema.

Figure 8.3 illustrates the typical Entity-Relationship diagram of a core sub-schema, including one core entity, two proper, non-shared internal components, and one shared component.

Note that a shared component may be part of one or more concepts, but it is not treated as an independent object. In hypertext design, such a consideration will drive the conception of the site views, which will always present or manage components as parts of their "enclosing" core concepts, and not as stand-alone objects.

8.3.2   Designing an Interconnection Sub-schema

Interconnection sub-schemas are patterns of relationships introduced in the data schema for expressing semantic associations between the core objects. Connection sub-schemas stem directly from the semantic associations between core objects declared in the data dictionary produced during requirements specification. Each semantic association yields a relationship between the involved core entities, as illustrated in Figure 8.4. Unless otherwise specified by constraints in the data dictionary, relationships between core entities are many-to-many.

At the two extremes, it is possible that all core concepts are related, which produces a completely connected graph of relationships; on the other hand, it may also happen that all the core concepts of the application are unrelated. In the latter case, the interconnection sub-schema is empty, and the core concepts are isolated.

8.3.3   Designing an Access Sub-schema

Access sub-schemas are patterns of entities and relationships that support the location and selection of core concepts. Identifying the needed access sub-schemas

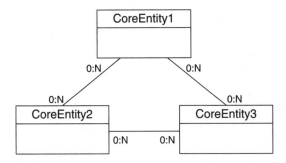

Figure 8.4 Typical connection sub-schema.

is less straightforward than identifying the other classes of sub-schemas. Hints as to the presence of access concepts can be found in the use case inventory, by carefully reviewing how users locate their objects of interest, and in the site view maps, which may refer to concepts used to categorize, specialize, or group into collections the core concepts.

An access sub-schema consists of two kinds of entities: categorizing entities and specialized sub-entities.

- A *categorizing entity* is an entity connected via a relationship to a core entity, which plays the role of the *categorized entity,* with the purpose of superimposing a classification hierarchy over the instances of the core entity. For example, the pieces of news can be classified into categories by introducing a NewsCategory entity into the Entity-Relationship diagram, as a categorizing entity, and connecting it with a relationship to the entity NewsItem, which plays the role of the categorized entity.

- A *specialized sub-entity* is an entity connected by an ISA association to a core entity. The instances of this sub-entity share some common property, which distinguishes them from the general case and can be exploited for facilitating access. Examples of this way of grouping special instances are commonly found in Web applications in the form of "highlighted items," like editor's choices, specials of the day, recent news, and so on. In this case, the sub-entity denotes the restricted sub-group of instances of the super-entity that are selected as members of the special collection.

Figure 8.5 pictorially represent a "canonical" access schema: a central entity, labeled Core, represents the core concept, and is surrounded by two entities representing access concepts, labeled Access1 and Access2, which denote alternative

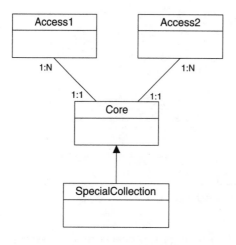

Figure 8.5 Typical access sub-schema.

categorizations. The diagram contains also a sub-entity, labeled SpecialCollection, which denotes a collection of representative core concepts.

Note that categorical concepts are treated as first-class entities, and not only as an internal property of the categorized entity, because they may themselves store several pieces of information, like a representative image, some descriptive text and so on, which illustrates the common features of core objects belonging to them. The organization of categorical concepts can reflect the following three recurrent patterns:

- Categorical concepts can themselves be categorized, resulting in a *hierarchy of categorizations*. For example, hardware products can be classified by category (computers or peripherals), then by family (PCs, servers, and laptops), then by commercial brand, and so on. Figure 8.6(a) shows an example of categorization hierarchy.

- The same core concept may be subject to more than one categorization, originating *multiple categorizations*. For example, fashion articles may be organized by target (man, woman, and child), and by season. Figure 8.6(b) illustrates this case.

- Finally, the same categorical concept can be used to classify more than one core concept, resulting in a *shared categorization*. For example, the entity Country may classify both news and products as shown in Figure 8.6(c).

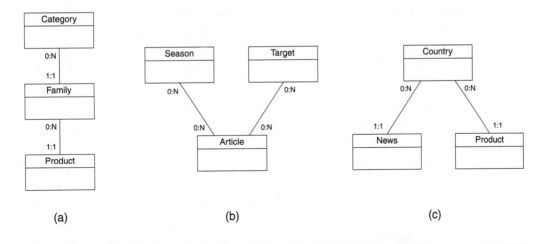

(a)   (b)   (c)

Figure 8.6   Three forms of categorization: hierarchical (a), multiple (b), shared (c).

8.3.4   Designing a Personalization Sub-schema

A personalization sub-schema consists of entities and relationships describing properties of the users, relevant to the personalization of the Web application. The properties captured by the personalization sub-schema typically comprise:

- User profile data, which are the attributes, possibly complex, that characterize the individual users. Examples of general-purpose profile attributes may be the name, address, sex, and age of a user. Profile data may also be application specific; for instance, in e-commerce applications profile attributes may include the total amount of expenditure, the date of the last visit or purchase, and so on.

- User groups, which represent the identified clusters of users with homogeneous requirements. The group may be treated as a mere property of users, or as a first-class object, with its own attributes.

- Personalization relationships, which are semantic associations between core objects and the users or groups, denoting aspects such as the access rights of users or groups over core objects, the ownership of core objects by users or groups, or the preference of users or groups for selected core objects.

The personalization sub-schema may be also used to represent the default rules for assigning users to the available site views. For instance, each user group may be connected to an instance of a SiteView entity, representing the available site views, to denote the semantic association between each group and the site view designed to fulfill the requirements of the group members.

The configuration in Figure 8.7 is an example of a basic, yet typical, personalization sub-schema.

- Entity User specifies information about the individuals who access the application; it includes basic properties like the name, password, and e-mail.

- Entity Group specifies information about the clusters of users with homogeneous requirements; it includes collective properties like the group name, the number of members, and so on.

- A many-to-many relationship (called Membership) connects User to Group, denoting that a user may belong to multiple groups, and that a group clusters multiple users.

- A one-to-many relationship (called Default) connects User to Group, denoting that a user may have one group as the default one among the groups he/she belongs to. This additional information is useful for assigning the user to the default group after he/she logs into the application. Note that in those applications where users are associated with a single group there is no need of the Default relationship.

- A one-to-many relationship (called Access) connects entity Group and entity SiteView, to denote the site view associated to a group. Thanks to the Default and Access relationships, each user can be associated to a unique default site view, which is the site view of the default group of the user.

The simple data schema of Figure 8.7 can be augmented with further elements, to represent user information needed in a specific application domain. Figure 8.8 shows for example a data schema in which the User entity includes

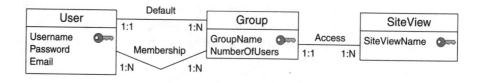

Figure 8.7   User and Group representations in the data schema.

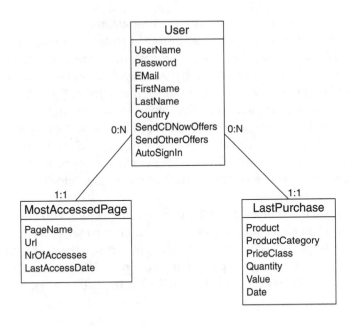

Figure 8.8   Domain-specific user profiles data for an e-commerce Web site.

additional profile attributes, inspired to the profile attributes requested to the user in the CDNOW Web site, such as FirstName, LastName, and Country. Some flag attributes also indicate if users are willing to receive announcements about special offers, or if they prefer to sign in automatically through IP identification when accessing the Web site. Further entities can be included for modeling complex data of the user profile. For instance, in order to provide users with personalized links to their preferred pages, the entity MostAccessedPage can be added for representing the user's most visited pages. The entity records the page name, its URL, the number of times the user has accessed it, and the date of the last access. The entity LastPurchase can be instead added for recording data about the last purchased products, like the category and price class of the purchased product, the ordered quantity, the total order value, and the purchase date. The information stored by this entity can be useful for determining the user's preferences about the products sold in a Web site.

Personalization relationships permit designers to express in the data schema a popular form of personalization, based on the users' preferences, stored as attribute values in the User entity or as instances of a relationship between the User entity and a core entity. In some cases, user preferences are implicitly computed from records of past interactions with the Web site (for example, in e-commerce applications, from the user's purchase history), or by means of sophisticated marketing business rules. In other cases, users have the possibility of explicitly indicating some preferences, which can be used to give them personalized content. An example of personalization relationship is illustrated in Figure 8.9 in the context of a personalized application publishing local information, like weather reports, events, and city guides. The preference expressed by the user about the city he/she wants to be informed about is represented by a relationship between entity User and the core entity City, which permits the selection of personalized content, denoted by the Forecast, LocalNews, and CityGuideItem components connected to entity City.

A personalization relationship may also denote information objects owned by individual users. The meaning of such a relationship may be that only the user who owns the personal objects can access and manipulate them. This happens for example for the shopping cart content in e-commerce Web applications. In other cases, personal objects are created and managed by their authors, but are avail-

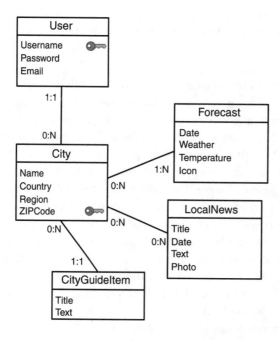

Figure 8.9 Example of personalization relationships.

able also to other users. This happens for example in Web boards, where users create messages for other users to read.

The data schema of Figure 8.10 includes two personalization relationships, which associate each user with the discussions and messages he/she has created. Messages are also connected to the discussion they are posted for.

Not all applications require a personalization sub-schema, and not all personalized applications require the same degree of sophistication in representing personalization data. Modeling user, group, and customization requirements in the data schema is *not necessary* when the following conditions are met:

- The application should serve the requirements of a single, homogeneous group of users.

- No page in the application should deliver content that depends on the user's identity.

- User authentication and access rights verification are either irrelevant, because there are no security and privacy issues, or dealt with outside the application. In the latter case, some other application must filter users' requests and ensure that the access rights are enforced.

- No page in the application should be adapted to the user's interaction context, for example, by modifying its layout and graphical resources.

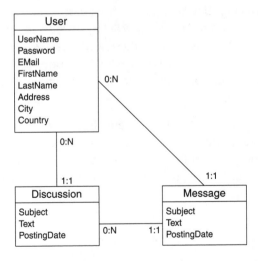

Figure 8.10 Web board data schema.

8.4 Running Example

The Acer-Euro Web application manages two main information assets: products and news. In this section, we show how to progressively construct the data schema by following the design process described in the previous section.

8.4.1 Identification of Core Entities

From the data dictionary defined during the Acer-Euro requirement specification, we initially pick the two concepts that play the role of core objects, namely *NewsItem* and *Product*. The data design activity therefore starts from the inclusion of two entities in the data schema, as shown in Figure 8.11.

8.4.2 Design of Core Sub-schemas

In the second step, the core sub-schemas centered on the core entities Product and NewsItem are detailed.

Entity NewsItem is characterized by a number of simple properties (Headline, SubHeadline, Date, Textdate, Place, etc.), all of which have a single value of a primitive type. Therefore all these properties are simply represented as attributes of the NewsItem entity, as shown in Figure 8.12(a).

Conversely, entity Product has both simple and complex properties. Various simple properties (name, short description, long description, small image, normal image, large image, and so on) are modeled by introducing attributes of the proper type in entity Product. Besides these attributes, Product has also some multi-valued properties (Benefit, ProductConfiguration, TechSpecItem), which require the introduction of proper internal components of the entity Product. In particular:

■ *Benefit* represents the main advantages offered by a product, which must be highlighted in the product page. It is described by means of the attributes Description, a short text summarizing the benefit (for example "ultra-portability"), and DescriptionLong, a text explaining the benefit in detail.

NewsItem

Product

Figure 8.11   Core entities of the Acer-Euro application.

■ *ProductConfiguration* represents a particular product configuration (for instance, "128 MB RAM, HD 9 GB, . . ."). One product family can have many product configurations. Each configuration is described by means of the ModelName, PartNumber, Description, and Price.

■ *TechSpecItem* represents an item from the technical specifications of a product. It includes the attribute Description, which is a short textual explanation.

All the entities stemming from these complex properties are connected to the core entity Product by mandatory one-to-many relationships, to highlight that they are proper sub-parts of the Product concept, as shown in Figure 8.12(b).

Entity Product includes also the shared components Logo and Award which represent other two complex properties:

■ *Logo* represents the commercial logos used site-wide and Europe-wide (for example the "Windows CE" logo, the "Intel Inside" logo, and so on), which give indications about the characteristics of the hardware and software components that make up a product; a logo is described by attribute Name (for example, "Intel inside"), used for internal use only, and by attribute Image, for graphically displaying the logo.

■ *Award* represents the awards won by the company for its products (for example, the "Cebit Best in Show" prize). An award is characterized by an image and a title.

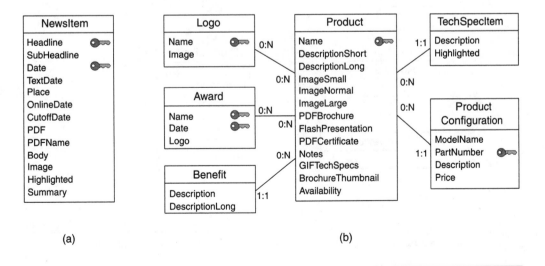

(a)

(b)

Figure 8.12 Core sub-schema for the NewsItem (a) and the Product (b) core objects.

Strictly speaking, Logo and Award are not proper sub-parts of Product. A logo and an award may exist independently of a product connected to them, or be associated with more than one product. However, they are treated as part of the core sub-schema of a product, to stress the fact that in the Acer-Euro application they are normally presented and managed inside the boundaries of a product. The resulting core sub-schema is reported in Figure 8.12(b).

8.4.3   Definition of the Access Sub-schema

At the end of the first data design step, the core sub-schemas are in place. Next, access to the core objects must be accommodated.

From the use cases associated to the external users, produced in Chapter 7, we deduce that the access to news should be supported through a categorization concept. Therefore, the entity NewsCategory is introduced and connected via a relationship to the NewsItem entity, as shown in Figure 8.13(a). NewsCategory is described by means of attribute Name (a string expressing the name of the category). Because the NewsCategory entity serves just the purpose of supporting a hierarchical access to news, the category name is the only piece of information to be represented.

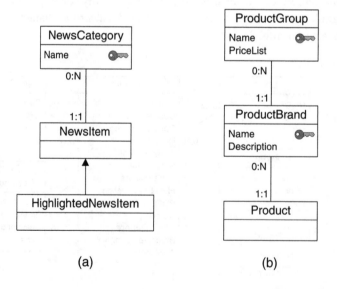

(a)   (b)

Figure 8.13   Access sub-schemas for the NewsItem and Product core object.

A second element is introduced in the access schema of the News concept: a sub-entity HighlightedNewsItem specializes entity NewsItem, and contains the highlighted news, published in the home page, as specified by the use cases and site view map for the external users illustrated in Chapter 7.

A two-level categorization hierarchy supports the access to the Product instances, as illustrated in Figure 8.13(b), where two categorizing entities appear:

- *ProductGroup* represents the broadest product categorization (for example, notebooks, desktops, and so on). It is described by attribute Name, which holds the name of the group, and by attribute PriceList, listing representative prices of selected articles of the group.

- *ProductBrand* represents a sub-categorization of products by commercial brand (for example, Travelmate). Each product group may cluster different product brands. Each brand is described by means of the Name, and of a short textual description highlighting the main features common to all the products of a brand.

The schema in Figure 8.13 represents the organization of content for a single European subsidiary (for example, Acer Italy, Acer UK, etc.). However, the main goal of the Acer-Euro application is to centralize the content of all the European subsidiaries. Therefore, the instances of all the entities of the data schema designed so far are to be considered multi-lingual; the external users should receive the version of the content written in their mother tongue, and the internal users should administer the version of the content for which they are entitled (for example, product managers of the Spanish subsidiary should update local news for Spain only).

To support the localization of content, the access schema is enriched with a further categorical concept, entity Country, which stores information about the different European countries for which the Acer-Euro Web site is developed. As shown in Figure 8.16, entity Country is characterized by several attributes: Name, its name in the local language, Isocode, the standard country code, like IT, UK and so on, Charset, representing the set of characters used for text encoding, Absolute_URL, that is, the canonical URL of the national Web site (for example *www.acer.it* for the Italian Web site), EnglishName, to be displayed in the international versions of the Acer-Euro pages, and Keywords, which is a text including localized keywords to be inserted into the national pages for facilitating their indexing by search engines.

Ideally, entity Country must be put in relationship to all the other entities of the design schema defined so far, to denote the fact that each instance (say an instance of some product) is a version for a given country. However, a

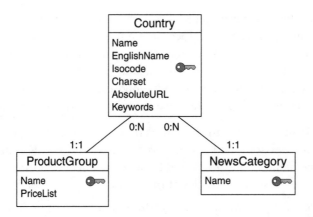

Figure 8.14 Inclusion of the entity Country into both access sub-schemas.

few observations show that a limited number of relationships with entity Country are sufficient:

- The product and news taxonomies are strict containment hierarchies: an Italian product group contains Italian brands only, which contain Italian products; a Spanish news category characterizes only Spanish news.

- Proper internal components (benefits, technical specifications) of products are not reused: the benefits and technical specifications of an Italian product are in Italian and cannot be reused in another country.

- Shared components (logos and awards) need not be localized, because they contain simple images or international titles.

Thus, connecting the categorizing entity Country to the root of the categorization hierarchy of products and news, as shown in Figure 8.14, enables the access to the "slice" of content associated with a specific country.

At the end of the third design step, the data schema of Figure 8.15 includes two core and two data access sub-schemas, centered on the core entities Products and News. The entity Country is shared by both access sub-schemas.

8.4.4 Definition of Interconnection Sub-schemas

The next step of data design introduces the relevant connections between the core concepts. News items are associated with the products they refer to. Also, a product award can be associated with one or more news announcing it. Therefore,

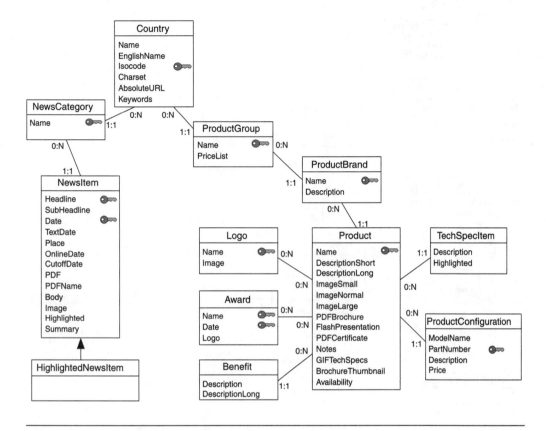

Figure 8.15 Core and access sub-schemas of the Acer-Euro application.

the two core sub-schemas are interconnected by means of two many-to-many re-lationships, one associating NewsItem and Product, the other associating Award and NewsItem. This addition leads to the data schema in Figure 8.16.

8.4.5 Design of Personalization Sub-schema

The last step of data design adds the needed elements of the personalization sub-schema. The Acer-Euro application makes a limited use of personalized features. External users are not registered, and thus no profile data about them are col-lected, and no personal content can be addressed to them.

Conversely, internal users must be registered and assigned to one or more groups. When they log into the application, the list of site views they are entitled to access must be determined.

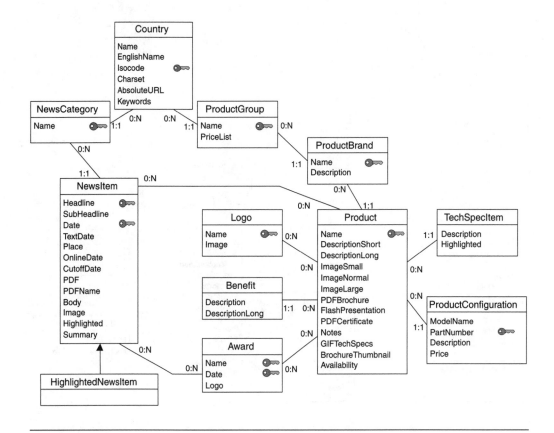

Figure 8.16 Inter-connection schema between Product and NewsItem core concepts.

To meet these requirements, a personalization sub-schema including the entities User, Group, and SiteView is added (Figure 8.17): instances of entity User represent Acer internal users, instances of entity Group denote the identified groups (External users, Administrators, Mar-Com managers, and Product managers), and instances of entity SiteView denote the identified site views, one for each group of internal users, plus one for external users.

The profile data of internal users are represented as attributes inside entity User, and include the relevant login and contact information: username, password, first name, last name, e-mail, and so on. Besides profile data, a personalization relationship is exploited, which associates each internal user with his/her personal set of administered countries, so that after the login the system can present him/her an index of countries among which to choose. After selecting a country, the user can start a content management session, limited to the core ob-

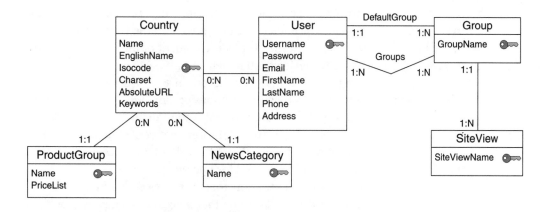

Figure 8.17   Personalization sub-schema of the Acer-Euro application.

jects associated with the selected country. Therefore, the personalization sub-schema includes a personalization relationship between entity Country and entity User, as illustrated in Figure 8.17.

Summary

This chapter has shown that the data schema of a Web application generally presents a regular structure, in which some recurrent inter-connected sub-schemas can be recognized. In particular, objects in the data schema can be characterized as core, access, inter-connection, and personalization objects, depending on the role they play in the application. Taking into account this characterization, the data schema results naturally decomposed into well-identified sub-schemas, centered on core objects.

This regularity facilitates building and maintaining the data schema, as well as designing hypertexts on top of it. As it will be shown in Chapter 9, designing the data schema while keeping in mind the role of the information objects makes it easier the hypertext design phase, in which standard hypertext patterns can be constructed on top of the different sub-schemas of the Entity-Relationship diagram.

Bibliographic Notes

Conceptual data modeling dates back to 1976, the year in which the famous article by Peter Chen "The Entity-Relationship Model—Toward a Unified View of

Data" appeared on the first issue of the *ACM Transactions on Database Systems* journal [Chen76]. Ever since, conceptual data modeling with the Entity-Relationship language has become a cornerstone of the development of information systems. Conceptual database design is described in detail in [BCN92].

The idea of using Entity-Relationship in conjunction with hypertext design has been explored by a few Web design methods proposed in the research community, including HDM [GPS93], RMM [ISB95], and Araneus [AMM97, AMM98, AMM98a]. These methods have underlined the importance of structure modeling in the design of Web sites, and have highlighted the differences between data modeling for traditional applications and for hypertexts.

An important empirical verification that Web sites are defined on top of content structures organized as a collection of specialized sub-schemas appears in a paper on the "self-similarity" of the Web, by Dill et al. [DKMRST01]. The main finding of the paper is that the Web can be decomposed into cohesive sets of pages, connected via a "navigational backbone," with several other pages pointing *into* the backbone or being reachable *out* of the backbone. This topology parallels the sub-schema organization illustrated in Figure 8.2, with the Web backbone being similar to the interconnection sub-schema linking the core entities, "into" pages matching the access sub-schema, and "out" pages mirroring the components of the core entities. The paper also shows that the Web structure is fractal and thus repeats itself recursively, which means that the Web seen "in the large" presents a structure similar to that of its cohesive sub-portions, which are the individual Web sites. This prompts the authors to say that "to design effective algorithms for data services at various scale of the Web it is sufficient to understand the structure that emerges from one fairly simple stochastic process." We believe that the typical topology of Web sites, which are built on top of core, access, and interconnection objects, may explain the deep reason of the fractal structure of the Web.

9 CHAPTER   Hypertext Design

9.1   Introduction

Hypertext design specifies the site views to be constructed on top of the data schema defined in data design, to realize the content publishing and manipulation services identified during requirements analysis. As illustrated in Figure 9.1, hypertext design starts from three essential sources of input: the conceptual data schema, which expresses the structure of data, the functional requirements, which indicate the functionality to be delivered, and the site view maps, which sketch the organization of the hypertexts offered to the users.

Hypertext design turns these inputs into a WebML specification, which gives a high-level view of the application front-ends, independent of any implementation detail, but precise enough to be used as a roadmap for the implementation.

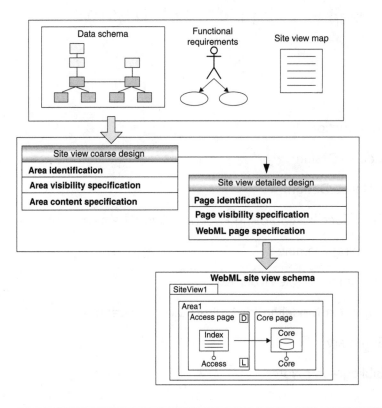

Figure 9.1   Hypertext design activities, inputs and outputs.

As the last part of the book will show, the transformation of a WebML site view into the application code is a very systematic process, which lends itself to be effectively supported by software tools. The workflow of hypertext design proceeds top-down, from *coarse design* to *detailed design*.

Coarse design aims at establishing a first draft of each site view, by mapping the elements of the data schema to the areas of the site views where they are used. The areas listed in the site view maps produced during requirements analysis are consolidated and assigned the visibility level of landmark, default, or internal areas. The designer also specifies the area content, in terms of the entities and relationships of the data schema that will be used to build each area. In doing so, special attention is paid to the role played by the various data elements, which may be exploited for accessing information, for publishing the content of core objects, for interconnecting core objects, or for personalization purposes. Coarse design produces a very high-level specification of site views, which exploits an informal textual notation to express the binding between the data elements and the areas where they are used.

Detailed design is a top-down refinement of coarse design, in which the draft schemas of site views are progressively revised until they become collections of WebML pages and units compliant with the user's requirements. The first step of detailed design is to identify pages and classify them as home, landmark, or internal pages. Then, the content elements and operations associated to areas are expressed as patterns of units and links. Detailed design exploits *WebML hypertext sub-schemas,* which are "canonical" configurations of pages and units, built on top of the core, access, interconnection, and personalization sub-schemas.

This chapter presents the fundamental activities of coarse and detailed hypertext design, and shows them at work on the Acer-Euro running case. The chapter also addresses two complementary issues: the design of usable hypertexts and of multi-device applications.

9.2 Coarse Design

In site view coarse design, the hypertext architect applies to each site view a sequence of refinement steps, shown in Figure 9.1, to consolidate the site view map into a set of WebML areas, and specify the content and visibility of each area.

The first activity consists of the *identification of areas.* The identification of areas starts by reexamining the functional requirements and the site view maps, which embody a preliminary idea of the division of the application into modules. From these inputs, the designer establishes the consolidated list of the site view areas to be developed, and produces a first WebML representation of each site view (Figure 9.2).

Once areas are established, the next step is to express *area visibility.* An area can be:

- A *default area,* if it is accessed by default when its enclosing site view is accessed. Typically, the default area within a site view is the one including the site view home page.

- A *landmark* area, when it is globally accessible from any other area within the Web site. Typically, the notion of being "landmark" is physically translated into the construction of some menu of landmark areas included in all pages of the Web site, which permits the user to "jump" to the landmark area from any page of the application.

- An *internal* area, when it corresponds to a piece of hypertext that can be reached only by means of explicit, point-to-point navigation links from some pages of other areas.

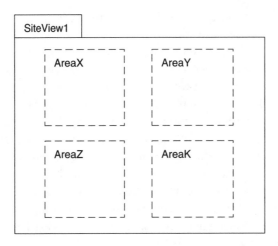

Figure 9.2   Consolidating the site view map by introducing areas.

The visibility of areas is expressed by applying the WebML landmark and default notations. In Figure 9.3, area X is the default area; therefore, it is the one accessed when the site view is entered. Area X and area Z are landmark areas; therefore, links to their default pages will be included in any page of SiteView1. Areas Y and K are instead internal areas, reachable by explicit links from specific pages.

The last step of coarse design is the *specification of content* associated with each area. The site view maps collected during requirement analysis contain an informal textual description of the services offered by each area. Content specification further details the assignment of content and functions to areas, by highlighting the role that the objects of the data schema play in building the area. The content of an area is expressed in terms of hypertext fragments, which are classified as follows:

- *Core hypertexts,* which publish the content of specific entities or groups of entities representing core information objects.

- *Access hypertexts,* which support various forms of access to core concepts.

- *Interconnection hypertexts,* which are used to interconnect core concepts.

- *Personalization hypertexts,* which are used for personalization purposes, like user identification, access rights management, personalized content delivery, and personal objects management.

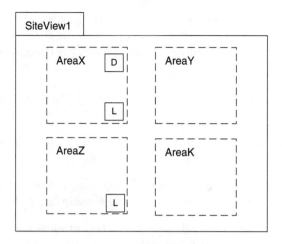

Figure 9.3   Specifying the visibility of areas.

- *Content management hypertexts,* which support content management operations like the creation, deletion, and updating of entities and the creation and deletion of relationships.

The hypertext fragments included in areas are expressed using an informal textual notation; the following statements included inside the boundaries of an area specify its enclosed hypertext fragments:

- Core(CoreEntity,Component1, ... ,ComponentN) denotes the publishing of content about core entity CoreEntity and its sub-component entities Component1, ... ,ComponentN.

- Access(CoreEntity,AccessEntity1, ... ,AccessEntityN) denotes the access to one or more instances of entity CoreEntity, by means of a step-by-step selection through the categorizing entities AccessEntity1, ... ,AccessEntityN. When the categorizing entities are not specified, the hypertext fragment supports the access to the core entity by means of search mechanisms.

- Interconnection(Role1, ... ,RoleN) denotes the navigation from the instances of Entity1 to the instances of EntityN, where Entity1 and EntityN are core entities connected by the sequence of relationship roles Role1, ... ,RoleN.

- **Create&Connect(Entity1,Role1, ... ,RoleN)** denotes the creation of a new instance of entity **Entity1**, and possibly the connection of the new instance to N existing entities through the relationship roles **Role1, ... ,RoleN**.

- **Modify(Entity1)** denotes the modification of instances of entity **Entity1**.

- **Delete(Entity1)** denotes the deletion of instances of entity **Entity1**.

- **Connect(Role1),Disconnect(Role1)** respectively denotes the creation and deletion of instances of the relationship role **Role1**.

- **Set(ContextInformation)** denotes the setting of some global piece of information, which is made available to all the pages of the site view. The context information is typically an attribute value, for instance the OID of an entity instance.

Figure 9.4 shows an example of content specification for an area dedicated to creating, deleting, and modifying news items. The core entity News is accessed through the categorizing entity NewsCategory, and the news in the selected category can be deleted and modified; the area also includes the possibility to create a piece of news within the selected category and to set the current category as a global parameter, to be made available in all the pages and areas of the site view.

News_ContentManagement Area
Access (News, NewsCategory)
Delete (News)
Modify (News)
Create&Connect (News,NewsToNewsCategory)
Set (NewsCategory)

Figure 9.4 Example of area content specification.

9.3 Detailed Design

Once the draft schema of a site view is in place, it is possible to refine it by transforming the generic textual descriptions of each area into a WebML specification supporting the features expressed by the coarse design. The process of detailed design applies iteratively the refinement steps illustrated in Figure 9.1, namely page identification, page visibility specification, and page content specification, to the individual areas of a site view.

Page identification addresses the division of an area into pages. Each page is assigned a portion of the content and functions of the enclosing area, and this allotment aims at optimizing the usability and effectiveness of the hypertext, by keeping together content elements and functions that have a high degree of cohesion, and separating loosely coupled features.

As an example of page specification, consider the coarse specification of the area illustrated in Figure 9.4. The content of the area can be assigned to three distinct pages, as shown in Figure 9.5: the first page (NewsAccess&Deletion) permits

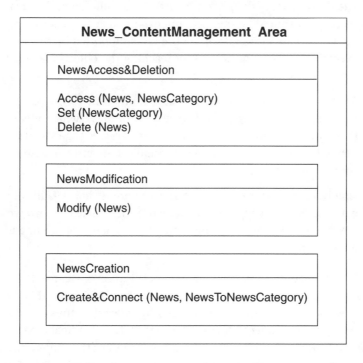

Figure 9.5 Example of page identification.

the access to news by means of their category, the choice of a category as the current category, and the deletion of a news item for the current category; the second page (NewsModification) allows the modification of an individual piece of news; the third page (NewsCreation) supports the creation of a novel piece of news. This allotment of functions and content to pages is justified by reasons of space and of logical cohesion, because keeping all content management functions in the same page is impractical, and thus each content management operation is assigned to a dedicated page.

The definition of *page visibility* designates each page as a home, default, landmark, or internal, based on its importance.

- The *home page,* which is presented by default when the user accesses the URL of a public site view or logs in into a protected site view, should be the page that contains those pieces of content and services that are the most important of the entire site view, or that are preliminary for accessing the other pages.

- The *default page* is the page presented by default when the area is accessed. It should be the most important page of the area, providing the entry points for performing the tasks supported by the area, for example the access primitives for reaching the objects managed or published in the area.

- A *landmark page* is globally reachable from all the other pages in the same enclosing module (site view or area), which means that a link to it appears in all the other pages. A page should be defined as landmark if it provides useful, frequently accessed content or services.

- Finally, an *internal page* is one that is not home, nor default, nor landmark. These pages typically implement subordinate content, which is presented only after accessing some other content, or intermediate steps of an interaction process.

Figure 9.6 adds page visibility to the specification of Figure 9.5. In particular, the page NewsAccess&Deletion is designated as the default page; this choice is motivated by the fact that accessing the news by category is the central step of the news content management process. The page is also a landmark, because it must be reachable from the other pages of the area, to restart the content management process for another news category. The remaining pages are internal; they are reached only by means of explicit links from the NewsAccess&Deletion page.

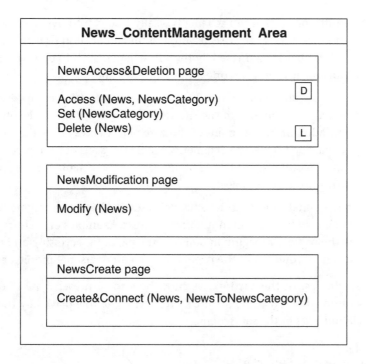

Figure 9.6 Example of page visibility specification.

9.4 Page Specification Using Hypertext Sub-schemas

Once pages and their visibility have been identified, it is possible to proceed with *page specification,* which consists of the detailed specification of units and links necessary to deliver the content and services established in the coarse hypertext design. Page specification is facilitated by the existence of some typical *hypertext sub-schemas,* which are hypertext design patterns supporting the use of the core, access, interconnection, and personalization data sub-schemas introduced in data design.

The publication of the different kinds of data sub-schemas into the areas of a site view follows a few general principles:

- A core sub-schema is typically used to define one area, which is devoted either to present or manage the content of the core object of the sub-schema. Defining areas over multiple core objects is possible, but less frequent.

■ An interconnection sub-schema typically results into hypertext fragments distributed inside the areas devoted to the publication or management of the core objects connected by the sub-schema. Such hypertext fragments enable navigation from one area to another one.

■ An access sub-schema typically results in hypertext fragments distributed inside the default area of the site view, and inside the area devoted to the publication or management of the core object accessed by the sub-schema. Such hypertext fragments enable the access to the core objects from top-level pages, like the home page or the default page of the area devoted to the core object.

■ The personalization sub-schema yields several hypertext fragments, which may be distributed in different areas. Examples of such fragments are the pages for logging in and out, the pages for accessing and updating personal content, and the pages for managing personal profile data.

In the rest of this section, we show how to turn each type of data sub-schema into a hypertext fragment coherent with the role played by the entities and relationships in the sub-schema.

9.4.1   Access Hypertext Sub-schema

Figure 9.7 recalls the typical configuration of an access sub-schema: two categorizing entities (Access1 and Access2) are related to a categorized entity (Core), and a sub-entity (SpecialCollection) introduces a specialization useful for identifying instances of the core entity with some relevant properties.

The normal use of access objects in a hypertext is to construct mechanisms for reaching the desired instances of the core concept. Thus, instances of the categorizing entities are included in the hypertext and connected to the associated instances of the categorized entity. Navigation occurs from the categorizing to the categorized entity, following a top-down path. Additional access primitives can be provided by inserting in the hypertext instances of a specialized sub-concept, which are used as "representatives" of the core concept. To complete the design, it is also possible to incorporate in the hypertext a search function, whereby keywords input by the user are used to locate a list of matching core objects.

Figure 9.8 shows a coarse specification, in which the Access area encloses a hypertext fragment supporting the access to instances of the entity Core, based on the entities and relationships of the access data schema shown in Figure 9.7. The access occurs via the categorizing entities Access1 and Access2, the specialized

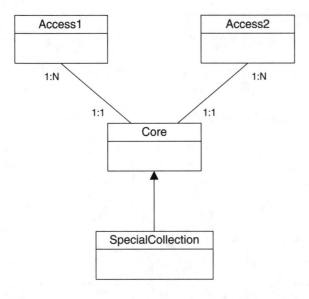

Figure 9.7   Typical configuration of access objects in the data schema.

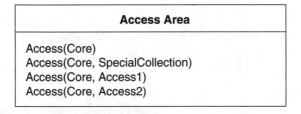

Figure 9.8   Area including access functions.

sub-entity SpecialCollection, and directly through a search over the instances of entity Core.

The specification of Figure 9.8 can be translated into a detailed hypertext as shown in Figure 9.9. The access hypertext consists of five pages. Page AccessEntry gathers all the entry points of the access paths for reaching the core entity, and is defined as landmark and default. In this way, the entry points of the access paths are located in a page with a high visibility, which is easily reachable from the other pages in the same area and from the other areas.

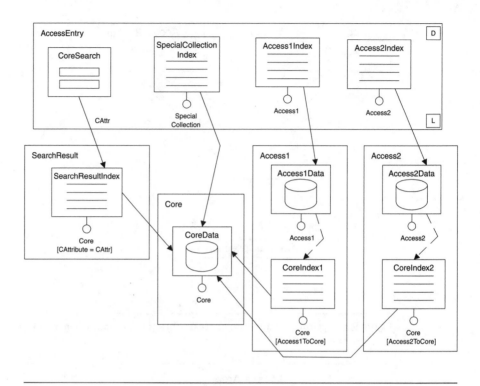

Figure 9.9 Typical hypertext associated with an access sub-schema.

The AccessEntry page includes two indexes (Access1Index and Access2Index) over the two access entities Access1and Access2. These indexes are the starting points of two independent navigation chains organized according to the cascaded index pattern. In the example, the indexes at the second step (CoreIndex1 and CoreIndex2) are placed in a distinct page, which also contains a data unit over the access entity, used to show information about the currently selected access category. Alternative patterns may avoid the intermediate data unit (if the access category has no useful data) or use a hierarchical index unit in the home page. The AccessEntry page also contains an index unit (SpecialCollectionIndex) showing a collection of representative core concepts, from which it is possible to jump to the page with the full details of one of the instances of the core entity. An entry unit (CoreSearch) also provides a keyword-based search. The results of the search are shown in an index unit (SearchResultIndex), placed in a separate page, from which it is possible to access the full details of the core concept.

9.4.2 Core Hypertext Sub-schema

The main function of a core sub-schema is to publish the content of core entities and of their components. Figure 9.10 recalls the typical organization of a core sub-schema, which consists of one core object, connected to several components.

Normally, in a hypertext for browsing core entities, the user selects one instance of a core entity, obtaining some data; then he/she navigates within the boundaries of the core sub-schema to access the features of the related components.

Figure 9.11 shows a coarse specification, in which the Core Area encloses a hypertext fragment supporting the browsing of an instance of entity Core and of its sub-components mentioned in Figure 9.10.

A possible hypertext fragment corresponding to such a specification is shown in Figure 9.12. The WebML schema provides alternative ways of accessing the core entity components, by using multidata, index, and scroller units. Instances of Component1 are kept in the same page as the core object instance they refer to; whereas instances of Component2 are browsed by means of an indexed guided tour pattern, with the index unit in the same page as the core object instance, and the scroller and data units in a separate page. Note the use of a set and a get unit for passing the

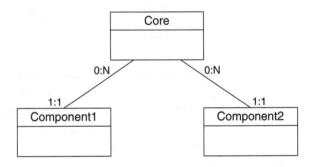

Figure 9.10 Typical configuration of core objects in the data schema.

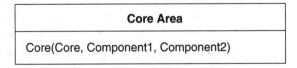

Figure 9.11 Area including core object browsing functions.

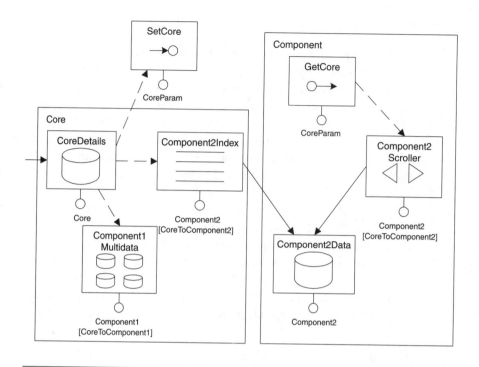

Figure 9.12   Example of hypertext associated with a core sub-schema.

identifier of the current instance of the core entity from Core page to Component page, where it is used in the selector condition of the scroller unit, to restrict scrolling only to the components of the current instance of the core entity.

9.4.3   Interconnection Hypertext Sub-schema

The role of the interconnection sub-schema is to provide navigable connections between core concepts. Figure 9.13 shows an example of interconnection data sub-schema involving three core entities and three relationships.

The typical use of the interconnection sub-schema is to construct hypertexts for moving from one core object to another one. Generally, each core object is bound to a specific area, and thus the interconnection hypertext typically permits the user to navigate from one area to another one. If each core entity must be connected to all the other core entities, the resulting hypertext schema contains a connected graph of navigation links. In some cases, not all the navigation possibilities need to be exploited, and the resulting navigation graph is simpler.

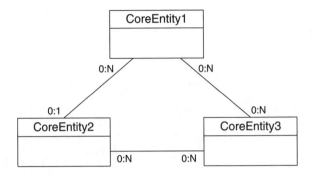

Figure 9.13 Typical configuration of interconnection concepts in the data schema.

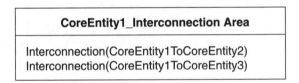

Figure 9.14 Area including core object interconnection functions.

Figure 9.14 shows the specification of an area enclosing a hypertext connecting the instance of entity CoreEntity1 to the instances of entities CoreEntity2 and CoreEntity3.

Figure 9.15 shows a typical hypertext built over such an interconnection sub-schema; it consists of three areas, each one centered over a specific core entity and containing one page with a central data unit showing the details of a core entity instance. From such a data unit two kinds of links may emanate: direct links to the single connected instance of a related core entity, or links to indexes of instances of a related core entity. These indexes are normally kept in the same page as the core entity instance, so that the user can access the features of the core entity and at the same time have a preview of the set of related objects.

9.4.4   Personalization Sub-schema

Personalization is a transversal feature, which results into several hypertext configurations serving different personalization-related purposes.

The key factor in the design of personalized hypertexts is the recognition of the user identity, and the delivery of functions and services based on it. The notion

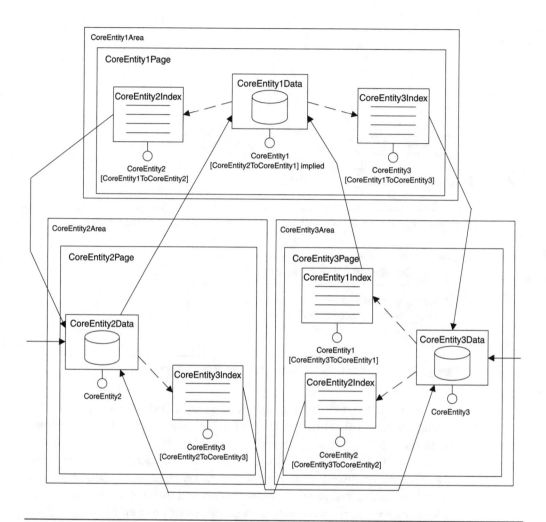

Figure 9.15   Typical hypertext associated with the interconnection sub-schema.

of user identity is interpreted in a broad sense: it may either refer to a registered user, whose personal details are recorded in the application, or to an anonymous user, who is temporarily identified by means of a session number.

Figure 9.16 recalls the form of a personalization sub-schema, which comprises the entities for modeling users, groups, and site views, and the relationships denoting the ownership and preferences of users with respect to the core objects of the application. This data schema is used for composing hypertext specifications with the following purposes:

■ Permitting the explicit collection and editing of personal profile data of users.

■ Enabling user login, credential verification, and the forwarding of the authenticated user to the appropriate site view.

■ Allowing the selective publishing and manipulation of content owned by the user or determined by preferences expressed in the user profile.

Figure 9.17 exemplifies a hypertext for user self-registration, which can be part of a site view offered to anonymous users for letting them subscribe to the

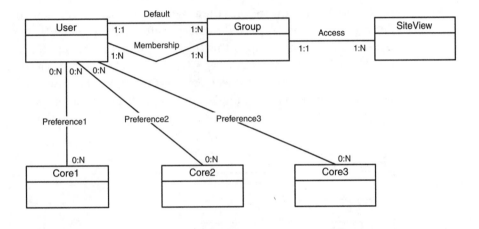

Figure 9.16 Personalization data sub-schema.

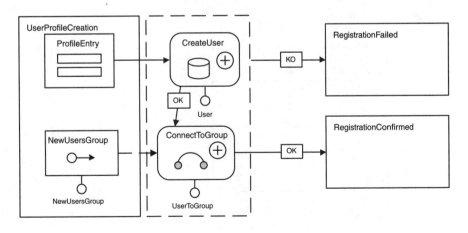

Figure 9.17 The user profile creation via a self-registration process.

application. The UserProfileCreation page contains an entry unit (ProfileEntry), whereby a user can insert his personal data, and a get unit (NewUsersGroup), which holds the OID of the specific group to which newly registered users are assigned. From the entry unit, an outgoing link activates a create and connect operation chain, which creates a new instance of entity User and connects it to the group that clusters all the newly registered users.

In an alternative to self-registration, users can be created by the administrator. In this case a hypertext similar to that of Figure 9.17 is added to the siteview of the administrator group.

The User entity can store the credentials for accessing the application and have a relationship that records the assignment of users to a default group, which determines the site view served to the user after login. Figure 9.18 represents the hypertext specification supporting the login process: a site view (PublicSiteView) is published for the generic non-registered users and includes a page (Login page), which contains an entry unit whereby users can insert their username and password. From the entry unit, a link activates the login operation, which looks up

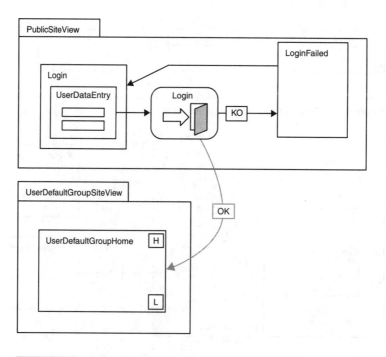

Figure 9.18   Login process modeled in WebML.

the user's default group and determines the destination site view. Then, the login operation leads the user to the home page of the site view of the default group. If the credentials of the user are invalid, the login operation displays an error page, which may include an error message and a link to the home page of the public site view.

Personalized applications provide users with content customized according to their preferences, and give the possibility of creating and managing "personal" objects. For such a form of personalization, the identity of the user currently browsing the Web application must be exploited in the selector of WebML units, to retrieve their content based on the user and on the group he/she belongs to. As already mentioned in Section 5.6.1, the two global parameters CurrentUser and CurrentGroup respectively hold the OID of the current user and group, and make them available to the units of the hypertext schema.

Figure 9.19 shows an example of personalized page, built on top of the personalization data sub-schema discussed in Chapter 8, which records data about the city where a user lives. Personalization is achieved by means of the GetUser unit, which retrieves the CurrentUser global parameter and feeds its value to the UserData unit, showing User personal information (for example, the user name). The MyCityData unit shows information about the city of the current user,

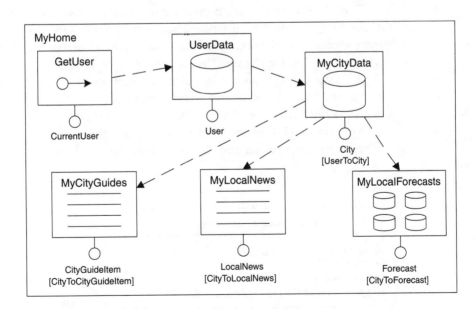

Figure 9.19 Hypertext schema with preference-based content.

thanks to a selector defined over the relationship role UserToCity, which denotes the preferred city of the user. Personalized content related to the preferred city is then published in the MyCityGuides and MyLocalNews index units, and in the MyLocalForecasts multidata unit.

9.4.5   Content Management Hypertext Sub-schema

Content management addresses the creation, deletion, or modification of entities, and the connection and disconnection of pairs of entities belonging to relationships. Content management hypertext sub-schemas are typically centered around the core objects, which can be created, deleted, and modified, connected to their components, attached to access entities, and associated with other core entities, to make the interconnection sub-schema navigable.

Figure 9.20 illustrates an area offering content management functions for creating, modifying, and deleting instances of entity CoreEntity, and for associating them to instances of the categorizing entity AccessEntity.

Figure 9.21 shows the WebML specification of a typical content management area dedicated to a core entity. The schema includes two distinct pages: one for deleting and modifying existing instances of the core entity, and one for creating new instances and associating them to a specific access entity instance.

Page CoreDelete&Modify is declared as default and landmark, and permits the user to access the core instances associated with a specific AccessEntity instance, selected from the AccessInstances index. Once a CoreEntity instance is selected and visualized in the CoreDetails unit, the user can delete or modify it.

A link departing from the AccessDetails unit leads to the CoreCreate page, where a create and connect pattern allows creating a new CoreEntity instance, and associating it to the previously selected AccessEntity instance.

The area could be extended with further pages for supporting the creation of CoreEntity components and the interconnection with other core entities.

CoreManagement Area
Access(CoreEntity,AccessEntity) Delete(CoreEntity) Modify(CoreEntity) Create&Connect(CoreEntity,AccessEntity)

Figure 9.20   Area including content management functions.

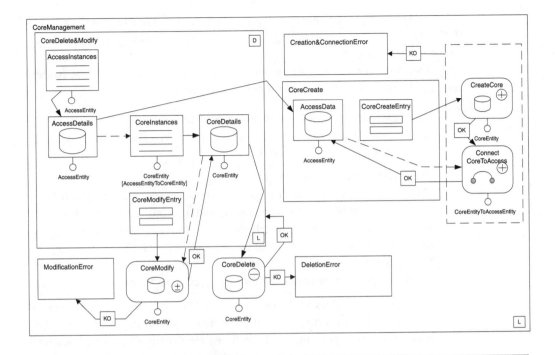

Figure 9.21 Typical hypertext for content management.

Such pages would exploit the same content management patterns illustrated in Figure 9.21.

9.4.6 Factoring Out Replicated Units Using OR Sub-pages

For a hypertext to be usable, content access must be facilitated as much as possible, by designing a rich set of navigation facilities. Access sub-schemas tend to be replicated in several pages, because users must be supported in the location of core objects in all the pages of an area. However, duplicating identical units in different pages is undesirable, because the replicated units must be implemented and maintained.

A trade-off between the usability of page design and the efficiency and maintenance requirements is granted by the appropriate use of nested sub-pages. In particular, *nested OR sub-pages* permit the designer to organize the content of a page into a fixed part (the units placed in the outer portion of the page), and a variable part, corresponding to the units placed inside the alternative OR sub-pages. The fixed part can host the access sub-schema common to all the pages of an area, eliminating the need of replicating the same units in multiple pages.

As an example, consider the access data sub-schema illustrated in Figure 9.22, where the entity Core is categorized by means of the two access entities Category and SubCategory.

The design of an area for presenting the instances of entity Core is illustrated in Figure 9.23. The area consists of three pages:

- Page1 includes an index of categories, and an entry unit representing a search form over the instances of the Core entity; a link from the Categories index unit leads to Page2.

- Page2 represents a second step for zooming into the instances of entity Core. It contains a data unit displaying the selected category, which is the destination of the link from Page1, and a second index over the access entity SubCategory, which shows the subcategories of the category selected in Page1. For improving usability, Page1 includes a duplicate of the entry unit and of the category index, so that the user can change category and perform searches without going back to Page1.

- Page3 represents the last step for accessing the instances of entity Core. It contains a data unit displaying the selected subcategory, which is the destination of the link from Page2, an index over entity Core, which shows the core instances belonging to the subcategory selected in Page2 or matching the search keyword, and a data unit displaying the details of the selected core entity instance. Page3 includes a duplicate of the entry unit and of the category index, so that the user can change category and perform searches without restarting from Page1, and a duplicate of the subcategories index computed using a get unit over the currently selected category, so that the user can change subcategory inside the current category, without going back to Page2.

As clearly illustrated in Figure 9.23, several units are duplicated to ensure that the redundant access mechanisms are available in all the pages. An equivalent hypertext, which avoids unit duplication, is illustrated in Figure 9.24. The

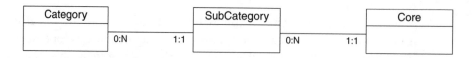

Figure 9.22   Data sub-schema with two-level access hierarchy.

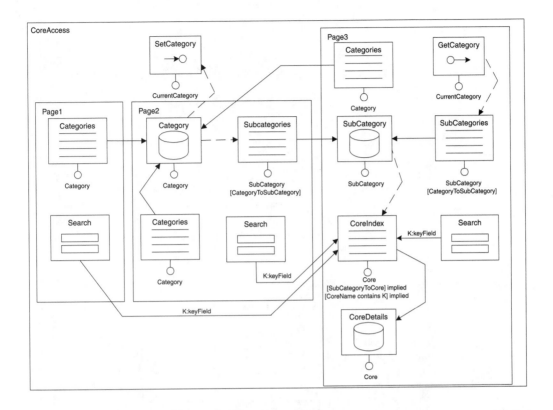

Figure 9.23   Hypertext design of an area for accessing and presenting core objects.

area now consists of a single page (Page1), which collects the units that must be visible in the entire area and are duplicated in all the three pages of Figure 9.23 (the Categories index unit and the search entry unit). The page comprises two OR sub-pages: Page1.1 is the default sub-page, and is empty or, more likely, contains some static content; this means that when Page1 is accessed only the index of categories and the search form are displayed. The second OR sub-page (Page1.2) is accessed when the user selects a category: it factors out two units (the Category data unit and the SubCategories index unit), which are common to two nested alternative sub-pages. Page1.2.1 is empty or contains static content, and is displayed by default. Page1.2.2 contains the selected subcategory, the index of core instances, and the details of the selected core instance. Thanks to the nesting of pages, when accessing the page with the details of the core instance, also the common units are visible, and the user can change category and subcategory.

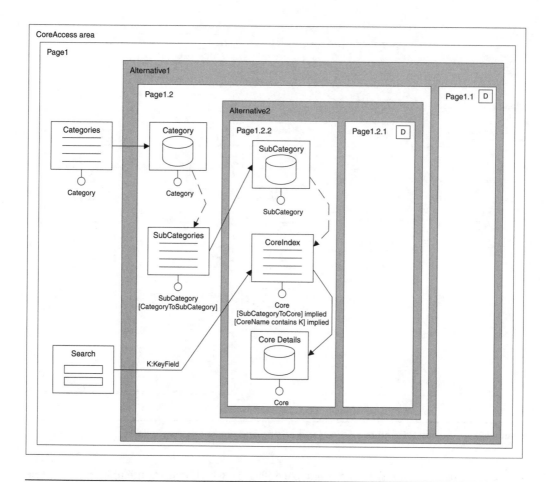

Figure 9.24   Revised hypertext design using nested OR sub-pages.

9.5 Running Example

In this section we will describe the hypertext design of a limited portion of the Acer-Euro application, the External Users site view, whose requirements specification and data design have already been introduced in Chapters 7 and 8.

9.5.1 External Users Site View

The External Users site view publishes contents about products and news targeted to the users of a specific country. It consists of four areas, called Home, What's New,

Products, and About Us, and its site map is shown in Chapter 7. The About Us area consists of one only page containing static content that illustrates the company mission and will not be discussed further. The coarse design of the site view, specifying the visibility and content of each one of the other three areas, appears in Figure 9.25.

The content of each area depends on the initial choice of the country, because content is translated into the local language. When the application is accessed, the current country is explicitly chosen by the user by means of a European home page, not modeled in this running example, or implicitly deduced by the URL typed by the user into the browser, thanks to a mapping from external addresses of the form *http://www.acer.XX* to internal URLs including a query string parameter corresponding to the country with attribute Isocode equal to the string "XX".

When the Home area of a specific country is accessed, the OID of the country is stored in a global parameter, to be reused in the other pages of the site view. The Home area also provides two alternative access mechanisms for reaching the instances of the NewsItem entity, and one for reaching the instances of the Product entity. The What's New and Products areas focus on the NewsItem and Product core entities, respectively, and permit the user to access and browse the

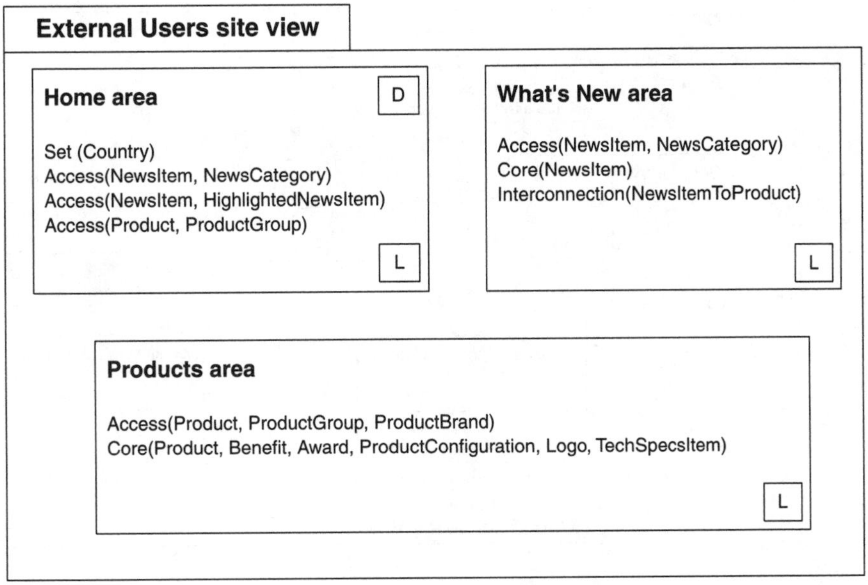

External Users site view

Home area   D

Set (Country)
Access(NewsItem, NewsCategory)
Access(NewsItem, HighlightedNewsItem)
Access(Product, ProductGroup)

                                                 L

What's New area

Access(NewsItem, NewsCategory)
Core(NewsItem)
Interconnection(NewsItemToProduct)

                                                 L

Products area

Access(Product, ProductGroup, ProductBrand)
Core(Product, Benefit, Award, ProductConfiguration, Logo, TechSpecsItem)

                                                 L

Figure 9.25 Coarse design for the External Users site view.

instances of these core objects. The What's New area also supports the interconnection between news items and products.

The *Home area,* elected as the default area of the External Users site view, contains a single page, whose detailed hypertext schema is illustrated in Figure 9.26. A central data unit over entity Country (CurrentCountry) holds the OID of the current country, which is used in the selector of several indexes of objects pertinent to the current country (LocalProductGroups, LocalNewsCategories, LocalHighlightedNews). The Home page also includes the index of all the other countries, for changing the current country and correspondingly the visualized content. The index of countries is replicated in all the other pages of the site view, and linked to the Country data unit in the Home page. A set unit is used to "record" the OID of the current country when the home page of a particular

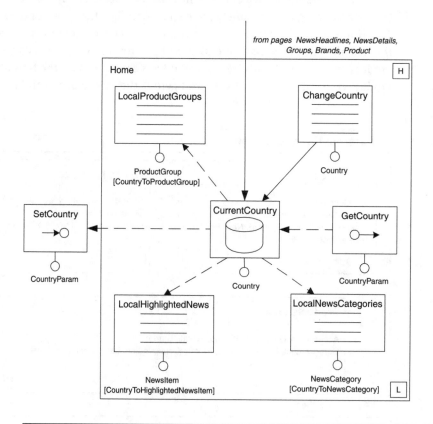

Figure 9.26 Detailed hypertext schema of the Home area of the External Users site view.

country is entered; then, a get unit feeds the OID of the current country to the CurrentCountry data unit, when the home page is accessed from the other areas.

The rendition of the home page of the UK national Web site of the Acer-Euro application, having URL *http://www.acer.uk,* is shown in Figure 9.27.

The *What's New area* publishes content about news items, grouped into news categories. It is a landmark area, reachable from all the other site view areas. The area consists of two pages: the NewsHeadlines page, supporting the access to news items by means of news categories, and the NewsDetails page, showing the detailed content of a single piece of news. Figure 9.28 shows the content of the two pages and their visibility.

Figure 9.29 shows the detailed design of the NewsHeadlines page. The page is the default of the area and provides only access mechanisms for reaching the core objects managed in the area. In particular, it includes a cascaded index pattern constructed on top of the access sub-schema defined by the Country, NewsCategory, and NewsItem entities, and the ChangeCountry index, which

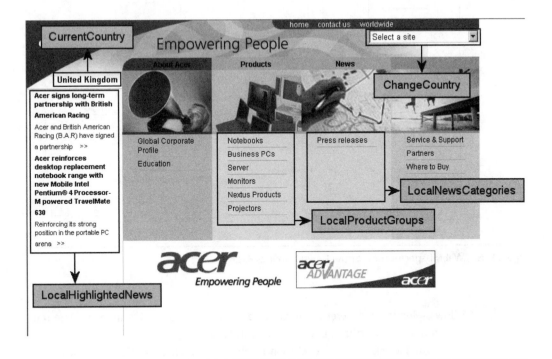

Figure 9.27   Home page of the UK site of the Acer-Euro application.

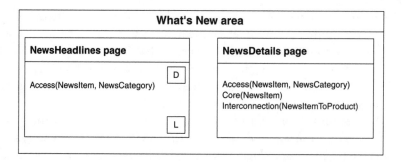

Figure 9.28   Page identification and visibility for the What's New area.

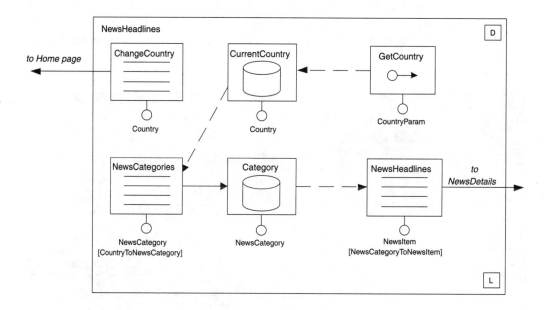

Figure 9.29   WebML specification of the NewsHeadlines Page.

allows selecting a different country and going back to the Home page. The rendition of NewsHeadlines page is shown in Figure 9.30.

The NewsDetails page, shown in Figure 9.31, displays the core content of the area. It is built using a very simple core hypertext sub-schema centered on the NewsItem entity, which has no sub-components. The page also includes a replica

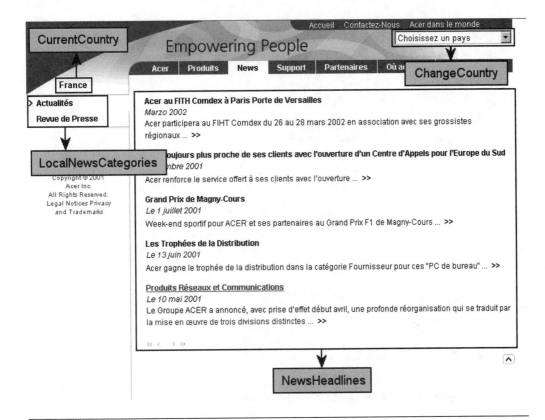

Figure 9.30   Rendition of the NewsHeadlines page.

of the index of local news categories, whereby the user can access the news of a different category without stepping back to the NewsHeadlines page, and an interconnection sub-schema between the core objects NewsItem and Product, represented by the RelatedProducts index; the selection of an item from this index leads to the Products area, specifically to a product associated with the current news item by the NewsItemToProduct relationship role. Finally, the page comprises the index for selecting another country. The rendition of the NewsDetails page is shown in Figure 9.32.

The *Products area* publishes the information about the products of the currently selected country. It is organized into four pages: Groups page, Brands page, Product page, and TechSpecs page. The first two pages realize an access hypertext sub-schema built on top of the entities Country, ProductGroup, and ProductBrand. The last two pages are instead devoted to browsing the Product

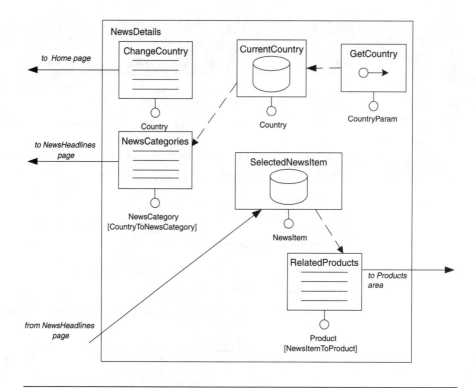

Figure 9.31   WebML specification of the NewsDetails page.

core entity. Figure 9.33 shows how the functionalities of the area are distributed among the four pages.

To facilitate access to products, the Groups and Brands pages allow a step-wise selection of a product through the product groups and product brands of the current country. In particular, the Groups page, whose WebML schema is shown in Figure 9.34, is the default page for the Products area, and provides the entry point of the access sub-schema defined over the categorizing entities Country, ProductGroup, and Brand. The page includes a get unit containing the OID of the current country previously set in the Home page. The OID of the country is used for retrieving the name of the current country in the CurrentCountry data unit, and for populating the index of product groups of the current country, from which a contextual link leads to the Brands page, opened on the chosen group. The usual index for changing the country is also included.

The rendition of Groups page is shown in Figure 9.35.

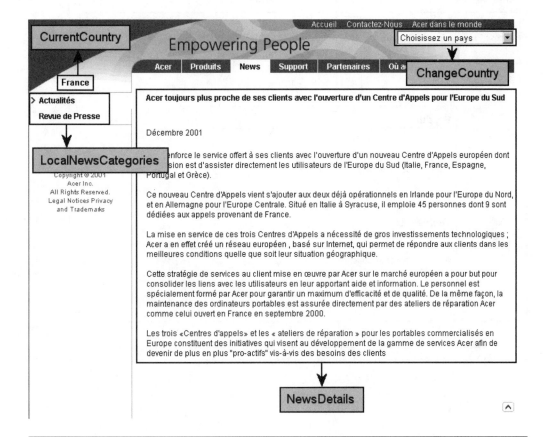

Figure 9.32 Rendition of the NewsDetails page.

The Brands page is accessed by clicking on one of the product groups shown on the left in Figure 9.35. The WebML schema of the page, shown in Figure 9.36, includes the ProductGroup data unit, which is the destination unit of the link from the Groups page. This data unit is linked to two hierarchical indexes, showing all the brands of the selected group, and all the products of each brand. These two hierarchical index units represent the prosecution of the access sub-schema started in page Groups page, whereby the user progressively reaches the actual product he/she is interested in. The page also includes a replica of the index of groups for the current country (ProductGroups), which can be used to select another group, without returning back to the Groups page. This secondary access pattern exploits a get unit containing the OID of the current

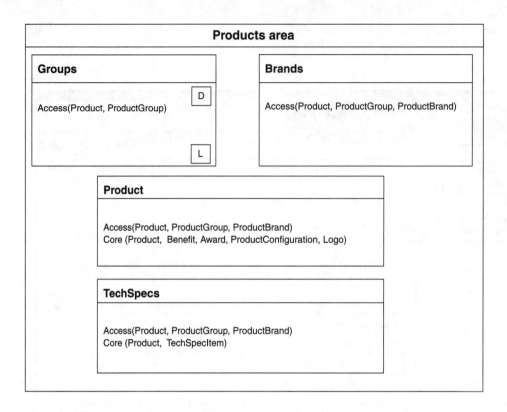

Figure 9.33 Page identification and visibility for the Products area.

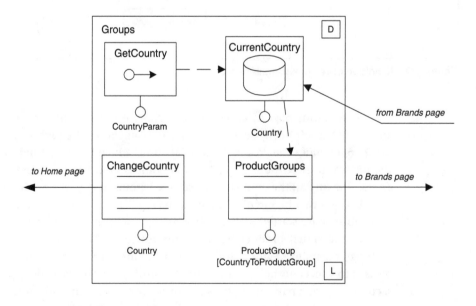

Figure 9.34 WebML schema of the Groups page.

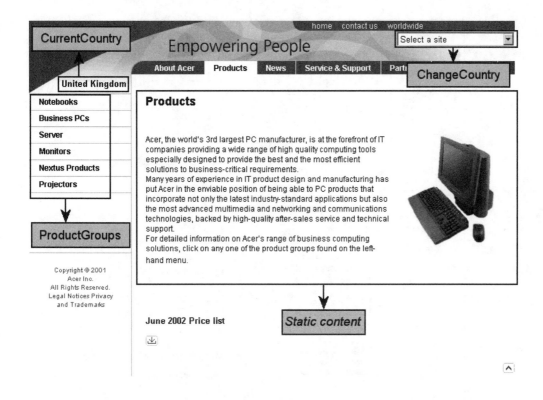

Figure 9.35   Groups page of the UK Web site.

country, which is passed to the CurrentCountry data unit, and from this unit down to the Groups index unit. The get unit ensures that the selection of the current country is preserved when accessing the Brands page, so that the content of the ProductGroups index unit reflects the past user selection in the Home page. Finally, a set unit is exploited to record the OID of the currently visualized group. This solution is analogous to the memorization of the OID of the current country in the Home page and permits recording the user's selections during the progressive "descent" toward the page that displays the details of a product.

The rendition of the Brands page is shown in Figure 9.37. Note that the reason why the hierarchical index over Product is repeated twice is that the list of products is displayed both in the left navigation bar and in the central area of the page, with different attributes. Clicking on the name of a product in the left index or in the central area of the screen leads to the ProductPage, opened on the selected product.

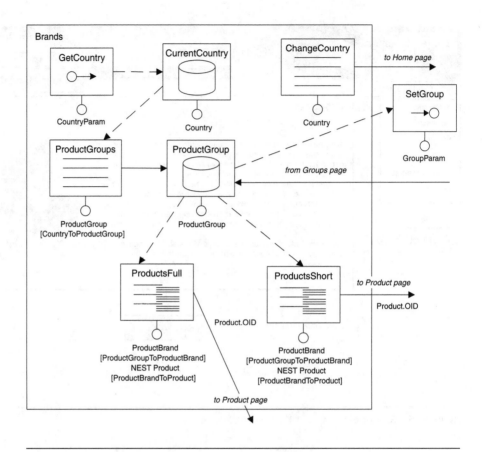

Figure 9.36   WebML schema of Brands page.

The Product page displays the details of a selected product, together with some of its internal components, namely benefits, configurations, logos, and awards (if any). The technical specifications are published separately in the TechSpecs page.

The WebML schema of the Product page, shown in Figure 9.38, contains a classical core hypertext sub-schema, consisting of a central data unit over the core entity Product, linked to several multidata units detailing the various features of a product.

The page also contains two redundant access sub-schemas, for quickly changing the current group and product; these access sub-schemas exploit the

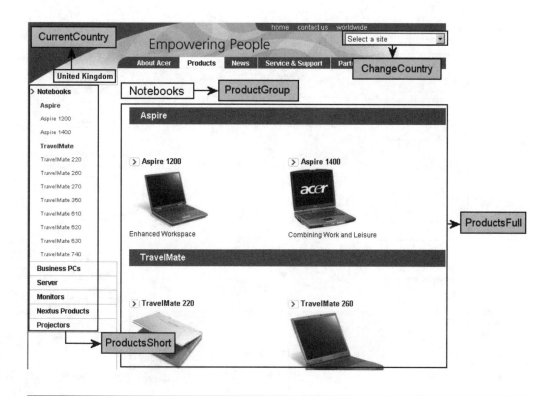

Figure 9.37 The Brands page, open on the Notebooks group.

previously saved country and group OID, to rebuild the index of product groups of the current country and the nested index of brands and products of the current group. The outgoing link exiting the ProductGroups index points back to the Brands page, and the outgoing link of the hierarchical index unit changes the visualized product. A link departing from the Product data unit leads to the TechSpecs page, which contains a multidata unit defined over the tech specs items for the selected product. Finally, the Product page includes the usual index of countries, with an outgoing link pointing back to the Home page.

The rendition of Product page is reported in Figure 9.39, where the most relevant content units are highlighted.

To conclude the illustration of the running example, we show two examples of use of OR sub-pages for factoring out common patterns of units. Consider again the pages of the What's New area, whose WebML schemas are shown in

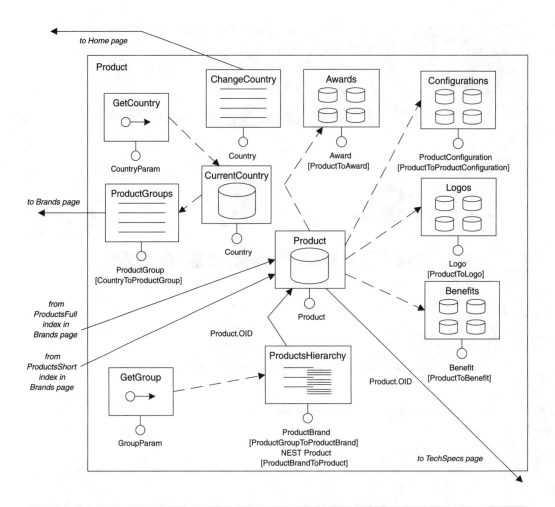

Figure 9.38 WebML schema of the Product page.

Figure 9.29 and Figure 9.31. Both pages include two replicated patterns of units: the access sub-schema consisting of the CurrentCountry data unit and of the NewsCategories index unit, and the index unit for changing the current country. A more efficient design can be achieved by factoring out the replicated units using OR sub-pages. As shown in Figure 9.40, a top-level page is introduced in the What's News area (NewsBrowsing), which contains the replicated units, that is, the index of countries, the data unit of the current country and the index unit of the local news categories. The NewsBrowsing page includes also two nested OR

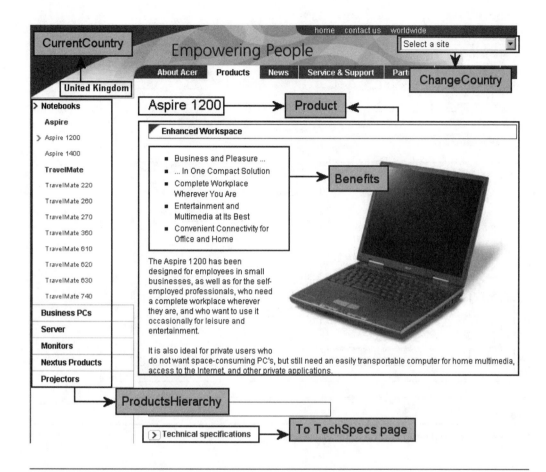

Figure 9.39 The Product page, open on the Aspire 1200 product.

sub-pages, respectively containing the news headlines and the news details. In this way, the index of countries and the index of local news categories appear both when reading the headlines (Figure 9.30) and when reading an individual piece of news (Figure 9.32).

As shown in Figure 9.41, OR sub-pages can be also adopted for refining the design of the Products area, in which the common features of the three pages Groups page, Brands page, and Product page, respectively represented in Figure 9.34, Figure 9.36, and Figure 9.38, are factored out using OR sub-pages. The resulting schema has a single page, which includes the index of countries, the CurrentCountry data unit, and the index of local product groups, which are the

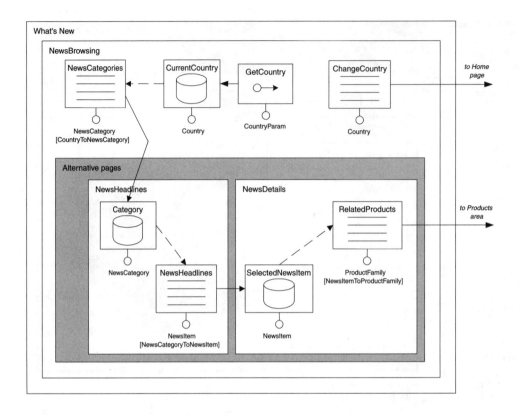

Figure 9.40   Revised design of the What's New area.

common content units. Then, two alternative OR sub-pages are introduced, with the units necessary for displaying the specific content of Brands page and Product page. After the redesign of the pages, the final hypertext schema of the Home, What's New, and Products areas of the External Users site view is represented by the pages shown in Figure 9.26, Figure 9.40, and Figure 9.41.

9.6   Designing Usable Hypertexts

Usability is a fundamental quality factor of software systems, particularly relevant in Web applications, where it is essential to attract users and facilitate them in visiting a site.

Hypertext usability may be enhanced by carefully choosing the most suitable patterns of pages and units, based on the user requirements and on the func-

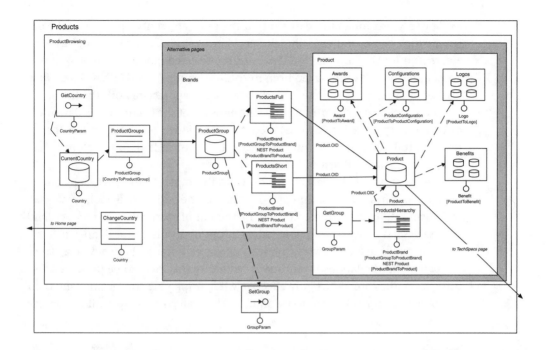

Figure 9.41   Revised design of the Products area, using OR sub-pages.

tion delivered by a page or area. In the rest of this chapter, we briefly overview some criteria for improving the usability of data-intensive Web applications and show them at work in pages of real Web sites.

9.6.1   Choice of Access and Core Patterns

As already discussed, the access to the core content of a Web application is supported by dedicated hypertext configurations, which allow users to progressively reach the objects they are looking for. When one object is located, the most appropriate hypertext configuration must be designed for presenting its content. In principle, any of the content publishing patterns illustrated in Chapter 3 can be used, but the choice of the most appropriate solution must take into account the structure and meaning of data, and the user requirements.

Multidata and plain index units are best used when the number of instances to show is limited, and when such instances are described by means of few attributes (typically, some descriptive properties for an index, and an image and some explanatory text for a multidata unit). If the unit represents a preview of the objects, which can be individually selected, then an index must be used, linked to a data unit for showing the full details of the selected object. Figure 9.42 shows an example of index unit taken from the online front page of *The New York Times*. The set of latest news is presented: the reader can appreciate both the list of latest news, which gives him/her a quick impression of the events of the day, and a brief summary of each individual piece of news, which may prompt him/her to read the full details in the internal pages. Each object is then linked to a data unit, showing the full text of the piece of news.

A *hierarchical index* pattern can be fruitfully employed to convey a hierarchy of logical or physical containment. For example, the outline of a book or tutorial, the organization chart of a company, or the bill of materials of a product lend themselves naturally to be represented by means of the hierarchical index pattern.

Hierarchical indexes are extremely expressive, because they show at a glance the parent-child relationships of the set of entity instances to be presented. For this reason, they are particularly effective when displaying core entities and their components, and chains of access indexes that categorize core entities. On the

Figure 9.42   Index pattern from the online front page of *The New York Times*.

other hand, computing a hierarchical index is generally expensive, because the corresponding query must exploit table joins to reconstruct the parent-child relationships. If the hierarchical index is recursive, the computation is even more expensive, because the number of levels is not known a priori, and must be determined at runtime. If the hierarchical data sets to be presented are not too large or do not change too frequently (so that the application pages can be cached) the hierarchical index pattern is the preferable choice for presenting nested data. Figure 9.43 shows an example taken from the Microsoft Developer Network online library, where technical articles are hierarchically organized based on their subjects. The left frame of the page permits the user to browse the article hierarchy, while the right frame displays the currently selected article. In this case, the nesting of instances according to their part-of relationship using a hierarchical index is the best way of organizing a large collection of resources.

As an alternative to hierarchical index, access paths over large sets of instances can be presented by means of a cascaded index pattern. A cascaded index has the advantage of letting the user reach the object(s) of interest by progressively selecting instances of some access entities. At each selection step, the user has a preview of the existing instances of the access entity, and can choose the instance that leads towards his/her search objective.

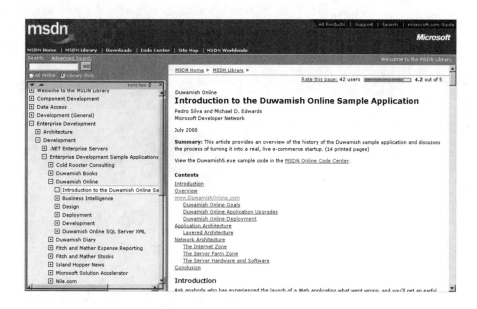

Figure 9.43   Hierarchical index pattern from the Microsoft Developer Network library.

Figure 9.44 shows an example of *cascaded index pattern* from the popular Lonely Planet traveling Web site. A destination is selected by using two cascaded indexes. The first index permits the user to select the region of the world he/she is interested in. After a region is selected, the second index shows the list of destinations for that region.

9.6.2   Navigation Aids

Navigation aids are all those auxiliary mechanisms that help users in exploring the Web site, by providing access shortcuts to the most important areas and pages. The first aid to navigation is the proper definition of the hierarchical structure of the site view, which is specified using areas, sub-areas, and the landmark, default, and home properties.

Area and page landmarks permit the definition of *navigation bars,* which group the links pointing to the landmarks; navigation bars can be global to the entire site view, when they refer to the top level areas, or local to a specific area, when they point to the landmark pages of the area. Figure 9.45 shows the navigation bar of the Amazon Web site, which includes a set of global landmark links, available in every page of the site, and a set of local landmark links, providing access to the landmark pages of the currently selected area (Books in the figure).

In large applications navigation shortcuts can be designed to reach the pages that are accessed most frequently, or pages that are too deep in the hierarchies

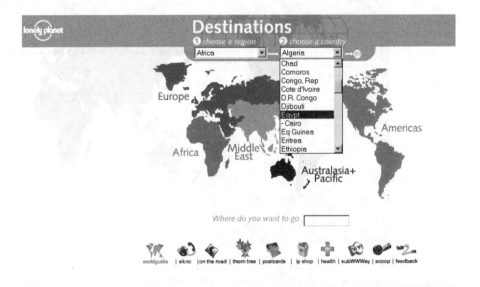

Figure 9.44   Multi-step index pattern from the Lonely Planet Web site.

defined using cascaded indexes. Such shortcuts are generally offered in the home page, with the aim of reducing the number of navigation steps. Depending on the information to be highlighted, different design solutions can be adopted. For example, sub-entities in the data schema can be used to create collections (like the best-selling products in an e-commerce site) presented as indexes in the home page.

Figure 9.46 shows two examples of shortcut index, which facilitate access to special products, such as new releases or recommended books.

Figure 9.45   Navigation bar within the Amazon Web site.

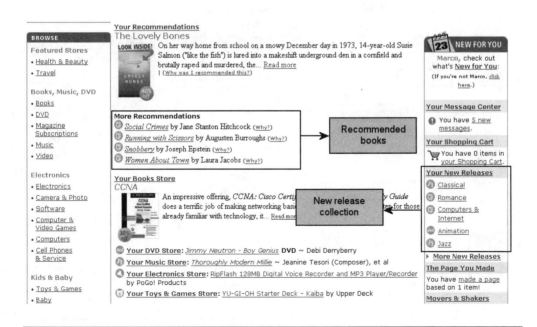

Figure 9.46   Shortcuts defined in the Amazon home page.

9.6.3   Orientation Aids

Orientation refers to the possibility of the user of evaluating the actual status of his navigation, and the position of the current page within the global structure of the hypertext.

A simple mechanism for improving orientation is to assign meaningful titles to pages and links that hint at the content that can be found in the current page, or reached by following a link.

User orientation can also be enhanced by the appropriate use of *breadcrumb links,* which are textual anchors placed in a visible region of the page that mirror the hierarchy of pages whose navigation led the user to the current point; breadcrumb links show the followed navigation path and help the user tracing his navigation steps.

Figure 9.47 shows the breadcrumb links in the Amazon Web site: the current page of the Books area, which displays books in the Database Design category, has been reached by browsing through different pages related to book categories and subcategories.

Orientation is relevant also to the navigation of the objects belonging to an ordered collection. Plain or indexed *guided tours* can be used for this purpose. As

Figure 9.47   Use of breadcrumbs links within the Amazon Web site.

already described in Chapter 3, a guided tour exploits a scroller unit, which provides browsing commands ("to the previous," "to the next," "to the first," "to the last," etc.), and shows the currently reached position in the sequence ("3 of 10"). The use of guided tours is particularly effective when there is the need for immediately showing a representative object of the collection, and when there is a very "strong" criterion for ordering the instances, so that the user can immediately grasp the meaning of going to the previous or next element in the sequence.

Figure 9.48 shows an example of an *indexed guided tour,* from the archive Web site of the dbworld mailing list, a very popular mailing list of the database community. Each message is displayed together with the commands to scroll to the previous/next one. The sorting of the archive is based on the time at which messages are posted to the mailing list, so that the meaning of "next" is immediate.

9.6.4 Search

In large data-intensive Web applications it is essential to provide search facilities, to let users bypass navigation and rapidly zoom in to the desired object. Keyword search is a very popular access mechanism, but it is also a double-edge sword: if the data items are well characterized by a few descriptive keywords, so that the expected precision of the search results is high, searching is the most concise and

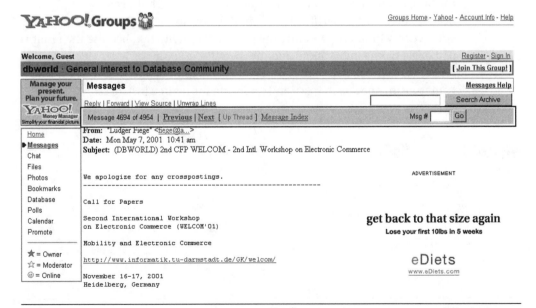

Figure 9.48 Indexed guided tour pattern from the archive Web site of the dbworld mailing list.

intuitive access mechanism. However, if data content is generic and the average number of irrelevant results can be expected to be high, then search tends to become frustrating, and navigation-based access paradigms are preferable.

Another fundamental observation before deciding on a search-based pattern is the heterogeneity of the content elements over which the search is performed. If the user-supplied keywords are to be searched in the instances of a single entity, it is then easy to present an index of results with homogeneous entries, so that when the user selects one entry it is possible to present him/her a page with both the details of the instance containing the searched keywords and its "semantic context" (for example, indexes to related concepts). Conversely, if the search is performed "blindly" on all the objects of the application, it is more difficult to present a list of homogeneous results, and reconstruct the semantic context of the retrieved item.

As a general rule, a well-designed access schema, with a rich set of categorization entities and special collections, should make it easy for the designer to provide hypertext design patterns based on the structural and relational properties of data, making keyword-based search a secondary access mechanism. However, when the scope of the search and the subject of the content are well defined and not too broad, keyword search may be the primary and most effective access mechanism. For example, Figure 9.49 shows an example of *filtered index pattern* taken from the digital library of the ACM Software Interest Group on Database Systems (ACM Sigmod). The library hosts a huge collection of technical and scientific publications on a very well defined topic. In this case, using a search form is the most effective way of directly locating the publication of interest, because the result is of a single type (a publication) and the specialist user can easily provide meaningful keywords (for instance, the last name of an author or a technical term), which help reducing the search space and retrieving the desired instances.

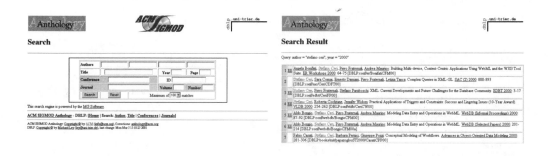

Figure 9.49 Filtered index pattern from the ACM Sigmod Anthology.

In case of large amount of data matching the search condition, a *filtered scrolled index* can be used for organizing results in different pages and avoid scrolling a long index on a unique page. An example of filtered scrolled index is shown in Figure 9.50, which reproduces a page from the Yahoo search engine, presenting the results of a keyword-based search. Twenty items per page are displayed, and scrolling commands allow moving through the result pages.

9.6.5 Consistency

Consistency is a fundamental principle of good design, and means that conceptually similar problems should be given comparable solutions. Referring to hypertext organization, the consistent use of composition and navigational patterns help users build reliable expectations about how to access information and perform operations, by applying past experience to predict the organization of an unfamiliar part of the application. Consistency applies not only to composition and navigation, but also to presentation, and in particular to the layout of pages. As will be further discussed in Chapter 13, presentation consistency can be greatly enhanced by using standard presentation rules, possibly embodied in CSS and XSL style sheets uniformly applied to all the pages of the application.

As an example of the importance of consistent page design, Figure 9.51 and 9.52 show two pages taken from the Cisco Web site. Both pages belong to the

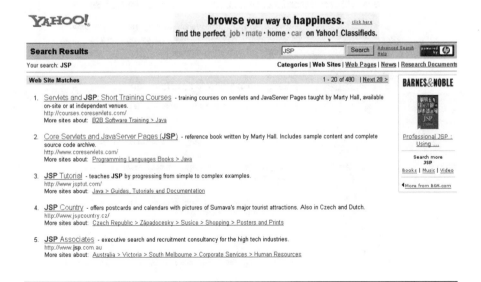

Figure 9.50   Presentation of search results in Yahoo.

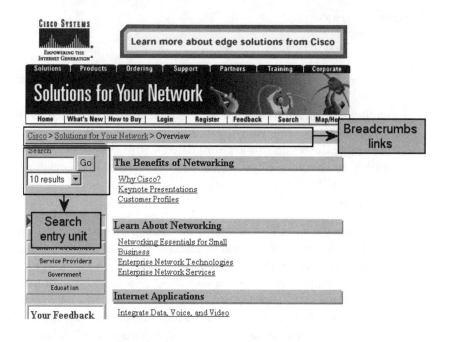

Figure 9.51 A page from the Solution area of the Cisco Web site.

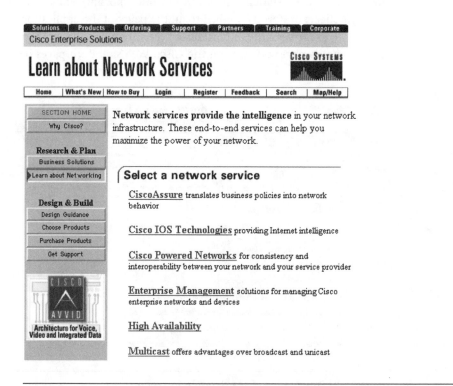

Figure 9.52 A second page from the Solution area of the Cisco Web site.

Solution area, which presents content about Cisco solutions. The page shown in Figure 9.51 includes breadcrumbs links, supporting user orientation, and an entry unit for keyword-based search. Other pages in the same area, as shown in Figure 9.52, do not include comparable features, although they address similar publishing and navigation requirements.

9.7 Hypertext Modeling for Multi-Device Applications

Site views may also serve the purpose of expressing alternative forms of content presentation targeted to different devices. Each site view may cluster information and services at the granularity most suitable to the rendition capabilities of a particular class of devices. To better appreciate this aspect, let us consider two versions of the CDNOW site used as a running example in the first part of the book, respectively available at the address *www.cdnow.com* and *wap.cdnow.com*. Both sites present information about artists and their albums, with the objective of selling them to customers. However, the two versions are accessed with different devices (the PC and a WAP-enabled cellular phone) and thus are very different:

- The HTML version of Web site, for personal computers, provides extensive information about musical albums and artists, and the site attracts also those users that do not want to buy albums but are interested in music.

- The WML version, addressed to WAP phones, provides very concise information about records, and is conceived for purchasers. Given the difficulty of browsing with a small screen, the hypertext is much simpler, and the interactions required to locate a given title are minimized.

The different organization of the two versions can be appreciated in Figure 9.53, where the home pages are contrasted.

Figure 9.54 shows the rendition of the same content (the list of albums available for a given artist) in the Web and the WAP version of the site. The WAP page is much simpler, and omits the links to the additional content not directly aimed at buying the product, such as the artist's biography, reviews and news, album tracks, etc., which are instead provided in the Web page.

The hypertext schema of the WAP application is described in Figure 9.55. The hypertext consists of three simple pages. The user is presented with a data entry unit for searching artists, followed by an index unit showing the names of artists, produced by the search. Finally, a page shows all the artist's albums, in a multidata unit. Compared with the hypertext of Chapter 3, describing the HTML version of the CDNOW Web site, it is easy to see that WAP pages are much simpler and consist of at most one or two units.

Figure 9.53 The home page of the CDNOW sites for PCs and for cellular phones.

Figure 9.54 The pages displaying albums in the CDNOW sites for PCs and for cellular phones.

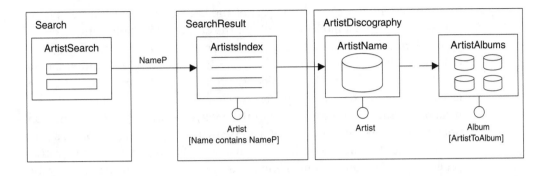

Figure 9.55 Hypertext of the WAP CDNOW application.

Hypertext modeling can be applied to multi-channel applications, by devising the site view structures most suited to the specific delivery medium. WAP is only one of the channels that can be used in alternative to the traditional Web browsers. The same design approach would apply to Web sites for PDAs, or for the digital television, by taking into account the specific requirements and constraints of each device with respect to the amount of information that can be placed within pages, and to the complexity of navigation. Once the hypertext schema for each device is established, producing the actual pages in the proper markup language, which can be HTML, WML or any other language, is a matter of implementation. In Chapter 13 we will address advanced techniques based on the use of XSL, which ease the production of markup code for multi-device applications.

Summary

This chapter concludes the third part of the book, in which we have discussed how the modeling concepts of Entity Relationship and WebML integrate in the "upper" part of the development process of a data-intensive Web application. In particular, we have shown the activities involved in the collection and formalization of the application requirements, and how these requirements are progressively turned into a more and more precise model of the application to be developed. In this chapter, we have zoomed in on the transformation of requirements into WebML hypertexts, according to a two-step process: first a coarse hypertext is drafted, and next it is turned into a detailed specification. We have also discussed a number of guidelines and design principles to make hypertext design more effective.

The essential aspect of this part of the book is the significant emphasis placed on conceptual modeling, both for the data and for the hypertexts of the application. The reason for this emphasis is that all the most important design decisions that do not depend on the physical architecture of the application should be taken during data and hypertext design, and expressed formally and at a high level. The resulting data and hypertext schemas are a fundamental piece of specification. As shown in the next part of the book, they drive the implementation phase; even more important, they are essential for application evolution and maintenance. If changes occur in the requirements, having a high quality, precise, yet easy to understand documentation of the application is key to mastering the implementation of changes, which must be planned and designed at the conceptual level and, only when fully understood, applied to the implementation code. In the last part of this book, we will show how implementation proceeds, once the conceptual model of the application is established.

Bibliographic Notes

Conceptual hypertext design is a novel discipline, and the available literature on this matter is still rather limited. Web design has been addressed from a different perspective, more oriented towards the communication issue of design-in-the-small. A number of books focus for example on page design, by introducing processes and methods for the effective production of HTML pages. Such methods are generally based on the principles of visual communication and interaction design, and adapt them to the features of Web design. For example, Sano proposes a number of visual design techniques for Web sites, to visually reflect a given organizational framework identified during a preliminary design preparation phase [Sano96].

The already mentioned book by Conallen [Conallen00] addresses the hypertext design phase as well. Conallen's approach is based on the Web Application Extension of UML, conceived for modeling Web applications independently of implementation details. Web pages are represented as UML components, by specifying both their server-side aspects (like their relationship with middle tiers, databases, and other resources) and their client-side aspects (like their relationships with browsers, Java applets, ActiveX controls and so on). The proposed UML-based approach is different from the conceptual hypertext modeling of WebML, because the UML representation of pages is still bound to a low-level vision of the hypertext.

Conceptual hypertext modeling is a subject intensely investigated also by the research community. WebML is the product of more than one decade of research on the subject of hypertext and hypermedia design, which has produced a wealth of new ideas, design notations, development methods, and prototype development tools. An overview of the various proposals can be found in [Fraternali99].

Among the pioneering works on hypermedia modeling, the HDM language [GPS91, GMP93, GPS93, GMP95] introduced a notion of model-based design, clearly separating the activities of authoring in-the-large (hypertext schema design) and authoring in-the-small (page and content production). Another influential work is RMM [ISB95], which proposed a hypermedia modeling language built upon the Entity-Relationship model, supported by a seven-step hypermedia design lifecycle in the tradition of software engineering. RMM also included guidelines for the typical hypermedia design tasks.

Among the recent proposals, Araneus [AMM97, AMM98], a project developed by researchers of Università di Roma Tre, aims at defining an environment for managing unstructured and structured Web content in an integrated system, called Web Base Management System (WBMS). Araneus adopts a mix of database and hypermedia concepts, both in the modeling notations and in the development lifecycle. The structure of the application domain is described by means of the Entity-Relationship model, whereas the navigation aspects of the application are specified using the Navigation Conceptual Model (NCM). Conceptual modeling is followed by logical design, using the relational model for the structural part, and the Araneus Data Model (ADM) for the navigation aspects. ADM is based on the notion of page scheme, a language-independent page description notation based on such elements as attributes, lists, link anchors, and forms. Development proceeds according to a structured process organized along two tracks: database and hypertext. Database design and implementation are conducted using the Entity-Relationship model and mapping it into relational structures. Hypertext design consists of conceptual modeling, which formalizes navigation by turning the Entity-Relationship schema into a NCM schema, and of hypertext logical design, which maps the NCM schema into ADM page-schemes. Finally, implementation requires writing page-schemes as declarations in the Penelope language, which specifies how physical pages are constructed from logical page schemes and content stored in a database.

Another innovative proposal is the Strudel project of AT&T Labs [FFL98], which aims at experimenting a novel way of developing Web sites based on the declarative specification of the site's structure and content. In Strudel both the schema and the content of a site are described by means of a set of queries over a data model for semi-structured information. Content is represented using the Uniform Graph Model, a graph-based data model capable of describing objects with partial or missing schema. The design of a Web site is done in a declarative way, by writing one or more queries over the internal representation of data, using the Strudel query language (StruQL). Such queries identify the data to be included in the site, and the links and collections of objects to be provided for navigation. In this way, Strudel separates the description of content from the definition of the structure and navigation of the site. Presentation is added as a separate dimension by means of HTML templates, which specify the rendering of the site definition queries in HTML.

Much emphasis has been recently posed over usability engineering, as a new design paradigm able to increase the acceptance of applications by users. The proposed methods encourage incorporating explicit usability goals during the design process, because the less expensive way for obtaining usable applications is to address usability requirements early in the development process. Sources about usability engineering are some classical Human-Computer Interaction books [Nielsen93, PRSBHC94, DFAB98]. A recent book by Nielsen [Nielsen00] proposes a comprehensive guide to usability engineering for Web sites. The book discusses many usability principles and guidelines about page layout organization, content, and access design, which derive from the analysis of experimental data collected by observing a large number of Web users. The reader's comprehension is facilitated by a large number of examples taken from real sites, which show critical situations to be avoided when designing Web applications.

IV PART

IMPLEMENTATION OF WEB APPLICATIONS

10 Architecture Design

10.1 Introduction

Architecture design marks a change of viewpoint in the development process. Compared to requirements collection and data and hypertext design, which focus on the progressive specification of the application, architecture design concentrates on the choice of the hardware, network, and software components that make up the system, to find the mix of these components that best meets the application requirements, and at the same time respects the technical and economic constraints of the project.

As Chapter 1 pointed out, a data-intensive Web application relies on many different technical ingredients, including protocols, languages, and software systems, which do not always fit together well. This heterogeneity makes architecture design a complex task, which requires mastering a large spectrum of problems and solutions. The work of the designer is driven by such technical objectives as performance, scalability, availability, state preservation, and security, and is constrained by economical and organizational factors, including the availability and skill of human resources, the allowed costs, the outsourcing policies, the availability of hardware and software licenses, and so on. In this chapter, we do not consider the organizational factors, and concentrate instead on the technical aspects of architecture design.

Rather than proposing a comprehensive checklist of the decisions to consider in architecture design or discussing formal methods for sizing up the architecture, we proceed pragmatically, by contrasting a number of *increasingly sophisticated architectures,* ranging from the simple single-host solution, sufficient for small applications, to a four-layer, fully replicated configuration, suitable to large applications with heavy workloads and strict availability requirements. The progression from each architecture schema to the next one introduces a new server or architecture layer, and/or increases the level of replication of one of the existing layers. Each configuration is analyzed with respect to the various design objectives.

We complete the chapter with an overview of the techniques for *testing and improving performance,* which are one of the most challenging topics of architecture design. In particular, we pay special attention to *caching,* a very promising technology for enhancing performance with low-cost infrastructures.

Although in most real-life situations the architecture is decided at project start, and possibly revised after completing data and hypertext design, we have delayed the discussion of architecture design after the analysis and design phases, just prior to introducing implementation. This choice underlines the architecture-independence of the activities of data and hypertext design, which can be conducted at a high level, whereas the subsequent tasks of data and hypertext implementation are closer to the physical level, and thus depend on the architectural choices.[1]

The rest of the book zooms in on the various components of the architectures illustrated in this chapter, and shows how to "fill" them with the implementation of a data-intensive application.

---

[1]Quite luckily, the progress of technologies and standards is making implementation less architecture-dependent, because different software platforms and development environments are converging toward common features, and the non-homogeneous aspects are hidden by interoperability products.

- Chapter 11 focuses on the data tier, and shows how to fit the data schema of the Web application inside the existing enterprise information system.

- Chapter 12 discusses the middle tier, and focuses on the implementation of WebML hypertexts; it illustrates how to dynamically publish content using page templates, and how to update data through operations.

- Chapter 13 extends the solutions discussed in Chapter 12 to exploit advanced software solutions, namely the Model-View-Controller (MVC) design pattern, distributed business objects (specifically, Enterprise Java Beans), and XSL presentation rules.

- Finally, Chapter 14 demonstrates a CASE tool embodying most of the discussed implementation techniques for mastering the complexity of large data-intensive Web applications.

Although less present than in the first chapters of the book, the Entity-Relationship (E-R) and WebML models play an important role also in this conclusive part. They guide developers during implementation by offering a high level view of the application structure, which fosters the development of a more regular and qualitative solution. However, the implementation techniques illustrated in Chapters 11, 12, and 13 are very general, and can be applied to the development of a data-intensive Web application also in absence of a conceptual model.

10.2 Dimensions of Architecture Design

In this section, we consider the main goals, constraints, and scenarios of architecture design.

10.2.1 Goals of Architecture Design

The definition of the application architecture must ensure the achievement of the adequate level of service with respect to the following dimensions:

- *Performance:* the application must sustain the expected workload, expressed by parameters like the maximum number of concurrent users, the number of page requests served per unit of time, or the maximum time for delivering a page to the client.

- *Scalability:* the architecture must be extensible, so that, when the workload increases, it is possible to add more computation power and keep the performance stable.

- *Availability:* the application must work continuously, and faults should not affect significantly the service delivered to users. Ideally, failure of any of the architecture components should be tolerated and not interrupt the service.

- *State maintenance:* the state of the user interaction (represented, for instance, by the session data maintained at server-side) must be preserved, even when the application is distributed on multiple machines or failures occur.

- *Security:* the information hosted in the data tier and transmitted between the application and its users should be protected, and users should be identified and granted access only to the content and functions they are entitled to.

10.2.2   Constraints of Architecture Design

Architecture design is not only a matter of goals, but also of constraints, physical, financial, and organizational. The following variables affect decision-making:

- *Cost:* each resource costs, thus every configuration requires a different investment, in terms of processors, network infrastructure, interfaces, and software licenses. The application budget may limit the choice of the hardware resources and of the software products.

- *Complexity:* some configurations are simpler than others to set up and maintain. The unavailability or the cost of specialized technical skills may constrain the architecture design.

- *Corporate standards and infrastructures:* the application must be deployed within the corporate IT infrastructure, which may constrain the selection of processors and software products.

10.2.3   Scenarios of Architecture Deployment

One of the most important decisions to make is where to maintain the designed architecture. In recent times, a push is observed toward the outsourcing of the IT infrastructure, even by large enterprises. Three different scenarios are possible:

- *Internal:* the application architecture is kept inside the enterprise and maintained by the internal IT department.

- *Housed:* the application architecture is maintained by the internal IT department of the enterprise, but is physically installed at an external service provider.

- *Hosted:* the application architecture is located at the premises of an external service provider, who also maintains it.

Choosing the most appropriate deployment scenario is a very critical decision, which has great impact on the organization of the enterprise. We restrain from giving guidelines for this fundamental decision but nonetheless stress the fact that architecture design remains essential also when the infrastructure is housed or hosted, because it sets the required level of service that must be met irrespective of where the application runs and of who maintains it.

10.3 Designing the Hardware and Network Architecture

In Chapter 1 we addressed the various technologies and languages for building dynamic Web pages, and in particular we showed that the most comprehensive architecture includes four components: the Web server, the script execution engine, the application server, and the database server (Figure 10.1).

In the next sections, we show a gallery of possible configurations, from the simplest to the most complex, and discuss the pros and cons of each one in terms of performance, scalability, availability, session management, and security. Initially, we consider only the three essential components, namely the Web server, the script execution engine, and the database server; then we add the application server, which is required for applications with mid or high complexity.

10.3.1 Single Server Configuration

Figure 10.2 shows the simplest configuration, which we call *single server*. In such a configuration, the basic components of the architecture, namely the Web server, the program execution engine, and the database, are installed on the same machine. The host resides in the intranet and may be connected to the Internet via a router, which permits Internet users to address HTTP requests to the Web server.

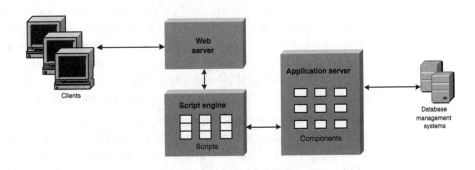

Figure 10.1   Components of a data-intensive Web Application.

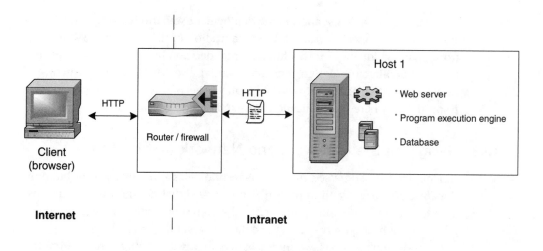

Figure 10.2 Single server configuration.

If such a connection is not provided, only internal users inside the corporate intranet can access the application.

The router between the Internet and the intranet acts as the so-called *firewall,* which is the element that separates the potentially hostile external environment from the internal network. The firewall is typically equipped with *access control rules,* which filter the incoming or outgoing requests and decide which ones to admit and which ones to forbid.

The single-processor configuration can be evaluated in the light of architecture design goals and constraints:

- *Performance:* the sustainable throughput is bound by the configuration of the host, in terms of CPU speed, available memory, and disk access latency. The server machine can be a PC, a workstation, up to a mainframe system, with a progression of performance, but also of costs. In general, the performance of the single server architecture is limited by the fact that the script engine and the database management system are both memory and CPU-intensive applications, and thus conflict in the use of machine resources, which may produce a bottleneck.

- *Scalability:* scaling the system requires adding power to the server machine, or choosing a more sophisticated class of hardware, and augmenting the number of concurrent processes. The maximum scalability is thus bound by the hardware architecture of the selected server, for example by the maximum number of CPUs. In general, PCs and workstations, which are not conceived for massive parallelism, offer limited scalability.

- *Availability:* in the simplest configuration, with a single CPU and one process for each software component, every software and hardware element is a single point of failure: if it breaks, the entire system hangs. Fault-tolerance can be improved to the price of increased cost and complexity, by adding redundant hardware resources, for example multiple CPUs and mirrored disks, and by installing multiple processes running different instances of the Web server, script engine, and database. The replication of processes is treated later, in Section 10.3.3.

- *State maintenance:* as explained in Chapter 1, user session data can be stored in the main memory by the program execution engine. Because there is a single server, which processes all the incoming requests, the data of the user session are locally available to the server handling the request.

- *Security:* this is the weakest aspect of the single server architecture, because attackers breaking the firewall and the Web server can take control of the host and gain direct access to the database, violating data protection.

- *Cost:* cost is low, as far as massive parallelism is not required. Adding more processors, RAM, and faster disks to the server, or shifting to a more sophisticated class of hardware, increases the cost, and may sometimes exceed the expenditure for an alternative configuration, made of multiple low-cost hosts.

- *Complexity:* the single server configuration is clearly the simplest option. In particular it spares all the technical chores of setting up a complex intranet and of connecting together the machines hosting the different tiers of the architecture.

The single server solution, implemented on low-cost PCs or workstations, is viable for small-scale, non-critical Web applications, where simplicity and limited IT investment are the prominent goals, and data security is not essential. Many low-end Web hosting providers indeed offer a similar configuration, by renting to their customers a single machine, or even a portion of a machine hosting multiple applications of different customers. Another use of the single server architecture may be the deployment of an intranet application, enabling, for example, the browser-based access to corporate data residing in a mainframe system. However, if performance, availability and secure access from the Internet are requested, a more articulated architecture is needed. The next sections present increasingly sophisticated architectures, which improve on all the design goals, at the price of extra costs and management complexity.

10.3.2 Separation of the Database Server

The first step for improving the architecture is devoting a dedicated machine to the database management system, as shown in Figure 10.3.

This solution positively impacts performance, scalability, availability, and security:

- *Performance:* besides the positive impact due to an extra processor, the physical division of the database and Web server permits a more adequate sizing of the involved machines, whose configuration can be tuned to the requirements of the installed software.[2] For example, fast access and mirrored disks can be added to the host in the data tier and exploited by the database management system. The performance gain introduced by the dedicated host in the data tier may be somewhat reduced by the network communication overhead required by the two separate machines; however, normally this downside is more than compensated by the performance increase due to separate hosts.

- *Scalability:* scalability improves because now it is possible to act separately on the middle and data tier. Normally, the first bottleneck is in the

---

[2]In Unix systems, it is not infrequent that the installation of a database system is preceded by a reconfiguration of the operating system kernel, for supporting faster access to disks.

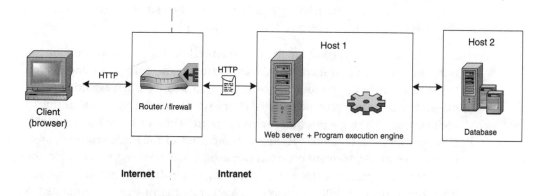

Figure 10.3 Separate database configuration.

middle tier, where the Web server and program execution engine reach their maximum capability before fully exploiting the capacity of the data tier. In this case, the middle tier can be scaled to ensure that more workload passes down to the data tier and the overall throughput augments. Section 10.3.3 discusses alternative techniques for scaling the middle tier and database tier.

■ *Availability:* although faults in the middle tier and in the database tier are insulated, availability is still impaired by the fact that each component is a single point of failure. The replication techniques discussed in Section 10.3.3 not only improve performance and scalability, but also availability, because redundant resources are introduced.

■ *Security:* security significantly improves. A second firewall can be added to insulate the data tier from the Web server, creating a so-called *demilitarized zone* (DMZ) between the Internet and the corporate intranet, which hosts the database, and possibly other corporate applications that do not use the Web (Figure 10.4). The inner firewall may disallow HTTP requests at all and let only database requests pass, making it more difficult for attackers to reach the data tier.

10.3.3 Exploiting Replication and Parallelism

The configuration of Figure 10.4 is limited in scalability and fault tolerance, due to the presence of a single instance of the Web and database servers. The next configurations exploit the classical principles of *replication and parallelism* to increase

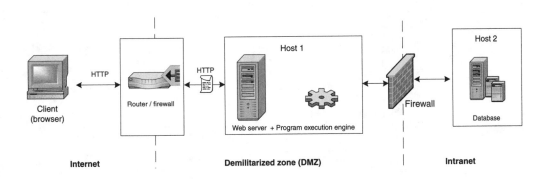

Figure 10.4 Demilitarized zone.

performance, scalability, and availability. Figure 10.5 shows two alternative ways of using parallelism:

■ With *vertical cloning,* a single server machine includes several independent processors and hosts multiple processes dedicated to the application.

■ With *horizontal cloning,* entire servers are replicated.

The two solutions are not mutually exclusive, because it is possible to replicate hosts that make use of vertical cloning. The tradeoff between vertical and horizontal cloning is a matter of hardware choices and budget constraints. In general, horizontal cloning may be more economical and provides the maximum scalability at the price of increased complexity in managing the architecture.

Irrespective of the tier and component to which it is applied, cloning positively affects performance, scalability, and availability:

■ *Performance and scalability:* cloning permits *load balancing:* the incoming workload is spread over the various processes, and each process receives a well-balanced fraction of the total incoming traffic. If load balancing is used in conjunction with horizontal cloning, *clustering* is required. A cluster is a loosely coupled group of servers (also known as *nodes*) that provide a unified view of the services that they individually offer.

■ *Availability:* cloning enables *fail-over:* if a process or a cluster node fails, its workload can be redistributed to the other processes or nodes of the same

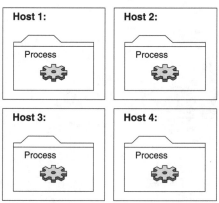

Figure 10.5   Vertical and horizontal cloning.

cluster, which produces a performance degradation but avoids a complete stop of the application.

Parallelism applies to all levels of the architecture of a Web application. The first example of horizontal cloning is the architecture illustrated in Figure 10.6, in which the middle tier contains multiple machines, each hosting a replica of the Web server and execution engine. In this solution, the router/firewall acts as a *network dispatcher,* and spreads the incoming HTTP requests to the different Web servers, to balance their workload, and augment the throughput toward the database server. In case of failure of one machine, the network dispatcher continues to use the remaining available servers, thus increasing availability.

The replicated architecture of Figure 10.6, which duplicates the Web server and the server-side scripting engine, affects the management of the interaction state, when such a state is maintained in the form of session data by the scripting engine. As described in Chapter 1, a session is a sequence of requests from one client to one server, during which the server-side execution engine may exploit user-oriented information stored in the session object, typically implemented in the main memory of the server, for fast access. This way of handling state information assumes that the user interacts with a single server, which may not be the case in a replicated architecture, where multiple cloned servers may respond to different requests of the same user. Therefore, state management in a replicated architecture requires reproducing or simulating the one-to-one relationship between

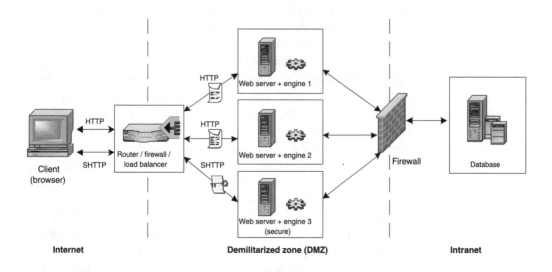

Figure 10.6   Replicated Web server configuration.

the client and the server, even with horizontal clones and load distribution. Otherwise, if the request of a user, who started an interactive session with clone A, is sent to clone B, then clone B does not recognize the session identifier communicated by the user and treats him/her as a new user, thus loosing the state of the interaction.

To preserve the integrity of user sessions, the load balancing policy must guarantee that the state information stored in the user session, including the session identifier, is available to the server selected for responding to the request. The most common technique for achieving this goal is the exploitation of *session affinity,* which is a mapping, maintained by the load balancer, between each active session and the server that originated it and holds its state data. The load balancer uses such a mapping to send all the incoming requests pertinent to a given session consistently to the same server. This procedure is also known as the provision of *sticky sessions.* To implement sticky sessions, the load balancer must be able to analyze the content of the incoming request, for instance, to extract the session identifier from a cookie or from a parameter of an encoded URL. Note that simply using the IP address of the client emitting the request may not be sufficient to identify the user, either because the requests of different clients may have the same IP address (this may happen, for instance, when client requests are mediated by a proxy), or because a client changes IP address during a session (this may happen, for example, in the case of dial-up connections).

State management affects not only load balancing, but also the fail over procedures. The user session may be lost when the server that handles it fails, and the user's request is forwarded to another server. In this case, the newly appointed server ignores the session identifier received from the user and starts a new session, and the session data kept in the main memory of the failed server are lost.

Providing fail-safe session management requires the persistent memorization of session data, for example in a *session database,* so that any server can recover them after a failure. This solution is rather expensive in terms of performance, because each user action affecting session data, for instance each change to the shopping cart, requires database access. For optimizing performance without preventing fail-safe session management, a mixed solution can be implemented: session data are kept in the main memory of the scripting engine, and backed up in the database for fail-safety purposes. In this way, the normal read access to session data requires only an inexpensive main memory lookup, and only updates to the session data cause database access. The copy to the database can be done either in real-time, or in a "lazy" way, for example periodically, or upon completion of the server-side program that computes the page requested by the user. When the frequency of read accesses to session data is higher than the frequency of updates, the lazy alignment of the database substantially reduces the overhead of persistent session management.

Cloning the Web server may be exploited also to improve the *security of data transmission:* one of the replicated Web servers (for instance, server 3 in Figure 10.6) may be equipped with *secure HTTP,* a variant of the normal HTTP protocol for handling cryptographic protection of the data transmitted by the HTTP request. The network load balancer may be configured to send all requests needing cryptographic protection to the secure Web server, without affecting the performance of the remaining Web servers, which handle normal requests. Secure HTTP could be implemented also in the one machine configuration, for example by installing two Web servers on different ports of the same host. However, secure HTTP slows down the Web server's response and is better delegated to a separate HTTP server.

10.3.4 Separation of the Web Server and Scripting Engine

The evolution of the architecture of Figure 10.6 is the separation of the Web server from the scripting engine. The former receives HTTP requests, delivers static HTML pages, and routes requests for dynamically computed pages to the script engine; the latter executes the server-side programs for dynamic page computation, which may generate requests to the database for retrieving the data necessary to produce the response page. Cloning can be applied separately to the Web server and to the program execution engine, obtaining the configuration shown in Figure 10.7.

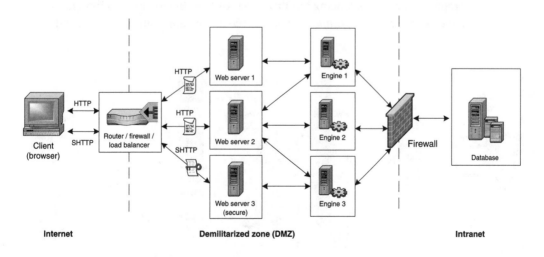

Figure 10.7 Replicated Web server and engine configuration.

This separation further improves scalability and fault-tolerance, because now the Web server and the scripting engine can be replicated independently. The separation introduces two levels of load balancing, one across the HTTP servers and one across script engines. Normally, the processing at the program execution engine is much heavier than that of the HTTP server, and thus a well-balanced configuration may require more machines for the scripting engines than for the Web servers. Separating and independently clustering the two functions allows optimizing the number of hosts.

From the technical standpoint, the separation of the engine and Web server impacts the implementation of the communication protocol between the two components; the communication overhead introduced by the separation must be compensated by the performance increase due to the horizontal cloning.

10.3.5 Configuration with an Application Server

The architecture of Figure 10.7 can be made more scalable and modular by extending the middle tier with an application server, whose characteristics have already been discussed in Chapter 1.

Figure 10.8 shows an instance of the application server architecture in which all the various tiers, from the Web server to the database server, use replication and clustering.

The benefit of application servers is the centralization of the business logic in a dedicated sub-tier, which manages shared resources, transparent object-level replication, load balancing, and fail-over. Unlike the previous architectures, *parallelism inside the application server is dynamic:* the application server decides the

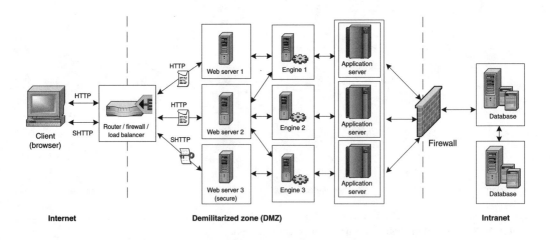

Figure 10.8 Application server configuration.

number of processes to allocate to each business component at run time, based on the *real* traffic. In this way, more applications can co-exist on the same host, because the application server regulates their contention, giving more resources to the application that is experiencing more workload.

The architecture of Figure 10.8 grants the maximum configuration flexibility, because each function is mapped to a distinct physical tier, which can be independently replicated, and a virtually unlimited scalability, because components can be added to each tier, preserving the overall balance of the configuration.

A further benefit of the application server architecture is that it fosters the development of reusable business objects, which are independent of the context where they are used. The objects hosted in the application server can be called by the page templates in the middle tier, and also by non-Web applications distributed across the enterprise, for example by standalone Java applications. In other words, the business objects in the application server are a platform for *enterprise application integration;* enterprise-wide business functions can be developed and deployed in the application server, and then used consistently by any kind of clients.

For coping with the different security requirements of the heterogeneous clients, the application server may be embedded in a *separate demilitarized zone* (labeled DMZ2 in Figure 10.9). Internet clients access the application server through the DMZ and have to cross two firewalls; more trusted clients, for instance intranet or extranet clients accessing the enterprise applications over a secure network like a Virtual Private Network, may live inside the second demilitarized zone, having privileged access to the application server, but still remaining separate from the inner intranet hosting the data tier.

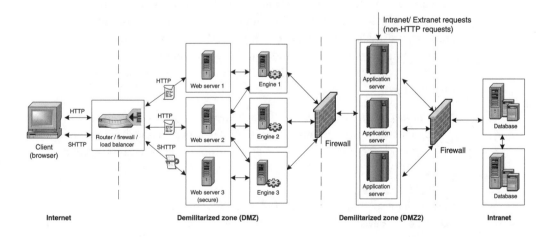

Figure 10.9   Application server configuration, with insulated application server.

10.4   Techniques for Testing and Improving Performance

At the end of this gallery of architectures, and before entering the discussion on how to implement the various features of a data-intensive Web application, we zoom in on a specific and very important topic in the design of the application architecture: the methods and tools for testing and improving performance.

10.4.1   Estimating the Workload

The starting point for dimensioning the architecture and verifying its performance is the specification of *performance requirements,* which typically amounts to predicting the number and type of page requests that clients will make, and the response time needed to answer to these requests acceptably. Estimating the workload is not an exact discipline, and the margin of error greatly increases moving from B2B and intranet applications to B2C applications offered to Internet users.

For B2B or enterprise applications, the number of users can be determined with a good approximation, and the use cases elicited during requirements analysis permit one to turn these numbers into a sensible guess of the page requests to expect. For example, if a use case specifies that a user group consisting of 10,000 users daily accesses a site view by issuing an average of 30 page requests, the number 30×10,000=300,000 of page accesses per day can be taken as a rough estimate of the workload for the site view. Such a number will obviously fluctuate, but not dramatically, unless there is a substantial change in the number of employees or in the workflow described by the use case.

Conversely, a B2C application is far less predictable, because the number of hits depends on the success of the application, a factor hard to estimate beforehand. In this case, the business requirements of the application, including marketing analysis, sales forecasts, and competitor's reviews, could help estimate the expected number of customers and hence the volumes of requests.

In any case, the workload should be characterized by means of a spectrum of parameters:

- *Number of page requests:* the average and peak number of requests emitted by clients, expressed, for instance, in pages per second.[3] This number expresses the *throughput* of the application as perceived by the client.

---

[3]A common rule of thumb is the so-called 80/20 rule, which estimates that 80% of the total traffic is received in the 20% of the time. In other words, peak traffic is roughly four times the average traffic.

■ *Number of concurrent users:* this number differs from the number of page requests, because it expresses the prediction of the average and maximum number of users that will access the application simultaneously. The number of concurrent users affects especially the application back-end, where queues may occur in the business and data tier.

■ *Response time:* the maximum number of seconds that the client should wait for the response. Ideally, the response time should not exceed the user's thinking time (let's say 3 seconds), and should be relatively stable in peak conditions. Response time could be further distinguished in *time to first byte* (TTFB) and *time to last byte* (TTLB). The former gives an indication of the performance of the back-end processing, because it ignores any network latency due to the transmission of the entire page; the latter is more significant for the client, because it measures the time needed to receive the complete response.

■ *Request mix:* given that an application is made of many different pages, with different complexity, the bare number of requests per second is insufficient to characterize the load. To make performance testing more trustable, it is necessary to estimate the user's behavior, and then generate an artificial workload that matches the real one. The request mix can be expressed by associating to each application page a "weight," which denotes the probability that the user accesses the page in an average interactive session. Page probabilities can be used during test sessions to construct realistic workloads.

10.4.2 Setting Up the Test Environment

Performance testing should be done on the actual hardware, software, and network infrastructure, using the real application.

The real application, of course, is available only at the end of implementation. However, deferring performance assessment to such a late time is dangerous, because it delays the verification of the architecture to the very end of the development process. To anticipate performance analysis, it may be possible to build an application prototype and make it available during the architecture design phase. The prototype may implement only a subset of the application pages, corresponding to the most critical use cases, and should reproduce as faithfully as possible the data access and update queries of the real application.

Also, to minimize hardware and licensing costs, the real hardware and software is usually provisioned only at the end of the implementation. In this case, analysis can start from a preliminary test configuration, pragmatically selected based on past experience and economical and organizational constraints (for example, based on existing hardware and infrastructure), and then proceed by trial and error, following the experimental cycle based on bottleneck identification and removal illustrated in Section 10.4.4. The results obtained with the preliminary architecture could be projected on the real configuration, to gain confidence that the ultimate architecture will meet performance requirements.

However, performance must be reevaluated prior to the application deployment on the real software and hardware.

10.4.3 Verifying Performance

Once a configuration is in place, it must be stress-tested in order to determine performance. Performance evaluation entails: 1) defining the test sessions and testing tools; 2) running the experiments; 3) collecting and analyzing test data.

Testing a Web application requires simulating the clicking behavior of clients, by generating a suitable number of requests for the application pages. This task is supported by specialized testing tools, which offer functions for the following:

- Defining the mix of page requests that simulate a usage session. For each usage session it is possible to specify a set of pages to call, and the percentage of requests that should be addressed to each page in the mix.

- Defining the maximum number of concurrent clients that send requests to the application and fine tune the clicking behavior of each client, for example by setting a *thinking time* between consecutive requests, or by simulating different bandwidths of the client connections (for instance, slow modem, ISDN, and ADSL).

- Scheduling and running the test sessions.

- Collecting reports about various performance parameters. Typically, Web stress tools chart parameters like the number of pages per second, the total duration of the test session, the number of communication and server errors, and so on.

As a concrete example, Figure 10.10 and Figure 10.11 show the interface of a Web application-testing tool called WAS (Web Application Stress), by Microsoft.[4] Figure 10.10 shows the window for setting the parameters of the test session; Figure 10.11 displays the report produced after executing the test.

---

[4]The tool can be downloaded free of charge from *webtool.rte.microsoft.com/*.

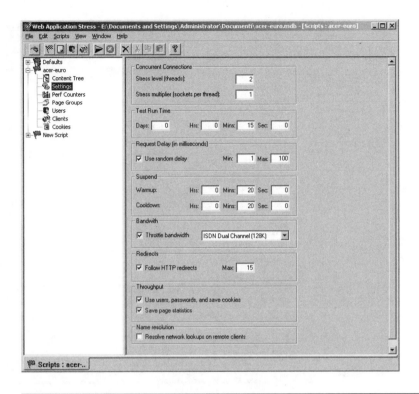

Figure 10.10 Setting test session parameters in WAS.

10.4.4 Identifying and Removing Bottlenecks

The hardest part of performance tuning is understanding the behavior of the application and of the selected configuration, which requires identifying problems and taking the necessary countermeasures for removing them.

In a complex system, like a data-intensive Web application, performance is determined by the slowest component, which is the so-called *bottleneck*. Bottlenecks may hide in any of the elements of the architectures illustrated in Figure 10.9, including the Web server, the scripting programs and page templates, the business components, and the database, and also in the connections between the various components and tiers. In a well-designed architecture, the workload should be harmonically distributed across the different tiers and components, so that there is no single bottleneck, and each component should work at a reasonable fraction of its maximum capacity, so that some extra power is available to accommodate exceptional events, like the anomalous increase of the workload or the failure of some components.

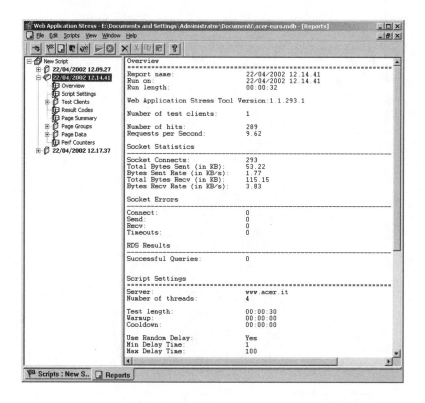

Figure 10.11   Test session report in WAS.

Tuning performance involves a cyclic process comprising the tasks shown in Figure 10.12: the process consists of defining a configuration, verifying that it satisfies the performance requirements, and, in the negative case, identifying and removing bottlenecks.

A pragmatic approach to identifying performance problems is to progressively stress the system, until one of the components reaches a saturation point and manifests itself as the performance bottleneck. Saturation can be discovered by running a set of experiments in which the stress level, for example the number of simulated concurrent users, is increased and by monitoring the system throughput. The occurrence of a bottleneck typically shows in the performance/load diagram presenting a curve like the one in Figure 10.13, where the throughput increases almost linearly with the workload until one of the components "breaks," and then either remains constant or even decreases, revealing a situation of over-stress.

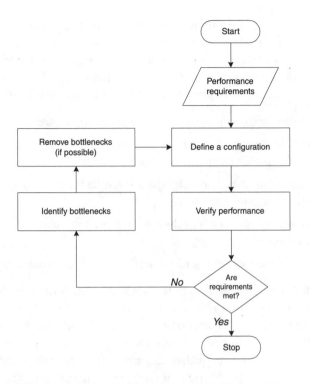

Figure 10.12 The performance tuning process.

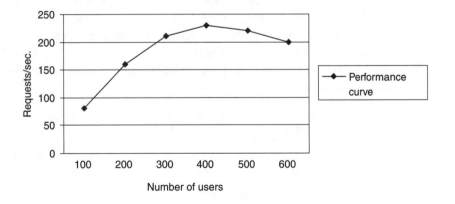

Figure 10.13 Performance diagram showing system saturation.

When saturation is encountered, the next step is identifying the saturating component. An indication may come from the analysis of performance indicators in the different physical machines. For instance, any component that in the stress tests runs constantly at a high level of CPU utilization (say, above 75%) is a candidate bottleneck. The most frequently encountered situations include:

- The Web server being unable to serve the incoming requests.
- The server-side scripting interpreter being overloaded due to the execution of complex programs or page templates.
- The business components used by the server-side scripts or page template being overloaded.
- The database connection being slowed down by too many concurrent requests.
- The database processor taking too much to execute a complex query.

If the tested configuration is such that each machine hosts a single component, then the machine where the over-stress has occurred clearly points to the component to revise. If the over-stressed machine hosts multiple components, for example the Web server and the database, then separating the components on different machines and running further tests may permit to make the diagnosis. Sometimes, isolating components is not feasible, but still some insight may be acquired with more detailed measurements. For example, if the machine that hosts the Web server and the scripting engine saturates, it is possible to verify who is slowing down the system by looking at the request queue of the Web server; if the number of requests waiting in queue increases in correspondence to the slowdown, it is likely that the scripting programs or page templates are forced to wait, because the business object to which they address requests are overloaded.

When the bottleneck is identified, there are different applicable strategies to solve the problem:

- Acting on the application code to fix problems and optimize execution time.
- Adding more resources to the configuration, as illustrated by the replicated architectures discussed in the preceding sections.
- Introducing caching mechanisms.

In principle, intervening on the application code is the most appropriate solution, as there should be no bottlenecks due to the ill design of application components. Optimization is particularly relevant in the data tier, where well-established database tuning techniques are available, which may yield substantial reductions in the execution time of database queries. However, optimizing the implementation code is a complex task, and a sensible compromise must be reached between achieving 100% implementation efficiency, which is an ideal goal, and the effort spent in code optimization. When the application code is reasonably efficient, further performance improvement can be gained by increasing the number of resources and/or introducing caching mechanisms.

10.5 Web Caching

The first two solutions for improving the performance of a Web application, namely code optimization and architecture scaling, demand highly qualified technical skills and massive investments in the IT infrastructure. A third way to obtain low-cost and low-impact performance improvement is granted by the careful use of caching.

Caching consists of temporarily storing resources in a fast access location, for later retrieval; it is a very consolidated practice in computer and software architectures. For example, caching is exploited in computer architectures, where the instructions with a high probability of being executed next are stored in a fast access memory close to the processor, to avoid costly memory accesses.

In the Web context, caching applies to any resource involved in the computation of the response to a user request, from the entire HTML page, to the result of an individual data query. Web caching amounts to temporarily storing such resources, to minimize their computation when a client request needs them.

Web caching provides two fundamental benefits, which are somewhat orthogonal:

- *Reduction of network latency:* if the cache is closer to the client than the origin server owning the resource, the route that the resource must traverse to reach the client is shorter, which reduces bandwidth consumption and response time.

- *Reduction of computation effort:* if the resource is dynamically built, using a cached copy minimizes the effort of reassembling it from the raw data.

As illustrated in Figure 10.14, Web caching can be seen as a way of *decoupling content delivery from content generation.*

In its most general form, a Web cache intermediates between the user requests and the application producing the response. Client requests, which can be in the order of millions, are addressed to a dedicated infrastructure hosting cached copies of resources. If a request can be served with a cached copy, it does not

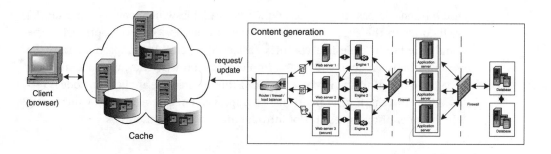

Figure 10.14   Web caching decouples content delivery and production.

reach the application; otherwise, the caching infrastructure calls the application to get the resource, stores a copy of it, and sends it to the client. In this way, only a fraction of the incoming requests (which may be less than 10% in practical cases)[5] is served in realtime by the application.

Decoupling content delivery and generation greatly reduces the investments in architectures, because the caching infrastructure is built using multiple but inexpensive machines, and the application architecture for content generation can be scaled down, because it must sustain less traffic.

Setting up a proper Web cache entails answering the questions of what to cache, and when and where to cache objects.

10.5.1   What to Cache

Anything that contributes to the response can be cached, including:

- Static HTML pages and multimedia files.

- Fragments of pages computed by scripting programs.

- Intermediate data consumed by the scripting programs for producing page, for example XML files.

- The result of database queries or other application commands.

Static resources are always cacheable, irrespective of the application code and architecture. For the remaining objects to be cacheable, suitable measures

---

[5]IBM reports that less than 2% of the client requests addressed to the 2000 Olympics Web site reached the application servers. The remaining percentage was serviced by the cache infrastructure.

must be adopted in the application code and/or in the architecture, to ensure the proper handling of data updates, which could invalidate the cached copies.

10.5.2 Where to Cache

Caching is ubiquitous in the architecture of the Web, as illustrated in Figure 10.15.
There are four fundamental ways in which a caching mechanism can be implemented:

- *Browser caching:* every browser contains a cache of HTML pages and multimedia files used to speed up the rendition of pages that contain cached objects. The cache is a directory in the user's hard disk, which can be filled with objects up to a certain space limit. Browser-based caching is simple and universally diffused; it applies only to static resources, and can be by-passed by the content provider, who can add suitable HTTP headers to the response or directives to the HTML page, which force the browser not to use the cache.

- *Proxy caching:* a proxy cache is a server-side cache, interposed between a large community of users, for example a corporate intranet, and the

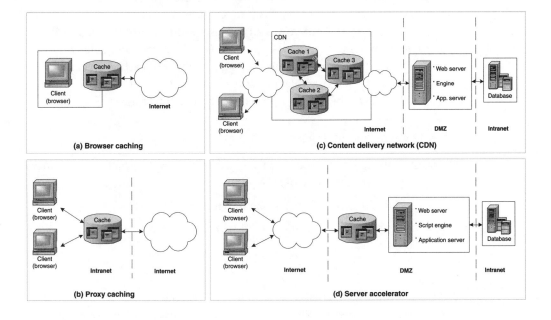

Figure 10.15 Alternative Web caching strategies.

public Internet. Proxy caches store a local copy of each resource requested by users, and avoid accessing the Internet for retrieving frequently asked pages.[6] The benefits are reduced bandwidth consumption and response time. Proxy caches are sometimes implemented together with the firewall, because the firewall controls the requests flowing from the intranet to the Internet and vice versa. Proxy caches, as well as browser caches, are placed at the side of the content consumer.

- *Content delivery networks* (CDN): CDNs are caching infrastructures, usually managed by service providers, located between the content consumers and the content producers. A CDN is typically used to serve a large number of geographically distributed Internet users. When a client requests a page to the origin server, the server returns a page with rewritten links that point to the nodes of the CDN, so that the further client requests are managed by the CDN. The CDN serves requests using multiple cache nodes and sophisticated content delivery policies, which select the optimal copy of the page by taking into account the geographical location of the user and the real-time traffic conditions. With the CDN approach, cache management is typically outsourced; this is a quite costly solution, typically paid on a per-megabyte basis.

- *Server accelerators:* a server accelerator is a caching solution implemented by the content producer. A server accelerator is a buffer placed in front of a server cluster that intercepts all requests addressed to that cluster, by caching copies of the objects produced by the servers, and delivering them to the subsequent requests. As the number of cached objects increases, the server accelerator cuts more and more server workload, which reduces the need for powerful server architectures.

10.5.3   When to Cache and to Refresh the Cache

The most challenging aspect of implementing a cache infrastructure is the management of cached content, which requires addressing two issues:

- *Cache population,* that is, the way in which the cache is populated.
- *Cache refreshing,* that is, the way in which cached content is invalidated and refreshed.

---

[6]More precisely, proxy servers use special-purpose HTTP headers for verifying the validity of a cached page with respect to the original one. If the cached copy has expired, they transparently access the origin server on the Internet.

Cache population can be done either by pushing or pulling content, as pictorially illustrated in Figure 10.16.

The *push approach* requires the bulk transfer of content from its original location to the cache. Such a transfer is typically done offline on a periodic basis, and is independent of the client requests. A typical example of push-based caching is *Web site materialization,* which produces a static version of a dynamic Web site, by requesting all the pages to the Web server and storing them in the cache. Site materialization can be performed with the help of dedicated tools, called *offline browsers,* which are able to navigate an entire dynamic Web site and save all the retrieved pages as static HTML files. Another instance of push-based cache management occurs in databases, where one or more replicated databases are made available to the Web application or to the enterprise information system, to accelerate data access. In Chapter 11, we show how to apply this solution to the data tier of a Web application.

The *pull approach* is the classic way of managing the cache. Content is transferred from the origin server to the cache upon a client request: if the requested object is already in cache (cache hit) it is returned, otherwise (cache miss) the request is routed to the origin server, which produces the object and updates the cache content. In the pull-based approach, content is not refreshed periodically,

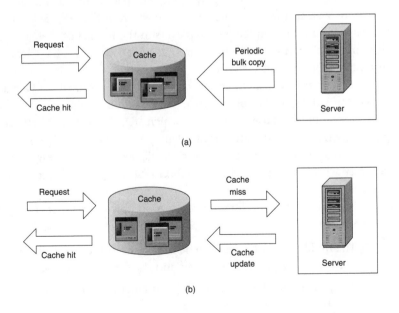

Figure 10.16 Push (a) and pull (b) cache population.

but each object is managed individually and resides in the cache for a duration established by the *cache invalidation protocol.*

Cache invalidation protocols are sets of rules for the exchange of requests and responses between the cache and the server, aimed at ensuring the validity of the resources sent to the client. Protocol rules depend on the nature of the cached objects.

For instance, HTTP 1.1 contains an invalidation protocol for caching static objects, which specifies two kinds of rules:

- *Expiration rules:* dictate the duration of an object in the cache.

- *Invalidation rules:* establish criteria for verifying if the cached object is not conformant to the original object.

Invalidation protocols are more complex for the caching of dynamic objects, like JSP pages, which may depend on content updated independently by multiple applications. In this case, the problem amounts to intercepting the content updates and notifying the cache, which refreshes the copy of the cached object.

10.5.4   Caching Dynamic Content Using a Server Accelerator and Caching Directives

We conclude this section with one significant example, which exposes some of the technical aspects of caching dynamic Web pages, the most interesting application of Web caching. The example is drawn from the Edge Side Includes (ESI) initiative, jointly prompted by top players in the market of Web application development platforms and architectures, like Akamai, ATG, BEA, Circadence, Digital Island, Oracle, and Vignette.

ESI comprises an architecture, an invalidation protocol, and a mark-up language for defining cacheable fragments of dynamic Web pages.

ESI requires the use of *surrogates,* which are intermediaries that act on behalf of an origin server. Surrogates may be deployed close to the origin server, as server accelerators, or throughout the network, as elements of a CDN. Figure 10.17 shows a server accelerator architecture based on JESI, the Java implementation of the ESI concept.

The architecture is an enhanced version of the three-tier configuration, in which:

- The middle tier includes a cache manager, positioned in front of the machine hosting the Web server and the servlet container.

- The page templates in the servlet container include special-purpose tags, which specify caching directives.

- The cache manager includes an ESI processor, capable of executing cache management commands.

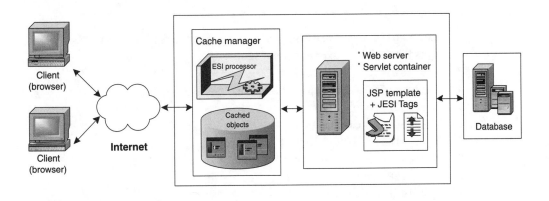

Figure 10.17 Caching architecture using ESI.

All the relevant aspects of caching, including the page fragment to cache and the expiration rules, are expressed by incorporating JESI tags in the JSP template. JESI tags permit the developer to divide the JSP page templates into fragments, with different caching requirements. For example, a page may include static content, an index of products, which varies weekly, and an index of news, which is updated daily. With JESI, the three page fragments can be cached separately using different refresh policies.

Figure 10.18 shows the flavor of JESI tags. The figure illustrates a JSP page template, which intermixes static content, corresponding to the HTML blocks numbered 1, 2, and 3, and some dynamic content, represented by the JSP fragments numbered 1 and 2. The entire templates is enclosed by a custom tag, called `jesi:template`, which sets the default caching parameters, for instance the expiration time, which amounts to 3,600 seconds in the example. The JESI processor treats all the static HTML blocks as a single cacheable object, with a time-to-live interval equal to the template default. Inside the template, the JSP code for producing dynamic content is surrounded by the `jesi:fragment` tag. Each tag delimits a portion of dynamically produced content, which is treated by the processor as a distinct cacheable object, managed based on the parameters expressed in the `jesi:fragment` tag.

The JESI processor can also handle the explicit invalidation of cache objects, for instance as a consequence of data updates. For this purpose, the invalidating operation must be wrapped by a JSP template containing a `jesi:invalidate` tag. The objects to invalidate are identified by means of a selector, which is an expression evaluated by the JESI processor to obtain the set of objects to remove from the cache.

```
1   <%@ taglib uri="WEBINF/jesitaglib.tld" prefix="jesi" %>
2   <jesi:template expiration="3600">
3     .. static HTML block # 1 ..
4     <jesi:fragment expiration="600">
5     .. JSP code block # 1
6     </jesi:fragment>
7     .. static HTML block # 2 ..
8     <jesi:fragment expiration="60">
9     .. JSP code block # 2
10    </jesi:fragment>
11    .. static HTML block # 3 ..
12  </jesi:template>
```

Figure 10.18   JSP template with JESI tags defining cacheable fragments.

Summary

In this chapter we have addressed the design of the architecture supporting a data-intensive Web application, which is a fundamental task prior to starting the implementation activities. Architecture design requires many inter-dependent decisions, which affect the most disparate issues, from hardware and software selection to network topology.

For tackling such decisions, it is important to understand the goals of architecture design and the variables that affect such goals. In this chapter, we have discussed such design factors as performance, scalability, availability, session maintenance, and security. In the light of these variables, we have introduced and contrasted four architectures (single server, separated database, separated/replicated Web server and execution engine, and application server). We have also discussed the fundamental problem of performance analysis and tuning, which is probably the most challenging goal to meet in deploying a Web application, and shown the use of caching to balance the needs of performance improvement and cost reduction.

In the following chapters, we will zoom in on the various "boxes" of the illustrated architectures, and show how to fill them with the implementation of a data-intensive application.

Bibliographic Notes

Web application architectures are a particular case of distributed systems. A good starting point for getting the essentials of computer networking is the classical book by Andrew Tanenbaum [Tanenbaum96], which can be complemented by the more recent title by Tanenbaum and Van Steen on the principles of distributed systems [VT02], which covers the most recent protocols and architectures, including the Web. An alternative source of information on the configuration of Web architectures can be found in the documentation of the most popular middleware and application server products. For instance, the IBM Redbooks Series contains the IBM WebSphere V4.0 Advanced Edition Handbook (*www.redbooks.ibm.com/pubs/pdfs/redbooks/sg246176.pdf*), which includes a wealth of information on Web application topologies and design principles.

Load balancing and the dimensioning of Web architectures are treated by several books, for instance [Bourke01, Kopparapu02], which discuss the key factors for supporting the growth of Web-based corporate infrastructures. In particular, the book by Kopparapu provides an in-depth technical discussion about how load balancers can be used for handling Web traffic demands, and for solving a multitude of network and server bottlenecks.

Performance analysis and capacity planning is treated in the book by Menasce et al. [MA01], which proposes an analytical model helping the skilled architecture designer forecast the Web applications workload and address performance optimization. A completely different explanation of capacity planning and architecture configuration can be found in the documentation of the popular "Duwamish Book Store" sample application, by Microsoft (see the Enterprise Development section at the Microsoft Developer Network library site *msdn.microsoft.com/library/*). The development of this reference application is followed from analysis to deployment, and special attention is devoted to capacity planning and architecture design. Another useful source of information is the Web site of the TCP-W benchmark (*www.tpc.org/tpcw/*), which stores the results of the benchmark for Web applications defined by the Transaction Processing Performance Council. The site contains the detailed specification of the most efficient architectures implemented by hardware and middleware vendors, which provide many useful insights on how to develop a scalable architecture.

Web caching is a very hot topic, both in the industrial arena and in the research community. A very comprehensive bibliography on the subject is maintained by Brian D. Davison, in a Web site dedicated to the Web caching (*www.web-caching.com*).

Web caching is discussed in two books [Wessel01, RS02], which provide technical hints about how to design, deploy, and operate a Web caching service. Wessel's book also covers some non-technical aspects of Web caching, including privacy, intellectual property and security; Rabinovich et al.'s book specifically addresses some replication issues, such as the mechanisms for request distribution, secure content access, and server selection.

The ESI initiative is presented in the official Web site of the Consortium (*www.esi.org*), which stores the current status of the ESI specification.

An innovative approach to caching is described in a VLDB paper [FVYI00], where the authors propose a multi-level caching systems, capable of caching database queries, XML fragments, and HTML, and discuss the trade-offs of caching at each of these levels.

11 Data Implementation

11.1   Introduction

Data implementation is concerned with the mapping of the conceptual data schema to concrete data sources, which enables the publishing (and sometimes the management) of content on the Web. Data implementation occurs in a variety of different scenarios; in most cases, content preexists to the development of the Web application and has to be extracted from external data sources.

From the viewpoint of the database supporting the application, we consider the following cases:

- *Dedicated database:* this situation occurs when the content *does not exist prior to the development of the application.* In this case, the development of the Web application comprises also the construction of a dedicated database, purposely built for storing the content to be published. Content maintenance is done with an ad hoc application, for example, with content management site views specified in WebML. Typical applications with dedicated databases are B2C and corporate portals, which are conceived specifically to collect and deliver content that is not reused outside the Web application.

■ *Replicated database:* this situation occurs when the content is stored in one or more corporate data sources, for example in relational databases or legacy systems, and is periodically copied into a database dedicated to the Web application. The *Web application owns and publishes a read-only copy of the corporate data* and the original content continues to be created and updated in its native location. An example of this scenario could be an e-commerce Web site that publishes content maintained in the corporate retail management system.

■ *Online database: the Web application has direct access to the corporate data,* to publish the current version of the content. In this case, the Web application has no dedicated database but connects directly to the external data sources, for either reading or writing content. An example of this category of applications is a Web-based reservation system, allowing Web users to see and change the up-to-date version of the reservation database.

Table 11.1 summarizes the differences between the three scenarios.

A further distinction, of a more technical kind, concerns the systems used to manage the data external to the Web application, which can be based either on relational database technology, or on legacy sources. In the former case, standard query languages and data distribution technology can help access the data; in the latter, the Web application must be able to extract data from the legacy systems, or to connect to them by means of appropriate software gateways.

Table 11.1 Scenarios of data implementation

Solution	Dedicated database?	Owned content?	Read access?	Write access?
Dedicated	Yes	Yes	Yes	Yes
Replicated	Yes	A copy of the content of the original data sources	Yes	No
Online	No	No, content remains in the original data sources	Yes	Yes

Real applications may exhibit a mix of all the above scenarios, because part of the content may be proprietary to the application, part may be extracted from data sources and replicated, and part may be accessed with a live connection to the enterprise information system. In all cases, the Entity-Relationship schema of the application defined in the data design phase plays a central role in the data implementation phase:

■ With a dedicated or replicated database, it is used as a starting point for deriving the schema of the database used by the Web application.

■ With online databases, it helps the design of the application programming interfaces for connecting to the remote sources and performing read and write operations.

The central role of the Entity-Relationship schema motivates the *data mapping architecture* illustrated in Figure 11.1. The core of the architecture is the *standard relational schema*, obtained by applying standard mapping rules to the Entity-Relationship schema. The standard schema comprises the definition of the tables that best match the entities and relationships of the application data

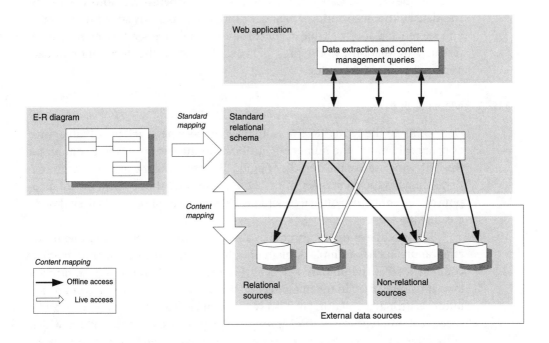

Figure 11.1   Data mapping architecture.

model. The standard relational schema offers to the web application a uniform view of the content, which facilitates writing the data retrieval and update queries necessary to implement content units and operations.

In this chapter, we discuss the issues involved in the implementation of the architecture of Figure 11.1, starting from the simplest solution in which the standard schema is directly used as dedicated database, and then continuing with the cases in which the standard schema facilitates the mapping to external sources, required by the replicated and online database architectures.

11.2 Standard Mapping

Deriving a relational schema from an Entity-Relationship diagram is a classical database design problem, treated in most database textbooks, which entails the following:

- Mapping entities and their attributes (BLOB).
- Mapping relationships.
- Mapping generalization hierarchies.

Entities are translated into relational tables, whereas relationships can be translated either into "bridge" tables, or into extra columns added to one table and referencing another table. Generalization hierarchies lend themselves to alternative translations, whose pros and cons depend on the distribution of data and on the expected queries.

11.2.1 Mapping Entities

Each entity in the Entity-Relationship diagram becomes a relational table, with as many columns as the number of attributes in the entity, plus one column for the OID, which serves the purpose of uniquely identifying the instances of the entity, defined as the *primary key* of the table. Figure 11.2 shows the standard mapping of one entity into one table, and provides an example of the SQL syntax for creating the table.

If one of the entity attributes has already the role of object identifier in the application and has a simple domain (like, for instance, the code of a product), it could be used as the primary key, omitting the OID column; however, primary keys are heavily used in the mapping of relationships, so we suggest avoiding applicative attributes and using instead system-managed attribute types, such as the special column type called *serial* or *autonumber,* provided by some DBMSs, which ensure that the system creates a distinct value of the column for each row of the

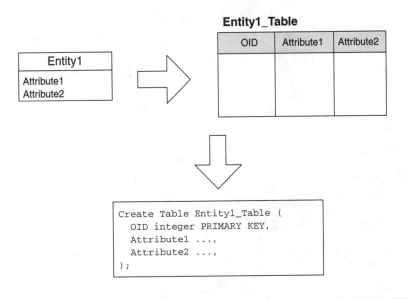

Figure 11.2   Mapping entity to relational tables.

table, freeing the application code from the burden of producing distinct values. Moreover, OID values should never be updated, because they denote the identity of an object, not an applicative property. Identifying attributes of the entity can be defined as a *secondary key* of the table, to stress that they are alternative means for identifying the objects.

11.2.2   Mapping BLOB Attributes

BLOB attributes contain large values, like images, videos, long texts, and documents, which make their storage more complex than for the attributes of simple types. BLOB values can be stored internally in the database or externally in the file system, and each alternative admits two further cases, pictorially illustrated in Figure 11.3.

Internal storage in the database can be:

- *In the same table,* when the BLOB attribute is mapped into a suitable column of the entity table as shown in Figure 11.3(a).

- *In a separate table,* when BLOB attributes are stored in a dedicated table, which contains at least two columns: a numerical primary key, for identifying the BLOB, and a column for storing the BLOB value as shown in Figure 11.3(b).

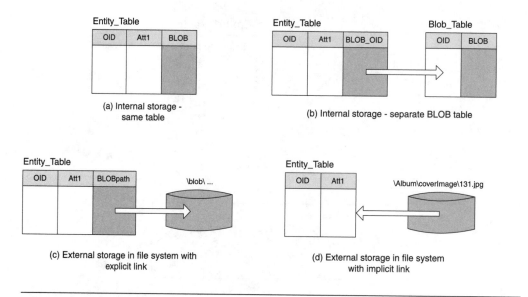

Figure 11.3 Alternative ways of storing BLOB attributes.

The first approach enables the retrieval of BLOB objects without requiring a join of different tables, but it can be impossible in certain database products that forbid multiple BLOB values in the same row. The storage in a separate table requires a join between the entity table and the BLOB table, but may save space by avoiding the storage of duplicates when several objects share the same value of the BLOB attribute.

With the external storage, each BLOB value is mapped to a file in the file system. This solution admits two options with respect to the way in which the file is linked to the entity instance that owns it:

- *Explicit link:* the pathname of the BLOB file is included in the entity table as an extra column as shown in Figure 11.3(c).

- *Implicit link:* there is no database column storing a reference to the BLOB file, but this reference is inferred by the application code, based on some file and directory naming convention, which establishes a sort of implicit link as shown in Figure 11.3(d). For example, a pathname like `\Album\coverImage\131.jpg` may denote the implicit link between the cover image attribute of the album object having OID = 131 and the file `131.jpg`, which contains the actual BLOB value.

The explicit link solution is more flexible than the implicit link one, because it permits storing BLOB attribute values as files with arbitrary names and positions in the file system.

Storage of BLOBs in the database has the advantage of centralizing the management of application content and facilitating its maintenance, because the added-value database services, like backup and recovery, are used also for the multimedia content. However, the lack of a file associated with the multimedia content makes programming the Web application more complex:

■ The storage and retrieval of BLOB values from the database, for example with such interoperability libraries as ODBC and JDBC involves complex sequences of statements, which may vary from database product to database product.

■ When building the HTML page, the construction of URLs referencing the BLOB becomes more complicated, because there is no file to point to. Normally, such URLs must point to a server-side program, for example a servlet, which is in charge of extracting the BLOB value from the database and serving it back to the browser.

■ Building the HTTP response, after a request for downloading the BLOB, requires setting extra HTTP headers, so that the browser is able to handle the file name and extension, when the user requires saving the BLOB value as a file on disk.

Storage of BLOBs in the file system facilitates the abovementioned programming tasks, because the BLOB value needs not be extracted from the database and is a "real" file, which can be referenced directly by the appropriate HTML tags and handled by the Web server and browser in a standard way. However, file system storage also has disadvantages: the BLOB application content does not benefit from the back up and recovery services of the database. Moreover, if the architecture includes several replicated Web servers and scripting engines, it is necessary to provide a shared file server in the data tier.

11.2.3 Mapping Relationships

The mapping of relationships depends on their cardinality; we separately address many-to-many and one-to-many relationships, whereas one-to-one relationships are treated as a special case of one-to-many relationships.

The mapping of *many-to-many relationships*, shown in Figure 11.4, requires the introduction of a dedicated table, called *bridge table*, consisting of the primary key columns of the two entities participating to the relationship.[1] The primary

---

[1]Note that we excluded N-ary relationships from the data model (see Chapter 2).

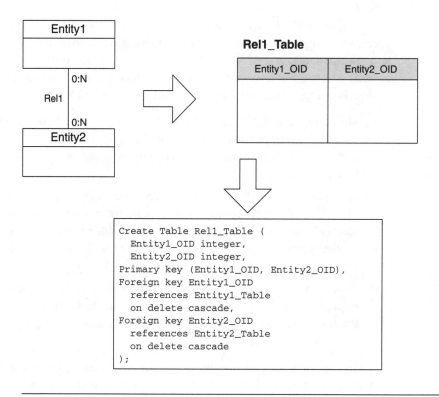

Figure 11.4 Translation of many-to-many relationship.

key of the bridge table comprises the primary key columns of the two participating entities; this reflects the meaning of a binary relationship, which requires that the same two objects cannot participate to the same relationship more than once.

The values stored in the columns of the bridge table represent references to the primary keys of the objects participating in the relationship. Therefore, these values cannot be chosen freely, but are constrained to be a subset of the primary key values appearing in the tables of the participating entities. This restriction is an example of *database integrity constraint,* that is, a property that must hold in every database state, for the content of the database to be valid. Integrity constraints are an important feature of databases, and are supported by the SQL language, which includes statements for expressing them in the definition of the database schema. A general treatment of SQL integrity constrains is outside the scope of this book, but the interested reader may find a full coverage of this topic in any database textbook and SQL manual. In the sequel, we illustrate only a few cases, in which integrity constraints help obtain a relational schema closer to the semantics of the Entity-Relationship schema.

The restriction needed for mapping relationships can be expressed in SQL using a *foreign key* integrity constraint in the definition of the bridge table. A foreign key constraint connects a child table to a parent table, imposing that the values of some columns of the child table, called referencing columns, match the values of selected columns of the parent table, called referenced columns. In the simplest case, the referencing columns include just one column, and the referenced column is the primary key of the parent table, which means that the rows of the child table include a "pointer" to the objects of the parent table.

Syntactically, a foreign key constraint is expressed in the definition of the child table. The statement:

```
foreign key Entity1_OID references Entity1_Table
```

in the declaration of the child table `Rel1_Table` specifies a referential integrity constraint between the referencing column `Entity1_OID` and the primary key column of the parent table `Entity1_Table` (see Figure 11.4 for a complete example of the syntax).

Relational database and the SQL language provide mechanisms for automatically restoring the database to a correct state, when a database update occurs, which produces a referential integrity violation. Referential integrity can be violated by four kinds of updates, which may produce rows in the child table with wrong values of the foreign key columns:

- The deletion or primary key update of rows in the parent table.

- The insertion or primary key update of rows in the child table.

In SQL, it is possible to express four actions to be taken by the database management system in response to a referential integrity violation:

- *Cascade:* the deletion or primary key update of the referenced row is propagated to the referencing row.

- *Set Null:* the foreign key column in the referencing row is set to the null value.

- *Set Default:* the foreign key column in the referencing row is set to a default value, established in the definition of the foreign key column.

- *No Action:* the transaction causing the integrity violation is aborted. This option is the default one.

Syntactically, the integrity repair action is added to the definition of the foreign key in the child table; for instance, the following SQL declaration specifies that a deletion of a row from the parent table (`Entity1_Table`) is followed by deletion of all the matching rows of the child table:

```
foreign key Entity1_OID references Entity1_Table
on delete cascade
```

Figure 11.4 shows the SQL code for creating the bridge table of a many-to-many relationship, comprising two referential integrity constraints from the bridge table to the tables of the participating entities; both constraints use the cascade action ensuring the deletion of dangling references upon deletion of the referenced entity instances. This is sufficient for protecting the database from integrity violations, because we assume that applications do not update the primary and foreign key of objects, and that the creation of an instance of the relationship always exploits the primary keys of two existing objects.

One-to-many relationships are translated by adding an extra column to the table of the entity participating to the relationship with maximum cardinality equal to one. Figure 11.5 shows an example of such translation: the relationship

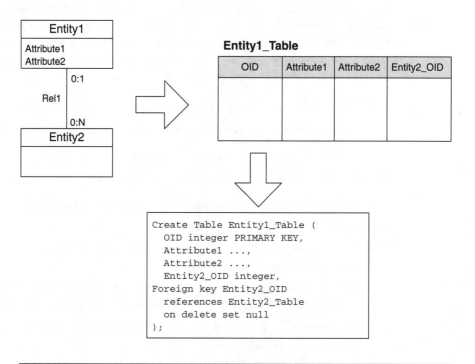

Figure 11.5 Translation of one-to-many relationships.

is mapped to the `Entity2_OID` column in the table of Entity1. Such column references the primary key of the table associated with Entity2. Note that if the relationship has minimum cardinality equal to one, then an integrity constraint, represented by the NOTNULL keyword, is added to the definition of column `Entity2_OID,` to force the presence of a value.

As for many-to-many relationships, a foreign key integrity constraint may be added to the definition of the child table, to express that the values of the referencing column are a subset of the primary key values of referenced table. To prevent integrity violations, a standard SQL repair action can be associated with the referential integrity constraint: such action could be SET NULL, if the relationship is optional (that is, minimum cardinality is equal to zero), or CASCADE, if the relationship is mandatory (that is, minimum cardinality is equal to 1). Note that the ON DELETE CASCADE option causes the deletion of the entire referencing row, which represents the whole object participating to the relationship, and not only the relationship instance. This may be appropriate, for instance, for automatically deleting all the lines of an order, when the order is deleted.

The case of *one-to-one relationships* is treated as the case of one-to-many relationships. The foreign key column mapping the relationship is preferably added to a table of the entity participating with 1:1 cardinality, if it exists, to avoid null values.

11.2.4 Mapping Generalization Hierarchies

Generalization hierarchies have been recently proposed in SQL 99,[2] an extension of the most widely adopted version of the SQL language, SQL 92, and have been implemented by a category of products called *object-relational databases,* which integrate the relational data model with selected features of the object-oriented model, including generalization. However, object-relational databases are less diffused than the purely relational ones, and their support to generalization varies from product to product.

As an alternative to using the built-in inheritance primitives of object-relational databases, generalization hierarchies can be mapped into a standard relational database schema, by transforming the super-entity and its specialized sub-entities into a set of correlated tables. Recall that in Chapter 2 we made a few simplifying assumptions on generalization hierarchies, excluding multiple inheritance and entities playing the role of super-entity in more than one hierarchy. Due to these assumptions, each generalization hierarchy assumes the topology of a tree

---

[2]SQL 99 provides a simple inheritance mechanism, whereby tables are associated with a type, and may inherit attributes from a supertype. Multiple inheritance is not supported.

of entities; thus, it is possible to express a mapping rule for a "parent-child" entity pair, and then apply such rule to all the entities in the tree, proceeding level-by-level; in this way, arbitrarily complex hierarchies can be mapped to tables.

Considering one level of the hierarchy, a generalization can be classified as total or partial:

■ It is *total* when every object of the super-entity is specialized into one of the sub-entities;

■ It is *partial* when some objects of the super-entity do not correspond to any object of one of the sub-entities.

Given one super-entity and its sub-entities, two alternative mapping strategies are possible:

1. Horizontal mapping, in which the generalization hierarchy is transformed into a single table, called *super-entity table,* which represents all the entities in the hierarchy.

2. Vertical mapping, in which the generalization hierarchy is partitioned into multiple tables, called *sub-entity tables,* each representing one entity.

Horizontal mapping is illustrated in Figure 11.6. The resulting table contains the attributes of all the entities in the hierarchy, plus one additional attribute (called `EntityType`), whose value permits one to distinguish the specific sub-entity to which an object belongs. If the specialization is *total,* the entity type assumes exactly N values, one for each specialized sub-entity; if it is *partial,* the entity type assumes N+1 values, one for each specialized sub-entity, plus one for the objects belonging only to the super-entity, which are not specialized. Consider, for example, entity Person and its derived sub-entities Male and Female: this specialization is total since each person is either male or female, and therefore the entity type may assume only two values (male or female). Conversely, if entity Person is partially specialized into the sub-entities Professor and Student, three values are needed for the entity type: one for the professor instances, one for the student instances, and one for all the persons that are neither professors, nor students.

The attributes of sub-entities typically assume many null values; more precisely, if one row represents an object of a given sub-entity, all the attributes associated with the other sub-entities are *null.* For example, supposing that professors have a department, the department attribute for all the persons that are not professors assumes a *null* value.

Vertical mapping is illustrated in Figure 11.7; in this approach, if the mapping is *total,* then the relational schema consists of one table per sub-entity. Each

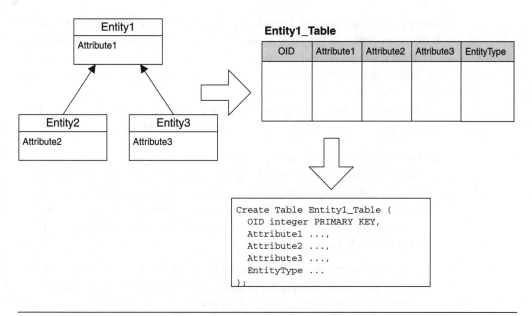

Figure 11.6 Horizontal translation of a generalization hierarchy.

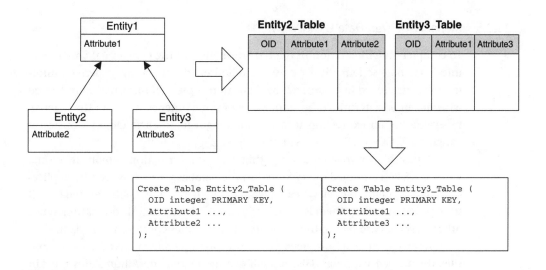

Figure 11.7 Vertical translation of a generalization hierarchy.

sub-entity table contains the columns representing its local attributes, plus the attributes inherited from the super-entity. If the specialization is *partial*, the resulting schema contains an additional table, having as columns the attributes of the
super-entity, and storing the instances of the super-entity that do not specialize
into any sub-entity.

The choice between horizontal and vertical mapping depends on the kind
of expected queries and on the number of attributes of the involved entities.

- Using *horizontal mapping is preferable* when the expected queries address
  most frequently all the objects of the super-entity irrespective of their
  specialization, and if the specific attributes of the sub-entities are few.
  A drawback of this translation is that the number of columns of the
  super-entity may be large, and the super-entity table may be filled
  with null values.

- Using *vertical mapping is preferable* when the most frequently expected
  queries separately address the objects of the sub-entities, and if the
  number of specialized attributes of the various sub-entities exceeds the
  number of the common attributes in the super-entity. The downside
  is that when an application accesses the attributes of the super-entity
  regardless of the partition of instances into sub-entities, then a union
  of all the sub-entity tables must be performed.

11.2.5 Mapping Derived Data Using Views

To complete the illustration of the transformation of the conceptual data model
into a database schema, it is necessary to address the mapping of derived information, introduced in Chapter 2. By definition, a piece of information is derived
when it can be determined from the value of some other elements of the schema,
by evaluating an expression in a suitable language, like the Object Constraint
Language (OCL) briefly discussed in Chapter 2.

A possible approach for computing derived information exploits relational
views. A *view* is a named query stored in the database, which is seen by applications as a regular table; views can always be queried, and sometimes updated, if
the query that defines them is sufficiently simple. A view definition may reference
other views or base tables; the latter are the real tables containing the data.

As an example of how views can be used to implement derived data, we consider the derived attributes /DiscountedPrice and /NumberOfAlbums illustrated in
Chapter 2, which we reproduce in Figure 11.8.

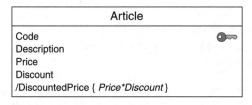

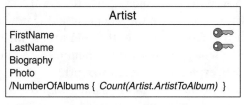

Figure 11.8 Derived attributes.

Attribute /DiscountedPrice, in entity Article, is defined as the product of the non-derived attributes Price and Discount. The mapping of entity Article may proceed as follows:

▪ First, a relational table is created, which maps all the non-derived attributes of the entity.

▪ Then a view is defined on top of such table, which extends the schema of the base relation with a column representing the derived attribute, calculated by means of a SQL expression.

The following pair of SQL statements performs the mapping of entity Article:[3]

```
CREATE TABLE ArticleBaseTable (
    Code number(10) primary key,
    Description varchar(100),
    Price float,
    Discount float
);
```

---

[3]We use attribute Code as primary key, instead of an ad hoc OID attribute, because such an attribute already identifies article instances and is a simple numeric value, which can be used efficiently as the primary key.

```
CREATE VIEW ArticleView AS
SELECT Code, Description, Price, Discount,
       (Price*Discount) AS DiscountedPrice
FROM ArticleBaseTable;
```

Syntactically, the declaration of the view is similar to the creation of a table, with the attribute list replaced by a SQL query. The effect of the CREATE VIEW statement is to define a virtual table, with the schema resulting from the column list of the SQL query. In the above example, the column list includes all the columns of table ArticleBaseTable, plus the virtual column DiscountedPrice, calculated by means of the SQL expression (Price*Discount).

The mapping of entity Artist proceeds in a similar way, but the SQL query is slightly more complex, because it involves the use of grouping and of aggregate functions, to count the number of albums published by an artist.

```
CREATE TABLE ArtistBaseTable (
    Oid number(10) primary key,
    FirstName varchar(50),
    LastName varchar(50),
    Biography clob,
    Photo varchar(100),
);
CREATE VIEW ArtistView AS
SELECT Oid, FirstName, LastName, Biography, Photo,
       COUNT(AlbumTable.Oid) AS NumberOfAlbums
FROM ArtistBaseTable, AlbumTable
WHERE ArtistBaseTable.Oid=AlbumTable.ArtistOid
GROUPBY ArtistBaseTable.Oid
```

The SQL query in the view definition joins the Artist base table and the Album table, using the foreign key column ArtistOid of table AlbumTable, which maps the one-to-many relationship ArtistToAlbum. The table resulting from the join, which contains as many rows for each artist as the number of albums he/she has published, is then grouped by artist OID, and then the aggregate function COUNT is used in the column list to determine the number of rows associated with each artist.

Other examples of derivation, like the total price of the shopping cart introduced in Chapter 4, can be treated in a similar way, by creating a SQL view that computes the derivation expression. Transforming a derivation expression into a SQL view is a rather technical task, which requires good knowledge of both the derivation language (for instance, OCL) and SQL. However, for the most commonly used derivations, such as those involving arithmetic calculations, counting, and relationship traversal, the translation into SQL is quite immediate and follows the patterns shown in the examples above. In Chapter 14 we will present a CASE tool which incorporates a compiler for automatically transforming derivation expressions, written using a subset of OCL, into SQL views.

11.2.6 Physical Design Tips

The design of the standard database illustrated so far leads to the construction of a *logical database schema,* which comprises the table definitions that best match the conceptual Entity-Relationship model of the application. These table definitions can be considered still at a high, "logical," level, because they do not include directives about the physical organization of data.

In the traditional lifecycle of a database application, logical design is followed by *physical design,* an activity concerned with the revision of the database schema, with the aim of optimizing the performance of queries.

Physical database design is a complex discipline, which requires an in-depth understanding of the way in which relational databases work, and also knowledge of the expected workload of database transactions and of the size of data. Even if treating physical database design is outside our aims, and is better left to a specialized textbook on database tuning, we provide in this section a few hints about the definition of indexes, which are the simplest, and often the most effective, mechanism for improving database performance. The proposed guidelines are necessarily very general and do not consider the distribution of data and transactions. However, they can be used as a starting point for physical database design, and complemented by more sophisticated database tuning actions.

The table definitions illustrated in the preceding sections can be complemented with the specification of indexes, which can be added to the database schema for speeding up the computation of the typical queries needed for publishing the content of the entities and relationships. The following indexes are of general utility:

- For each entity table, a unique index can be created on the primary key column (typically, on the OID column); such index may speed up the queries containing WHERE clauses of the form OID=<value>, like the query obtained by translating the default selector of data units.

- Additional indexes can be defined on the columns representing entity attributes used by units with attribute-based selector conditions. These indexes may accelerate the execution of the queries needed for retrieving the content of such units.

■ For a bridge table representing a many-to-many relationship, an index can be defined for each foreign key column; these indexes may speed up table joins between the bridge table and the entity tables, and the queries selecting the objects associated with a specific object via the relationship, which typically include a WHERE condition of the form `BridgeTable.EntityXOID=<value>`.

■ For an entity table including a foreign key column representing a one-to-many relationship, an index can be added on the foreign key column, which may accelerate the queries selecting the objects associated to a specific object via the relationship, which normally include a WHERE condition of the form `Entity1Table.Entity2OID=<value>`.

11.2.7 Running Example

This section presents the mapping to the standard relational schema of a portion of the Acer-Euro Entity-Relationship diagram. For the sake of brevity, we consider only the sub-schema shown in Figure 11.9, including entities NewsCategory, NewsItem, and Product, and the relationships among them. Obviously, the standard mapping can be extended to the whole schema of the Acer-Euro case described in Chapter 9.

By applying the standard mapping rules, each entity corresponds to a relational table, with as many columns as the number of attributes of the entity; since all entities lack a suitable candidate key, we add to each table a numeric OID column and define it as the primary key. Each relationship corresponds either to a bridge table (if cardinality is many-to-many) or to a foreign key (if cardinality is one-to-many). In the example, the standard schema contains three entity

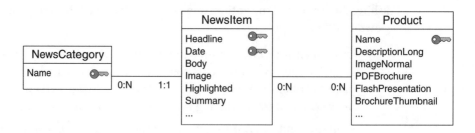

Figure 11.9 Part of the Acer-Euro structure model implemented in the example.

tables: NewsCategoryTable, NewsItemTable, and ProductTable. The one-to-many NewsItem_NewsCategory relationship is mapped to a foreign key in table NewsItemTable. Instead, the many-to-many relationship NewsItem_Product is implemented as a bridge table (NewsItem_ProductTable).

All the entity attributes are mapped into a column. BLOB attributes such as the ImageNormal attribute in the ProductTable and the Image attribute in the NewsItemTable could be mapped in different ways, as explained in Section 11.2.2: in this example, we suppose that they are stored in the file system, with an explicit reference in the entity tables.

Figure 11.10 gives the complete SQL definitions of tables NewsItemTable and NewsItem_ProductTable, inclusive of indexes.

Note that the primary OID column and the secondary key columns (Headline, Date) of table NewsItemTable are not null and unique (a unique index is defined), and that the NewsCategory_OID column is defined as not null, because it represents a one-to-many relationship with minimum cardinality equal to 1.

```
Create Table NewsItemTable (
  OID number(10) Primary Key,
  Headline varchar(50) NotNull,
  Date date  NotNull,
  Body clob,
  Image varchar(100),
  Highlighted boolean,
  Summary clob,
  NewsCategory_OID number(10) NotNull,
  Unique (Headline, Date),
  Foreign key NewsCategory_OID
       references NewsCategoryTable
       on delete cascade
);
Create Unique Index NewsItemOIDIndex on
  NewsItemTable(OID);
Create Unique Index NewsItemKeyIndex on
  NewsItemTable(Headline, Date);
Create Index NewsCategoryRefIndex on
  NewsItemTable(NewsCategory_OID)
```

```
Create Table NewsItem_ProductTable (
  NewsItem_OID number(10)
  Product_OID number(10)
  Primary key (NewsItem_OID, Product_OID),
  Foreign key NewsItem_OID
       references NewsItemTable
       on delete cascade,
  Foreign key Product_OID
       references ProductTable
       on delete cascade
);
Create Index NewsItem_Product_IndexNI on
  NewsItemTable(OID);
Create Index NewsItem_Product_IndexP on
  ProductTable(Product_OID);
```

Figure 11.10 Example of SQL for creation of tables and indexes.

This example shows that the mapping is almost mechanical and can be performed either manually or with the help of automatic code generation tools, like the one described in Chapter 14.

11.3 Data Management Issues and Architectures

Building the standard schema is a fundamental step for developing any one of the three data management architectures (dedicated, replicated, or online databases). In particular:

■ If the Web application manages and publishes its *dedicated database,* then the standard schema *is* the schema of such database and there are no further data integration issues. This situation is illustrated in Figure 11.11. The data of the Web application can be maintained by content-management site views, designed as discussed in Chapter 9 and implemented using the techniques that will be explained in Chapters 12 and 13.

■ Similarly, if the Web application exploits a *replicated database,* then the standard schema *is* the schema of the application database; however, the content is a copy of data residing in the external data sources. The problem is ensuring the periodic refresh of the data stored in the replicated database.

■ If the Web application must access *online databases,* the standard database defines the *view* of the external data sources required for

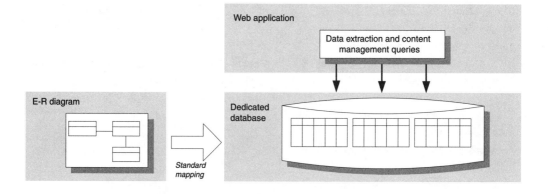

Figure 11.11 Architecture with dedicated database.

implementing the Web application. Depending on the nature of the external data sources, the view specified by the standard schema could be implemented using standard technology, for example distributed relational views, or should be reconstructed by ad hoc programming in the business tier.

The dedicated database architecture greatly simplifies the implementation of the data tier, because both the database schema and the content are new, and thus there are no problems related to the integration with existing data sources. The remaining data architectures pose more challenging problems, related to the existence of autonomous data sources, with their own schema and content. In this section we briefly discuss two fundamental questions to be addressed when implementing the data tier in the replicated and online architecture: *schema and data integration.*

11.3.1 Schema Integration

The standard schema expresses the "best" relational schema for supporting the Web application. In an ideal world, the Entity-Relationship diagram from which the standard schema is derived should perfectly match the schema of the existing data sources where content is stored, and thus the standard schema could be mapped onto the data sources simply by associating each entity and relationship table to the proper table in the preexisting databases. In reality, the data design conducted according to the method of Chapter 8 has *abstracted from the organization of data sources,* to avoid bias and obtain the schema of the database most suited to the Web application requirements. Thus, the problem of reconstructing the standard schema from the real data sources has been deferred on purpose to the data implementation phase. In order to minimize the schema integration efforts, an expert designer could use an intermediate approach and consider during data design both the requirements of the Web application and the constraints of the existing data sources. However, schema integration problems arise naturally in the design or re-engineering of information systems, whatever data analysis method is used, for various reasons:

■ *Analysis errors:* the data analysis phase may have overlooked the features of some of the involved data sources.

■ *Changes in the data schemas:* some data sources may have been changed, some may be no longer in use, or new ones may have been added.

In all the above cases, it is necessary to align the standard data schema to the real schema of the data sources. Two alternative approaches are possible:

■ *Adapting the standard schema* to make it consistent with the external data sources. This approach requires a sort of "upward propagation" of features from the physical level to the conceptual level. First, the standard schema is adapted, so that it becomes consistent with the schema of the existing data sources; next, the Entity-Relationship model is "reverse-engineered" to make it coherent with the updated relational schema. Finally, the part of the hypertext affected by the change in the Entity-Relationship model is aligned.

■ *Adapting the schema of the external data sources* to make it conform the standard schema. This option is more critical, because adaptation may affect preexisting applications that use the data sources; modifying such applications is unfeasible in most real situations, because they could be legacy or proprietary, or simply because changing them costs too much.

A possible solution, applicable if the external data sources are relational, is to adapt their schema to the standard schema using *views*, as shown in Figure 11.12. This approach, feasible when the standard schema can be reconstructed from the

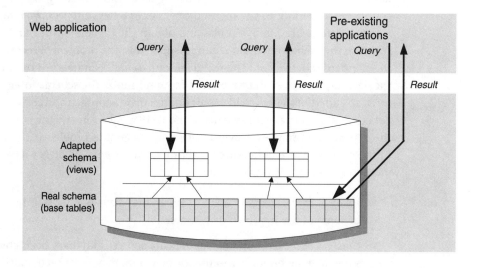

Figure 11.12   Using views to adapt the real database schema to the standard schema.

preexisting schema using SQL queries, lets the Web application work as if the standard schema existed, and at the same time leaves the source database and the preexisting applications unaffected.

11.3.2 Data Integration

Unifying different data sources is an instance of the well-known problem of *heterogeneous data integration,* which addresses the definition of coherent global views on top of multiple data sources, possibly heterogeneous. Heterogeneous data integration is an extremely challenging matter, because it requires not only the collection of data from multiple data sources, but also the reconciliation of conflicts and inconsistencies, which may arise at various levels:

- In the *physical format:* the data sources may exploit different technologies for storing data, like relational databases, repositories, text or XML files, and so on. Each format has its own query language or content retrieval API.

- In the *syntax:* the same information could be encoded using different syntaxes; for example, a date could be represented using the MM/DD/YYYY format in one data source, and the DD/MM/YYYY format in another one.

- In the *semantics:* data with the same name may have different interpretations in different data sources; for example, a field named "shipping date" could be interpreted as the shipping date from the manufacturer in one data source, and the shipping date from the retailer in another source.

Note that the above problems may occur also in the case of a single preexisting data source, when the inconsistencies arise between the preexisting schema and the standard schema obtained from the Entity-Relationship diagram. Discussing heterogeneous data integration in all its implications is outside the scope of this chapter. We provide several references in the Bibliographic Notes, and show in the next section concrete examples of data integration, performed with the help of commercial tools.

11.3.3 Implementation of the Replicated Database Architecture

The replicated database architecture addresses the integration problem by importing content from external data sources and integrating it into a database with the standard schema. Figure 11.13 shows this architecture.

The data transfer from the external data sources to the Web application database may range from a simple table copy, to complex transformations. In the

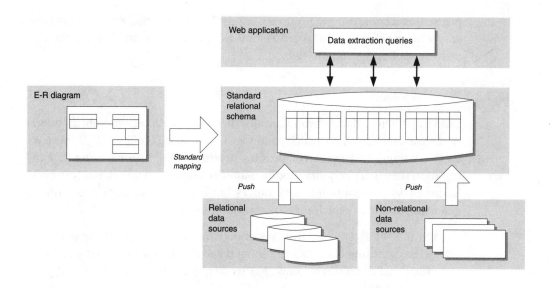

Figure 11.13   Architecture with replicated database.

following, we limit the discussion to data sources accessible using such interoperability standards as ODBC and JDBC. These data sources typically include relational databases and a few other formats, supported by ODBC or JDBC drivers. Accessing arbitrary non-relational sources requires implementing ad hoc programs that perform the same data transfer functions available in standard commercial products for relational databases.

Figure 11.14 pictorially illustrates the typical workflow of the data integration process, which involves extracting, transforming, and merging content taken from multiple data sources, and storing such content into the target database.

As a concrete example of the data integration process, we illustrate the use of *Microsoft Data Transformation Services (DTS),* a component of the Microsoft SQL Server 2000 database management system, which bundles a set of graphic tools and programmable objects for retrieving, transforming, and integrating information stored in heterogeneous data sources. DTS is activated from the management console of SQL Server 2000 (Figure 11.15) and includes a set of wizards for guiding the user through the data push process, which is seen as the export of information from one or more data sources, followed by the import of the exported elements into a destination data source.

The core concept of DTS is a *package,* a collection of data integration tasks, which can be applied to one or more data sources for moving database objects (for

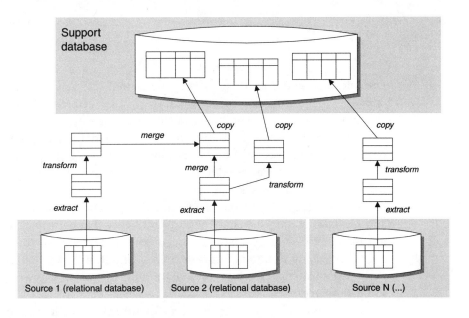

Figure 11.14 Data transformation workflow.

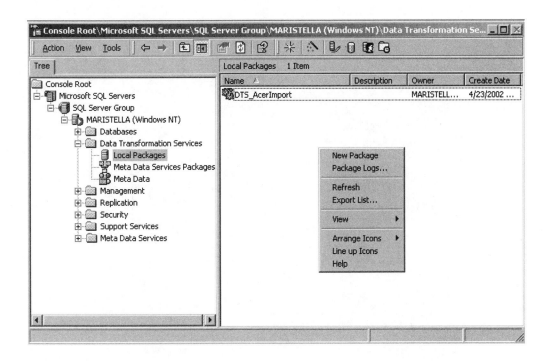

Figure 11.15 Activation of DTS Package Designer from SQL Server 2000 Enterprise Manager.

example, table definitions) and data to the desired destination. Each package is organized into one or more steps, which can be executed sequentially or in parallel. When executed, the package connects to the specified data sources, copies data and database objects, transforms data, and notifies specified users or processes of events occurred in the execution of the package. Packages are similar to modules: they can be edited, protected by passwords, scheduled for periodical execution, and versioned.

A package consists of four main elements: *connections, tasks, transformations,* and *workflows.* A *connection* is a link to a data source that participates to the data integration process, as a content provider or receiver. DTS uses Microsoft's OLE DB as the underlying technology of connections, and thus it can interact with any ODBC compliant data source. Figure 11.16 shows the wizard screen for attaching to a data source.

A *task* is a unit of work to be executed during the data integration process. DTS includes a set of predefined tasks, and can be extended by programming custom tasks using any language that supports the Microsoft COM object model. A

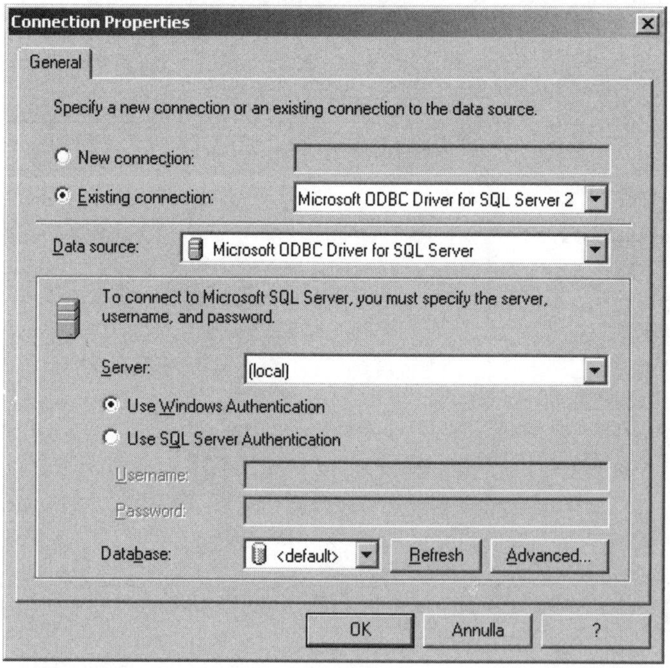

Figure 11.16 Definition of a connection with DTS Package Designer.

data transformation task moves data from a source table to a destination, and applies one or more transformations during such transfer, for example, adding a calculated column to a table. The most frequently used data transformation task is the Data Pump task (Figure 11.17), whereby it is possible to move selected content of one or more source tables into a destination table, either existing or newly created on the fly by means of a SQL statement.

A *transformation* is a conversion operation applied to the columns of a source table, typically during a data transformation task. DTS has a predefined set of column transformations, which can be extended by custom transformations written in Visual Basic. The provided transformations include column copy, date format conversion, string transformations (like case conversion, trimming, and sub-string selection), and file-based transformations, like the insertion of files in table columns.

A *package workflow* is a diagram representing the precedence constraints among the tasks of the package. Figure 11.18 shows an example of workflow diagram, consisting of three tasks and two precedence constraints. The workflow aims at moving a table from a source to a destination database. The first step is specified as a SQL statement dropping the target table from the destination database. The second step, represented as a solid arrow between two database icons, represents a data pump task for actually transferring the table; the first task is connected to the second one by an "On Success" link, which means that the second step is executed only after the successful completion of the first step. Finally

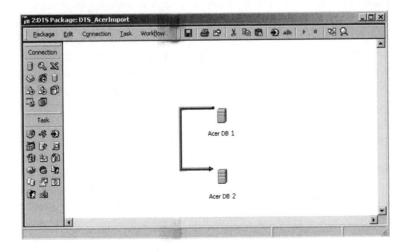

Figure 11.17   Creation of a Data Pump Task in the DTS Package Designer.

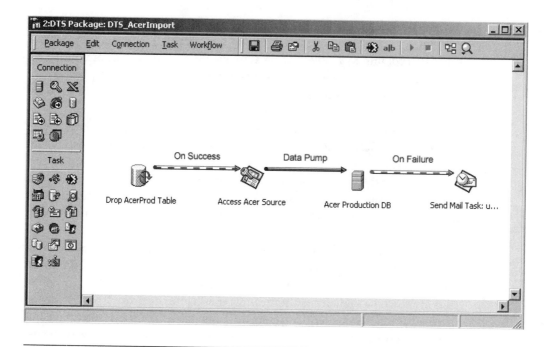

Figure 11.18   Workflow diagram of a DTS package.

a mail notification task is connected to the data pump task by a failure link, which makes the email notification to be sent only if the table copy fails.

DTS and similar tools can be applied also to the task of *data refreshing*, in which the data transformation workflow reduces simply to the scheduled copy of data from one or more preexisting data sources to the database supporting the Web application. In this way, corporate data is managed securely in the enterprise information system, and is copied to the database of the Web application for publication on the Web.

11.3.4   Implementation of Online Database Architectures

With the dedicated and replicated database architectures, the online publishing of content is decoupled from its maintenance, which occurs separately from Web access, within the enterprise information system. Such decoupling is not possible with the online database architecture, because the application needs live access to the corporate data.

From the application integrator's perspective, the best technological solution for the implementation of the online database architecture is to exploit *distributed database technology*, as shown in Figure 11.19. A distributed database is a

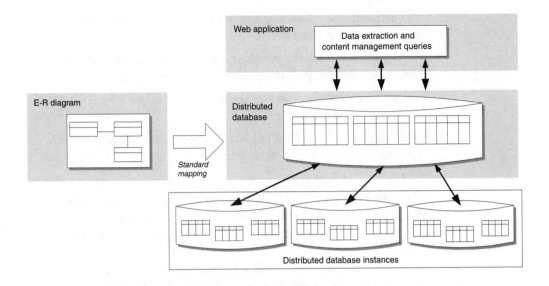

Figure 11.19 Distributed database architecture.

database system capable of managing in a unified manner data spread across multiple database instances; the client application interacting with the database is given the illusion of a unique centralized database, which is mapped by the distributed database management system onto multiple physical databases.

The most important benefits provided by distributed databases to the client applications are *location and fragmentation transparency;* thanks to these properties, an application is unaware of the physical place where the data reside, and of the fact that the data of a single logical table may be segmented into multiple physical tables; the query processor and a name binding service take care of reformulating a query on the logical tables into a query on the physical tables, and of addressing sub-queries to the host where the data are actually stored.

The services provided by distributed databases typically include:

- *Distributed views:* the possibility of defining views over multiple distributed data sources. Such views build the appearance of a centrally managed relational table, but the query that defines the distributed view collects data from different databases. In particular, the entire standard relational schema may appear as a set of distributed views over remote data sources.

- *Distributed query processing:* the ability to pose queries over multiple tables, hosted in different data sources. Queries on top of the standard relational schema are translated, by the view decomposition mechanism, into queries on the underlying data sources, and then executed by the distributed query processor.

■ *Distributed transactions:* the possibility of defining sequences of updates to be executed atomically on tables stored in different databases.

■ *Distributed administration services:* the availability of procedures for distributed backup and failure recovery.

■ *Scalable performance:* the best products apply special optimization techniques to distributed SQL queries, which ensure high performance and massive scalability.

Distributed database servers are offered by all major database vendors. The downsides of this technology are essentially the high cost, the need of being administered by skilled personnel, and the limited interoperability and proprietary nature.

In absence of a distributed database, linking the Web application to remote data sources requires establishing *explicit independent connections* to each data source, using interoperability standards like JDBC or ODBC; Figure 11.20 shows the resulting architecture. With this approach, the Web application manages

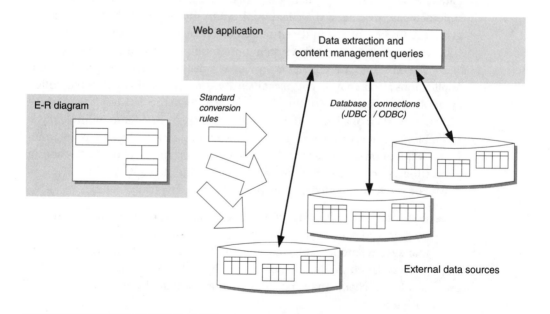

Figure 11.20   Online database architecture with explicit connection to multiple data sources.

multiple connections to the various data sources and uses such connections to execute queries and updates. In this architecture, there is not a single centralized database compliant to the standard relational schema, but the tables corresponding to the entities and relationships are scattered across the various data sources, and are individually accessed by the application to construct the content of pages and units.

The architecture of Figure 11.20 has the advantage of simplicity, because connecting to multiple preexisting databases does not require complex technology, but exploits the same mechanisms as for connecting to a single dedicated database, as long as the data sources are accessible using ODBC or JDBC. However, several disadvantages compensate architectural simplicity:

- *Location transparency is not possible.* The Web application must know exactly where each piece of content is stored to be able to dispatch the right query to the right place. As a consequence, a re-allocation of data in the data sources affects the code of the Web application.

- *Inter-database relationships between entities must be hand-programmed.* If the Entity-Relationship schema includes a relationship between entities mapped to different data sources, it is not possible to exploit the power of the SQL query processor for joining the remote tables, as required for navigating from one object to another related object. Cross-database relationships must be implemented in custom ways, for example by importing into one of the two involved databases the OIDs of the related objects. Doing this breaks the query optimization capabilities of the relational engine and forces the implementation of join algorithms in the code of the Web application, which is technically difficult and problematic for performance.

- *Lack of transactional atomicity.* If a content modification required by the Web application spans multiple data sources, the application code must ensure that the modification is applied atomically, which means that it either succeeds at all the involved data sources, or it fails and is rolled back at all sites. This property is technically difficult to implement, especially in a distributed environment, and requires the use of specialized software architectures and products.

The difficulty of interacting with multiple data sources is alleviated by middleware products and by enterprise application integration platforms. In Chapter 13 we will illustrate the use of Enterprise JavaBeans for wrapping relational data sources and exposing them as business objects in the middle tier.

Summary

In this chapter we have discussed data implementation, which is the activity aimed at providing persistent storage to the content of the Web application. We have illustrated how to transform an Entity-Relationship diagram into a standard relational schema, by applying transformation rules to entities, relationships, and generalization hierarchies. This transformation may take advantage of relational constructs like referential integrity constraints and indexes, which make both the resulting relational schema more adherent to the semantics of the Entity-Relationship and query processing more efficient.

The standard relational schema is used in different data integration architectures. We first discussed the situation in which a dedicated database is used and therefore the standard relational schema is directly exploited to store the content of the Web application. Next, we considered the scenario in which content preexists to the Web application, and discussed the replicated database architecture, in which data are periodically copied from the origin database to the database of the Web application, a task well supported by commercial data replication software. Finally, we addressed the online database architecture, in which the Web application directly accesses the information stored in the native data sources, and described a high-level solution based on distributed database technology, as well as a low-level approach, which requires programming the various connections and queries to the external data sources.

Real applications often exhibit a mix of the three data architectures, and therefore require a mix of the discussed solutions.

Bibliographic Notes

The process of transforming the conceptual design into a relational schema is described in several textbooks, including [ACPT99, BCN92]. In [ACPT99] the standard mapping rules for deriving a relational schema from an Entity-Relationship diagram are presented, and various design options are discussed; more general mapping rules are described in [BNC92], which addresses the mapping of Entity-Relationship schemas into different data models (relational, network, and hierarchical). The activity of integrating the schemas of existing or new databases into a global, unified schema is surveyed in [BLN86]. A comparative review of the work accomplished in this area is provided, which identifies the strengths and weaknesses of the various methodologies. Formal approaches to view integration are discussed in [BC86] and [GJM96]. The data transfer from heterogeneous data sources into a destination database can be realized with the help of transformation tools, like the Data Transformation Service (DTS) by Microsoft [Microsofte] shown in Section 11.3.3. Another example of data transformation tool is DataStage XE by Ascential [ASC], which permits extracting data from arbitrary data sources and progressively combining the extracted data through a variety of transformation operations. Data transformation can also be expressed directly in SQL99, by means of special operators [GP99].

The maintenance of replicated databases relates to the problem of maintaining materialized views. In [CKLMR97] the authors investigate a number of issues related to supporting multiple views with different maintenance policies.

Distributed database management systems are the subject of several textbooks, among which [CP84, OV99] provide a thorough overview of this technology; distributed transactions are described by several articles and books, like [GR93] and [WT02].

Several commercial products available on the market support database distribution. For example, the Oracle 9i database system includes two interoperability solutions, called Transparent Gateways and Generic Connectivity, that permit access to multi-vendor databases using an Oracle database as a front-end. These solutions offer location transparency, multi-site queries, SQL dialects translation, distributed views across heterogeneous databases, and distributed atomic transactions. As another example, Microsoft SQL Server 2000 offers the possibility of defining linked servers, which operate as a federation of distributed databases. In a cluster of linked servers it is possible to define distributed partitioned views, which are relational views with base tables distributed over different nodes of the cluster. The client can address queries to a single server, and query processing is automatically performed on the appropriate servers in the cluster.

12 Hypertext Implementation

12.1   Introduction

Hypertext implementation is the phase in which the conceptual specification of the front-end of the Web application must be transformed into a set of concrete software components, installable in one of the architectures illustrated in Chapter 10. These components dynamically build the pages of the application from the content stored in the data sources, using one of the data implementation architectures discussed in Chapter 11.

As a platform for exemplifying hypertext implementation, this chapter uses the Java programming language and its extensions for Web development, in particular the JSP server-scripting language and the JDBC database connection interface. However, the discussion proceeds as much as possible on general grounds, so that the illustrated techniques remain valid also in other contexts, for example in the Microsoft .NET architecture, or in a PHP-based Web server.

For simplicity of illustration, we will start explaining the implementation of the various hypertext constructs by associating all the functions needed to dynamically compute a page to a single JSP template. In this way, all the programming tasks necessary for page computation remain concentrated in a single source file, which simplifies the understanding of the implementation techniques.

All the JSP templates that we will discuss share a common structure, which comprises five main sections, each one addressing a specific problem of page computation: the fetching of parameters from the HTTP request, the connection to the database, the query execution and context propagation, the production of the HTML code, and the final disposition of temporary objects.

The progression of the examples follows the order of presentation of WebML primitives adopted in Chapters 3 and 4. We exemplify the JSP, JDBC, and SQL code necessary for implementing almost all the WebML primitives introduced in these chapters, but, most important, illustrate the general structure of a page template comprising the implementation of several linked units, so that readers may easily extend the provided examples and implement any combination of units they may need in their hypertext specification. Furthermore, appendix D at the end of the book provides a concise summary of all the main aspects of the implementation of each WebML construct.

This chapter presents the basic implementation techniques of units, pages, and links, using a single page template encompassing all the functions needed for page computation. This software organization is used for illustration purposes, but is not recommended as the best software modularization scheme for real projects, with many complex pages, because putting everything in a single page template results in a source code that is overloaded with many heterogeneous functions, and thus difficult to read and maintain.

A better software organization will be presented in Chapter 13, where we apply classical software engineering techniques and design patterns to achieve a better distribution of the responsibilities of dynamic page computation. The monolithic page templates of this chapter will be split into a set of reusable software components, to better exploit the object-orientation of the development language and the separation of concerns granted by a software design pattern called Model-View-Controller (MVC).

12.2 Overview of the Page Computation Steps

We start the explanation of hypertext implementation by recalling the typical workflow for dynamically computing a Web page from content stored in a database. The required activities are schematized in Figure 12.1.

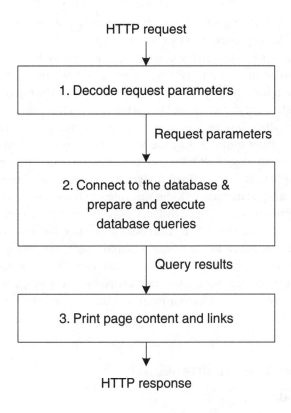

Figure 12.1   Computation of a dynamic page template from database content.

In the first step, the HTTP request is analyzed, to extract possible parameters, typically to be used by the database queries for retrieving the page content. In the second step, the connection to the database is established and the queries for extracting the content needed to populate the page are assembled and executed. In most cases, queries have a fixed structure and require only input parameters; in a few cases, the query source code must be assembled at runtime, just prior to executing the query. After a query is submitted to the database, its results are collected into suitable data structures, and may be used to determine the value of parameters used in some other content retrieval query. Therefore, query execution is iterated until all the queries needed to retrieve the page content have been processed. Finally, in the last step, when all the pieces of content necessary to construct the HTML page have been retrieved, the page is produced and returned as result of the HTTP call. Specifically, the query results are used to build the dynamic part of the page, which typically consists of content (texts, images, and so on), and links, expressed as HTML anchor tags.

The essential parts of the above page computation flow are the construction and execution of the content retrieval queries and the production of the HTML markup. Each unit in the page has its own rules for retrieving the content and for producing the markup code, and when the page contains multiple linked units, the order in which queries are executed is important, because a unit may require input from other units. It is in the solution of these problems that the WebML specification of pages helps: WebML classifies the content elements that may appear in the page in well-defined categories, corresponding to the different kinds of units, and establishes well-defined rules for the order in which units are computed, represented by the high-level page computation procedure explained in Chapter 5. Therefore, the general schema of activities illustrated in Figure 12.1 can be specialized to the case of a WebML page, consisting of several linked units, to obtain a page implementation road map, shown in Figure 12.2.

The first part of the page template implements the initial assignment of parameter values to page units. The navigation of a link by the user results in an

---

Part 1: Extract parameters from the HTTP request

Part 2: Connect to the database

Part 3: Prepare and execute queries:

    1. Construct query statement of current unit

    2. Execute query

    3. If there are dependent units, bind the output of the current unit to the input of dependent units, and repeat steps 1–3

Part 4: Produce the dynamic page content

    Build the HTML markup for rendering the current unit, from the result of the query associated to it

    Build the outgoing contextual links of the unit by:

    1. Building the fixed part of the URL

    2. Building the parameters associated with the link

Part 5: Dispose temporary resources

Figure 12.2 General schema of the JSP template for implementing a WebML page.

HTTP request, possibly containing the parameter values needed for initializing the units of the page. These parameters represent either the "fresh" values produced by the navigation of the link, used to obtain new content for some units, or "preserved" values, used to "remember" past choices made by the user in previous navigations of intra-page links. From the technical standpoint, the extraction of parameters from the request must cope with the different ways of encoding parameters in HTTP requests.

The second part of the page template addresses the connection to the database, preliminary to the execution of the data retrieval queries necessary to fetch the content of page units. This is a simple technical task, which requires knowledge of the chosen programming interface to the database.

Part 3 is the core of the template, which embodies the page computation semantics. Its goal is to compute all the computable units of the page, taking into account the fact that the page can be accessed along different links, which correspond to different parameters in the HTTP request. This section of the template reflects the computation procedure explained in Chapter 5: first, the initially computable units are determined and their queries are evaluated; then, the output of such queries is used as input for calculating the query of other dependent units. This part of the template must also resolve ambiguities caused by units with multiple alternative inputs. At the end of this part of the template, all the data retrieval queries of the computable units have been performed, and their results are stored in appropriate data structures, from which they can be extracted to produce the dynamic portion of the HTML mark-up.

Part 4 builds the HTML content of each unit, by intermixing the dynamically generated content with the static HTML mark-up of the page, to achieve the desired page layout. The construction of the units' mark-up addresses three aspects: the rendition of the unit's content, the construction of the unit's outgoing contextual links, and the construction of the page's non-contextual links. The construction of contextual links requires the definition of the URL associated to the link, which typically consists of a fixed part, depending on the page to which the link points, and of a dynamically assembled query string, which bundles the output parameters necessary to compute the destination page of the link. Instead, the construction of non-contextual links is straightforward, because the involved URLs have no parameters and are fixed, once the various pages of the site view have been associated to the JSP templates that implement them.

Finally, the last section of the template simply disposes the temporary object used in the previous phases.

We are now ready to show concrete examples of JSP pages built according to this general scheme.

12.3 Implementing Pages, Content Units, and Links

In this section, we concretely apply the computation illustrated in Figure 12.2 to several cases of JSP page templates, corresponding to typical WebML pages made of content units and links. We use the data structure and hypertext model of the Acer-Euro running case to build a gallery of representative examples. In particular, news categories and news will be used as running objects. For convenience, Figure 12.3 recalls the Entity-Relationship model of the news categories and news objects, and the equivalent relational tables.

12.3.1 Standalone Pages

Figure 12.4 shows a WebML *page consisting of a single context-free unit*. In particular the page contains an index unit, called NewsCategories, for publishing the list of all the news categories. In the example, we assume that each news category is

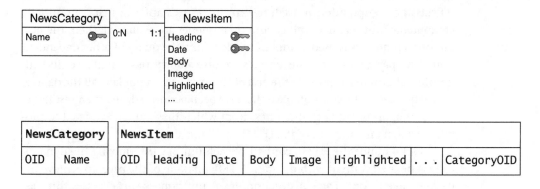

Figure 12.3   News and news categories: Entity-Relationship model and equivalent relational tables.

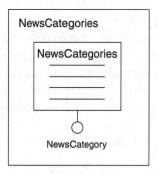

Figure 12.4   WebML page with a single index unit and no input links.

denoted simply by the category name, and the index is ordered by ascending category name.

Figure 12.5 shows the JSP page template implementing the page of Figure 12.4.

```
1   <%@page language="java" %>
2   <%@ page import= "java.sql.*" %>
3   <% // DATABASE CONNECTION
4   Class.forName("sun.jdbc.odbc.JdbcOdbcDriver");
5   Connection conn = DriverManager.getConnection("jdbc:odbc:acme",
6                      "acmeuser", "acmepwd");
7   // QUERY PREPARATION AND EXECUTION
8   Statement stmt = conn.createStatement();
9   ResultSet result = stmt.executeQuery(
10                     "SELECT NAME FROM NEWSCATEGORY ORDER BY NAME");
11  %>
12  <!-- CONTENT PRODUCTION -->
13  <html>
14  <head>
15  <title>News Categories Page</title>
16  </head>
17  <body>
18  <!-- INDEX UNIT MARKUP PRODUCTION -->
19  <table>
20      <% while (result.next()) { %>
21      <tr>
22          <td><%= result.getString("NAME") %></td>
23      </tr>
24      <%} %>
25  </table>
26  </body>
27  </html>
28  <!-- TEMPORARY OBJECTS DISPOSAL -->
29  <%
30  result.close();
31  stmt.close();
32  conn.close();
33  %>
```

Figure 12.5 JSP implementation of NewsCategories page.

With respect to the general structure illustrated in Figure 12.2, the organization of the template of Figure 12.5 is simpler, because several optional parts are not needed.

The extraction of the request parameters is not necessary, because unit NewsCategories has no input links, and thus the page is called with an HTTP request without parameters, for example, by navigating an URL like the following one (assuming that the page templates is saved in a file named `newsCategories.jsp`): *www.myserver.com/newsCategories.jsp*

Therefore, the page template starts directly from Part 2, which includes the code for connecting to the database. This code will remain the same in all the subsequent examples, and will be commented only for this first case. After a few preliminary JSP declarations (lines 1–2), at line 4 the database driver is loaded and automatically registers an instance of itself within the JDBC driver manager. In particular the Java class called `sun.jdbc.odbc.JdbcOdbcDriver` is a JDBC driver (called JDBC-ODBC bridge) for Windows-based systems, which implements JDBC functions by translating them into native ODBC operations.[1] The actual database connection is represented by a Java object of type `Connection`, which is created at line 5, by invoking the function `getConnection` of class `DriverManager`. The `getConnection` function accepts three input values: the data source name, the username and the password. In the rest of this chapter, we will connect to a database called `acme`, using the strings `acmeuser` and `acmepwd` as username and password, respectively. Part 2 ends with the creation of a connection object, whereby it is possible to start interacting with the database.[2]

After the connection to the database is established, the template continues with the formulation of the unit's query and its execution. In the present example, this task is particularly simple, because there is a single unit, and the code of its associated query is fixed and without input parameters. Obviously, parameter propagation does not occur inside the page, because there is a single unit.

At line 8, the `createStatement` function is invoked on the connection object, to create an empty statement object, called `stmt`, which represents an interface for executing queries. This statement object is used to pose the query to the database, by invoking the `executeQuery` function on it (lines 9–10). The

---

[1]Using a different JDBC driver entails a modification of the code at line 4, changing the Java class to the one required by the specific driver.

[2]In a real setting, the creation and closure of the database connection would be factored out of the page. The database connections would be initialized and pooled by the application server, and accessed as a shared resource by all the page templates of the application.

executeQuery function takes as argument the actual source code of the SQL query, and returns the query result in the form of a record set. In this example, the query is a simple SELECT statement and the result is assigned to the Java variable named result. Note that no selector is specified in the WebML index unit, and thus the SELECT statement does not include the WHERE condition, and extracts from the NEWSCATEGORY table all the existing rows. The SELECT statement has an attribute list containing the NAME column, which corresponds to the attribute shown in the index unit, and an ORDER BY clause, which mirrors the sorting criterion (ascending by NAME) of the WebML unit.

The production of the HTML mark-up starts at line 12. After some static HTML (lines 12–17), the page template contains the section for computing the dynamic portion of the page (lines 18–25). This portion comprises an HTML table, built from the result of the SQL query. In particular, the table contains one row for each record in the result set, and each row contains a single cell built from the value of the NAME attribute of the current record. To construct the table, a while loop is necessary (lines 20–24), which halts when the result.next() function returns false, meaning that there are no more rows to process. Inside the loop, an HTML row and cell are created containing the value of the NAME attribute of the current record (result.getString("NAME")). Therefore, executing the loop produces as many HTML rows as the number of rows in the NEWSCATEGORY table.

Finally, the last part of the JSP template (lines 28–33) simply closes the various Java objects used to communicate with the database.

The example of this section can be generalized also to *standalone multidata units* and to *units with selectors:*

- A standalone multidata unit would require the same data retrieval query as the one shown at lines 9–10. The HTML mark-up production part would be similar, possibly with a different layout of the unit's instances, for example, for tiling the instances of the multidata unit in a matrix, instead of arranging them in a list. The real difference between the index and multidata unit is in the implementation of their outgoing link; this difference will be clarified in Section 12.3.5.

- If an index or multidata unit has a selector, the SQL statement of the unit's query includes an appropriate WHERE clause. For example, the index unit shown in Figure 12.6 has an attribute-based selector, which retrieves only the news categories with attribute ApprovalStatus equal to 1, and corresponds to the following SQL query:

```
SELECT NAME FROM NEWSCATEGORY WHERE
APPROVALSTATUS = 1 ORDER BY NAME
```

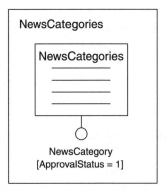

Figure 12.6 Index unit with attribute-based selector.

A slightly more complex code is required to handle hierarchical index units, which retrieve content from multiple entities and present the index entries in a hierarchical way. As an example, consider the example of Figure 12.7, where a hierarchical index unit shows the news items grouped by category.

The first modification is in the SQL query for retrieving the content of the unit, which must join the NEWSCATEGORY and NEWSITEM tables, to obtain a set of rows where the heading of each news item is paired to the name of the category it belongs to:

```
SELECT C.NAME, N.HEADING
FROM NEWSCATEGORY C LEFT JOIN NEWSITEM N ON C.OID =
N.CATEGORYOID
ORDER BY C.NAME, N.HEADING
```

Then, the result set of the query is used to produce the HTML mark-up, for example to build two nested HTML lists, showing the category names, and for each category, the heading of each pieces of news of that category. To this end, a loop with several nested conditional statements is required, as exemplified by the code in Figure 12.8.

12.3.2 Inter-page Links

The next example shows the implementation of links, starting with *inter-page contextual links*. In particular, the introduction of links raises two issues:

- The production of the HTML rendition of the link *in the source page*.
- The fetching of the parameters transported by the link and the assignment of the parameter's values to the input of the units *in the destination page*.

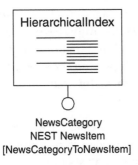

HierarchicalIndex
NewsCategory
NEST NewsItem
[NewsCategoryToNewsItem]

Figure 12.7 Hierarchical index unit with attribute-based selector.

```
<ul> <!-- CONTENT PRODUCTION: HIERARCHICAL INDEX UNIT -->
  <% String lastCategoryName = null;
    while (result.next()) {
      String categoryName = result.getString("NAME");
      String heading = result.getString("HEADING");
      if (!categoryName.equals(lastCategoryName)) { // NEW CATEGORY
          if (lastCategoryName != null) { // NOT FIRST CATEGORY %>
            </ul>
          </li>
          <%}
          lastCategoryName = categoryName; %>
          <li><%= categoryName %>
            <ul>
      <%} %>
      <% if (heading != null) { %>
              <li><%= heading %></li>
      <%} %>
    <%}
    if (lastCategoryName != null) { %>
            </ul>
          </li>
      <%} %>
</ul>
```

Figure 12.8 JSP implementation of a WebML hierarchical unit.

Figure 12.9 shows a WebML hypertext extending the example of Figure 12.4; *the index unit is now linked to a data unit* over entity NewsCategory, placed in a distinct page. The meaning of this configuration is that the selection of one element in the index opens the CategoryDetails page on the selected object.

To achieve this effect, the implementation discussed in the previous section is extended in two ways:

- A JSP template implementing the CategoryDetails page is introduced; this template is called by means of an HTTP request transporting the identifier of the news category object to show, and uses this parameter in the SQL query associated to the Category data unit.

- The JSP template for page NewsCategories is extended, by adding one HTML anchor for each row of the dynamically built index of categories. The href attribute of each anchor tag contains a different URL, concatenating the name of the template implementing the CategoryDetails page, and the declaration of a request parameter transporting the OID of the object used to construct the current row of the index.

Figure 12.10 shows the JSP template of page NewsCategories, with comments delimiting the fundamental code sections. As a first extension, the SQL query at line 10 has been augmented to retrieve also the OID column of table NEWSCATEGORY. The OID is used at lines 23–24 to construct the URL associated to each index row, by wrapping the name of each category inside an HTML anchor (`<a>` . . . `</a>`) tag. For each row of the index, the HTML anchor tag includes an href attribute consisting of a fixed part (`categoryDetails.jsp?categoryDU=`) and a variable

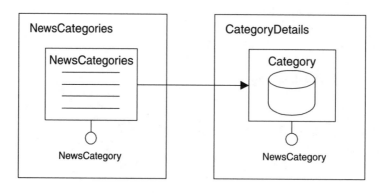

Figure 12.9   Two pages connected by a contextual link.

```
1   <%@page language="java" %>
2   <%@ page import= "java.sql.*" %>
3   <% // DATABASE CONNECTION
4   Class.forName("sun.jdbc.odbc.JdbcOdbcDriver");
5   Connection conn = DriverManager.getConnection("jdbc:odbc:acme",
6                       "acmeuser", "acmepwd");
7   // QUERY PREPARATION AND EXECUTION
8   Statement stmt = conn.createStatement();
9   ResultSet result = stmt.executeQuery(
10      "SELECT NAME,OID FROM NEWSCATEGORY ORDER BY NAME");
11  %>
12  <!-- CONTENT PRODUCTION -->
13  <html>
14  <head>
15  <title>News Categories Page</title>
16  </head>
17  <body>
18  <!-- INDEX UNIT MARKUP PRODUCTION -->
19  <table>
20  <% while (result.next()) { %>
21  <tr>
22  <!-- INDEX UNIT OUTPUT LINK PRODUCTION -->
23  <td><a href="categoryDetails.jsp?categoryDU=<%=result.getString("OID")%>">
24      <%= result.getString("NAME") %></a></td>
25  </tr>
26  <%} %>
27  </table>
28  </body>
29  </html>
30  <%
31  result.close();
32  stmt.close();
33  conn.close();
34  %>
```

Figure 12.10 JSP implementation of page NewsCategories.

part (`<%=result.getString("OID")%>`). The fixed part is file name of the template associated with the destination page (`categoryDetails.jsp`), followed by the constant part of the query string, which contains the name of the parameter (`categoryDU`). The variable part of the URL is built from the value of the `OID` column of the current row of the `NEWSCATEGORY` table, retrieved from the query result stored in the Java object named `result`. Executing the template produces a table of news categories, but this time, compared to the template of Figure 12.5, each category name is the anchor of an HTML link.

Note that the name of the parameter passed through the HTTP request (`categoryDU`) recalls the destination unit where the parameter is used, which is the Category data unit; having a consistent parameter naming convention is a good practice, because it helps the programmer of the source page construct the HTTP request, and the programmer of the destination page associate each request parameter to the query of the respective unit.

Figure 12.11 shows the JSP code in the file named `categoryDetails.jsp`, which implements page CategoryDetails.

The template shows the extraction of parameters from the HTTP request: at line 4, the instruction `request.getParameter("categoryDU")` retrieves from the predefined JSP object named `request`, which represents the HTTP request, the value of the parameter named `categoryDU`, and stores the extracted value into a Java variable associated to the unit's input parameter (`categoryDUInput`). The value fetched from the request is exactly the one appended to the URL constructed in page NewsCategories, as shown by line 23 of Figure 12.10.

The value of the `categoryDUInput` variable is used to compute the page content; in the present case, the page computation algorithm is trivial: there is a single unit (the Category data unit), which receives its expected input from the single parameter of the HTTP request. The value of this parameter is used to prepare the data retrieval query for the Category data unit, which extracts the name and description of the news category having the OID stored in the `categoryDUInput` variable. In this case, the source code of the SQL query is not fixed, as in the previous examples, because the value of the OID to use in the `WHERE` clause may vary, depending on the value in the HTTP request. This problem can be solved using *prepared statements,* which are a feature commonly found in the native application programming interfaces of database systems, and in the interoperability libraries like ODBC and JDBC. A prepared statement is defined as a query object that is sent to the database system in two steps: a first time for being compiled, and then, after compilation, for being executed. Execution can be repeated as many times as required without the need of recompilation, which saves execution time.

```
1   <%@page language="java" %>
2   <%@ page import= "java.sql.*" %>
3   <% // REQUEST PARAMETERS FETCH
4   String categoryDUInput = request.getParameter("categoryDU");
5   // DATABASE CONNECTION
6   Class.forName("sun.jdbc.odbc.JdbcOdbcDriver");
7   Connection conn = DriverManager.getConnection("jdbc:odbc:acme",
8                       "acmeuser", "acmepwd");
9   // QUERY PREPARATION
10  PreparedStatement pstmt = conn.prepareStatement(
11        "SELECT NAME, DESCRIPTION FROM NEWSCATEGORY WHERE OID =?");
12  pstmt.setString(1, categoryDUInput);
13  // QUERY EXECUTION.
14  ResultSet result = pstmt.executeQuery();
15  %>
16  <html> <!- CONTENT PRODUCTION ->
17  <head>
18  <title>News Category Page</title>
19  </head>
20  <body>
21  <% if (result.next()) {%> <!- DATA UNIT MARKUP PRODUCTION ->
22  <table>
23    <tr><td> Name </td><td> <%= result.getString("NAME")%> </td></tr>
24    <tr><td> Description </td>
25        <td> <%= result.getString("DESCRIPTION")%> </td></tr>
26  </table>
27  <%} %>
28  </body>
29  </html>
30  <% // TEMPORARY OBJECTS DISPOSITION
31  result.close();
32  pstmt.close();
33  conn.close();
34  %>
```

Figure 12.11 JSP implementation of the Category page.

The most common use of prepared statements is the execution of parametric queries, which are query statements that accept parameters. A parametric statement can be pre-compiled, and then executed multiple times, possibly with different parameter values.

The use of prepared statements is exemplified at line 10, where the connection object is used to create the parametric SQL query SELECT NAME, DESCRIPTION FROM NEWSCATEGORY WHERE OID =?, which extracts the name and description of the news category object identified by the OID passed as a parameter to the query. The value of the OID is represented by the question mark in the source code of the query. The prepared statement is incomplete, and must be bound to an actual parameter value before execution. This is done at line 12, where the instruction pstmt.setString(1, categoryDUInput) supplies the prepared statement object pstmt with the value of the categoryDUInput variable, as the first (and single) query parameter. After this instruction, the prepared statement is ready to execute, which is done at line 14.

The rest of the JSP code is devoted to content production: the result of the query is the single news category object having the specified OID, which is used at lines 23–25 to insert into an HTML table the category name and description.

Note that a real example would include error-checking code, for example to cope with HTTP requests not providing a value for the OID parameter, or with the failure of the SQL query. For brevity, we will skip error checking and exception handling code in the examples of content units discussed in this chapter.

The example of the Category page can be generalized, by replacing the data unit with other units accepting input parameters, like *index and multidata unit with relationship-based selectors,* as exemplified by the hypertext of Figure 12.12.

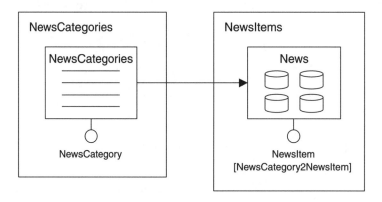

Figure 12.12   Unit with relationship-based selector.

The code of page NewsItems is shown in Figure 12.13. The only significant new aspect is the SQL query of the multidata unit (line 11), which implements the role-based selector condition. The query contains a selection on column CATEGORYOID in the WHERE clause. As explained in Chapter 11, this column maps in the relational schema the many-to-one relationship between a news item and its corresponding news category. Had the relationship between news categories and news been many-to-many, a bridge table would have been necessary; in this case the SQL query would require joining the entity table and the relationship bridge table, as in the following example, where table CATEGORY_ITEMS stores the OIDs of the pairs of objects connected by the hypothetical many-to-many relationship:

```
SELECT N.HEADING, N.BODY
FROM NEWSITEM N JOIN CATEGORY_ITEMS C ON N.OID = C.ITEMOID
WHERE C.CATEGORYOID = ?
```

12.3.3 Intra-page Links

The next example shows the implementation of *pages containing multiple units, connected by intra-page links*.

Figure 12.14 shows a WebML page, which contains an index unit connected to the data unit by an automatic intra-page contextual link.

The presence of intra-page links impacts the implementation in three ways:

- The page can be accessed in more than one way: by navigating an inter-page link,[3] and by using an intra-page link. This implies that the page can be called by different HTTP requests, including different parameters. The template must extract the parameters from the request and check their values, to understand which units are initially computable. Then, context propagation proceeds as explained in Chapter 5, from the initially computable units to their dependent units.

- The destination unit of the intra-page link may be computed with alternative input values: either from a fresh value transported in the HTTP request after the navigation of the intra-page link, or from the default value supplied by the source unit of the intra-page link. The template must contain a suitable conditional statement for deciding which input to use.

- The HTML construction part must build the anchor tag for an intra-page link, by appending to it all the parameters required to recompute the

---

[3]This case includes also the navigation of an implicit non-contextual link, if the page is a landmark.

```
1   <%@page language="java" %>
2   <%@ page import= "java.sql.*" %>
3   <% // REQUEST PARAMETER FETCH
4   String newsMDUInput = request.getParameter("newsMDU");
5   // DATABASE CONNECTION
6   Class.forName("sun.jdbc.odbc.JdbcOdbcDriver");
7   Connection conn = DriverManager.getConnection("jdbc:odbc:acme",
8                       "acmeuser", "acmepwd");
9   // QUERY PREPARATION AND EXECUTION
10  PreparedStatement pstmt = conn.prepareStatement(
11      "SELECT HEADING, BODY FROM NEWSITEM WHERE CATEGORYOID =?");
12  pstmt.setString(1, newsMDUInput);
13  ResultSet result = pstmt.executeQuery();
14  %>
15  <html> <!-- CONTENT PRODUCTION -->
16  <head>
17  <title>News Details Page</title>
18  </head>
19  <body>
20  <table> <!-- CONTENT PRODUCTION: MULTIDATA UNIT -->
21    <% while (result.next()) { %>
22    <tr>
23      <td><%= result.getString("HEADING") %></td>
24      <td><%= result.getString("BODY") %></td>
25    </tr>
26    <%} %>
27  </table>
28  </body>
29  </html>
30  <% // TEMPORARY OBJECTS DISPOSITION
31    result.close(); pstmt.close(); conn.close();
32  %>
```

Figure 12.13   JSP implementation of page NewsItems.

page, which may comprise both the "fresh" values determined by the navigation of the intra-page link, and the "preserved" values, appended to the HTTP request in order to restore the content of some units to the value preceding the navigation.

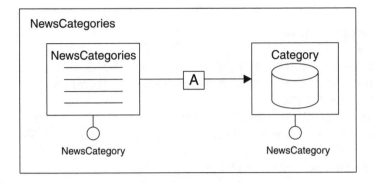

Figure 12.14 Index unit linked to a data unit.

The JSP template of Figure 12.15 starts with the decoding of the HTTP request. In the present example, the page has a single input parameter, which is the OID of the category object required by the Category data unit. The fetching of the request parameter is done at line 4: the parameter named `categoryDU` is extracted from the request and stored in the Java variable named `categoryDUInput`. Unlike in the previous examples, this variable may contain either a null value or a valid object identifier, depending on the way the page is accessed: if the page is accessed non-contextually, the `categoryDU` parameter is null; if the page is accessed by navigating the intra-page link, the `categoryDU` parameter stores the identifier of the selected news category to be displayed in the data unit.

After the usual part devoted to the database connection, the template continues with the preparation and execution of queries. The index unit is a context-free unit, as explained in Chapter 5, and its query can be executed irrespective of any input parameter, whereas the data unit is an internally dependent unit of the index unit. Therefore, the query for the index unit is executed first, and the query of the data unit follows.

The query of the index unit is processed at lines 10–13. The only difference with respect to the previous examples is the use of a JDBC 2 scrollable result set (lines 10–11),[4] which permits resetting the cursor's position before the first row (as done in line 17). This variation is required because the first row of the result set of the index unit must be accessed twice: once for extracting the OID to be used as default input for the data unit (line 16), and once for printing the HTML rendition of the index (lines 33–34). Scrollable results sets permit resetting the

---

[4]Scrollable result sets may not be supported by some JDBC drivers, but the same effect can be achieved also with normal result sets, at the cost of a bit more complex code.

```
1   <%@page language="java" %>
2   <%@ page import= "java.sql.*" %>
3   <% // REQUEST PARAMETER FETCH
4   String categoryDUInput = request.getParameter("categoryDU");
5   // DATABASE CONNECTION
6   Class.forName("sun.jdbc.odbc.JdbcOdbcDriver");
7   Connection conn = DriverManager.getConnection("jdbc:odbc:acme",
8                        "acmeuser", "acmepwd");
9   // QUERY EXECUTION: INDEX UNIT
10  Statement stmt = conn.createStatement(ResultSet.TYPE_SCROLL_SENSITIVE,
11                                  ResultSet.CONCUR_READ_ONLY);
12  ResultSet result = stmt.executeQuery(
13        "SELECT OID, NAME FROM NEWSCATEGORY ORDER BY NAME");
14  // CONTEXT PROPAGATION TO DATA UNIT QUERY
15  if ((categoryDUInput == null) && result.next()) {
16      categoryDUInput = result.getString("OID");
17      result.beforeFirst();
18  }
19  // QUERY PREPARATION AND EXECUTION: DATA UNIT
20  PreparedStatement pstmt = conn.prepareStatement(
21      "SELECT NAME, DESCRIPTION FROM NEWSCATEGORY WHERE OID =?");
22  pstmt.setString(1, categoryDUInput);
23  ResultSet result2 = pstmt.executeQuery();
24  %>
25  <html> <!-- CONTENT PRODUCTION -->
26  <head>
27  <title>News Categories Page</title>
28  </head>
29  <body>
30  <table> <!-- CONTENT PRODUCTION: INDEX UNIT -->
31    <% while (result.next()) {%>
32    <tr><td>
33      <a href="newsCategories.jsp?categoryDU=<%= result.getString("OID")%>">
34      <%= result.getString("NAME") %> </a>
35    </td></tr>
36    <%} %>
```

(continued)

Figure 12.15 JSP implementation of page News Categories.

Figure 12.15 *(continued)*

```
37  </table>
38  <!-- CONTENT PRODUCTION: DATA UNIT -->
39  <% if (result2.next()) { %>
40  <table>
41    <tr><td> Name </td><td> <%= result2.getString("NAME")%> </td></tr>
42    <tr><td> Description </td>
43        <td> <%= result2.getString("DESCRIPTION")%> </td></tr>
44  </table>
45  <%} %>
46  </body>
47  </html>
48  <% // TEMPORARY OBJECTS DISPOSITION
49  result.close(); stmt.close();
50  result2.close(); pstmt.close(); conn.close(); %>
```

position of the cursor after the first access (line 17), so that the loop producing the HTML rendition of the index starts from the first row.

After the index unit's query is executed, it is the turn of the data unit's query. Before preparing the query, the test at line 15 is performed, to ensure that the most specific input value is used. If the page has been accessed non-contextually, the value of categoryDUInput variable is null and default parameter propagation from the index unit to the data unit must take place: the first row of the result of the index unit's query is fetched to get a default input (line 15), the value of the OID column is assigned to the categoryDUInput variable (line 16), and the cursor is reset to the original position (line 17). If the page has been accessed navigating the intra-page link, the value of the CategoryDUInput variable is not null, and the default context propagation is skipped. In this case, the OID value that comes from the HTTP request is used. After this test, the data unit's query is executed, using as parameter the most specific value available, stored in the categoryDUInput variable (lines 22–23).

Then, the HTML code is built using the result sets of the two queries. For simplicity, we just construct two tables, one for the index unit and one for the data unit. In a real example, extra HTML formatting would be needed to obtain a more aesthetic result.

This example permits us to discuss the implementation of *scroller units*, which are typically implemented in the same way as the index unit of Figure 12.14. The difference between the implementation of an index unit and that of a scroller unit is in the produced HTML mark-up. The scroller unit uses the same query as the index unit, but exploits only selected objects in the result set: the *first* and *last* objects, the *current* object, defined as the object having the same OID as the input parameter of the data unit linked to the scroller unit, and the *previous* and *next* objects, defined as the objects coming immediately before/after the current object in the result set. The HTML production for a scroller unit amounts to the construction of four anchor tags (first, last, previous, next), whose URLs contain the OID of the appropriate object, determined by scanning the result set of the scroller unit's query.

The code of Figure 12.15 can also be adapted to cope with a *non-automatic* intra-page link. In this case, default parameter propagation does not apply. As a consequence, when the page is accessed non-contextually, the data unit's query is not executed, nor its content shown. To skip the construction of the data unit it is sufficient to condition the execution of the data unit's query at lines 20–23 and the production of the HTML code at lines 38–45 with the following test: `if (categoryDUInput != null)`, which checks that the intra-page link has been navigated.

12.3.4   Entry Units

The fourth example discusses the implementation of *entry units,* using the filtered multidata pattern shown in Figure 12.16. This example illustrates a second way of building links, based on HTML forms and on the HTTP POST method.

Entry units are different from other units for two reasons:

- They do not have an associated content retrieval query, but are directly translated into an HTML form in the body of the page template.

- Their outgoing link, which is always non-automatic and transports as parameters the values entered by users, is implemented using the action attribute and submit button of an HTML form, instead of an anchor tag. The parameters transported by the link are typically submitted using the HTTP POST method, instead of the default GET method. The different encoding of the HTTP request affects the HTML rendition of the link, but not the parameter extraction from the request; the predefined JSP `request` object, used in the previous examples, can be exploited to extract input parameters also from the POST request.[5]

---

[5]The transparent handling of POST method calls is possible only if the form is not used for file uploads. Otherwise, decoding request parameters requires handling multi-part messages, which is a quite technical task. We will return to this subject in paragraph 12.4.3.

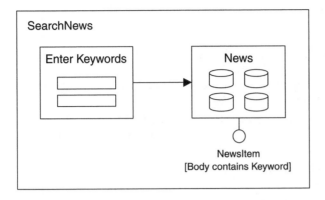

Figure 12.16 Filtered multidata pattern.

The JSP code for implementing page SearchNews appears in Figure 12.17.

At line 4, the request is examined to extract the request parameters, which, in this case, are the values entered by the user. The function for doing this is the same as seen before (`request.getParameter()`), even if in this case the HTTP request may be a POST request.

The subsequent part of the template contains the query preparation and execution code. The only unit requiring a data retrieval query is the multidata unit, which has one input parameter corresponding to the parameter of the unit's selector. The code at lines 12–17 wraps the data retrieval query with a test for checking if the unit is computable: the test verifies if there is a keyword submitted by the user, and if such keyword is not the empty string; if the test succeeds, the multidata unit's query is instantiated and executed. If the page has been accessed non-contextually or the user has left the input field blank, the test fails and the query is skipped.

Next, the content production part follows: first of all, the entry unit is rendered as an HTML form (lines 25–29), which contains an `<input>` tag of type text, named `keyword`. The outgoing link of the entry unit is implemented as the form's `action` attribute (line 25), which specifies the destination page of the link, and as an `<input>` tag of type `submit` (line 28), which is rendered as a confirmation button. When the user presses the button, the input of the keyword field is packaged as a request parameter named `keyword`, and the page is re-invoked.

After the HTML form, there is the JSP code for constructing the mark-up of the multidata unit from the results of the corresponding SQL query. Note

```
1   <%@page language="java" %>
2   <%@ page import= "java.sql.*" %>
3   <% // REQUEST PARAMETERS FETCH
4   String keyword = request.getParameter("keyword");
5   // DATABASE CONNECTION
6   Class.forName("sun.jdbc.odbc.JdbcOdbcDriver");
7   Connection conn = DriverManager.getConnection("jdbc:odbc:acme",
8                       "acmeuser", "acmepwd");
9   // PARAMETER PROPAGATION AND QUERY EXECUTION
10  ResultSet result = null;
11  PreparedStatement pstmt = null;
12  if ((keyword != null) && !keyword.equals("")) {
13  pstmt = conn.prepareStatement(
14      "SELECT HEADING, BODY FROM NEWSITEM WHERE BODY LIKE ?");
15  pstmt.setString(1, "%" + keyword + "%");
16  result = pstmt.executeQuery();
17  } %>
18  <html> <!-- CONTENT PRODUCTION -->
19  <head>
20  <title>News Search Page</title>
21  </head>
22  <body>
23    Enter a search keyword: <br>
24  <!-- CONTENT PRODUCTION: ENTRY UNIT -->
25  <form method="POST" action="searchNews.jsp">
26    Keyword: <input type="text" name="keyword">
27    <br>
28    <input type="submit" name="submit">
29  </form>
30  <!-- CONTENT PRODUCTION: MULTIDATA UNIT -->
31  <% if ((keyword != null) && !keyword.equals("")) { %>
32  <table>
33    <% while (result.next()){%>
34    <tr>
35      <td><%= result.getString("HEADING") %></td>
36      <td><%= result.getString("BODY") %></td>
```

(continued)

Figure 12.17 JSP implementation of the filtered multidata pattern in the SearchNews page.

Figure 12.17   *(continued)*

```
37    </tr>
38    <%} %>
39  </table>
40  <%} %>
41  </body>
42  </html>
43  <%    // TEMPORARY OBJECTS DISPOSITION
44  if ((keyword != null) && !keyword.equals("")) {
45       result.close(); pstmt.close();
46  }
47  conn.close();
48  %>
```

that the loop for constructing the HTML table is not entered if the page has been accessed non-contextually or with a null keyword, because in such case no query was executed and there are no results to display. In a real example, a further test would be needed in the HTML production part, to distinguish the case in which the query is executed but no results are found, and show an appropriate message to the user.

The implementation of more complex search forms and selector conditions is straightforward: the HTML form is extended with as many fields as required, and the WHERE clause of the SQL query of the multidata unit is extended with suitable sub-clauses using the values of the input fields in comparison predicates.

12.3.5   Multi-Choice Index Unit Linked to a Multidata Unit

This example shows the implementation of *multi-choice index units and of multi-data units with outgoing links*. These cases are actually the two sides of the same coin: the common problem is to pass over links a multi-value parameter, namely a set of OIDs. This problem has a very simple solution: if a URL is constructed which contains multiple parameter=value pairs referring to the same parameter, as for instance in the query string oid=12&oid=31&oid=345& . . . then the request object associated to the navigation of the URL contains a *set of values* associated to the multi-value parameter. The extraction of such values requires using the JSP function `request.getParameterValues()`, instead of the JSP function `request.getParameter()` seen so far. Function `getParameterValues()` returns an array of strings, instead of the single string returned by function `getParameter()`.

These concepts are clarified by the practical example in Figure 12.18, which shows a page where a multi-choice index over entity NewsItem points to a multidata unit over the same entity, placed in a separate page. When the user selects some instances in the multi-choice index and presses the submit button, the details of the various selected objects appear in the multidata unit.

The JSP code of page NewsChoice illustrates how a request transporting a multi-valued parameter can be assembled.

The first part of the JSP template is identical to the construction of a normal index. Lines 1–11 execute a fixed SQL query, which retrieves the entire set of news objects.

The HTML construction part is different, because a multi-choice index must be produced, and not a plain index. A multi-choice index is just an HTML form, containing one checkbox for every object. A few lines of code assemble this form from the output of the SQL query (lines 17–28): the form contains an HTML table, with one row for each element of the query result; each row consists of two cells: the leftmost cell contains the heading of the news items (line 21), and the rightmost cell includes an HTML input of type checkbox, which is rendered as a checkable box (lines 22–23). Each input of type checkbox has attribute `name` equal to the constant string "`chosenOIDs`", and attribute `value` equal to the

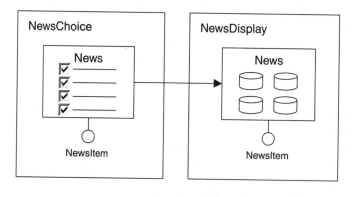

Figure 12.18   Multi-choice index linked to a multidata unit.

```
1   <%@page language="java" %>
2   <%@ page import= "java.sql.*" %>
3   <% // DATABASE CONNECTION
4   Class.forName("sun.jdbc.odbc.JdbcOdbcDriver");
5   Connection conn = DriverManager.getConnection("jdbc:odbc:acme",
6                      "acmeuser", "acmepwd");
7   // QUERY PREPARATION AND EXECUTION
8   Statement stmt = conn.createStatement();
9   ResultSet result = stmt.executeQuery(
10          "SELECT OID, HEADING FROM NEWSITEM ORDER BY HEADING");
11  %>
12  <html> <!-- CONTENT PRODUCTION -->
13  <head>
14  <title>News Choice Page</title>
15  </head>
16  <body> <!-- CONTENT PRODUCTION: MULTICHOICE INDEX -->
17    <form action="newsDisplayPage.jsp" method="POST">
18      <table>
19        <% while (result.next()) { %>
20        <tr>
21          <td><%= result.getString("HEADING")%></td>
22          <td><input type="checkbox" name="chosenOIDs"
23                     value="<%= result.getString("OID")%>"/></td>
24        </tr>
25        <%} %>
26      </table>
27      <input type="submit">
28    </form>
29  </body>
30  </html>
31  <% // TEMPORARY OBJECTS DISPOSITION
32  result.close();
33  stmt.close();
34  conn.close();
35  %>
```

Figure 12.19 JSP implementation of page NewsChoice.

OID of the current row of the result set. In this way, each checkbox contributes to building the composite value of the `chosenOIDs` request parameter, by appending the identifier of one object to it. When the user presses the confirmation button, all the OID values of the checked items are packaged into the value of the `chosenOIDs` request parameter. Then, the form's action attribute points to page `newsDisplayPage.jsp`, where the composite value of the `chosenOIDs` parameter can be properly disassembled.

The construction of the outgoing link of a multidata unit follows a similar pattern as for the multi-choice unit. The only difference is the way in which the query string is constructed. In the case of a multidata unit, the result set of the SQL query is used to build a single URL, by appending to the URL query string one term `chosenOIDs=<%=result.getString("OID")%>` for each object in the result set. Then, the HTTP request containing the multi-valued parameter `chosenOIDs` can be decoded in the same way as for a multi-choice unit, illustrated next.

The JSP code of page NewsDisplay, shown in Figure 12.20, demonstrates how a request transporting a multi-valued parameter can be decoded and used for constructing a data retrieval query. The tricky point of this page template is the way in which the SQL query is formed, which is the third example of how to do it, after the case of a fixed statement (Figure 12.5, lines 9–10), and of a statement containing a fixed number of parameters with unknown value (Figure 12.11, lines 10–12).

The difference in this case is that we need to write and execute a query of the form: `SELECT HEADING, BODY FROM NEWSITEM WHERE OID=value1 OR OID=value2, . . .` where `value1, value2 . . .` are all the OID values transported by the link, *the number of which is not known when writing the template*.

However, this problem also has a simple solution: in the page template it is possible to create the source code of the query on the fly! To do so, the array of strings returned by the invocation of function `request.getParameterValues()` (line 4) is used in a loop to append the variable part of the SQL query to the fixed part. The source code of the query is stored in a Java variable, called `query`, which initially contains only the fixed part (line 10). At each loop iteration, a sub-clause of the form `OID= . . .` is appended to the query, using the current OID taken from the array (line 14). In all iterations but the first one, also the SQL keyword `OR` is prefixed to the `WHERE` clause under construction (line 13), to properly concatenate the current sub-clause to the previous one. At the end of the loop, the dynamically built Java string contains the complete SQL query, which can be submitted for execution to the database in the usual way, as a parameter of the `executeQuery` function (line 19). When the query is executed, the result set can be exploited as usual to build the HTML.

```
1   <%@page language="java" %>
2   <%@ page import= "java.sql.*" %>
3   <% // REQUEST PARAMETER FETCH: MULTI VALUED PARAMETER
4   String[] oidSet = request.getParameterValues("chosenOIDs");
5   // DATABASE CONNECTION
6   Class.forName("sun.jdbc.odbc.JdbcOdbcDriver");
7   Connection conn = DriverManager.getConnection("jdbc:odbc:acme",
8                       "acmeuser", "acmepwd");
9   // QUERY PREPARATION
10  String query = "SELECT HEADING, BODY FROM NEWSITEM WHERE ";
11  if (oidSet.length != 0) {
12      for (int i = 0; i < oidSet.length; i++) {
13          if (i > 0) query += " OR ";
14          query += "OID="+ oidSet[i];
15      }
16  }
17  Statement stmt = conn.createStatement();
18  // QUERY EXECUTION
19  ResultSet result = stmt.executeQuery(query);
20  %>
21  <html> <!- CONTENT PRODUCTION -->
22  <head>
23  <title>News Details Page</title>
24  </head>
25  <body>
26  <table> <!- CONTENT PRODUCTION: MULTIDATA UNIT -->
27    <% while (result.next()) { %>
28    <tr>
29      <td><%= result.getString("HEADING") %></td>
30      <td><%= result.getString("BODY") %></td>
31    </tr>
32    <%} %>
33  </table>
34  </body>
35  </html>
36  <%  // TEMPORARY OBJECTS DISPOSITION
37    result.close(); stmt.close(); conn.close();
38  %>
```

Figure 12.20 JSP implementation of page NewsDisplay.

12.3.6   Areas, Landmark Pages, and Nested Sub-pages

Areas and landmarks do not affect implementation in a substantial way, because they are merely devices for modularizing a site view, and for better organizing the non-contextual links between pages. In practice, the references to areas and to landmark pages are implemented simply by inserting the appropriate non-contextual links in each page of the site view, using HTML anchor tags.

Nested AND sub-pages require the introduction of HTML frames. The JSP page template is divided into as many independent files as the number of AND sub-pages; then a master file containing an HTML <FRAMESET> tag is built, to put the frames together. HTML frames have not been presented in Chapter 1, but are a standard feature of HTML, although less popular than it used to be in the early days of Web design. The reader may refer to any good HTML manual for an explanation of the <FRAME> and <FRAMESET> HTML tags. From a purely implementation point of view, the use of frames does not influence the programming techniques for constructing page templates seen so far, and thus we do not dwell on the topic further.

Conversely, *nested OR sub-pages* require some extra coding effort. Nested OR pages show alternative pieces of content in the same region of the page, which entails the presence of some conditional instruction in the JSP template, to selectively enable alternative portions of content. As an example, consider the page in Figure 12.21, in which a data unit displays the details of a news category, from which it is possible to visualize either the index of all news of the category, or a multidata unit listing only the most recent news, but with the full details of each piece of news. The symbol (D) on the RecentNews sub-page denotes that this sub-page is the default one, shown when the News page is accessed non-contextually. Implementing a page with alternative sub-pages requires a conditional statement in the template code, to establish which sub-page must be processed. The chosen page may be the default one, if the page is accessed non-contextually, or the sub-page actually reached by a contextual link. To ease the implementation of such conditional statements, every link pointing to an alternative sub-page contains one extra URL parameter, say `subpage`, which explicitly carries the name of the alternative sub-page to display. The code in Figure 12.22 shows this implementation technique at work.

At lines 4–5, the HTTP request is analyzed to extract the two possible parameters: the OID of the category to display, and the name of the alternative sub-page that has been accessed. Then, after connecting to the database and performing the SQL query for the data unit (lines 6–15), a test is made to understand which alternative sub-page is required (line 18). If the non-default alternative page (AllNews)

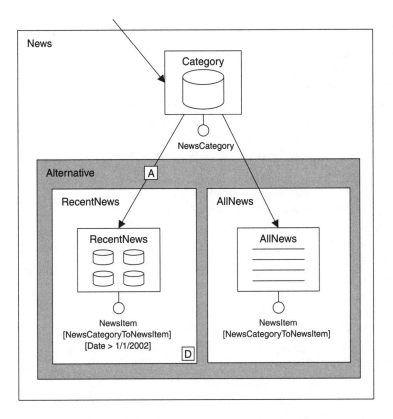

Figure 12.21 Alternative OR sub-pages.

is requested, a SQL query is composed, which retrieves the content of the AllNews index unit, that is, the heading of all the news items of the input category (lines 18–19). Otherwise, a SQL query is composed, which retrieves the content of the RecentNews multidata unit, that is, the heading and body of the news items issued after 1/1/2002 (lines 20–22). The query actually composed is next executed, at line 24.

In the HTML production part of the template, first the data unit is built in the usual way from the result of its SQL query (lines 28–38). Then the test on the `subpage` request parameter is repeated to determine which sub-page must be rendered (lines 39 and 45). If the parameter's value is equal to `all`, the content of the index unit is produced (lines 40–44), otherwise the content of the multidata unit is built (lines 46–51).

```
1   <%@page language="java" %>
2   <%@ page import= "java.sql.*" %>
3   <% // REQUEST PARAMETERS FETCH
4   String categoryDU = request.getParameter("categoryDU");
5   String subpage = request.getParameter("subpage");
6   // DATABASE CONNECTION
7   Class.forName("sun.jdbc.odbc.JdbcOdbcDriver");
8   Connection conn = DriverManager.getConnection("jdbc:odbc:acme",
9                       "acmeuser", "acmepwd");
10  // QUERY PREPARATION AND EXECUTION: DATA UNIT
11  PreparedStatement pstmt = conn.prepareStatement(
12     "SELECT NAME, DESCRIPTION, OID FROM NEWSCATEGORY WHERE OID =?",
13     ResultSet.TYPE_SCROLL_SENSITIVE, ResultSet.CONCUR_READ_ONLY);
14  pstmt.setString(1, categoryDU);
15  ResultSet result = pstmt.executeQuery();
16  // CONDITIONAL QUERY PREPARATION AND EXECUTION
17  PreparedStatement pstmt2 = null;
18  if ("all".equals(subpage)) pstmt2 = conn.prepareStatement(
19     "SELECT HEADING FROM NEWSITEM WHERE CATEGORYOID =?"); // INDEX UNIT
20  else pstmt2 = conn.prepareStatement(
21     "SELECT HEADING, BODY FROM NEWSITEM WHERE CATEGORYOID =?" +
22     " AND NEWSDATE >'1/1/2002' ");           // MULTIDATA UNIT
23  pstmt2.setString(1, categoryDU);
24  ResultSet result2 = pstmt2.executeQuery();%>
25  <html> <!-- CONTENT PRODUCTION -->
26  <head> <title>News Page</title> </head>
27  <body>
28  <% if (result.next()){%> <!-- CONTENT PRODUCTION: DATA UNIT -->
29  <table>
30    <tr><td> Name </td><td><%= result.getString("NAME")%> </td></tr>
31    <tr><td> Description </td> <td><%=result.getString("DESCRIPTION")%></td></tr>
32    <tr><td colspan="2"><a href="
33      newsPage.jsp?subpage=recent&categoryDU=<%=result.getString("OID")%>">
34      Recent News</a></td></tr>
```

(continued)

Figure 12.22   JSP implementation of News page and of its alternative sub-pages

Figure 12.22 *(continued)*

```
35   <tr><td colspan="2"><a href="
36      newsPage.jsp?subpage=all&categoryDU=<%=result.getString("OID")%>">
37      All News</a></td></tr>
38   </table> <%} %>
39   <% if ("all".equals(subpage)){ %>
40   <table> <!-- CONTENT PRODUCTION: ALL NEWS SUBPAGE -->
41      <% while (result2.next()) { %>
42      <tr><td><%= result2.getString("HEADING") %></td></tr>
43      <%} %>
44   </table>
45   <%} else { %>
46   <table> <!-- CONTENT PRODUCTION: RECENT NEWS SUBPAGE -->
47      <% while (result2.next()) { %>
48      <tr><td><%= result2.getString("HEADING") %></td></tr>
49      <tr><td><%= result2.getString("BODY") %></td></tr>
50      <%} %>
51   </table> <%} %>
52   </body></html>
53   <% // TEMPORARY OBJECTS DISPOSITION
54      result.close(); result2.close(); pstmt.close();
55      pstmt2.close();conn.close(); %>
```

12.4 Implementing Operations

The implementation techniques seen so far address the various ways of publishing content in a hypertext; we now turn to the problem of implementing content updates and generalized operations.

Implementing a hypertext with operations requires two distinct steps:

- Building the page template from which the operation is invoked: this step reuses all the implementation techniques illustrated in the previous examples, with some minor extensions.

- Implementing the operations: this task requires the actual implementation of the business logic of the operation, and the result checking code necessary to decide which link to follow after the operation completes.

In the following examples, we will adopt the simplifying assumption that operations are implemented as JSP templates, which we call *operation templates,* to distinguish them from page templates. From the programming style point of view, this solution is not the most appropriate one, because, unlike page templates, operation templates do not display anything, but have only a side effect, and thus no HTML mark-up construction is required. A more correct approach would be to encode operations as servlets, and call such servlets from the JSP page containing the operation's activating link. However this would require introducing in this already dense chapter servlet programming, which has a slightly different flavor with respect to JSP coding. We will revise the style in which operations are implemented in Chapter 13, where we introduce a more sophisticated implementation architecture.

12.4.1   General Schema of Operation Implementation

An operation is inserted in a hypertext by establishing a link between a unit in a page and the operation, with the meaning that navigating the link fires the operation. This basic configuration can be extended by defining sequences of multiple operations, and by drawing transport links from the page whereby the operations are activated to any unit in the operation chain.

Therefore, the implementation of operations deals with two aspects: 1) how to code a sequence of operations; 2) how to build the link that activates such sequence.

Operations sequences (including single operations as a special case) are implemented by writing an appropriate JSP operation template, according to the general schema illustrated in Figure 12.23.

The first part of the template deals with *request parameters fetching,* and is identical to the corresponding part of a page template. The parameters transported by the navigated link that triggered the operation must be extracted from the request, to be used in the execution of the operations.

The second part of the operation template deals with *the preparation and execution of the operation queries.*

If *the operation chain contains a single operation,* the template simply initializes the code of the query, executes it, and checks the result, to determine if the OK or the KO link must be followed. Each kind of WebML operation requires appropriate instructions for executing the operation and for verifying the outcome of execution.

If *the operation chain consists of multiple linked operations,* the operation template must address three further issues: the execution of the operations in the

---

Part 1: Extract parameters from the HTTP request

Part 2: Prepare and execute queries:

1. Start transaction

2. Instantiate parameters of query for current operation

3. Execute query of current operation

4. If (error)
   {rollback current transaction;
    forward control to destination
    of KO link of current operation}

5. If current operation != last goto 2

Part 3: Display result page

6. Commit current transaction;

7. Forward control to destination of OK link of current operation

---

Figure 12.23   General schema of an operation template.

proper order, the passage of parameters between operations, and the atomicity of transactions:

- The order of execution of operations is determined by the topology of links between them: if an operation A is the destination of an OK or KO link exiting from an operation B, the execution of B precedes the execution of A.

- The passage of parameters depends on the input links of each operation. An operation may take input values either from parameters associated with input links exiting the page whereby the operation chain is activated, or from the output of an operation preceding it. In the former case, the parameter values are fetched from the HTTP request triggering the operation chain, in the latter they are drawn from some value computed by the execution of a preceding operation.

- The atomic execution of multiple operations must be ensured when the sequence of operations is enclosed inside a transaction. The atomicity of sequences of create, delete, modify, connect, and disconnect operations can be implemented by exploiting database transactions. In this case, the central part of the operation templates assumes the form illustrated in Figure 12.23: at the beginning, a new database transaction is started, which provides an atomic execution context for all the operations; then, for each operation, the associated query is instantiated with the proper input parameters and executed; if execution fails, the whole transaction is aborted; otherwise, execution proceeds to the next operation. In the last part of the template, reached if all the operations succeed, the transaction is committed, to make the effect of the entire operation chain persistent, and control is forwarded to the destination page of the OK link of the last operation. Atomicity can be hard to implement for generic operations executed outside the context of a database system; the use of Enterprise JavaBeans, briefly discussed in Chapter 13, may help achieving atomicity of sequences of arbitrary operations.

The implementation of operations chains affects also the coding of the page from which the operation chain is activated. In particular, the HTML implementation of the link activating the operation chain must obey the following rules:

- The link must carry, besides its parameters, also all the parameters transported by transport links reaching operations in the same chain. This can be done in two ways, based on how the link activating the operations is implemented in HTML:
  - If the link is implemented as an anchor tag, appropriate parameters are added to the query string of its URL.
  - If the link is implemented as the submit button of an HTML form, input fields of type hidden are added to the HTML FORM tag.[6]
- If any of the operations has a link pointing back to the page whereby the operation chain is activated, the activating link must also transport the extra parameters needed to "remember" the input of externally dependent units, as explained in Chapter 5.

Note that transport links pointing to the operations of the chain are not rendered; the parameters associated to them are added to the implementation of the link activating the operation chain.

---

[6]Input fields of type "hidden" are <INPUT> tags used in HTML forms, not shown in the rendition of the <FORM> tag, but passed along with the HTTP request.

12.4.2 Deletion of an Object Chosen from an Index

As a starting example, we discuss the implementation of *delete operations, with OK and KO links*. Consider the hypertext in Figure 12.24, in which the selection of an item in the index unit invokes the deletion of a news category.

Supposing that the delete operation is implemented as a JSP operation template named `delete.jsp`, the implementation of page NewsCategoryDelete is identical to the code illustrated in Figure 12.10, but for URL constructed at line 23, which now points to the JSP template wrapping the delete operation. The revised version of line 23 includes the following URL:

```
href="delete.jsp?OID=<%=result.getString("OID")%>
```

The operation template is shown in Figure 12.25. After the request parameter extraction (line 4) and the connection to the database (lines 6–8), the command for the delete operation is prepared, using a DELETE command instead of a SELECT query (line 11). After the preparation, the query is executed. To trap possible errors, the update is executed inside a Java *try-catch block* (lines 14–18): the meaning is that the statement inside the block (line 15) is tentatively executed; if it succeeds, the computation restarts after the try-catch block (line 19); if the execution raises an SQL error, the exception is trapped and control passes to the instructions inside the catch block (line 17). The transfer of control after operation execution is implemented by using the built-in JSP function `forward` of the `pageContext` object, which, as the name suggests, transfers the control to another JSP template. In Figure 12.25, upon success, the control is transferred back

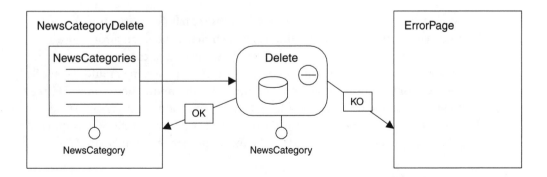

Figure 12.24   Index unit linked to a delete operation unit.

```
1    <%@page language="java" %>
2    <%@ page import= "java.sql.*" %>
3    <% // REQUEST PARAMETERS FETCH
4    String selectedOID = request.getParameter("OID");
5    // DATABASE CONNECTION
6    Class.forName("sun.jdbc.odbc.JdbcOdbcDriver");
7    Connection conn = DriverManager.getConnection("jdbc:odbc:acme",
8                        "acmeuser", "acmepwd");
9    // QUERY PREPARATION
10   PreparedStatement pstmt = conn.prepareStatement(
11           "DELETE FROM NEWSCATEGORY WHERE OID =?");
12   pstmt.setString(1, selectedOID);
13   // QUERY EXECUTION AND ERROR TRAPPING
14   try {
15       pstmt.executeUpdate();
16   } catch (SQLException e) {
17       pageContext.forward("errorPage.jsp");    // KO LINK
18   }
19   pstmt.close();   // TEMPORARY OBJECTS DISPOSITION
20   conn.close();
21   pageContext.forward("newsCategories.jsp");   // OK LINK
22   %>
```

Figure 12.25   JSP implementation of a delete operation.

to page newsCategories.jsp (line 21); in case of failure, control is passed to the page named errorPage.jsp (line 17), which may contain an error message.

As a conclusive comment, we note that the examples in Figure 12.24 and Figure 12.25 can be easily extended to implement the deletion of multiple objects selected using a multi-choice unit: in this case, the multi-choice unit is implemented as explained in section 12.3.5, and the operation template can delete several objects by assembling on the fly the WHERE condition of the SQL command with multiple OR sub-clauses, using the technique presented in Figure 12.20.

12.4.3   Entry Unit Linked to a Create Unit

As the second example, we demonstrate the implementation of *create operations*, focusing also on *file uploading and on the update of database columns containing large objects*. Most of the discussion applies also to *modify operations*.

The example of create operation appears in Figure 12.26. The NewsCreation page, which permits the user to enter the heading and the body of a piece of news, simply contains an HTML form, shown in Figure 12.27, with an action attribute pointing to page createNews.jsp, which includes the code of the create operation.

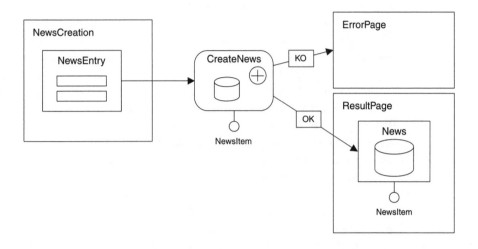

Figure 12.26 Create operation after entry unit.

```
1   <html>
2   <head>
3   <title>Enter heading and body</title>
4   </head>
5   <body>
6     <form method="POST" action="createNews.jsp">
7       Heading: <input type="text" name="heading"><br>
8       Body: <textarea name="body"></textarea><br>
9       <input type="submit">
10    </form>
11  </body>
12  </html>
```

Figure 12.27 HTML implementation of page NewsCreation.

The JSP code of the create operation has a structure very similar to that of the delete operation, but must cope with the creation of unique identifiers. A possible approach for *creating a unique identifier* for the newly created object is to leave this task to the end user, who must provide the identifier via the HTML form, as for regular attribute values, and then rely on the database integrity checking mechanisms to ensure that no duplicate identifiers are produced. However, as discussed in Chapter 11, this approach is not applicable to those objects that lack a primary key meaningful to the user, and is not recommended in general. Therefore, it is better to let the create operation manage the production of unique OIDs. This problem is so frequently encountered in database applications that most relational products offer a built-in primitive for facilitating OID invention. For example, the Oracle database management system includes *sequence generators* for creating a batch of unique values to use as the primary key of a table, and in the Postgres database a table column can be declared of type *serial,* to have the system invent a unique key value at each object insertion. These mechanisms are more efficient than ad hoc solutions, like the one described next, but are not always portable from a database to another one.

The example in Figure 12.28 presents a simple OID invention technique, which exemplifies the tasks required for the creation of unique values and can be used in absence of more efficient native data types usable for system-generated primary keys. The illustrated syntax is vendor-dependent in some aspects (specifically, in the instructions for setting table locks), but all the major database products include equivalent primitives for achieving the same effect. The solution is based on an auxiliary COUNTER table, which is a one row, one column table, storing the maximum OID value currently used in all the entity tables; when the application is initialized, a tuple is inserted into the COUNTER table, which stores an initial OID value (typically 0). The create operation is implemented as a sequence of three SQL commands: the first query is a SELECT statement, which calculates the next available OID, by looking up the COUNTER table (lines 14–15); the second statement increments the COUNTER table to record the new maximum OID value (lines 18–19); the last command is the actual INSERT statement (lines 21–22), which uses the calculated OID value as the primary key for the new object (line 23). For this approach to work correctly, some extra work must be done, because multiple clients can access the database concurrently, and thus it may happen that, after one client selects the maximum OID value, and before it completes the INSERT statement, another client reads the same maximum OID value. In such a case, the two clients would use the same number as the primary key of a new object, producing an integrity violation. The solution to this problem consists of performing the SELECT, UPDATE, and INSERT statements inside an atomic transaction and setting an exclusive lock on the COUNTER table until the transaction has completed. An exclusive lock is a mechanism of the database management system, whereby a transaction may request the exclusive access to a table, thus preventing other concurrently executing transactions to access the same table until the lock is released, either explicitly or implicitly at the end of the transaction. Setting the lock on the COUNTER table ensures that, while the sequence of the SELECT, UPDATE, and INSERT statements is being processed, no other transaction can read or write to the table, which avoids the abovementioned concurrency problems.

The example of Figure 12.28 shows how to declare the boundaries of a transaction and set a lock in JDBC. The instruction at line 11 turns off the so-called *autocommit* mode of the database connection, in which each individual SQL statement is a distinct transaction. As a consequence, the statement of line 11 implicitly starts a transaction that ensures that the subsequent queries are executed atomically. Then, the statement at line 13 sets an exclusive lock on the COUNTER table. After the execution of the insert command (line 28), the transaction must be explicitly terminated, either by "committing" its operations, as done at line 34, or by undoing the entire batch of work, using a rollback statement (as done at line 30, in case of failure of the INSERT statement). Executing the SELECT, UPDATE, and INSERT statements of Figure 12.28 in the context of the same transaction and with an exclusive lock on the COUNTER table ensures that the OID invention procedure is safe with respect to concurrent create operations.

A second issue in the implementation of create and modify operations concerns the *use of complex data types, like large textual or binary objects,* as the type of entity attributes and database columns, because in this case the instructions for performing the database update may require some extra programming work, typically dependent on the specific database product. The create unit in Figure 12.27 could provide an example: if the text for the news body exceeds the dimension of the standard SQL "varchar" column type, a nonstandard column type may be needed.[7]

The problem gets even more complicated when the value for an entity attribute must be created or modified using a file uploaded from the client.

---

[7]Examples of data types used by database systems for storing large amounts of data are BLOBs (binary large objects), CLOBs (character large objects), TEXT, and so on.

```
1   <%@page language="java" %>
2   <%@ page import= "java.sql.*" %>
3   <% // REQUEST PARAMETERS FETCH
4   String heading = request.getParameter("heading");
5   String body = request.getParameter("body");
6   // DATABASE CONNECTION
7   Class.forName("sun.jdbc.odbc.JdbcOdbcDriver");
8   Connection conn = DriverManager.getConnection("jdbc:odbc:acme",
9                       "acmeuser", "acmepwd");
10  // START TRANSACTION
11  conn.setAutoCommit(false);
12  Statement stmt = conn.createStatement();
13  stmt.executeUpdate("LOCK TABLE COUNTER IN EXCLUSIVE MODE");
14  ResultSet result = stmt.executeQuery(
15  "SELECT 1 + MAX(OID) AS NEWOID FROM COUNTER");   // INVENT NEW OID
16  result.next();
17  String newOID = result.getString("NEWOID");
18  result = stmt.executeUpdate(
19   "UPDATE COUNTER SET OID=1+OID");                // INCREMENT COUNTER
20  // QUERY PREPARATION: CREATE UNIT
21  PreparedStatement pstmt= conn.prepareStatement(
22  "INSERT INTO NEWSITEM(OID, HEADING, BODY)  values (?, ?, ?)");
23  pstmt.setString(1, newOID);
24  pstmt.setString(2, heading);
25  pstmt.setString(3, body);
26  // QUERY EXECUTION: CREATE UNIT
27  try {
28      pstmt.executeUpdate();
29  } catch (SQLException e) {
30      conn.rollback(); result.close();            // ERROR: ROLLBACK
31      pstmt.close();      conn.close();
32      pageContext.forward("errorPage.jsp");   // FOLLOW KO LINK
33  }
34  conn.commit();                                  // SUCCESS: COMMIT & UNLOCK
35  result.close();
36  pstmt.close();
37  conn.close();
38  // FOLLOW OK LINK
39  pageContext.forward("resultPage.jsp?newOID=" + newOID);
40  %>
```

Figure 12.28 JSP implementation of a create operation.

Dealing with large attribute values transmitted as uploaded files requires addressing three questions:

■ The upload of a file from the user's browser, to use as the value of the BLOB attribute.

■ The decoding of the transmitted content at the server side.

■ The storage of the decoded content together with the object it belongs to.

The *upload of a file* is achieved by using HTML forms, already seen at work for string and text input. An HTML form can be used also for submitting files, as the HTML lines in Figure 12.29 demonstrate.

The code in Figure 12.29 causes the browser to display a form containing an input box with a "Browse . . ." button; clicking the button makes a dialog box appear, whereby it is possible to explore the client's file system and choose the file to submit, as shown in Figure 12.30.

After the selection of a file, clicking the submit button causes the chosen file to be uploaded to the Web server as an attachment to the HTTP POST request, encoded in a format known as the *multipart MIME format.*

The *decoding of a multi-part attachment* at the server side is quite a technical task, but several commercial and open source libraries exist that alleviate the job.[8] The typical task done by the multi-part handling library is to manage the retrieval of the different segments of a multi-part attachment and to re-assemble it as a stream, available to the page template for manipulation, for instance for insertion into a database column, or for storage in the server file system.

```
<form action="acceptFile" enctype="multipart/form-data" method="post">
    Upload a file : <br>
    File <input type="file" name="submit-file"><br>
    <input type="submit" value="Submit">
</form>
```

Figure 12.29 Implementation of a form with a field for file uploading.

---

[8]A popular multi-part handling library is the O'Reilly MultipartRequest and Multipart-Parser Java classes, included in the com.oreilley.servlet Java package, available at *www.servlets.com/cos/index.html.*

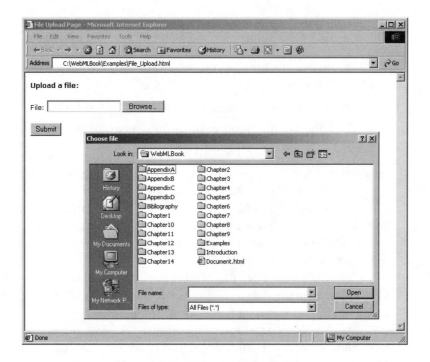

Figure 12.30   Use of input tag of type file in HTML.

BLOB storage varies based on the solution adopted for archiving the BLOB, which can be one of the options discussed in Chapter 11:

1. Storage of the BLOB in the same entity table that stores the regular attributes of the object.

2. Storage of the BLOB in a separate database table, and of the OID of the BLOB value in the entity table.

3. Storage of the BLOB in the file system, with the pathname of the BLOB file stored in the entity table.

4. Storage of the BLOB in the file system, using directory and file naming conventions to link the file to the object it belong to.

Case 3 is the most common: the code in Figure 12.31 illustrates the essential instructions requested for saving an uploaded file in the server file system and for storing the pathname of the uploaded file in the table column corresponding to the BLOB attribute. The example assumes the existence of a Java class for multipart handling, called `MultipartRequest`. Lines 1–2 construct a utility

```
1   MultipartRequest multi =
2       new MultipartRequest(request, "uploadDir");
3   Enumeration files = multi.getFileNames();
4   while (files.hasMoreElements()) {
5       String name = (String) files.nextElement();
6       String filename = multi.getFilesystemName(name);
7       if (filename != null) {
8           // store the value of "filename" in the database column
9           // containing the pathname of the BLOB value
10      }
11  }
```

Figure 12.31   Storage of attributes of type BLOB using a multipart handling library.

object of class `MultipartRequest`, which wraps the actual HTTP request including the multipart attachment. The object constructor invoked at line 2 has two input parameters: the original HTTP request and the name of the directory where the uploaded files must be stored. The execution of the constructor automatically reads the uploaded files from the HTTP request and saves them with their original names in the directory specified as the value of the second parameter. Then, at line 3, function `getFileNames` is invoked on the multipart request object, to retrieve a Java enumeration container storing the symbolic names of all the files submitted by the user in the input form.[9] Finally, the loop at lines 4–11 iterates over the symbolic file names to extract one by one the physical pathnames of the files that have been stored in the server file systems. These pathnames can be saved in the appropriate columns of the database table storing the entity instances (lines 8–9).

12.4.4   Create and Connect Pattern

As discussed in Chapter 5, operations can be linked to form *operation chains*. In this section, we address the implementation of a *create and connect pattern;* we also cover the implementation of *multiple input links pointing into operation chains.*

---

[9]The symbolic name is typically the name of the input field used in the HTML form, which is normally different from the filename of the uploaded file. In this way, the same file can be uploaded in two distinct input fields of the same form.

The example in Figure 12.32 contains a create and connect operation pattern. The NewsCreation page includes an entry unit, for inputting the heading and body of the piece of news, and a data unit, displaying the current news category. The outgoing link of the entry unit activates the create operation, which is linked to a connect operation for creating an instance of the relationship between the news category and the news item. The transport link exiting from the CurrentCategory data unit carries the OID of the current news category in input to the connect unit. After the transaction is executed successfully, the OK link of the connect unit leads back to the NewsCreation page, transporting the OID of the current category back to the page. If any of the operations fail, an error page is diplayed.

The template of page NewsCreation is shown in Figure 12.33. The most remarkable aspect is the construction of the form fields, which comprises a hidden field representing the context information associated with the transport link, which is not rendered. The hidden field (lines 33–34) adds to the HTTP request the OID of the category displayed in the data unit, needed by the connect unit in the operation chain.

The operation template implementing the create and connect transaction is illustrated in Figure 12.34. The transaction consists of a sequence of two operations: the create operation, followed by the connect operation. The create operation takes

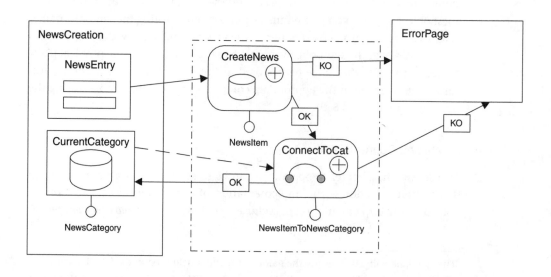

Figure 12.32   A create and connect pattern.

```
1   <%@page language="java" %>
2   <%@ page import= "java.sql.*" %>
3   <% // REQUEST PARAMETERS FETCH
4   String categoryOID = request.getParameter("OID");
5   // DATABASE CONNECTION
6   Class.forName("sun.jdbc.odbc.JdbcOdbcDriver");
7   Connection conn = DriverManager.getConnection("jdbc:odbc:acme",
8                         "acmeuser", "acmepwd");
9   // QUERY EXECUTION
10  PreparedStatement pstmt = conn.prepareStatement(
11      "SELECT OID, NAME, DESCRIPTION FROM NEWSCATEGORY WHERE OID = ?");
12  pstmt.setString(1, categoryOID);
13  ResultSet result = pstmt.executeQuery();
14  %>
15  <html> <!-- CONTENT PRODUCTION -->
16  <head><title>News Creation Page</title></head>
17  <body>
18  <!-- CONTENT PRODUCTION: DATA UNIT -->
19  <% if (result.next()){ %>
20  <table>
21    <tr>
22      <td><%= result.getString("NAME") %></td>
23      <td><%= result.getString("DESCRIPTION") %></td>
24    </tr>
25  </table> <br>
26  <%} %>
27  <!-- CONTENT PRODUCTION: ENTRY UNIT -->
28  Enter heading and body: </br>
29    <form method="POST" action="createAndConnect.jsp">
30      Heading: <input type="text" name="heading"><br>
31      Body:    <input type="text" name="body"><br>
32      <input type="submit">
33      <input type="hidden" name="categoryOID"
34        value="<%=result.getString("OID")%>">
35    </form>
36  </body>
37  </html>
38  <%    // TEMPORARY OBJECTS DISPOSITION
39  result.close(); pstmt.close(); conn.close();
40  %>
```

Figure 12.33 JSP implementation of page NewsCreation.

```
1   <%@page language="java" %>
2   <%@ page import= "java.sql.*" %>
3   <% // REQUEST PARAMETERS FETCH
4   String heading = request.getParameter("heading");
5   String body = request.getParameter("body");
6   String categoryOID = request.getParameter("categoryOID");
7   // DATABASE CONNECTION
8   Class.forName("sun.jdbc.odbc.JdbcOdbcDriver");
9   Connection conn = DriverManager.getConnection("jdbc:odbc:acme",
10                      "acmeuser", "acmepwd");
11  // START TRANSACTION
12  conn.setAutoCommit(false);
13  Statement stmt = conn.createStatement();
14  stmt.executeUpdate ("LOCK TABLE COUNTER IN EXCLUSIVE MODE");
15  ResultSet result = stmt.executeQuery(
16    "SELECT 1 + MAX(OID) AS NEWOID FROM NEWSITEM"); // INVENT NEW OID
17  result.next();
18  String newOID = result.getString("NEWOID");
19  result = stmt.executeUpdate(
20  "UPDATE COUNTER SET OID=1+OID");              //INCREMENT COUNTER
21  // QUERY PREPARATION: CREATE UNIT
22  PreparedStatement pstmt= conn.prepareStatement(
23  "INSERT INTO NEWSITEM (OID, HEADING, BODY) VALUES (?,?,?)");
24  pstmt.setString(1, newOID);
25  pstmt.setString(2, heading);
26  pstmt.setString(3, body);
27  // QUERY EXECUTION: CREATE UNIT
28  try {
29      pstmt.executeUpdate();
30  } catch (SQLException e) {
31      conn.rollback(); result.close();        // ERROR: ROLLBACK
32      pstmt.close(); conn.close();
33      pageContext.forward("errorPage.jsp");   // FOLLOW KO LINK
34  }
35  // QUERY PREPARATION: CONNECT UNIT
```

(continued)

Figure 12.34 JSP implementation of the create and connect operation chain.

Figure 12.34   *(continued)*

```
36  PreparedStatement pstmt2 = conn.prepareStatement(
37  "UPDATE NEWSITEM SET CATEGORYOID =? WHERE OID =?");
38  pstmt2.setString(1, categoryOID);
39  pstmt2.setString(2, newOID);
40  // QUERY EXECUTION: CONNECT UNIT
41  try {
42      pstmt2.executeUpdate();
43  } catch (SQLException e) {
44      conn.rollback(); result.close();              // ERROR: ROLLBACK
45      pstmt.close(); pstmt2.close(); conn.close();
46      pageContext.forward("errorPage.jsp");         // FOLLOW KO LINK
47  }
48  conn.commit();                                    //SUCCESS: COMMIT
49  result.close();
50  pstmt.close(); pstmt2.close();
51  conn.close();
52  // FOLLOW OK LINK
53  pageContext.forward("newsCreation.jsp?OID=" + categoryOID); %>
```

input from the HTTP request (the heading and body of the piece of news to create); the connect operation takes one input parameter from the create unit (the OID of the new object), and one parameter from the HTTP request (the OID of the current category).

The operation template of Figure 12.34 has the general structure described in Figure 12.23. Lines 35–39 demonstrate the SQL query of the connect operation, which in this case is an update on the table column that represents the one-to-many relationship between a piece of news and its category. If the relationship is many-to-many, the SQL query of the connect operation requires the creation of a row of the bridge table, storing the OIDs of the two connected objects.

After the successful commit of both the create and connect operation, the contextual OK link of the connect unit is navigated and control passes back to the NewsCreation page (line 53). Because the OK link is contextual, the parameters needed for computing the destination page must be passed along the link; in this case, the OID of the current category, which was received in input by the operation template, is re-emitted in output along the OK link.

The example of Figure 12.34 can be easily adapted to obtain the implementation of the disconnect operation, whose SQL query does the opposite as the query of lines 35–39: it sets to null the relationship column, for one-to-many relationships, or it deletes a row of the bridge table, for many-to-many relationships.

12.4.5   Login, Logout, and Global Parameters for the Current User and Group

We turn now to other frequently used features of Web applications: login and logout, and the storage of global parameters about the current user and his/her group. A *login* operation has three purposes:

- Verifying the credentials of the user.

- Forwarding the user to the site view of his/her default group, if the credentials are verified, or to an error page, if verification fails.

- Setting the global parameters `CurrentUser` and `CurrentGroup` to the OID of the user and group objects that represent the currently logged user, and his/her default group.

Global parameters, including those needed for storing the OID of the currently logged user and of his/her group, can be implemented using the *session object,* a standard feature of the Java servlet and JSP API, which is available in all server-side platforms. As explained in Chapter 1, the session is a Java object automatically created by the servlet container at the first request of a client, and maintained for certain amount of time, to create a binding between the HTTP client and the server. Each session has a distinct identifier, which is communicated back and forth between the client and the server, to keep the section active. The session object can be used to store *state information* at the server-side, to be made available to all the pages of a given application, during an active session. We will use the session object to store and retrieve the global parameter corresponding to the OID of the currently logged user and of his/her default group.

The operation template in Figure 12.35 implements the login operation, exploiting the relational schema for representing profile data illustrated in Chapter 8. The login operation is typically called by an HTML form containing two input fields, one for the username and one for the password. The operation template retrieves the value of the username and password from the HTTP request (lines 4–5). Then, it uses these values to instantiate the prepared statement shown at lines 9–12. The SQL statement verifies that the given username and password do exist in the USER table, and retrieves the OID of the user associated to the credentials, and the OID of his/her default group, obtained by joining the USER and GROUP tables. The outcome of credential verification is examined by the IF statement at line 16. If the SQL query did not find any object matching the username and password,

```
1   <%@page language="java" %>
2   <%@ page import= "java.sql.*" %>
3   <%
4   String username = request.getParameter("username");
5   String password = request.getParameter("password");
6   Class.forName("sun.jdbc.odbc.JdbcOdbcDriver");
7   Connection conn = DriverManager.getConnection("jdbc:odbc:acme",
8                        "acmeuser", "acmepwd");
9   PreparedStatement pstmt = conn.prepareStatement(
10      "SELECT U.OID AS USEROID, G.OID AS GROUPOID " +
11      "FROM USER AS U LEFT JOIN GROUP AS G ON G.OID = U.GROUPOID " +
12      "WHERE U.USERNAME =? AND U.PASSWORD =?");
13  pstmt.setString(1, username);
14  pstmt.setString(2, password);
15  ResultSet result = pstmt.executeQuery();
16  if (!result.next()) {                       // NO VALID USER DATA FOUND
17      result.close();
18      pstmt.close();
19      conn.close();
20      pageContext.forward("loginError.jsp");
21  } else {                                    // VALID USER DATA FOUND
22      session.setAttribute(
23         "CurrentUser", result.getString("USEROID"));
24      session.setAttribute(
25         "CurrentGroup", result.getString("GROUPOID"));
26      result.close();
27      pstmt.close();
28      conn.close();
29      pageContext.forward("home.jsp");
30  } %>
```

Figure 12.35   JSP implementation of the login operation.

the connection is closed and control is transferred to page loginError.jsp, which may request the username and password again. If verification succeeds, the OID of the user and group are stored in two session attributes, CurrentUser and CurrentGroup (lines 22 and 24), and control is forwarded to the home page of the site view associated with the default group of the user.

Note that in Figure 12.35, the name of the home page to jump to is hard-wired in the JSP code, at line 29. This works if there is only one group and a single protected site view. In a more realistic scenario, where multiple groups and site views are involved, the database schema representing users and groups can be extended to store also the URL of the site view of each group and the URL of its home page, as discussed in Chapter 8; then, the SQL query of lines 9–12 can retrieve such URL, and use it in the forward instruction of line 29.

The *logout* operation is much simpler than the login operation: it amounts to invalidating the session and forwarding control to the home page of the public site view.

A last conclusive remark concerns security: the transmission of the user's password via a plain HTTP request is highly insecure, because no encryption is used by the HTTP protocol. However, using a secure version of the HTTP protocol, like Secure HTTP, ensures that the password transmission is protected, and does not require any extra programming effort, because the Secure HTTP protocol is transparent to the template programmer.

12.5 Implementing Set and Get Units and Complex Pages

The final examples of this chapter show the use of *set and get units* and summarize the procedure for implementing a complex page. The first hypertext chosen for illustration is shown in Figure 12.36.

A first page, NewsCategories, includes the index of all news categories and a data unit (NewsCategory) displaying the details of one category. A second page, NewsItems, contains a multidata unit, which lists the pieces of news of the category selected in the previous page, and includes a non-contextual link for getting back to the NewsCategories page. In the NewsCategories page, the NewsCategory data unit is linked to a set unit, for storing the OID of the currently displayed category into a global parameter, and has an incoming link from a get unit, defined on the same global parameter as the set unit. In this way, the OID of the current category is preserved by a global parameter, and can be used to restore the content of the NewsCategory data unit, for instance, when navigating the non-contextual link pointing back from the NewsItems page to the NewsCategories page.

The implementation of page NewsCategories includes all the features of the page computation algorithm explained in Chapter 5, and also addresses the treatment of get and set units. We use this example to summarize the general design workflow of complex pages.

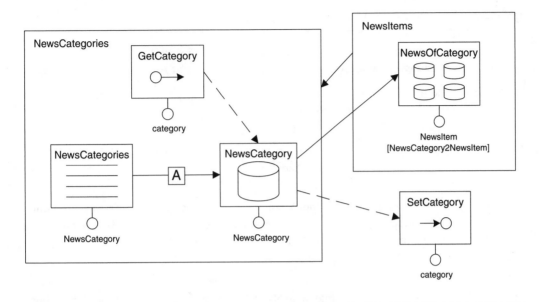

Figure 12.36 Page with set and get units for remembering the selection in an index.

First, we examine the ways in which the page can be accessed, to understand the parameters present in the HTTP request and the content of the global parameter. The page can be accessed in three ways:

- *Non-contextually for the first time:* the request contains no parameters and the global parameter has no value.

- *Non-contextually for the second time:* the request contains no parameters and the global parameter has the value of the last displayed category.

- *Navigating the intra page link:* the request contains as parameter the fresh value of the new category to display, and the global parameter stores the value of the last displayed category.

From the observation of the page access modalities, the input and output of each unit can be determined; for the NewsCategory data unit, which may have multiple alternative inputs, the specificity rule tells which input must be used. Table 12.1 summarizes the content of the request and the relevant input and output of units, for the three different accesses to the page.

The next step is the definition of the order in which units are evaluated, which is independent of the way in which the page is accessed, and depends on the

Table 12.1   Alternative accesses to page NewsCategories.

	Request parameters	Index unit: input/output	Get unit: output	Data unit: input
NC 1st time	None	Input: none Output: first object	Empty	Output of index unit
NC 2nd time	None	Input: none Output: first object	Last displayed	Output of get unit
Intra-page	Fresh OID value for the NewsCategory data unit	Input: none Output: selected object	Last displayed	Fresh value from HTTP request

topology of intra-page links. The NewsCategories index unit and the GetCategory get unit are context-free, as they do not require input, and can be evaluated first; next, the NewsCategory data unit can be considered, which depends on the index and get units; finally the set unit can be evaluated, which depends on the data unit.

The evaluation of the data unit must be wrapped by means of a test for selecting the most specific input parameter; the data unit has two input links, and the input link from the index unit may carry either a default or a fresh value. Considering the cases illustrated in Table 12.1, the input of the data unit can be decided with the following test:

```
IF the HTTP request contains a fresh value for the category OID
  Input = fresh value from the HTTP request
ELSE IF the global parameter contains a value for the category OID
  Input = value of the global parameter
ELSE
  Input = OID of the first object of the NewsCategories index unit
```

The template of page NewsCategories is shown in Figure 12.37; we comment only the relevant sections:

- The HTTP parameter fetching section extracts the single parameter from the request (lines 3–4).

- The NewsCategories index unit is evaluated first (lines 9–13).

- After the index unit evaluation, the test for deciding the input of the data unit is performed (lines 14–21); the test directly accesses the global parameter in output from the get unit, which requires just a lookup in the session object (line 18).

- Next, the data unit is evaluated, using the most specific input value (lines 22–26).

- Then, the set unit is considered, which requires storing the OID used in the data unit in the session object (line 27).

- Finally, the HTML content production part follows; it is very similar to the example of Figure 12.15, but for the presence of the outgoing link of the data unit, which is implemented as an HTML anchor (lines 46–48) consisting of a fixed part and of a variable part extracted from the result set of the data unit's query.

Figure 12.37 illustrates the JSP instructions for implementing *set and get units*. The set unit is translated into an instruction that stores a value in the session object:

```
session.setAttribute("global-parameter-name", "value")
```

and the get unit is translated into a lookup in the session object:

```
value = session.getAttribute("global-parameter-name")
```

As a last example of implementation, we conclude by recalling in Figure 12.38 the complex page discussed in Chapter 5; we only show the relevant design decision and leave to the reader writing the actual JSP code.

Table 12.2 summarizes the page accesses highlighted in Figure 12.38, showing the parameters of the HTTP request and the input and output of units.

The implementation of the page is a single JSP template. However, the order of unit evaluation is not unique, because there are multiple context-free units; therefore, the programmer is free to choose a specific order among the possible ones (a possible sequence is: ArtistIndex, NewAlbumIndex, NewAlbumData, ArtistData, AlbumIndex, and AlbumData). The units with multiple inputs are all the data units (NewAlbumData, ArtistData, AlbumData); their implementation must exploit the most specific OID, which is different based on the way the page is accessed. The specificity tests for such units are sketched on page 452[10]:

---

[10] The actual code of the tests may exploit the value of the request parameters, as done for instance in lines 16–21 of Figure 12.37. Alternatively, if the number of possible accesses to the page is very large, the programmer may opt for using extra request parameters explicitly showing the navigated link, which may make the code of the tests more readable.

```
1    <%@page language="java" %>
2    <%@ page import= "java.sql.*" %>
3    <% // REQUEST PARAMETER FETCH
4    String categoryDUInput = request.getParameter("categoryDU");
5    // DATABASE CONNECTION
6    Class.forName("sun.jdbc.odbc.JdbcOdbcDriver");
7    Connection conn = DriverManager.getConnection("jdbc:odbc:acme",
8                         "acmeuser", "acmepwd");
9    // QUERY EXECUTION: INDEX UNIT
10   Statement stmt = conn.createStatement(
11       ResultSet.TYPE_SCROLL_SENSITIVE, ResultSet.CONCUR_READ_ONLY);
12   ResultSet result = stmt.executeQuery(
13       "SELECT NAME, OID FROM NEWSCATEGORY ORDER BY NAME");
14   //SPECIFICITY TEST WITH EVALUATION OF GET UNIT
15   String dataUnitOID;
16   if (categoryDUInput != null)  // INTRA PAGE LINK NAVIGATED
17       dataUnitOID = categoryDUInput; //USE SELECTED OID
18   else if (session.getAttribute("category") != null)  // USE GET UNIT'S OUTPUT
19       dataUnitOID = (String) session.getAttribute("category");
20   else { result.next(); dataUnitOID = result.getString("OID");
21       result.beforeFirst();}  // USE DEFAULT PROPAGATION FROM INDEX UNIT
22   // QUERY EXECUTION: DATA UNIT
23   PreparedStatement pstmt = conn.prepareStatement(
24       "SELECT OID, NAME, DESCRIPTION FROM NEWSCATEGORY WHERE OID = ?");
25   pstmt.setString(1, dataUnitOID);
26   ResultSet result2 = pstmt.executeQuery();
27   session.setAttribute("category", dataUnitOID); // SET UNIT EXECUTION
28   %>
29   <html> <!-- CONTENT PRODUCTION -->
30   <head> <title>News Categories Page</title> </head>
31   <body>
32   <table> <!-- CONTENT PRODUCTION: INDEX UNIT -->
33     <% while (result.next()) {%>
34     <tr><td><a href=
35         "categoryPage.jsp?categoryDU=<%=result.getString("OID")%>">
36         <%= result.getString("NAME") %> </a></td></tr>
37     <%} %>
38   </table>
39   <% if (result2.next()) { %>
```

(continued)

Figure 12.37 JSP implementation of page News categories.

Figure 12.37 *(continued)*

```
40  <table> <!-- CONTENT PRODUCTION: DATA UNIT -->
41    <tr><td> Name </td><td> <%= result2.getString("NAME")%> </td></tr>
42    <tr><td> Description </td>
43      <td> <%= result2.getString("DESCRIPTION")%> </td></tr>
44      <!-- CONTENT PRODUCTION: DATA UNIT'S OUTGOING LINK -->
45    <tr><td colspan="2">
46      <a href=
47      "newsItems.jsp?newsMDU=<%= result2.getString("OID")%>">
48      News of this category</a></td></tr>
49  </table>
50  <%} %>
51  </body>
52  </html>
53  <%          // TEMPORARY OBJECTS DISPOSITION
54  result.close(); stmt.close();
55  result2.close(); pstmt.close(); conn.close();%>
```

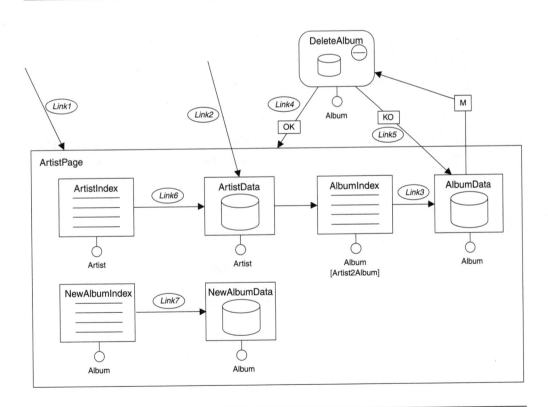

Figure 12.38 A complex page with multiple accesses.

Table 12.2 Alternative accesses to page ArtistPage

Link	Request parameters	ArtistIndex, NewAlbum Index	NewAlbum Data
1	None	Input: none Output: first object	Input/Output: output of NewAlbum Index
2	Fresh OID for ArtistData	Input: none Output: first object	Input/Output: output of NewAlbum Index
3	Fresh OID for AlbumData, preserved OID of ArtistData, NewAlbum Data	Input: none Output: first object	Input/Output: preserved OID from request
4	Preserved OID of ArtistData, NewAlbum Data	Input: none Output: first object	Input/Output: preserved OID from request
5	Preserved OID of AlbumData, ArtistData, NewAlbum Data	Input: none Output: first object	Input/Output: preserved OID from request
6	Fresh OID of ArtistData, preserved OID of NewAlbum Data	Input: none Output: first object	Input/Output: preserved OID from request
7	Fresh OID of NewAlbum Data, preserved OID of ArtistData, AlbumData	Input: none Output: first object	Input/Output: fresh OID from request

```
NewAlbumData:
    IF the HTTP request contains a fresh/preserved Album OID
        Input = OID from the HTTP request
    ELSE
        Input = OID of the first object of the NewAlbumIndex unit
ArtistData:
    IF the HTTP request contains a fresh/preserved Artist OID
        Input = OID from the HTTP request
    ELSE
        Input = OID of the first object of the ArtistIndex unit
```

ArtistData	AlbumIndex	AlbumData
Input/Output: output of ArtistIndex	Input: artist of ArtistData Output: first album of input artist	Input: output of AlbumIndex
Input/Output: fresh OID from request	Input: artist of ArtistData Output: first album of input artist	Input: output of AlbumIndex
Input/Output: preserved OID from request	Input: artist of ArtistData Output: first album of input artist	Input: Fresh OID from request
Input/Output: preserved OID from request	Input: artist of ArtistData Output: first album of input artist	Input: output of AlbumIndex
Input/Output: preserved OID from request	Input: artist of ArtistData Output: first album of input artist	Input: preserved OID from request
Input/Output: fresh OID from request	Input: artist of ArtistData Output: first album of input artist	Input: output of AlbumIndex
Input/Output: preserved OID from request	Input: artist of ArtistData Output: first album of input artist	Input: preserved OID from request

```
NewAlbumData:
    IF the HTTP request contains a fresh/preserved Album OID
        Input = preserved oid from the HTTP request
    ELSE
        Input = OID of the first object of the AlbumIndex unit
```

Summary

In this chapter we discussed the implementation of the WebML primitives for hypertext modeling. We started by illustrating how the algorithm for the computation of a page, explained at a high level in Chapter 5, can be translated into concrete code for a server-side scripting platform like JSP. With this focus, we have presented the general structure of the JSP template implementing an arbitrary WebML page, and progressively introduced a gallery of examples, moving from the simplest page, with only one index unit, to more complicated cases, including multiple units, intra-page links, entry units, and multi-choice units.

After completing the explanation of the WebML primitives for content publishing, we devoted a section to content management operations, showing the implementation of delete, create, and connect operations, both alone or linked to form transactions. The discussion of operations has also illustrated the problems inherent to the management of file uploads and BLOB storage.

Finally, we presented the implementation of a few advanced features, like global parameters, login and logout operations, and the use of set and get units for preserving the state of pages during inter-page navigation.

The designer can use the present chapter to get a clear vision of how to turn his/her site view into a dynamic Web application; the guidelines for implementing all WebML primitives are further summarized in Appendix D. More generally, any developer faced with the challenge of implementing a data-intensive Web application may benefit from the implementation techniques discussed in this chapter, which provide suggestions on how to solve commonly encountered application problems.

Bibliographic Notes

The implementation of data-intensive and dynamic Web applications is the subject of many textbooks, especially books targeted to the developers of a specific platform.

In the Java world, JSP and servlet programming are treated by many texts, among which is the popular title by Marty Hall [Hall00]. Another book entirely devoted to JSP programming is [Bergsten00], which guides the developer from the installation of the Java development environment to such advanced topics as the programming of JavaBeans and custom tags.

Database connectivity in Java and Java Server Pages is discussed in the annotated reference manual of JDBC, the second edition of which covers also the features of JDBC 2.0 [WFCHH99]. The technical issues of working with large objects are mostly vendor-dependent and thus the most appropriate source of information is the technical documentation of the specific product. For example, the Oracle Technology Network contains a section dedicated to the JDBC technology, which publishes technical papers and code samples demonstrating the use of Oracle JDBC with different complex data types, like large objects (LOBS) and binary files (BFILES); see, for example, the Sample Code area at: *otn.oracle.com/ sample_code/tech/java/sqlj_jdbc*.

The problem of managing file uploads and multi-part attachments is treated in many technical articles and Web sites. The popular com.oreilley.servlet Java package (*www.servlets.com/cos/index.html*) comprises several utility classes for this job, and includes the technical documentation for putting the libraries to work quickly. The full file upload specification is contained in experimental RFC 1867, available at *www.ietf.org/rfc/rfc1867.txt*.

13 Advanced Hypertext Implementation

13.1 Introduction

In the previous chapter, we discussed how to implement WebML hypertexts, by translating WebML pages and operations into JSP templates. Any WebML specification, even complex pages accessed in multiple ways, can be implemented by following the guidelines and examples of code presented in Chapter 12. However, the resulting programming style is based on "all-inclusive" templates, intermixing the business logic, the data access code, and the presentation, which impairs application maintenance and code reuse.

Improving the quality of the implementation requires the adoption of a more modular software architecture enforcing the principle of *separation of concerns*. The monolithic page templates of Chapter 12 should be broken down into smaller components, and each component should address only one specific aspect, for example data access, business logic, or presentation, so that each aspect could be modified separately, with great benefits on maintenance and evolution.

To this end, the examples of this chapter adopt a software architecture called *Model-View-Controller (MVC)*, expressly conceived for improving the separation of concerns and modularity of software applications. With this reorganization, the page and operation templates of Chapter 12 are partitioned into reusable components, which are easier to produce and maintain.

In addition to the revision of the software architecture according to the MVC design pattern, we also explain other advanced techniques suited to very large applications: the definition of generic unit and operation services using XML descriptors, the development of distributed business objects with the Enterprise JavaBeans standard, and the centralized management of presentation with the help of CSS and XSL rules. All these design principles and techniques are shown at work on examples drawn from Chapter 12, to let the reader appreciate the difference between the implementation of a small-size application, and a software design targeted to large, enterprise-class applications.

13.2 Improving the Software Architecture

Designing the overall architecture of an application requires addressing not only the hardware and network configuration, but also the software architecture. By this term, we mean the allocation of the different application functions to the various processes running in the selected deployment architecture, and the distribution of responsibilities among the software components that compose each module. Before proceeding with the discussion, we highlight software-specific design objectives that drive the decision-making process. These criteria add up to and complement the architectural factors discussed in Chapter 10.

- *Separation of concerns:* application functions normally developed by different professionals should remain separate also in the application code.

- *Evolvability:* changes in requirements or software maintenance needs should be confined to the affected modules, and not propagate outside them.

- *Reusability:* software should be organized into reusable components. The most important principle for achieving reuse is that each module should know as little as possible about the way in which it will be used by client modules, and each client should ignore the internal details of the module it uses.

■ *Software scalability:* the software architecture should support very large applications, with thousands of modules. There should be the possibility of applying bulk modifications to the software, without manual intervening on each affected program.

We open the discussion about software architectures with a revision of the template-based solution adopted in Chapter 12. For this purpose, we consider again the JSP template of Figure 13.1, which implements a WebML page containing an index unit. The reader should not be misled by the apparent simplicity of this example; in Chapter 12 we have shown that more complex pages yield much more elaborated JSP templates.

The page template of Figure 13.1 concentrates into a single module a variety of different responsibilities:

■ *Data management:* the template contains the code for the dialog with the data sources, the formulation of the data extraction queries, and the storage of the query results into appropriate structures.

■ *Presentation:* the HTML section of the template contains the static markup and the code for dynamically producing the display of the results of the data extraction queries.

■ *Control handling:* the template also incorporates the knowledge of the actual page to display after a user's click, represented by the URL of the various links emanating from the page. Control issues are more evident in the case of operation templates discussed in Chapter 12, which contain conditional statements for deciding which link to follow after the execution of an operation.

The problems of maintaining templates like the one in Figure 13.1 are manifold.

■ *Dispersion of the business logic.* Global changes to the data extraction or update logic, and more generally to the business logic behind the presentation layer, propagate to all pages, because they are not centralized in a dedicated module, but scattered and replicated in all the page templates.

■ *Dependence of page templates on data structures.* Changing the structures used to store the results of data queries breaks the presentation code, which is aware of such data structures. This may happen simply by changing the library used to connect to the database and execute queries.

■ *Dependence of page templates on link topology.* Changing the link topology of the hypertext, or even changing the name of a JSP template, requires

```
1   <%@page language="java" %>
2   <%@ page import= "java.sql.*" %>
3   <% // DATABASE CONNECTION
4   Class.forName("sun.jdbc.odbc.JdbcOdbcDriver");
5   Connection conn = DriverManager.getConnection("jdbc:odbc:acer",
6                       "aceruser", "acerpwd");
7   // QUERY PREPARATION AND EXECUTION
8   Statement stmt = conn.createStatement();
9   ResultSet result = stmt.executeQuery(
10                      "SELECT NAME FROM NEWSCATEGORY ORDER BY NAME");
11  %>
12  <!-- CONTENT PRODUCTION -->
13  <html>
14  <head>
15  <title>News Categories Page</title>
16  </head>
17  <body>
18  <!-- INDEX UNIT MARKUP PRODUCTION -->
19  <table>
20      <% while (result.next()) { %>
21      <tr>
22          <td><%= result.getString("NAME") %></td>
23      </tr>
24      <%} %>
25  </table>
26  </body>
27  </html>
28  <!-- TEMPORARY OBJECTS DISPOSAL -->
29  <%
30  result.close();
31  stmt.close();
32  conn.close();
33  %>
```

Figure 13.1   Example of page template.

intervention on the source code of all the affected pages. For instance, changing the file name of a landmark page would require updating the code of all the pages of the site view!

■ *Lack of isolation of presentation aspects.* Presentation must be handled by a programmer and not by a graphic designer, because the page mark-up is mixed with server-side scripting instructions. The graphic designer who works on the page template in his/her favourite WYSIWYG HTML editing tool sees a mix of graphics and programming instructions, and can hardly assess the graphic quality of the page without actually executing it on real data, which requires technical skills. Moreover, while working on the presentation, he/she may unconsciously remove lines of code, breaking the consistency of the template.

■ *Lack of scalability.* The software architecture is not scalable, because every page deals with all aspects as if it were a standalone module, which makes it impossible to separately replicate and reuse functions. For example, it is impossible to share the same component for executing database queries across different pages, because every page addresses this problem by itself.

These observations clearly motivate a different software organization.

13.3 Model-View-Controller Architecture

Most of the problems highlighted in the previous section are not specific to data-intensive Web applications, but are general, and relate to the modularization of any application. One of the most powerful software architectures proposed by the software engineers to cope with these problems is the so-called *Model-View-Controller design pattern* (*MVC* for short). The MVC is conceived to better separate and insulate the three essential functions of an interactive application:

■ The business logic of the application (*the Model*).

■ The interface presented to the user (*the View*).

■ The control of the interaction triggered by the user's actions (*the Controller*).

In the MVC architecture, the typical flow of control is the one represented in Figure 13.2.

The computation is activated by a user's request for some content or service. The request is intercepted by the Controller, who is responsible of deciding which action to take for servicing it. The Controller dispatches the request, in the form of a "request for action," to the suitable component of the Model. The Model

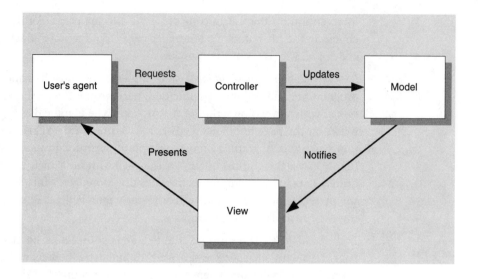

Figure 13.2   MVC architecture.

incorporates the business logic for performing the action, and executes such logic, which updates the state of the application and produces a result to be communicated to the user. The change in the Model triggers the most appropriate View, which builds the presentation of the response. Such presentation typically embodies interaction objects, whereby the user may pose a new request and reactivate the computation process.

The MVC architecture prescribes a sharp distinction of responsibilities among the components of the application:

- The Model encapsulates the business actions required for answering a user's request and keeps the state of the application. The Model should ignore the format in which requests are posed, and the way in which the response is constructed and presented to the user.

- The View embodies the presentation logic for assembling the user interface. An application may have a single View or multiple Views, and a View may be composed of sub-Views, relevant to different types of results. The View should ignore where the results to present come from and the details of the request originating such results.

- The Controller is the traffic cop of the architecture, responsible for interpreting the user's request, producing the appropriate request for action, examining the result of each action, and deciding what to do next. The Controller is totally unaware of the business logic of the action it invokes, and of the presentation logic of the View.

▓ The Actions are the actual components that implement the business logic. They are designed for being reusable by different applications, possibly using different front-ends.

13.3.1 Model-View-Controller Architecture Applied to Web Applications

In recent times, the MVC architecture has been claimed as an effective pattern for organizing the architecture of Web applications. The leader of such a line of thought is the popular *Struts* project of the *Apache Software Foundation (jakarta. apache.org/struts*), which offers an open-source implementation of the MVC architecture fitting the Java 2 Enterprise Edition platform. The discussion that follows is inspired by the concepts and terminology of Struts, but is independent of the particular incarnation of the MVC architecture, and can be applied to any Web application development platform.

In the Web context, the original MVC scheme must be somehow adapted to take into account the peculiarity of HTTP as a client-server protocol, especially the lack of mechanisms for maintaining the state of the interaction, and the asymmetric nature of the protocol, which makes it impossible for the server to

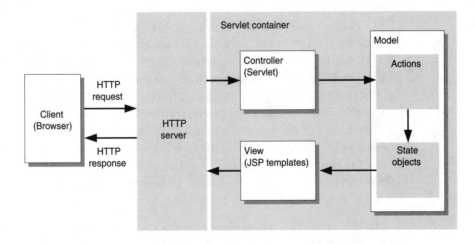

Figure 13.3 The MVC architecture applied to Web applications.

notify the client of changes in the application state. Figure 13.3 shows the adaptation of the classical MVC architecture to the Web context, using Java as a reference platform. The illustrated scheme is sometimes called *MVC 2 architecture.*

The emitter of service requests in the MVC 2 architecture is the Web browser. When the user clicks on a hyperlink in the HTML page, an HTTP requests is addressed to the HTTP server, which may route it to the servlet container, where a program acting as the Controller intercepts it. The Controller decides the course of action necessary to service each request. The possible actions are contained in the Model in the form of object-oriented components (sometimes called *action classes*). The Controller maps the HTTP request to the suitable action, by creating an object of the action class and calling one of its functions.

Each *action class* is a Java class wrapping a particular application function, operating on the state of the application. In the simplest situations, an action class implements all the business logic needed to serve the HTTP request. In more complex scenarios, the action class may collaborate with other objects for fulfilling its tasks. Example of actions could be execution of a database query, the sending of e-mail, or the authentication of the user. If the invoked action needs to update the state of the application, it may create or modify appropriate objects of the Model, called *state objects,* which represent the state of the application. State objects may last just the time needed for servicing the request, or persist between consecutive requests; for example, they may store the result of a data retrieval query, or the shopping cart items of the user. After completion, the action communicates the outcome of execution to the Controller, which decides what to do next.

In the typical flow of control of a Web MVC application, after an action completes, the Controller invokes a JSP page template, which is part of the View. The JSP template is responsible for presenting the updated state of the application to the user; for doing so, it accesses the state objects of the Model, where the current state of the application is stored, and builds the HTML page, which is sent back to the browser. Examples of views built after the execution of an action could be the display of the result of a database query, the notification that e-mail has been sent, and the home page of the Web site after the successful login of the user.

In a concrete implementation of the MVC 2 architecture, for instance in the Struts application framework, further technical components and mechanisms contribute to the architecture. These components are illustrated in Figure 13.4.

■ The Controller, which dispatches the client requests to the actions that serve them, is typically implemented as a *configurable servlet,* which reads the binding between HTTP request and actions from a *configuration file.* With this solution, the page to display after executing an action can be

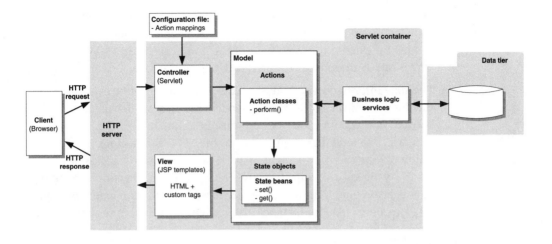

Figure 13.4 Concrete components of the MVC 2 architecture.

changed simply by editing the action mapping in the configuration file, without updating the code of the Controller.

■ The Action Classes, which are invoked by the Controller to serve requests, expose to the Controller a very simple interface, typically consisting of a *single function with a fixed name.*[1] In this way, the Controller needs to know only the name of the action class to call for any given request, and remains unaware of the details for invoking the real business services. Such details are known only to the action class, which "wraps" the business functions and plays the role of a "mediator" between the Controller and the business services.

■ The effect of executing action classes and business functions is recorded in the Model, as a set of state objects. These are typically very simple objects, with a standard interface consisting of functions for setting property values (called *setters*) and for getting the value of properties (called *getters*). In the Java world, objects of this kind are called *JavaBeans*. The JavaBeans representing the application state are typically produced by the execution of actions, and consumed by the JSP templates of the View.

■ The JSP templates in the View transform the content of the state objects into the HTML mark-up of the page, by calling the getter functions of

---

[1] In Struts, all actions classes expose a function called `perform`.

JavaBeans. A particularly effective way of organizing the JSP templates exploits *custom tags,* which, as explained in Chapter 1, mask the code needed for extracting the content of the JavaBeans behind XML tags, which can be intermixed to the HTML tags of the page.

■ The state information embodied by the JavaBeans must be available for the duration of the entire request-servicing process, and sometimes between consecutive requests, and must be stored into some data structure available to all the components of the MVC architecture. Two JSP utility objects can be used as containers of JavaBeans: the *request object* stores JavaBeans used within a single request, like, for instance, the result of a database query; the *session object* records information across multiple HTTP requests, like, for instance, the content of the user's shopping cart.

13.4 Mapping WebML to the MVC Architecture

The mapping of a WebML application into the MVC 2 architecture is pictorially illustrated in Figure 13.5, which fills the generic "boxes" of Figure 13.4 with WebML-specific elements. In the rest of this section, we discuss how the implementation of the fundamental WebML primitives (pages, units, links, and operations) uses the components appearing in Figure 13.5.

13.4.1 Mapping WebML Pages to the MVC Architecture

Each *WebML page* is mapped into four elements: 1) a *page action* in the Model, 2) a *page service* in the business tier, 3) a *JSP template* in the View, and 4) a *page action mapping* in the Controller's configuration file.

■ The page action is an instance of an action class: it extracts the input from the HTTP request and calls the page service in the business tier, passing to it the needed parameters. When the invoked page service terminates, the page action notifies the Controller of the outcome of page computation.

■ The page service is a business function supporting the computation of a page. It exposes a single function `computePage()`, invoked to carry out the parameter propagation and unit computation process according to the algorithm illustrated in Chapter 5. The page service updates the state objects in the Model: at the end of the page service execution, all the JavaBeans storing the result of the data retrieval queries of the page units (called *unit beans*) are available to the View.

■ The page template in the view computes the HTML page to be sent to the user, based on the content of the Model. The page template contains the static HTML needed to define the layout where the units are positioned, and *custom tags* implementing the rendition of WebML units.

■ The action mapping is a declaration placed in the Controller's configuration file that ties together the user's request, the page action, and the page view.

We now illustrate each one of these parts in detail, using as a running example the NewsCategories page implemented by the JSP template of Figure 13.1.

Figure 13.6 shows the code of the page action associated to the NewsCategories page, which illustrates the interaction between page actions and page services. The page action is a Java class, which extends the base class called Action (line 1). The action class defines a standard function, called perform (line 3), which is invoked by the Controller for computing the page.

The perform function encapsulates the interaction with the business tier: in the example of Figure 13.6, first of all a service for the NewsCategories page is created (line 7); then, such a page service is queried, by means of a utility function (getPageParameterNames), for retrieving the names of the parameters to be fetched from the request (line 9); these parameters are actually copied from the request into an auxiliary data structure, called state, (line 10), which is used for communicating between the page service and the page action, and for storing the state of the page; such a data structure is a Java map, that is, a set of name-value pairs. Next, the actual page business logic is triggered, by calling the computePage

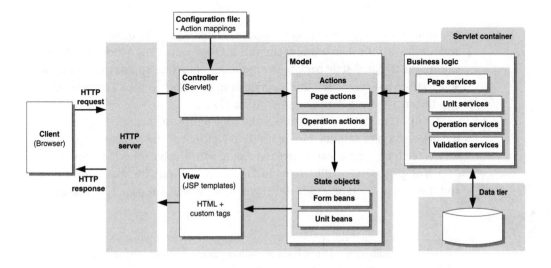

Figure 13.5   Mapping WebML concepts to the MVC architecture.

```
1    public class NewsCategoriesAction extends Action {
2
3    public ActionForward perform(ActionMapping mapping, ActionForm form,
4              HttpServletRequest request,
5              HttpServletResponse response) {
6    // build the page service
7    NewsCategoriesPageService pageService = new NewsCategoriesPageService();
8    // extract values of page's input parameters from the HTTP request
9    String[] parametersToFetch = pageService.getPageParameterNames();
10   Map state = copyFromRequest(request, parametersToFetch);
11   // compute the page
12   pageService.computePage(state);
13   // store state inside the HTTP request
14   // (for forwarding them to the view)
15   storeState(request, state);
16   // return control to Controller
17   return mapping.findForward("success");
18   }
19  }
```

Figure 13.6   Page action for page NewCategories, exemplified in Struts.

function of the page service (line 12): the function takes in input the state map, and fills it with the data beans of the various page units. The action concludes by storing the updated state back to the request object (line 15), so to make it available to the View templates, and by returning an object to the Controller, denoting the outcome of action execution (line 17).[2]

With respect to the structure of the page template illustrated in Figure 13.1, the page action exemplified in Figure 13.6 factors out the code for request parameters fetching, and encapsulates the dialog with the business logic services.

The page service, illustrated in Figure 13.7, covers the execution of units and the propagation of parameters, which, in the case of page NewsCategories,

---

[2]For sake of simplicity we do not consider failures in the computation of pages. Thus, the result returned by the page action (line 17) is always "success".

```
1   public class NewsCategoriesPageService extends PageService {
2
3       /** List of page parameters (empty for this page) */
4       public static final String[] PAGE_PARAMETERS = new String[0];
5
6       /** Return the list of page parameters */
7       public String[] getPageParameterNames() {
8           return PAGE_PARAMETERS;
9       }
10      /** Compute the page */
11        public void computePage(Map state) {
12      // execute services of content units
13          NewsCategoriesService unitService = new NewsCategoriesService();
14          unitService.execute(state);
15          }
16
17  }
```

Figure 13.7   Page service for page NewsCategories.

are rather trivial, because the page contains a single context-free unit. The page service is a Java class (NewsCategoriesPageService), which implements the two functions called by the page action class shown in Figure 13.6. Function get-PageParameterNames simply returns an empty array of strings, because page NewsCategories requires no input for its units; function computePage creates an instance of the unit service for the NewsCategories index unit (line 13), and calls its execute method (line 14), which computes the content of the index unit. In such an invocation, the state object is passed to the unit service, which stores in it the result of the data retrieval query. Unit services are objects encapsulating the behavior of WebML units; they are described in Section 13.4.2.

A skeleton of the page template for page NewsCategories is shown in Figure 13.8. The template starts with the inclusion of a custom tag library. The included library is named "webml" and all its tags have a name that starts with the webml: prefix, which distinguishes them from the regular HTML tags. Then, the template contains regular HTML mark-up for the static part of the page. When the index unit must be presented, the custom tags of the WebMLtag library are used, as we will show in Figure 13.11.

```
<%@ taglib uri="/WEB-INF/webml.tld" prefix="webml" %>
<html>
<head>
<title>News Categories Page</title>
</head>
<body>
<!-- INDEX UNIT CUSTOM TAG -->
   ...
   ...
</body>
</html>
```

Figure 13.8   View template of page NewsCategories, using a custom tag library.

```
<action path="/NewsCategories" type="NewsCategoriesAction">
    <forward name="success" path="/NewsCategories.jsp"/>
</action>
```

Figure 13.9   Configuration file of page NewsCategories.

In the Controller, page NewsCategories contributes the XML fragment shown in Figure 13.9 to the configuration file[3].

The first line of the action mapping declares a binding between client requests with a URL containing the string "NewsCategories" and the action class named "NewsCategoriesAction". When the Controller receives a request matching that specification, it constructs an object of the NewsCategoriesAction class (illustrated in Figure 13.6) and calls its perform() function. The forward element nested inside the action tag declares what to do after the action has completed. In the case of a page, we have assumed for simplicity that the data retrieval queries do not fail, and thus define a single possible outcome ("success"), which corresponds to calling the View associated to the page, represented by the JSP template named NewsCategories.jsp. Note that, according to the

---

[3]In Struts, the configuration of the Controller is written in the XML file named struts-config.xml.

MVC division of responsibility, the Controller decides what to do next, and not the action class, which returns to the Controller an object symbolizing the outcome of the action, but does not know about the View template named `NewsCategories.jsp`.

13.4.2 Mapping Content Units to the MVC Architecture

Units have a partition of responsibility similar to pages, but on a smaller scale.

- From the View perspective, units are responsible for the *production of content*. This content can be dynamic, for index, multidata, scroller, and data units, or static, for entry units.

- From the Model perspective, each unit contributes to the *state information* used by the View to build the response. Index, multidata, scroller, and data units contribute a data bean, whereas entry units are associated with a *form bean*. A form bean is an object that collects and maintains the values entered by the user in the form. Data and form beans differ only in the origin of their content: from the data layer in the case of data beans, from user's input in the case of form beans.

- From the business logic point of view, units with dynamic content encapsulate the *data retrieval logic*, whereas entry units encapsulate the *input validation logic*.

Each unit maps into two components of the MVC2 architecture: a unit service in the business layer, and a custom tag in the View. Note that units do not contribute actions in the Model, because the Controller knows only about pages, and is unaware of the units contained in them, which are not exposed as individually callable actions.

A *unit service* is a Java class, which is responsible for computing the unit's content and producing a collection of JavaBeans, filled with such a content. The class encapsulates the instructions needed to assemble the data retrieval query, executes it, and packages the results into an array of JavaBeans. Figure 13.10 shows the Java class implementing the service for the NewsCategories index unit, which retrieves the name of all the category objects.

Compared to the template of Figure 13.1, the unit service shown in Figure 13.10 encapsulates the business logic for computing the content of the index unit, including the code of the data retrieval query and the format of the result data bean.

In the View, content units map to *custom tags* transforming the content stored in the unit beans into HTML. Such tags could be generic tags taken from a

```
1    public class NewsCategoriesService extends IndexUnitService {
2
3      public void execute(Map state) throws SQLException {
4        // DATABASE CONNECTION
5        Connection conn = getConnectionFromPool();
6        // QUERY PREPARATION AND EXECUTION
7        Statement stmt = conn.createStatement(
8          ResultSet.TYPE_SCROLL_SENSITIVE, ResultSet.CONCUR_READ_ONLY);
9        ResultSet result = stmt.executeQuery(
10           "SELECT NAME FROM NEWSCATEGORY ORDER BY NAME");
11       // DETERMINE THE NUMBER OF CATEGORIES
12       result.last();
13       int count = result.getRow();
14       result.beforeFirst();
15       // CONSTRUCT THE ARRAY OF JAVABEANS
16       Category[] categories = new Category[count];
17       int i = 0;
18       while (result.next()) {
19         Category category = new Category();
20         category.setName(result.getString("NAME"));
21         categories[i++] = category;
22       }
23       // STORE THE COLLECTION OF BEANS INTO THE STATE MAP
24       state.put("NewsCategories", categories);
25     }
26   }
```

Figure 13.10   Unit service for an index unit.

standard tag library, or WebML-aware tags, defined on purpose to match the features of WebML units. Figure 13.11 shows an example of custom tags designed for presenting the content of a WebML index unit. These tags may be part of a broader tag library conceived for presenting all WebML units.

The presentation of the index unit is achieved by means of three tags, called webml:indexUnit, webml:iterator, and webml:attribute. The webml:indexUnit tag delimits the content of the index unit and references (in the unitID attribute) the data bean where the content of the unit is stored. The webml:iterator tag has the effect of iterating over all the objects included in

```
<%@ taglib uri="/WEB-INF/webml.tld" prefix="webml" %>
<html>
<head>
<title>News Categories Page</title>
</head>
<body>
<!-- INDEX UNIT CUSTOM TAG -->
<webml:indexUnit unitID="NewsCategories">
  <table>
    <webml:iterator>
      <tr>
        <td> <webml:attribute attributeID="name"/> </td>
      </tr>
    <webml:iterator>
  </table>
</webml:indexUnit>
</body>
</html>
```

Figure 13.11 Custom tags for presenting the NewsCategories index unit, embedded into the JSP template of page NewsCategories.

the data bean associated to its enclosing `webml:indexUnit` tag: at each iteration, the static mark-up and the mark-up produced by custom tags nested inside the `webml:iterator` tag is added to the HTML page. The `webml:attribute` tag prints the value of the data bean property mentioned in its `attributeID` attribute. When nested inside a `webml:iterator` tag, the actual data bean object used by the `webml:attribute` tag is the current element of the collection of data beans over which the iteration is performed.

WebML *data, multidata,* and *scroller units* can be implemented in the same way as index units, by defining a unit service encapsulating the data retrieval logic, and suitable custom tags presenting the content of the JavaBeans built by the unit service.

13.4.3 Mapping Entry Units to the MVC Architecture

Entry units are implemented differently for the other units, because they do not require a data retrieval service, but only accept user input. This function is normally supported by HTML forms (as shown in the page template of example 4 in Chapter 12), but with a number of limitations. For example, an HTML form does not remember previous user's choices when the page is accessed for the second time, and does not support input validation and error messages. A better implementation may exploit a custom tag library, for enhancing the capability of HTML forms.

The JSP template in Figure 13.12, which implements the EnterKeyword entry unit shown in Chapter 12, uses the Struts HTML tag library for extending the functions of HTML forms.[4] First of all, the template declares the inclusion of a library of tags, named "struts-html" (line 1): all tags of the included library have a name that starts with the html: prefix, which distinguishes them from the reg-

```
1   <%@ taglib uri="/WEB-INF/struts-html.tld" prefix="html"  %>
2   <html:html>
3   <html:errors/>
4   <html:form action=" searchNews">
5   <table border="0" width="100%">
6     <tr>
7       <td>Keyword</td>
8       <td><html:text property="keyword"/>
9       </td>
10    </tr>
11    <tr>
12      <td align="right" colspan="2">
13        <html:submit> Submit </html:submit>
14      </td>
15    </tr>
16  </table>
17  </html:form>
18  </html:html>
```

Figure 13.12 Page with custom tags for user input.

---

[4]Alternatively, it is possible to define custom tags in the webml tag library, implementing functions similar to those supported by the Struts tags used in the example. However, because JSP templates can use multiple independent tag libraries, we prefer to show the use of an existing and popular library.

ular HTML tags. The HTML section of the page includes a form for submitting a keyword (lines 4–17), implemented using the Struts tags instead of the plain HTML tags. In particular, custom tags replace the HTML form and input tags (lines 4, 8, and 13). The custom tags extend the standard HTML tags with "memory" and error checking. If the page is re-accessed for the second time, the input fields re-display the previously submitted keyword. Moreover, the `html:errors` tag, placed in front of the form (line 3), prints any error message produced by the action invoked after the submission of the form, for example a warning message after the submission of an empty keyword.

The "intelligent" behavior of the form tags is granted by the underlying MVC architecture. Each Struts form is supported by a dedicated object in the Model (called a *form bean*), which stores the state of the form, that is, the previous user's input. Form beans are automatically created and populated upon the form submission, and can be passed to the action for validation and elaboration. In the example of Figure 13.12, the action is represented by the module named `searchNews`, mentioned at line 4, which contains the business logic for validating the input keyword and for retrieving the matching NewsCategories.

To support *validation in the business tier,* the `perform()` function of a Struts action class, exemplified in Figure 13.6, accepts a parameter named `form`; this parameter holds the form bean storing the input submitted with the form, which can be passed down for validation to the service in the business tier. The form bean is also available to the View template, which can use its content to redisplay previously submitted values and error messages. All these sophisticated features are exposed to the View designer simply as tags, which can be mixed to the standard HTML layout and presentation elements.

13.4.4 Mapping Operations to the MVC Architecture

Operations are the last piece of WebML to map to the MVC architecture; we illustrate their mapping by sketching the implementation of the example of create and connect pattern, discussed in Chapter 14, which we recall in Figure 13.13.

We start by showing the *configuration file* of the Controller, which illustrates the actions involved and the flow of control, in presence of potential operation failure and OK or KO links. Each operation contributes an *operation action mapping* to the configuration file of the Controller. The configuration file for the hypertext of Figure 13.13 is illustrated by the XML fragment in Figure 13.14. The XML contains two `action` tags, one for the create operation and one for the connect operation. Each action tag contains the attributes for mapping the HTTP request to the proper action class (path, type, name) and two `forward` sub-elements.

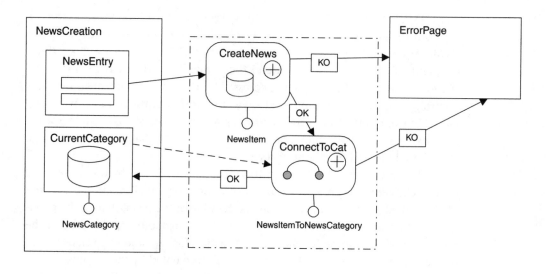

Figure 13.13   Create and connect pattern.

```
<action path="/createNews"
        type="CreateNewsAction"
        name="createNews">
  <forward name="OK" path="/connect2Category"/>
  <forward name="KO" path="/errorPage.jsp"/>
</action>
<action path="/Connect2Category"
        type="Connect2CategoryAction"
        name=" Connect2Category">
  <forward name="OK" path="/newsCreation.jsp"/>
  <forward name="KO" path="/errorPage.jsp"/>
</action>
```

Figure 13.14   Configuration file for create and connect pattern.

Each forward sub-element corresponds to a possible outcome of the operation (OK or KO) and specifies the component to call next.

Each WebML operation requires an operation action class and a service; the former encapsulates the details of calling the latter, which is responsible of actually performing the operation.

The *operation action class* is a simple variant of the page action class shown in Figure 13.6: the difference is in the type of business service to create, which is an operation service instead of a page service, and in the handling of the result of service execution, which can be OK or KO. Figure 13.15 shows the action class for the CreateNews operation.

After creating the operation service associated to the create operation (line 7) and copying the appropriate parameters from the request into the state object (lines 9–10), the action class invokes the service passing to it the current state object (line 12); the invocation returns a data bean, called `result`, storing the result of the create operation, that is, a result code and the OID of the newly created category. The result of the operation is used to enrich the state object, which is forwarded to the next operation (lines 14 and 17), as well as to build the result code returned to the Controller (line 19).

```
1   public class CreateNewsAction extends Action {
2
3     public ActionForward perform(ActionMapping mapping, ActionForm form,
4                     HttpServletRequest request,
5                     HttpServletResponse response) {
6       // build the operation service
7       CreateNewsService opService = new CreateNewsService();
8       // extract values of operation's input parameters from the HTTP request
9       String[] parameters2Fetch = opService.getOperationParameterNames();
10      Map state = copyFromRequest(request, opParameterNames);
11      // execute the operation
12      CreateNewsResult result = opService.execute(state);
13      // put the OID of the newly created news into the state
14      state.put("newsOID", result.getOID());
15      // store state inside the HTTP request
16      // (for forwarding them to the next operation or page)
17      storeState(request, state);
18      // perform a JSP forward based onto the result code
19      return mapping.findForward(result.getResultCode());
20    }
21  }
```

Figure 13.15 Operation action for CreateNews operation.

The action class for the *ConnectToCategory* operation is represented in Figure 13.16. The only remarkable aspect is the handling of the parameter passed along the OK link of the connect operation, which uses the request object as a "transportation vehicle." The result returned from the operation service (line 12), which comprises the OID of the category connected to the newly created piece of news, is put into the state object (line 14), which in turn is stored into the request (line 17); in case of success, the Controller transfers the control to the NewsCreation page and forwards the HTTP request filled by the connect operation to the action class associated to such a page. The action class can fetch from the request the OID of the category needed to populate the CurrentCategory data unit, as requested by the contextual OK link between the connect operation and the data unit.

The *operation services* associated to the create and connect operations of Figure 13.15 and Figure 13.16 wrap the SQL statements for implementing the operations and have a structure similar to that of a unit service, shown in Figure 13.10.

```
1    public class ConnectToCategoryAction extends Action {
2
3      public ActionForward perform(ActionMapping mapping, ActionForm form,
4                      HttpServletRequest request,
5                      HttpServletResponse response) {
6        // build the operation service
7        ConnectToCategoryAction opService = new ConnectToCategoryAction();
8        // extract values of operation's input parameters from the HTTP request
9        String[] parametersToFetch = opService.getOperationParameterNames();
10       Map state = copyFromRequest(request, opParameterNames);
11       // execute the operation
12       ConnectToCategoryResult result = opService.execute(state);
13       // put the OID of the news category into the state
14       state.put("categoryOID", result.getCategoryOID());
15       // stores state inside the HTTP request
16       // (for forwarding them to the next operation or page)
17       storeState(request, state);
18       // performs a JSP forward based onto the result code
19       return mapping.findForward(result.getResultCode());
20     }
21   }
```

Figure 13.16 Operation action for the ConnectToCategory operation.

The data retrieval query is replaced by the code necessary to perform the operation, which is the same that appeared inside the JSP templates in the example of Chapter 12.

13.5 Managing Very Large Applications

The MVC architecture is a big step forward in the direction of facilitating the maintenance of data-intensive Web applications. However, there is still room for improvement. When the application is very large,[5] the MVC solution discussed in the previous section does not alleviate the problems associated with the size of the application:

- Every unit and operation requires a *dedicated service* in the business tier. If units are many, a very large number of services must be developed and maintained. All the services of individual units of the same kind (for instance, index units, or create units) are very similar, because they differ only for the details of the data retrieval or update query, and possibly for the properties of the data bean storing the query result. However, this similarity is not exploited to reduce the amount of code to build and maintain.

- Every page requires a *distinct page service*. These services are numerous and all similar, because they differ only for the parameters fetched from the HTTP request, and for the sequence in which unit services are invoked and parameters are passed from one query to another one. Again, similarities are not factored out.

- The business services are implemented as *programs executed inside the servlet container*. It would be more appropriate to implement them as full-fledged business components living in the application server, using a distributed object technology like Enterprise JavaBeans.

- The look and feel of the application is *hardwired to the JSP templates*. Changing the presentation style requires manual intervention on a large number of files. For example, updating the graphic style of all index units, for instance adding a mouse-over JavaScript effect, requires locating and manually updating the relevant mark-up in all pages.

---

[5]The real Acer-Euro application is integrated with an extranet for managing the product distribution channel. At the time of writing, the integrated application features 22 site views, 556 page templates, and 3068 units, for a total of over 3000 SQL queries.

We start by considering the first two problems, which are solved with the same technique, and address the remaining two in the next sections.

To avoid the proliferation of page and unit services, it is possible to exploit *genericity,* a classical principle of software design. Unit services can be reorganized according to the pattern shown in Figure 13.17.

For each type of unit, a single *generic service* is designed, which factors out the commonalities of unit-specific services. This generic service is parametric with respect to the features of individual units, like the SQL query to perform, the input parameters of such a query, and the properties of the output data bean produced by the query. The unit-specific information can be stored in a *descriptor file,* for instance written in XML, used at runtime to instantiate the generic service into a concrete, unit-specific service.

Figure 13.18 shows an example of XML descriptor for specifying the features of the NewsCategories unit implemented by the unit service of Figure 13.10. The descriptor declares that the unit has an empty set of input parameters (denoted by the empty tag `<input-parameters/>`), and one output parameter stored as a property of the unit data bean, namely the name of the category object. The descriptor also contains the source code of the data extraction query associated to the unit. This information can be used by the generic index unit service to build a specific unit service bound to the NewsCategories index unit.

Separating generic and individual features of unit services using descriptors makes application maintenance easier, because descriptors can be updated separately from the source code of the generic service, and only one service per type of unit needs to be implemented, tested, and maintained.

The same design practice can be applied to page services, but in this case the descriptor associated to an individual page is more complex, because it must describe the topology of the page units and links, which is needed for executing the page computation algorithm. However, designing a generic page service and a

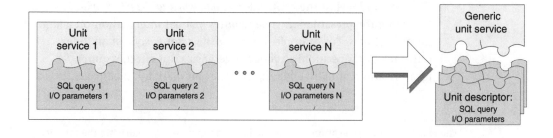

Figure 13.17   Unit-level services versus generic unit service plus descriptor.

```
<descriptor>
  <info>Descriptor of NewsCategories index unit </info>
  <generic-service>webml.runtime.IndexUnitService</generic-service>
  <input-parameters/>
  <output-parameters>
    <output-parameter name="name" position="1" type="Text"/>
  </output-parameters>
  <query>
    SELECT NAME FROM NEWSCATEGORY ORDER BY NAME
  </query>
</descriptor>
```

Figure 13.18   XML descriptor of the NewsCategories index unit.

descriptor syntax for pages pays in the long run, because it centralizes the semantics of page computation into a single point, which is easier to implement,
debug, and evolve.[6]

13.6   Using Enterprise JavaBeans to Implement the Business Logic

The page action classes and the page and unit services embody the business logic
of a WebML application: they control the computation of a page, the operations
needed to prepare the content of a unit, or to update the application data. In the
MVC architecture described in Figure 13.5 and used so far, the business logic components are implemented as Java classes executed inside the servlet container.

---

[6] The benefits of implementing generic services can be appreciated on a concrete example.
As already mentioned, the integrated Acer-Euro applications consist of 22 site views, fea-
turing 556 pages and 3068 units. A conventional MVC implementation would requires
556 Java classes for page services and 3068 Java classes for unit services. Using generic services and XML descriptors dramatically reduces these numbers: in the real implementation, only one generic page service exist (accompanied by 556 page descriptors, encoded
as XML files) and 11 unit services (for the basic WebML units: data, index, multidata,
multi-choice, scroller, entry, create, delete, modify, connect, disconnect), accompanied by
3068 unit descriptors.

This approach imposes several limitations to the scalability and reusability of the implementation:

- ■ Page and unit services live in the servlet container and cannot be called by other applications, for example by a non-Web application needing the same services. Therefore, non-Web applications do not share the business logic with Web applications, and must re-implement it, which introduces duplications, opens the way to errors and misalignments, and impairs maintenance.

- ■ Cloning the machine where the servlet container resides duplicates also all the services of the application. The number of clones must be decided statically, and cannot be adapted at runtime. If the traffic of a certain application reduces, the objects implementing its services remain in main memory and occupy resources, potentially impacting other applications running on the same server.

A better software organization can be obtained by exploiting the application server architecture presented in Chapter 10. In such architecture, the middle tier is split into the servlet engine and the application server. The latter offers a service-rich execution environment, ideal for deploying reusable business components. The MVC 2 architecture can be *embedded within the application server architecture,* as shown in Figure 13.19. In particular, the role of the Model can be shared between the action classes living in the servlet container and business components implementing the page and unit services, deployed in the application server. In this case, the action classes call the appropriate business objects, which implement the actual application functions.

Figure 13.19 shows a concrete realization of the application server architecture, fitting the Java2EE platform. In this context, the business components are implemented as Enterprise JavaBeans.[7]

Enterprise JavaBeans (EJB) are an open standard for building server-side distributed components in the Java programming language. EJBs are deployed into the application server, which is called *EJB container,* and can be accessed by Web applications and other enterprise applications. The EJB specification defines three types of enterprise beans, which address distinct application needs: session, messaging, and entity beans.

---

[7]Enterprise Java Beans must not be confounded with "plain" Java Beans. The former are distributed objects living in the application server; the latter are normal Java objects living in the servlet container.

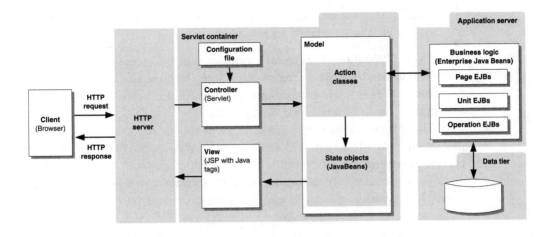

Figure 13.19 The MVC 2 architecture embedded in the application server architecture.

Session and messaging beans model business processes,[8] including algorithms, workflows, and business rules. Session beans can be *stateless,* if they do not retain state across multiple requests of the same client, or *stateful,* if they retain state across client invocations. Stateless beans are insufficient for developing stateful applications, but are easily pooled and scaled, whereas stateful beans can be used to implement persistent sessions without using a database, but are more complex to implement, replicate, and distribute.

Entity beans wrap business data and expose them as persistent objects. There are two categories of entity beans, based on the way in which persistent operations, like saving an object into the database, or loading an object, are implemented:

- ▣ *Bean-managed persistent (BMP):* the code for all persistency-related operations is hand-written by the programmer.

- ▣ *Container-managed persistent (CMP):* the implementation of persistent operations is carried out automatically by the EJB container. In this case, each bean is implemented as an *abstract class,* accompanied by

---

[8]Message-driven beans are called through *messaging,* whereas session bean through *remote method invocation.* Remote method invocation (RMI), a modern variant of remote procedure call (RPC), is the technology for synchronously invoking a function from one machine to another one. RMI is contrasted to messaging, which is asynchronous and based on message queues.

a *deployment descriptor,* used by the application server for automatically generating the actual data access code.[9]

Figure 13.20 shows the typical organization of EJB components, in which entity and session beans play different roles. Entity beans wrap the persistent data and expose them as persistent distributed objects. Session beans *use* entity beans and implement the business logic on top of them.

The software architectures of Figure 13.20 applies also to the MVC implementation of data-intensive Web applications, and yields the hierarchy of components represented in Figure 13.21.

The action classes in the servlet container interact with page and operation session beans, which replace the page and operation services illustrated in Section

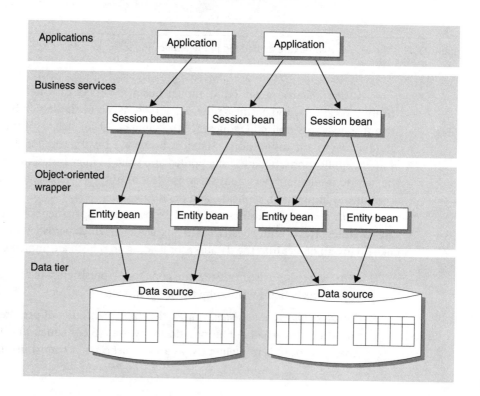

Figure 13.20   Typical organization of EJB business objects.

---

[9]Although less mature than BMP entity beans, in this section we use CMP entity beans. CMP coding examples are simpler, because database-related operations need not be hand-written.

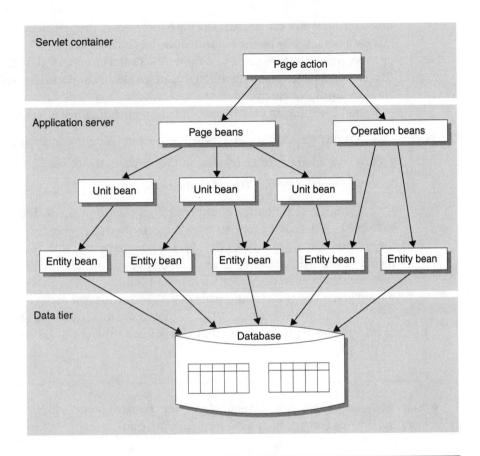

Figure 13.21 EJB components in a data-intensive Web application.

13.4. Page beans invoke the functions of unit beans, which correspond to the notion of unit service. Finally, operation and unit beans interact with a set of entity beans, which expose the persistent data as objects.

In the remainder of this section we provide some guidelines to transform pages, units, and operations into a set of business components using the EJBs.

13.6.1 Wrapping Persistent Data with Entity Beans

The wrapping of persistent data as object-oriented components requires packaging all the tables that represent one entity and its outgoing relationship roles as an entity bean.

The entity bean exposes persistent attributes, possibly set-valued, and standard functions for accessing and updating them. The implementation of such functions must take care of mapping the object state to the persistent data, which is done automatically by the EJB container, for CMP beans.

As an example, Figure 13.22 shows the CMP entity bean class that wraps the relational tables mapping the NewsCategory entity and its relationship role NewCategoryToNewsItem.

Implementing an enterprise bean requires writing three pieces of code:

- A utility class, called *home,* which is used to create instances of the bean.

- A Java interface, to be used by all the clients of the bean.

- The actual class implementing the bean.

Figure 13.22 shows the code of the class that implements the bean. The example uses a CMP bean, and thus the class NewsCategoryBean is abstract (line 1) and contains no fields (line 2); the concrete class, with the real implementation of the functions, is generated automatically by the EJB container from the deployment descriptor associated with the bean. The class contains setter and getter functions, that is pairs of get/set methods for each column of the database table (in the example, OID and name), and for each foreign key column or bridge table representing a relationship role of the entity (in the example,

```
1   public abstract class NewsCategoryBean implements javax.ejb.EntityBean {
2       // no fields, this is a CMP enterprise bean!
3
4       // abstract get/set methods
5       public abstract String getOid();
6       public abstract void setOid(String oid);
7       public abstract String getName();
8       public abstract void setName(String name);
9       // abstract get/set methods for outgoing relationships
10      public abstract Collection getNewsItems();
11      public abstract void setNewsItems(Collection newsItems);
12      // other EJB required methods
13          ...
14  }
```

Figure 13.22   EJB implementation of the NewsCategory entity.

NewsItems).[10] Note that, since the relationship role has maximum cardinality N, both the return value of the getNewsItems method and the input argument of the setNewsItems method are a collection of objects, and not a single object.

From the abstract class in Figure 13.22 and from the deployment descriptor, the EJB container produces a concrete sub-class, which includes the implementation of all the abstract functions. These functions comprise all the JDBC and SQL code necessary for reading and writing the persistent data of the bean.

Figure 13.23 shows a fragment from the EJB deployment descriptor, which is an XML file listing all the persistent fields and relationship roles that the container will map into code in the concrete sub-class.

The <ejb-name> tag includes the nickname for this particular bean (line 5), useful for referring back to the bean later in the deployment descriptor. The <ejb-class> tag contains the name of the enterprise bean class (line 6), which is the class illustrated in Figure 13.22. Next, the descriptor includes a <cmp-field> tag for each persistent field for which the EJB container will generate the set and get functions in the concrete subclass (lines 7–12); the names of the fields declared in the deployment descriptor must match the names of abstract get/set methods in the class of Figure 13.22. The descriptor includes also the declaration of a <primkey-field> tag, which informs the EJB container that a particular field is the primary key of the class instances (line 13).

Primary key declarations are used for retrieving selected instances of the entity bean. Retrieving an instance requires accessing the bean's *home*, which represents an entry point to all the instances managed by the EJB container.

When the home is located, it can be used to find objects by their primary key, as shown in the following fragment:

```
// Look up the bean's home interface using the directory service
    . . . // omitted for brevity
// Use the home to retrieve the entity bean instance with given OID
NewsCategory newsCategory = home.findByPrimaryKey(oid);
```

The deployment descriptor proceeds with the section devoted to the relationships (line 16), which contains the declaration of the NewsCategoryTo-NewsItem relationship role (line 12). The <ejb-relationship-role> section

---

[10]The real class would include a few additional functions, necessary for technical reasons. We omit them for brevity.

```
1   <ejb-jar>
2     <enterprise-beans>
3       <entity>
4         <!-- NICKNAME ASSIGNED TO THE BEAN -->
5         <ejb-name>NewsCategory</ejb-name>
6         <ejb-class>NewsCategoryBean</ebj-class>
7         <cmp-field>
8           <field-name>oid</field-name>
9         </cmp-field>
10        <cmp-field>
11          <field-name>name</field-name>
12        </cmp-field>
13        <primkey-field>oid</primkey-field>
14      </entity>
15    </enterprise-beans>
16    <relationships>
17      <ejb-relation>
18        <!-- NICKNAME ASSIGNED TO THE RELATIONSHIP ROLE -->
19        <ejb-relation-name>NewsCategory-NewsItems</ejb-relation-name>
20        <!-- RELATIONSHIP ROLE DECLARATION -->
21        <ejb-relationship-role>
22          <!-- NICKNAME ASSIGNED TO THIS RELATIONSHIP ROLE -->
23          <ejb-relationship-role-name>CategoryToItems</ejb-relationship-role-name>
24          <!-- CARDINALITY -->
25          <multiplicity>Many</multiplicity>
26          <!-- name of the bean corresponding to this relationship role -->
27          <relationship-role-source>NewsCategory</relationship-role-source>
28        <!-- container-managed relationship (CMR) field -->
29        <cmr-field>
30          <cmr-field-name>newsItems</cmr-field-name>
31          <cmr-field-type>java.util.Collection</cmr-field-type>
32        </cmr-field>
33      </ejb-relationship-role>
34    </ejb-relation>
35    </relationships>
36 </ejb-jar>
```

Figure 13.23 Portion of the EJB deployment descriptor specifying persistent fields.

specifies the name assigned to the role (line 21), the maximum cardinality (line 25), and the source entity bean that includes the set/get functions implementing the relationship role (line 27). Finally the `<cmr-field>` tag, where `cmr` stands for Container Managed Relationship, tells the container which get/set functions of the entity bean class implement the relationship (lines 30–31), as well as the Java type to use for representing sets of objects, which can be `java.util.Collection,` if duplicates are removed, or `java.util.Set,` if duplicates are allowed (line 31).

The deployment descriptor illustrated in Figure 13.23 does not mention the actual database tables where the persistent content is stored. This specification requires a further configuration file, whose syntax varies based on the application server product.

13.6.2 Implementing Page Services and Content Unit Services as Enterprise Java Beans

A page service of the architecture of Figure 13.5 maps to a *page session bean* of the architecture of Figure 13.21. A page session bean is created and used by the page action class in the servlet engine, and encapsulates the algorithms for the propagation of the context and the calls to the session beans corresponding to unit services. The implementation of a page session bean is similar to the code illustrated in Figure 13.17, with the Java class replaced by a session bean.

A unit service in the architecture of Figure 13.15 maps to a *unit session bean* in the EJB-enabled architecture of Figure 13.21. A unit bean queries, filters and composes the data of one or more entity beans, and returns a result bean to be stored in the application state by the page action class. Unit beans do not directly interact with the underlying data storage, as the unit services illustrated in Section 13.4; instead, they work on entity beans, which provide an object-oriented vision of the relational data. The manipulation performed by unit beans over entity beans depends on the type of unit. For example, a data unit showing the NewsCategory instance with a given OID maps to the rather trivial session bean shown in Figure 13.24.

The session bean is a Java class that implements the `javax.ejb.Session-Bean` interface (line 1), which exposes a function for retrieving the instance to show in the data unit. The get function retrieves the home object, which serves as a factory of EJB objects, calls the predefined `findByPrimaryKey()` method of the home object, and returns the result to the invoker.

More sophisticated WebML primitives, like units with complex selectors, may exploit advanced primitives provided by the EJB specification, such as the EJB Query Language (EJB-QL), to simplify the retrieval of sets of entity beans satisfying the selector conditions.

```
1   public class NewsCategoryDataUnitBean implements javax.ejb.SessionBean {
2
3       // get the news category object with a given OID
4       public NewsCategory getNewsCategory(String oid) {
5           // look up the bean's home interface
6           .. omitted..
7           // retrieves the entity bean instance with a finder method
8           NewsCategory newsCategory = home.findByPrimaryKey(oid);
9           return newsCategory;
10      }
11  }
```

Figure 13.24   Session bean for a data unit.

13.6.3   Implementing Operation Units as Enterprise Java Beans

Section 13.4.4 explained how to fit an operation unit into the MVC architecture, assuming that an operation service in the business tier directly interacts with the database for updating data. When the business tier is implemented using EJB, operations units are exposed as session beans. As for content units, operation beans do not work on the database, but on entity beans. With the CMP technology, all the efforts for updating the data source is left to the bean container, freeing the developer from producing error-prone JDBC code. As an example, Figure 13.25 shows the session bean that implements the delete unit for removing an instance of entity NewsCategory having a given OID.

The code starts with the retrieval of the home object and of the desired bean instance; then, a call to the **remove()** method deletes the bean instance (line 10). Such call is translated by the EJB container into the JDBC and SQL instructions needed to delete the instance.

Using Enterprise JavaBeans to implement the business logic in the application server has a positive impact not only with respect to performance and scalability, but also on the data implementation architecture. EJBs alleviate the problems of the online-database architecture illustrated in Section 11.3.4:

■ *Lack of location and fragmentation transparency.* The deployment descriptors of the application server define the binding between the entity bean and its underlying table(s), freeing the client application from any knowledge of the physical location of data.

```
1    public class NewsCategoryDeleteUnitBean implements javax.ejb.SessionBean {
2
3        // remove the news category object having a given OID
4        public String removeNewsCategory(String oid) {
5            // look up the bean's home interface
6            .. omitted..
7            // retrieve the entity bean instance with a finder method
8            NewsCategory newsCategory = home.findByPrimaryKey(oid);
9            try { // attempt to remove the instance
10               newsCategory.remove();
11               return "success";
12       } catch (Exception e) {
13               return "error";
14           }
15       }
16  }
```

Figure 13.25 Session bean for a delete unit.

■ *Lack of inter-database relationships.* The programming of relationships between entities mapped to different data sources is confined to the set/get functions of the entity beans of the involved entities. This shields the Web application code from the burden of implementing this quite complex feature and make it reusable by multiple applications.

■ *Lack of transactional atomicity.* Updates to multiple EJBs can execute in the context of an atomic transaction, managed by the EJB container.

13.7 Using CSS and XSL to Manage Presentation

The last issue in the development of large applications is the reduction of the effort necessary for updating the look and feel of the application across a large number of pages. Dealing with presentation requires addressing two distinct concerns, *graphic properties* and *layout*.

The effective management of graphic properties requires some care in the use of HTML: graphic properties should not be coded as tag attributes in the HTML mark-up, but should be factored out into *Cascading Style Sheets* (CSS) stored in separate files. A good practice in the definition of CSS for WebML applications is to leverage the conceptual model to modularize the CSS rules. A set of rules can be designed for each WebML unit, by identifying the different graphic elements needed to present a certain kind of unit (labels of various kinds, cell backgrounds, and so on) and assigning to each element the proper graphic attributes using CSS. Figure 13.26 shows an example of CSS rules for the various graphic elements of index units (title, attribute labels and values in normal style and in highlighted style).

Factoring out the layout from the JSP template of a page is more difficult, but can be done. An extremely effective technique exploits XSLT for defining layout rules for pages and units. The fundamental idea is to define the layout of the page and of the different kinds of units separately from the JSP templates, as illustrated in Figure 13.27:

- Producing a *page template skeleton,* which includes all the custom tags corresponding to the units of the page, but only the minimal HTML mark-up needed to define the layout grid of the page and the position of the various units in such a grid.

- Using *XSLT presentation rules* for transforming the template skeleton into the final page template, embodying the real presentation mark-up.

Coding the page template skeleton is easy, but demands some care in writing the HTML markup. XSLT processing requires a well-formed XML input, and

```
.IndexUnit-Title {
     FONT-WEIGHT: bold; FONT-SIZE: 9px; COLOR: #ffffff; FONT-FAMILY: verdana;
}
.IndexUnit-Attribute-Name {
     FONT-WEIGHT: bold; FONT-SIZE: 10px; COLOR: #000000; FONT-FAMILY: verdana;
}
.IndexUnit-Attribute-Value {
     FONT-SIZE: 9px; COLOR: #000000; FONT-FAMILY: verdana;
}
.IndexUnit-Attribute-Name-Highlighted {
     FONT-WEIGHT: bold; FONT-SIZE: 10px; COLOR: #ff0000; FONT-FAMILY: verdana;
}
.IndexUnit-Attribute-Value-Highlighted {
     FONT-SIZE: 9px; COLOR: #ff0000; FONT-FAMILY: verdana;
}
```

Figure 13.26 CSS rules for index units.

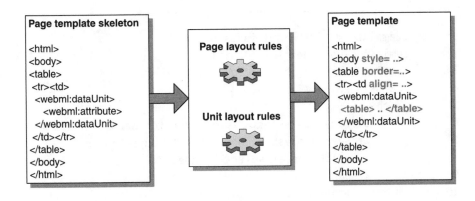

Figure 13.27 Factoring out page layout rules using XSLT.

thus the template skeleton should be defined using XHTML, instead of the more liberal HTML.[11]

The XSLT layout rules are a bit more technical. There are two kinds of such rules: *page rules* and *unit rules*.

- *Page rules* match the outermost part of the skeleton's layout (for example, the top-level HTML table) and transform it into the actual grid of the page, which may include multiple frames, images, static texts, and other kinds of embellishments. For facilitating the writing of page rules, page layouts could be classified into general categories (for instance, multi-frame pages, two-columns pages, three-columns pages, and so on), and different rule sets could be designed for each category of layout.

- *Unit rules* match a class of units (for instance, index units) and produce the markup for their presentation. Figure 13.28 illustrates an XSLT rule for index unit presentation. The rule applies to a "stripped down" version of the mark-up of the index unit, without presentation details, like the one shown in Figure 13.29, and transforms the custom tags of the index unit into a nested HTML table, using the attribute's names as heading, and the attribute's values as content.

Note that the HTML mark-up produced by the XSLT rule exploits the CSS styles associated to index units, so that the XSLT rule is concerned only with the layout and not with the graphic properties.

---

[11]XHTML is the redefinition of HTML according to the XML syntax. Several tools helping the transformation of HTML into XHTML are available; see for example the popular HTML Tidy (*tidy.sourceforge.net/*).

```
1   <xsl:template match="webml:indexUnit">
2     <webml:indexUnit unitID="{@unitID}">
3       <table>
4         <!-- heading (labels) -->
5         <th>
6           <xsl:for-each select="webml:iterator/webml:attribute">
7             <td><span class="IndexUnit-Attribute-Name">
8               <xsl:value-of select="@label"/>
9             </span></td>
10          </xsl:for-each>
11        </th>
12        <!-- content (values) -->
13        <webml:iterator>
14          <tr>
15            <xsl:for-each select="webml:iterator/webml:attribute">
16              <td><span class="IndexUnit-Attribute-Value">
17                <webml:attribute attributeID="{@attributeID}"/>
18              </span></td>
19            </xsl:for-each>
20          </tr>
21        </webml:iterator>
22      </table>
23    </webml:indexUnit>
24  </xsl:template>
```

Figure 13.28 XSL layout rule for index units.

```
<webml:indexUnit unitID="NewsCategories">
  <webml:iterator>
    <webml:attribute attributeID="name" label="Category's Name"/>
  </webml:iterator>
</webml:indexUnit>
```

Figure 13.29 Presentation-less tags for the NewsCategories index unit.

The use of CSS and XSLT for managing the presentation features of a large application enforces a sound development workflow, which assigns distinct responsibilities to the various professionals in the development team:

- *The graphic designer* establishes the categories of page layouts, writes HTML mock-ups for each class of page layout, and produces HTML mock-ups for the different kinds of units. He/she defines "examples of presentation" and need not to worry about the actual coding of units or pages.

- *The XSLT programmer* transforms the page and unit mock-ups created by the graphic designer into XSLT style sheets. This activity is not difficult, because XSLT has an XML syntax, which blends well with the syntax of the HTML mock-ups. The XSLT programmer needs only to understand the structure of the custom tags representing the different kinds of units, and may ignore the way in which such tags are coded.

- *The application modeler* defines the application pages and the units in each page, and produces the template skeletons from the WebML model of the page, which is quite a trivial task.

- *The programmer* implements the custom tags and the business services behind them.

In practice, XSLT presentation rules automate the work of the graphic designer, who has the responsibility of defining the look and feel, but delegates to the XSLT processor the repetitive task of applying such look and feel to every page and unit of the application. This approach grants both the quality of the graphic design, which can be as accurate as in the manual coding of page templates, and the work automation needed in very large applications, where manually applying sophisticated style rules to hundreds of pages is unfeasible. During maintenance, the benefits of XSLT presentation rules are even more evident; for instance, changing the layout of all indexes in the application amounts to updating only one style rule and re-applying the modified rule to all pages, which is done automatically by the XSLT processor.[12]

---

[12]In the Acer-Euro application, factoring out presentation into CSS and XSL rules has granted a substantial reduction of the presentation management effort: for all the 556 pages the look and feel has been produced by only three XSL style sheets (one for the B2C site views, one for the B2B site views, and one for the internal content management site views). Less than 5% of the HTML code produced by the XSL style has been retouched manually to improve the rendition.

As a conclusive remark, we underline a further benefit of presentation management with XSLT, which lies in the possibility of applying the presentation rules either at compile time or at runtime:

- Applying the rules at compile time yields a set of page templates embodying the final look and feel of the application; this approach is more efficient, because no template transformation is required at runtime.

- Presentation rules can be applied also at runtime, by publishing in the application server the template skeletons and transforming them on the fly, when the HTTP request arrives. This approach is more expensive in terms of execution time, because XSLT processing takes place at runtime, but is more flexible and may be very effective for multi-device applications. Different XSL rules could be designed addressing the presentation requirements of alternative devices; then, the most appropriate rules could be dynamically applied at runtime, for instance, based on the user agent declared in the HTTP request. In this way, the actual pages seen by the user would have a presentation dynamically adapted to the access device, and the template skeletons plus the different XSLT rules would serve the needs of a broad spectrum of access devices.

Summary

In this chapter, we have shown that a classical design pattern proposed by software engineers, called Model-View-Controller (MVC), can foster an organization of the software functions, in which the aspects of control, state, and interface are more separated, more reusable, and easier to maintain. The subsequent discussion has proven that WebML concepts map naturally to the MVC architecture, which makes WebML applications effectively implementable on top of enterprise-class architectures.

As a further enhancement to the MVC-based implementation, we have discussed advanced solutions required for managing very large applications, namely the design of generic services, the implementation of the business logic in the application server using Enterprise JavaBeans, and the use of CSS and XSL presentation rules for factoring out the look and feel from the page templates.

Bibliographic Notes

The classic form of the MVC software design pattern is illustrated in the fundamental book by Erich Gamma et al [GHJV95]. The incarnation of the MVC architecture in the Web context, the so-called MVC 2 architecture, is discussed in several textbooks and technical articles on advanced Web architectures, like for instance [ACM01, Davis]. A source of useful resources about the MVC 2 architecture is the Web site of the Apache Struts project (*jakarta.apache.org/struts*), where the reader can find an open-source implementation of the MVC 2 architecture, and many technical resources for developing Web applications using this pattern. For example, the site contains a wealth of tag libraries contributed by independent developers, which demonstrate the variety of tasks that can be accomplished with this useful technology.

Architectural patterns for Web applications implemented in the Java 2 Enterprise Edition platform are collected and discussed in the section of Sun's Web site devoted to blueprint applications (*java.sun.com/blueprints/patterns/j2ee_patterns/index.html*). The site also contains the implementation of two "canonical" applications, the popular Java Pet Store and Smart Ticket demos, which can be used to familiarize with the design principles and the implementation techniques for advanced Web applications.

The official source for the Enterprise JavaBeans API is the Java 2 Enterprise Edition site at *java.sun.com/j2ee*, which contains the API specifications and several resources, like tutorials and technical papers. An advanced textbook on EBJ programming is the book by Ed Roman, Scott Ambler and Tyler Jewell, *Mastering Enterprise JavaBeans* (2nd edition) [RAJ01], which guides the developer from the basics of EBJ programming, to advanced topics like transaction management and clustering.

14 Tools for Model-Based Development of Web Applications

14.1 Introduction

In the previous chapters, the modeling notations, the development process, and implementation techniques for data-intensive Web applications have been explained independently of any specific development tool. As the chapters of this last part of the book have demonstrated, the Entity-Relationship schema of the data and the WebML site views can be manually mapped into implementation structures, for instance, into a relational database and a set of JSP templates or components of the MVC architecture. The guidelines provided in the previous chapters assist Web engineers along the entire application lifecycle in producing a working Web application using any development standard or platform. However, when a well-defined software engineering method is in place, development can be greatly helped by CASE tools, supporting and documenting the design and assisting the production of the implementation code. CASE tools allow developers to rigorously adhere to the methodology and help decrease the design and implementation time.

This chapter is dedicated to a specific tool, called *WebRatio Site Development Studio* (WebRatio, for short), which supports the WebML design process.[1] With respect to the WebML development workflow introduced in Chapter 7, WebRatio covers the phases of data design and hypertext design, and supports implementation by automating the production of the relational database and of the application page templates. More precisely, WebRatio focuses on five main aspects:

- *Data design:* supports the design of Entity-Relationship data schemas, with a graphical user interface for drawing and specifying the properties of entities, relationships, attributes, and generalization hierarchies.

- *Hypertext design:* assists the design of site views, providing functions for drawing and specifying the properties of areas, pages, units, and links.

- *Data Mapping:* permits declaring the set of data sources to which the conceptual data schema has to be mapped, and automatically translates Entity-Relationship diagrams and OCL expressions into relational databases and views.

- *Presentation design:* offers functionality for defining the presentation style of the application, allowing the designer to create XSL style sheets and associate them with pages, and organize page layout, by arranging the relative position of content units in the page.

- *Code generation:* automatically translates site views into running Web applications built on top of the Java2EE, Struts, and .NET platforms.

The diagram of Figure 14.1 summarizes the design flow of WebRatio, highlighting the design phases, together with their inputs and outputs. The different design steps will be described in more detail in the next sections.

Thanks to the automatic generation of code, the tool can be used for fast-prototyping, thus shortening the requirements validation cycle. Unlike traditional prototyping tools, which generate application mock-ups, the WebRatio code generator produces application modules running on state-of-the-art architectures, and can be used for implementation, maintenance, and evolution. Code generation starts from the outputs of conceptual design and therefore imple-

---

[1]Further information on WebRatio is available at *www.webratio.com.*

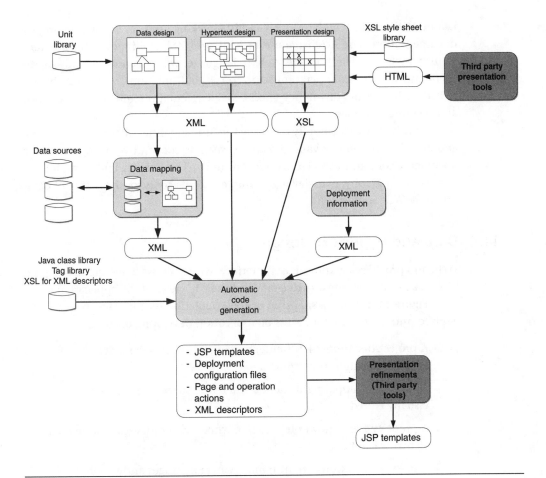

Figure 14.1 Design flow diagram of WebRatio.

mentation and maintenance benefit from the presence of a conceptual specification of the application.

The internal software architecture of the applications created by WebRatio exploits the design principles and techniques described in Chapters 12 and 13. In particular, applications are built using the Model-View-Controller pattern, generic components in the business tier, and CSS and XSL presentation rules for factoring out the look and feel from the page templates.

WebRatio internally uses XML and XSL as the formats for encoding both the specifications and the code generators: XML is used for describing data and hypertext schemas, whereas XSL is used for generating the graphic properties and layout of the page templates, for validity checking, and for automatic project documentation. The extensive use of XML and XSL facilitates custom extensions, which apply both to the WebML language, which can be extended with user-defined units and operations, and to the tool functions, which can be enriched with custom consistency checkers, documentation and code generators, and presentation rules.

In this chapter we briefly overview the functionalities offered by WebRatio, and also discuss some advanced features, such as cooperative work, automatic documentation, and user-defined custom units. The chapter ends with an annotated bibliography, overviewing a sample of other tools for the design of data-intensive Web applications.

14.2 Data and Hypertext Design

WebRatio provides a graphical user interface, which allows designers to compose both the Entity-Relationship diagram and the site views of the application.

Figure 14.2 shows a snapshot of the WebRatio user interface, which is organized into the typical four areas of application development tools:

- A project tree (upper left frame), organizing all the elements of the application project.

- A work area (upper right frame), where the specifications are visually edited.

- A property frame (lower left frame), where the properties of individual elements can be set.

- A message area (lower right frame), where messages and warnings are displayed.

In particular, Figure 14.2 shows a portion of the Entity-Relationship diagram of the running example. The work area visualizes the data schema, and the designer can define entities, attributes, relationships, and generalizations. The elements displayed in the diagram are also presented in the project tree, where they are hierarchically organized in folders. The properties of the currently selected element of the schema (the entity Product, in Figure 14.2) are displayed and can be edited in the property frame. The same organization of the graphical user interface supports also the editing of the site view diagrams.

A WebRatio application project consists of a single Entity-Relationship diagram and of a set of site views. A default structure schema consisting of the User and Group entities and their standard relationships, described in Chapter 8, is

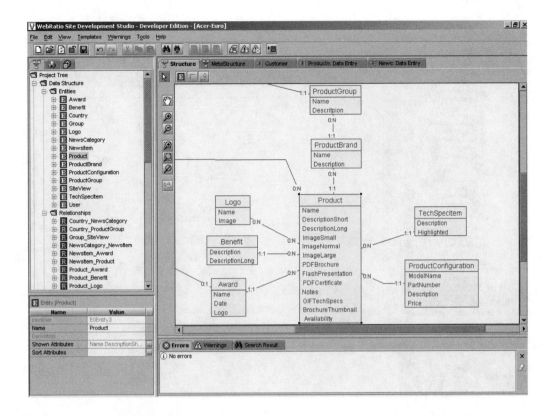

Figure 14.2 Data design in WebRatio.

automatically added to each project, and the developer can extend it with additional entities and relationships. The design of a site view is accomplished by visually manipulating hypertext elements such as units, pages, areas, links, selectors, and context parameters. Figure 14.3 shows the site view work area, with the focus on the Product page of the Acer-Euro application, which includes multiple units; these are also displayed in the project tree, and the properties of the currently selected unit (unit ChangeCountry in Figure 14.3) appear in the property frame.

WebRatio supports also the visual definition of derived data. A wizard (Figure 14.4) can be invoked to specify the expression for computing a derived entity, attribute, or relationship. Such expression, written in a subset of the OCL language, is automatically translated into a SQL view, and included into the application database.

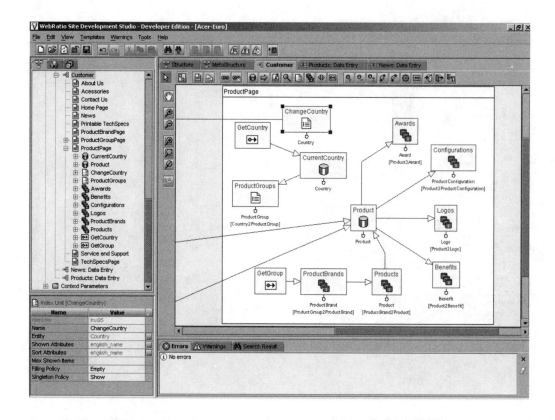

Figure 14.3   Hypertext design in WebRatio.

14.3 Data Mapping

WebRatio assists the data implementation phase, by associating the application to the data sources where content resides. All the three data implementation architectures described in Chapter 11 are supported (dedicated, replicated, and online database), with the highest level of assistance for the dedicated database solution. The connection to the data sources exploits the JDBC and ODBC programming interfaces; additional kinds of data sources can be added, by programming the services for connecting to them.

The data implementation activity proceeds by mapping the Entity-Relationship diagram onto the defined data sources; the user declares the data sources, and binds entities and relationships to tables. The mapping information, associating entities, relationships, and attributes with tables and columns, is stored in an XML file (see Figure 14.1).

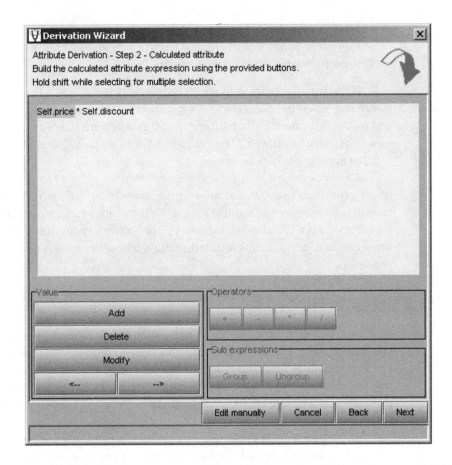

Figure 14.4 Derivation wizard, at work on the definition of a calculated attribute.

If the database for the application content does not exist, WebRatio can automatically create the default standard database, by applying the translation rules described in Chapter 12. To facilitate rapid prototyping, two alternative database generation commands are supported:

- *Creation of an empty database:* the tool automatically creates the standard tables and binds the entities and relationships of the project to them. Then the user populates the database manually or with a data replication tool.

- *Creation of a filled database:* the tool automatically creates the tables in the same way as for the empty mapping, but in addition it populates them with test data, for both entities and relationships. Entity tables are filled using column values sampled from user-defined test case files. In this way it is possible to produce large test databases, constructed from simulated data similar to the real data.

If the Entity-Relationship schema contains derived data, a third command (*Creation of views*) translates the OCL expressions of the derived schema elements, and produces a source file containing the SQL statements defining the relational views equivalent to the OCL expressions, which can be automatically installed into the appropriate data source.

All entities, relationships, and derived elements must be correctly mapped before generating the code and running the application, otherwise the code generation may produce incomplete results. As better illustrated in Section 14.6.1, WebRatio checks the alignment between the Entity-Relationship diagram and the physical databases, thus facilitating the tracking of changes in either of the two levels.

14.4 Presentation Design

Presentation design addresses the definition of *XSL style sheets,* embodying the presentation rules needed by the code generator to produce the page templates. WebRatio provides functionalities both for selecting from a library already available presentation styles and associating them to application pages, and for automatically transforming HTML mockups designed by graphic artists into XSL style sheets (see Figure 14.1).

An XSL style sheet encompasses a set of XSL rules that govern the way in which the page layout and the various kinds of units are rendered. To make XSL style sheets reusable across multiple pages with different content, the XSL rules do not reference the units of the individual pages, but include the specification of the positions in the page layout where units can be placed. Once a style sheet is selected for a page, WebRatio assists the coupling of page units to the locations exposed by the style sheet, with the drag-and-drop interface shown in Figure 14.5.

For each unit positioned in the page, and even for each attribute, contextual link, and field contained in a unit, a different XSL style sheet can be selected, which defines the specific presentation style to be used for rendering the element.

The XSL style sheets of pages and units may be handwritten by the XSL programmer, or automatically generated from HTML mockups. In the latter case, the graphic designer produces an annotated HTML file, which specifies an "example

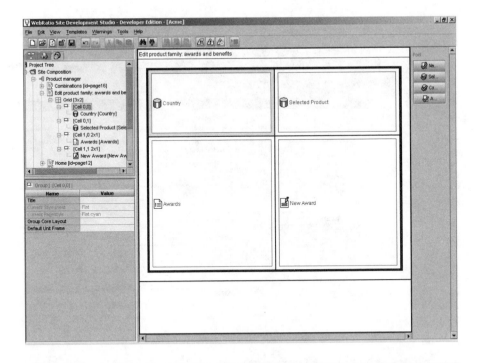

Figure 14.5 Positioning page units in the locations exposed by the XSL style sheet.

of presentation" for a given page or unit. The mock-up file contains custom XML tags, which permit WebRatio to convert it into an XSL style sheet, which can be added to the style sheet library.

Further refinements of the presentation can be applied directly to the page templates produced by the code generator. Standard WYSIWYG tools can be employed, either to modify the graphics and the layout, or to add static content to the page. WebRatio includes an extension file for Macromedia Dreamweaver, which makes WebML tags appear as special icons, as illustrated in Figure 14.6, where an HTML template from the Acer-Euro application is shown. The page template contains two data units (Country and Selected Product), one index unit (Awards) and one entry unit (New Award). The icons labeled with the symbol *A* denote a custom tag of the WebML tag library, specifically the tag representing data unit and index unit attributes. The graphic designer can edit the presentation properties of WebML tags, like those of regular HTML tags.

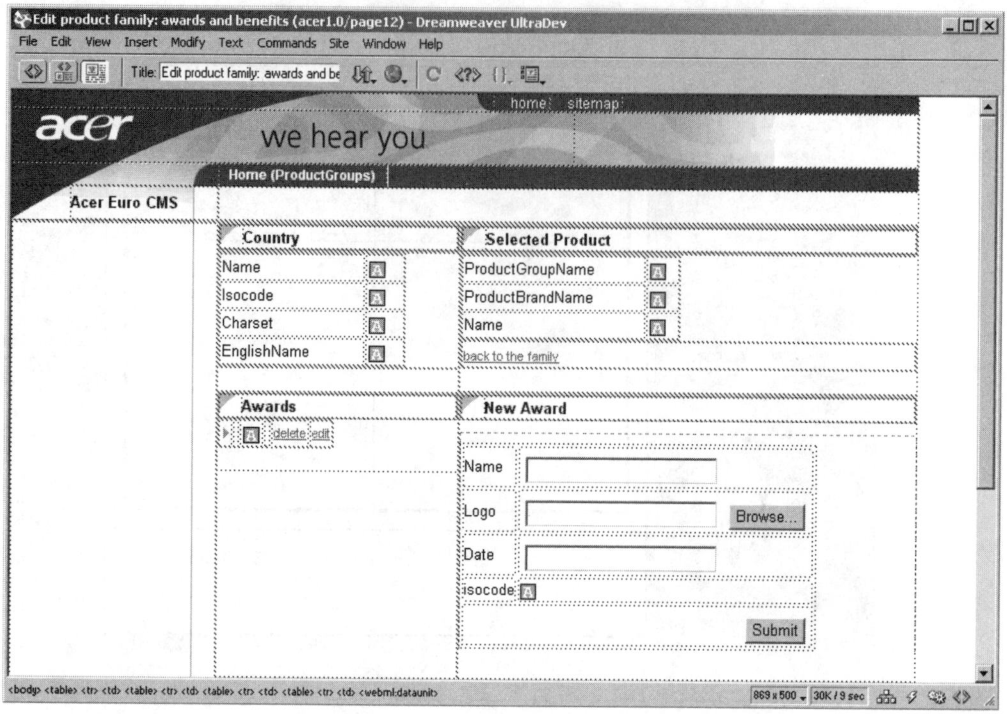

Figure 14.6   WebRatio-generated template edited with Macromedia Dreamweaver.

14.5   Code Generation

After specifying the Entity-Relationship schema and site view diagrams, mapping the data model to the data sources, and assigning style sheets to pages, it is possible to launch automatic code generation, transforming the site views into modules for the selected deployment platform, which may be JSP, Struts, and Microsoft .NET. Before generating the application code, the target platform and the deployment host must be set (see Figure 14.1).

The code generator implements the Model-View-Controller software architecture presented in Chapter 13. For instance, by choosing HTML as mark-up language and Struts as a deployment platform, the output of code generation includes:

■ A set of JSP page templates for the View, including HTML code and JSP custom tags. Two tag libraries can be used: the standard tag library of JSP (JSTL) or a WebML-specific library (WebML Taglib).

■ A set of page and operation actions, to be deployed in the Model.

■ The configuration file of the Controller.

■ A set of XML descriptors, which specify the properties of pages, units, and links for the generic page, unit, and operation services. Normally, the developer is not required to edit descriptors; however, if this need arises, for instance to optimize a SQL query, the updated descriptor can be stored in a special directory and will not be overwritten by subsequent invocations of the code generator.

The produced templates may use any mark-up language. Therefore, the code generator can be used to effectively deploy multi-device applications, in which the same content is served to multiple delivery channels, for instance to HTML browsers and WML-enabled mobile terminals.

14.6 Other Features

Further functionalities are available for correctness checking, cooperative work, automatic production of project documentation, and user-defined model extensions, as highlighted in the expanded design flow shown in Figure 14.7.

14.6.1 Correctness Checking

One of the benefits of conceptual modeling is the possibility of automatically checking for errors at the design level. This feature allows the early verification of the schemas produced by the designer, saving time in the code generation and in the debugging of the application. WebRatio provides error checking at three levels (see Figure 14.1):

■ *Model checking:* this function verifies the correctness of the Entity-Relationship diagram and of the WebML site views, and presents the detected problems with hints on how to fix them. An example of the errors detected by the model checker are the lack of required input for a unit, missing link parameters, the absence of OK or KO links of operations, and so on.

■ *Mapping checking:* this function controls if the elements of the data schema are correctly mapped to the data sources and signals if the databases are misaligned with respect to the Entity-Relationship diagram, due to changes in the specification or in the physical data sources, like the renaming or elimination of tables and columns. Detected problems with the associated hints are highlighted.

■ *Presentation and publishing checking:* this function checks if the pages of a site view are associated to a style sheet, if all the units composing the

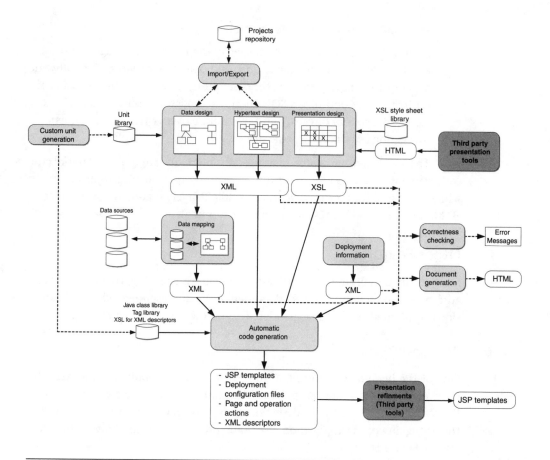

Figure 14.7   Design flow of WebRatio extended with additional features.

page have been positioned in the page layout, and if the deployment server contains all the components needed to run the application. If anything is missing, appropriate warnings are provided, with suggestions on how to solve problems.

14.6.2   Cooperative Work

WebRatio includes import and export functions, which facilitate the parallel development of an application by a work team. The typical workflow of a WebRatio project consists in developing the data model first, and then adding the specifications of the site views necessary to fulfill the application requirements. Site views are natural units of work to be independently developed by separate work teams. Therefore, WebRatio includes two functions for facilitating parallel development:

- The *import* function makes it possible to import the site views of another project into the current project, merging the two projects together. The import function performs a number of consistency checks and transformations, which ensure that the merged project is the correct union of the two merged sub-projects. Consistency checks and transformations are logged into a file and presented as a report to the user, who can accept them or undo the import.

- The *export* function makes it possible to export from the current project either the data model alone or the data model together with one or more site views. The export function creates a new project, consisting of the exported sub-schemas. The new project can be evolved in parallel with the original project and then merged back into the original project, using the import function.

14.6.3   Automatic Documentation

Another benefit of conceptual modeling is the possibility of producing high-quality documentation from the conceptual models of the application. WebRatio automatically generates *project documentation,* in a format called WebMLDoc, inspired to the popular JavaDoc documentation layout.

The produced documentation consists of a set of HTML pages, which describe every aspect of the project in an easy-to-browse format. A sample WebMLDoc page appears in Figure 14.8, which includes a clickable site view schema. Clicking on each symbol in the schema opens the WebMLDoc page associated to the selected concept. In the example, by clicking on the ChangeCountry index unit, the user accesses the detailed information of the selected element, as shown in Figure 14.9.

The WebMLDoc generator is written as a set of customizable XSL rules, which the designer can override and extend to obtain a personalized documentation format.

14.6.4   WebML Extensibility with Custom Units

WebRatio extends the capability of conceptual modeling and code generation beyond the set of predefined WebML units, because it allows developers to create and integrate into the development tool their own custom units and code generators.

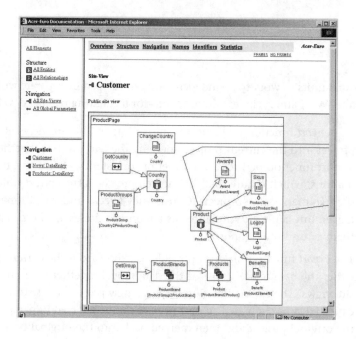

Figure 14.8   WebMLDoc page, showing a clickable site view diagram.

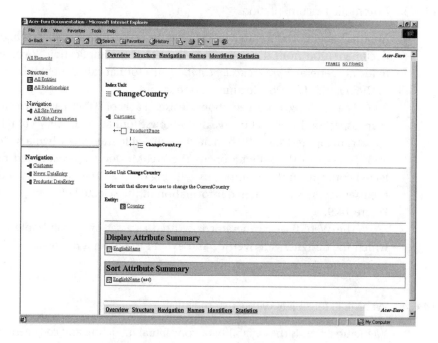

Figure 14.9   WebMLDoc page, showing the details of the ChangeCountry index unit.

Custom WebML units permit the designer to reverse-engineer his/her business components and make them part of the conceptual modeling and code generation process. Extending WebML requires defining a *plug-in unit* and deploying it in WebRatio Site Development Studio. Then, the model editor and code generator can use the new unit as any other WebML built-in unit.

Conceptually, a plug-in unit is a reusable component, characterized by a set of (required or optional) typed input parameters, and by a set of output parameters. The input parameters can be fed to the unit by input links, and the output parameters can be associated with output links of the unit, to be used in the selectors of other units.

A plug-in unit is defined by writing a few Java and XML/XSL files:

- One XML file describing the features of the unit visible to the designer, like its icon and the properties editable in the property frame.

- Two XSL rules, which extracts from each instance of the custom unit the description of its input and output parameters, needed to correctly link the custom unit to other units.

- One or more components (for instance, Java or C# classes) implementing the runtime service associated with the unit.

- One optional XSL file, which matches the instances of the custom unit and produces the XML descriptors required by the unit service. In this way, the unit service can be a single generic class, instantiated for a specific exemplar of the plug-in unit using the parameters provided by the descriptor.

- One or more custom tags for rendering the unit, if the unit presents some content.

- One or more optional XSL rules for expressing custom consistency checks.

An example of plug-in unit is the *calendar unit*, built using the standard Java class implementing a perennial calendar. Figure 14.10 shows the WebML diagram where the calendar unit is contextually linked to an index unit. The calendar unit exposes in output a value of type date, corresponding to the day selected by the user from the calendar; this value is associated as a parameter with the output link of the calendar unit, and used in the selector of the index unit, to produce the list of events that take place in the day selected by the user. Figure 14.11 shows the HTML page automatically generated by WebRatio, which includes the rendition of the calendar unit and of the linked index unit.

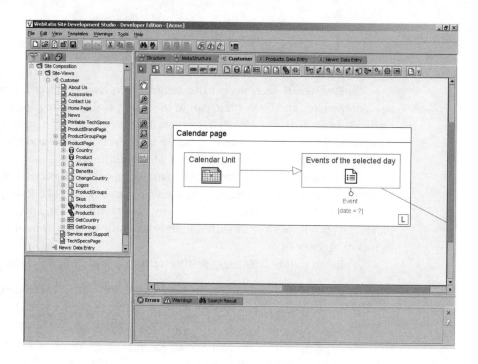

Figure 14.10 WebRatio page using the custom Calendar unit.

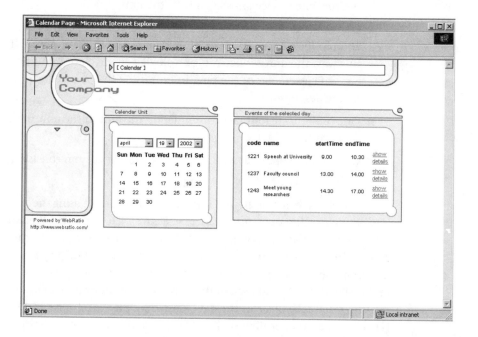

Figure 14.11 Rendition of the page with the Calendar unit.

Summary

In this chapter we have illustrated WebRatio, a tool specifically designed to support the development process of data-intensive Web applications. In essence, WebRatio consists of an Entity-Relationship and WebML editor, and of a set of XSL-based code generators, which transform an XML representation of the application into running page templates. WebRatio faces the classic dilemma of CASE tools between flexibility and automation by providing hooks for extending the core WebML primitives with custom units and style sheets, which can be integrated into the WebML diagrams and code generation process. The use of WebRatio enhances Web development productivity in two ways: it speeds up analysis and design, exploiting user-friendly schema drawing tools, automatic documentation generation, and fast prototyping based on one-click database and page template generation; and it enables the automatic implementation of page templates and unit services, which eliminates a substantial fraction of the development effort.

Applications produced with WebRatio exploit the MVC architecture and follow the guidelines for software design discussed in Chapter 13. Thus, the generated code meets the requirements of enterprise-class data-intensive Web applications.

Bibliographic Notes

After illustrating the features of WebRatio Site Development Studio [WebRatio02], we briefly review a sample of commercial tools for Web application development. We focus especially on those tools that exhibit some degree of conceptual modeling.

- *Hyperwave* [HIM98] is an advanced document management environment that permits remote users to browse, annotate, and maintain documents distributed over the Web. Hyperwave has a very basic, yet powerful, high-level model of a Web application, which is considered as a set of document collections organized hierarchically.

- Bluestone Software's *Sapphire/Web* [Bluestone] is a suite that integrates a Web server, a Java development environment, realtime systems and security monitoring applications. The tool is centered on conceptual modeling of client-server software components. In particular, Sapphire lets developers use drag-and-drop commands to tie together client, middle tier, and server-side objects inside a complex architecture. The tool exploits a high-level model of the application, which focuses mainly on architecture modeling and on the distribution of the application components.

■ *CodeCharge* [CodeCharge] provides automatic code generation based on an advanced Web site production wizard, which exploits a few predefined hypertext patterns. Developers can define a high-level model of the site, insert different pages with various patterns, and automatically produce page templates and SQL queries running in different platforms. The produced code follows a template-based software architecture.

Several software vendors offer end-to-end Web development suites, covering a large spectrum of tasks and technologies. Among the most comprehensive products, we cite the Oracle Web Development Suite [Gwyer96, BG96], which comprises *Oracle9i Designer* [Oraclec], a tool for generating Web applications from augmented Entity-Relationship diagrams, with a database-centric approach. Oracle Designer is an environment for business process and application modeling, integrated with software generators originally designed to target traditional client-server environments, namely Oracle Developer 2000 [Hoven97] and Visual Basic.

Oracle9i Designer tools are grouped in four categories, which reflect the needs of different types of user:

■ *The System Requirements Modeling* area includes tools for modeling business requirements, business processes and organization methods by means of diagrammatic representations of the data (using Entity-Relationship diagrams), functions and data flows in the systems that make up the organization.

■ *The Preliminary Designs Transformation* area includes a set of Transformers that generate preliminary designs from the models created earlier. For example, there are transformers for database creation from Entity-Relationship schemas, transformers for application design, and so on.

■ *The Design and Generation* area includes the Design Editor, which can be used to design a system that meets the business requirements of an organization and create server-side components and client-side applications from definitions recorded as system requirements.

■ *The Repository Tools* area contains the repository of all the defined resources, and provides administration and control primitives for repository maintenance.

From a Web design point of view, the third component is the most interesting of the tool suite, because it includes Oracle Web PL/SQL Generator, which is able to create Web applications for querying, updating, and entering information in an Oracle database from a Web interface, deployed on an Oracle9i Application Server instance. Specifically, three inputs drive the generation process:

- *A Web-enhanced database design:* database design diagrams, defined in the system requirements area, specify the structure of the database in terms of tables, views, foreign key relationships, and integrity constraints. These constitute the data schema of the future Web application.

- *The definition of applications and modules:* modules correspond to basic application units; each module consists of a sequence of tables, whose order determines the sequence of browsable pages that will be produced for that module. Navigation is established by drawing links between modules.

- *The user preferences:* user preferences are parameters that can be set to govern the presentation of the generated application; they can be defined either globally, at the module, or at the component level.

From these inputs, the Web Generator produces fixed-format Web pages, which can be refined by the designer; one set of related pages is generated for each module and links between different modules are turned into hyperlinks between the HTML startup pages of modules.

The Oracle suite does not exploit a specific notation for high-level hypertext modeling, but uses a mix of notations for information system modeling. It can be used to generate software components for Web publishing, starting from a broad set of conceptual models.

Summary of WebML Elements

WebML element	Brief description	Properties
AND sub-pages Page / Page1 / Page2	AND sub-pages are used to divide the page into portions. AND sub-pages are contained in a page or in a sub-page.	– Nested pages
Area Area	An area is a container of pages or, recursively, other sub-areas, which can be used to give a hierarchical organization to the site view.	– Name – Landmark – Content: pages, sub-areas – Default page or sub-area
Connect unit Connect	A connect unit creates new instances of a relationship.	– Name – Relationship role – Selector of the source entity – Selector of the target entity
Create unit Create	A create unit enables the creation of a new entity instance.	– Name – Source entity – Set of value assignments
Data unit Data unit	A data unit publishes a single object of a given entity.	– Name – Source entity – Selector (optional) – Included attributes

WebML element	Brief description	Properties
Delete unit	A delete unit deletes one or more objects of a given entity.	– Name – Source entity – Selector
Disconnect unit	A disconnect unit deletes instances of a relationship.	– Name – Relationship role – Selector of the source entity – Selector of the target entity

Entry unit	An entry unit supports form-based data entry.	– Name
		– For each field:
		  – Name
		  – Type
		  – Initial value (optional)
		  – Modifiability
		  – Validity predicate

Generic operation unit	A generic operation unit defines a generic operation: the input and output parameters must be defined by the designer.	Designer-defined
Get unit	A get unit retrieves the value of a global parameter.	– Global parameter
Global parameter	A global parameter stores information available to multiple pages for the duration of the session.	– Name – Type – Default value

WebML element	Brief description	Properties
Hierarchical index unit	A variant of index, in which the index entries are organized in a multi-level tree.	– Name – For each level: – Source entity – Selector (optional) – Included attributes – Order clause (optional)
Index unit	An index unit presents multiple objects of an entity as a list.	– Name – Source entity – Selector (optional) – Included attributes – Order clause (optional)
Link – automatic – transport	A link is an oriented connection between two units or pages. It abstracts the concept of anchor and allows the flow of information (by means of link parameters) between units. Links can be defined as – automatic: they are navigated without the intervention of the user – transport: they are not rendered as an anchor, but they only enable parameter passing	Normal, automatic and transport links: – Name – Source element (unit or page) – Destination element – Type of link (normal, automatic, transport) – Link parameters Link parameters: – Name – source-value
– OK link – KO link	Links exiting operations are distinguished into: – OK link: they are followed in case of operation success – KO link: they are followed in case of operation failure	OK/KO links: – Name – Source element (operation unit) – Destination element – Link parameters

WebML element	**Brief description**	**Properties**

Login unit

The login unit verifies the identity of a user accessing the site.

Parameters:
– Username
– Password

Logout unit

The logout unit forwards the user to a default page with no access control.

None

Modify unit

A modify unit updates one or more objects of a given entity.

– Name
– Source entity
– Selector
– Set of value assignments

Multi-choice index unit

A variant of index, where each element of the list is associated with a checkbox allowing the user to select multiple objects.

– Name
– Source entity
– Selector (optional)
– Included attributes
– Order clause (optional)

Multidata unit

A multidata unit presents multiple objects of an entity together, by repeating the presentation of several data units.

– Name
– Source entity
– Selector (optional)
– Included attributes
– Order clause (optional)

OR sub-pages

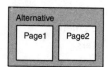

OR sub-pages specify that certain portions of the screen may contain *alternative* pieces of content, each one modeled as a distinct page.

OR sub-pages are contained in a page or in a sub-page.

– Nested pages
– Default nested page

WebML element	Brief description	Properties
Page Page	A page represents the actual interface browsed by the user. It contains units and/or sub-pages.	– Name – Landmark – Content: units, OR/AND sub-pages
Scroller unit Scroller unit	A scroller unit provides commands to scroll through the objects in a set.	– Name – Source entity – Selector (optional) – Block factor – Order clause (optional)
Sendmail unit SendMail	The sendmail unit provides the capability of sending e-mail messages.	Parameters: – Sender – Recipients – Subject – Body – Attachments
Set unit Set unit	A set unit assigns a value to a global parameter.	– Global parameter
Site view Site view	A site view represents a hypertext.	– Name – Content: pages, areas – Home page
Transaction	A transaction is a sequence of operations executed atomically, which means that either all the individual operations execute successfully, or the entire sequence is undone	None

WebML Syntax

miscellaneous

```
<Name>::= <Letter> {<Letter> | <Digit>}
<Number>::= <Digit> {<Digit>}
<Letter>::= ["A"-"Z"]|["a"-"z"]
<Digit>::= ["0"-"9"]
<Value>::= (<Letter>|<Digit>) { (<Letter>|<Digit>)}
<Type>::= <BuiltInType> | <EnumTypeName>
<BuiltInType>::= "String" | "Text" | "Integer" | "Float" | "Date" |
       "Time" | "Boolean" | "BLOB" | "URL"
<EnumTypeName>::= <Name>
<EntityName>::= <Name>
<AttrName>::= <Name> | OID
<RoleName>::= <Name>
```

data unit

```
<DataUnitDef>::= DataUnit <DataUnitName>
       "(" source <EntityName>
           [";" selector <SelectorDef> {","<SelectorDef>}]
           [";" attributes <AttrName> {"," <AttrName>}] ")"
<DataUnitName>::= <Name>
```

example:
```
DataUnit ShortArtist
(source Artist;
 attributes FirstName, LastName, Photo)
```

selector

```
<SelectorDef>::= (<AttrPredicate> | <RolePredicate>)
<AttrPredicate>::= <AttrPredLeft> <AttrPredOp> <AttrPredRight>
<AttrPredLeft>::= <AttrName> {"|" (<AttrName>)}
<AttrPredOp>::= "=" | "<" | "<=" | ">=" | ">" | "!=" | "in" |
       "contains" | "beginsWith" | "endsWith"
<AttrPredRight>::= (<Value> | <ParamName>)
```

```
            {"|" (<Value> | <ParamName>)}
<RolePredicate>::= <RoleName>"("<ParamName>")"
```

example:

```
   Year=2000;
   Title contains green|yellow
   Artist2Album(CurrArtist);
```

multidata unit

```
<MultidataUnitDef>::= MultidataUnit <MultidataUnitName>
      "(" source <EntityName>
            [";" selector <SelectorDef> {","<SelectorDef>}]
            [";" attributes <AttrName> {"," <AttrName>}]
            [";" orderby <OrderByDef> {"," <OrderByDef>}] ")"
<MultidataUnitName>::= <Name>
<OrderByDef>::= <AttrName> [ascending|descending]
```

example:

```
   MultidataUnit MultiAlbum
     (source Album;
      attributes Title, Artist, Photo;
      orderby Artist, Title)
```

index unit

```
<IndexUnitDef>::=
  IndexUnit <IndexUnitName> [multi-choice]
    "(" source <EntityName>
      [";" selector <SelectorDef> {","<SelectorDef>}]
      [";" attributes <AttrName> { "," <AttrName>}]
      [";" orderby <OrderByDef> {"," <OrderByDef>}]
      [";" (NEST <IndexUnitLevelDef> {"," NEST <IndexUnitLevelDef>}) |
        (RECURSIVE NEST <IndexUnitLevelDef>)] ")"
<IndexUnitName>::= <Name>
<IndexUnitLevelDef>::=
    <EntityName>
    selector <RolePredicate> {","<SelectorDef>}
    [";" attributes <AttrName> { "," <AttrName>}]
    [";" orderby <OrderByDef> {"," <OrderByDef>}]
```

example:

```
   IndexUnit AlbumIndex
   (source Album;
```

```
        attributes Title;
        orderby Title ascending)
```

scroller unit

```
<ScrollerUnitDef>::= ScrollerUnit <ScrollerUnitName>
        "(" source <EntityName>
            [";" blockFactor <Number>]
            [";" selector <SelectorDef> {","<SelectorDef>}]
            [";" orderby <OrderByDef> {"," <OrderByDef>}] ")"
<ScrollerUnitName>::= <Name>
```

example:
```
  ScrollerUnit AlbumScroll
  (source Album;
   blockFactor 1;
   orderby Title ascending)
```

entry unit

```
<EntryUnitDef>::= EntryUnit <EntryUnitName>
        ["(" fields <FieldDef>{";" <FieldDef>} ")"]
<EntryUnitName>::= <Name>
<FieldDef>::= <FieldName> <Type> ["," (fixed|modifiable)]
        ["," initiallyPreloaded <FieldPreloadValue>]
        ["," <FieldPredicate>]
<FieldName>::= <Name>
<FieldPreloadValue>::= <Value> | (<EntityName>.<AttributeName>) |
        (<LinkName>:<ParamName>)
<FieldPredicate>::=
    notnull | (<FieldName> <AttrPredOp> (<FieldName>|<Value>))
```

example:
```
  EntryUnit ArtistEntry
  (FirstName Text, modifiable;
   LastName Text, modifiable)
```

page

```
<PageDef>::=
    Page <PageName> [home] [landmark]
    "(" [units <ContentUnitName> {"," <ContentUnitName>}";"]
        [and-pages <PageName> {"," <PageName>} ";"]
```

```
        [or-pages <PageName> [default]{"," <PageName> [default]}]")"
<PageName>::= <Name>
<ContentUnitName>::= <DataUnitName> | <MultidataUnitName> |
        <IndexUnitName> | <ScrollerUnitName> |
        <EntryUnitName>
```

example:
```
    Page AlbumPage
    (units AlbumIndex, AlbumInfo)
```

link

```
<LinkDef>::= link <LinkName> [automatic] [transport]
        "(" from <LinkSource> to <LinkDest>
            [";" parameters <ParamDef> {"," <ParamDef>}]
            [";" type (automatic | manual)]
            [";" newWindow ":" (True | False)] ")"
<LinkName>::= <Name>
<LinkSource>::= <PageName> | <ContentUnitName>
<LinkDest>::= <PageName> | <ContentUnitName> |
        <OperationUnitName>
<OperationUnitName>::= <CreateUnitName> | <DeleteUnitName> |
        <ModifyUnitName> | <ConnectUnitName> |
        <DisconnectUnitName>
<ParamDef>::= <ParamName>":" ((["{"][<EntityName>.]<AttrName>["}"]) |
        (["{"]<FieldName>["}"]) |
        ([<LinkName>.]<ParamName>))
<ParamName>::= <Name> | "?"
```

example:
```
    link Pop2Jazz noncontextual
      (from PopArtistsPage to JazzArtistsPage)
    link ItemDetails contextual
      (from AllArtists to ArtistDetails;
       parameters CurrArtist:Artist.OID)
    link ArtistsDetails
      (from ArtistMultiChoice to ArtistsMultiData;
       parameters SelArtists:{Artist.OID})
```

OK-link

```
<OKLinkDef>::= OKLink <OKLinkName>
        "(" from <OKLinkSource> to <OKLinkDest>
```

```
            [";" parameters <ParamDef> {"," <ParamDef>}] ")"
<OKLinkName>::= <Name>
<OKLinkSource>::= <OperationUnitName>
<OKLinkDest>::= <PageName> | <ContentUnitName> |
      <OperationUnitName>
```

KO-link

```
<KOLinkDef>::= KOLink <KOLinkName>
      "(" from <KOLinkSource> to <KOLinkDest>
          [";" parameters <ParamDef> {"," <ParamDef>}] ")"
<KOLinkName>::= <Name>
<KOLinkSource>::= <OperationUnitName>
<KOLinkDest>::= <PageName> | <ContentUnitName> |
      <OperationUnitName>
```

site view

```
<SiteViewDef>::= siteview <SiteViewName>
      "(" [areas <AreaName> {"," <AreaName>} ";"]
         [pages <PageName> {"," <PageName>}] ")"
<SiteViewName>::= <Name>
```

example:
```
   siteview CompanySiteView
     (areas CorporateNews, CustomerInformation;
      pages HomePage)
```

area

```
<AreaDef>::=
   area <AreaName> [landmark]
      "(" [areas <AreaName> [default]{"," <AreaName> [default]} ";"]
          [pages <PageName> [default]{"," <PageName>}[default]] ")"
<AreaName>::= <Name>
```

create unit

```
<CreateUnitDef>::= CreateUnit <CreateUnitName>
      "(" source <EntityName>
          [";" <Assignment>{"," <Assignment>}] ")"
<Assignment>::= <AttrName> ":=" <ParamName>
```

example:
```
CreateUnit CreateArtist
  (source Artist;
    FirstName:=FName, LastName:=LName)
```

delete unit

```
<DeleteUnitDef>::= DeleteUnit <DeleteUnitName>
      "(" source <EntityName>
          [";" selector <SelectorDef> {","<SelectorDef>}] ")"
<DeleteUnitName>::= <Name>
```

example:
```
DeleteUnit DeleteAlbum
(source Album; selector [OID IN?])
```

modify unit

```
<ModifyUnitDef>::= ModifyUnit <ModifyUnitName>
      "(" source <EntityName>
          [";" selector <SelectorDef> {","<SelectorDef>}]
          [";" <Assignment>{"," <Assignment>}] ")"
```

example:
```
ModifyUnit ModifyBio
  (source Artist; selector OID=oidArtist;
    biographicInfo:=bio)
```

connect unit

```
<ConnectUnitDef>::= ConnectUnit <ConnectUnitName>
      "(" source <RoleName> ";"
          "[" <SourceSelectorDef> "]" ","
          "[" <DestSelectorDef> "]" ")"
<ConnectUnitName>::= <Name>
<SourceSelectorDef>::=
    <EntityName>"."<AttrName> <AttrPredOp> <AttrPredRight>
<DestSelectorDef>::=
    <EntityName>"."<AttrName> <AttrPredOp> <AttrPredRight>
```

example:
```
ConnectUnit AssignReview
  (source Artist2Review;
    [Artist.OID = Art], [Review.OID = Rev])
```

disconnect unit

```
<DisconnectUnitDef>::= DisconnectUnit <DisconnectUnitName>
     "(" source <RoleName> ";"
         "[" <SourceSelectorDef> "]" ","
         "[" <DestSelectorDef> "]" ")"
<DisconnectUnitName>::= <Name>
```

global parameter

```
<GlobalParamDef>::= globalParameter <GlobalParamName>
     "(" ((type <Type> [";" initialValue <Value>]) |
            (type OID ";" entity <EntityName>)) ")"
<GlobalParamName>::= <Name>
```

example:
```
GlobalParameter CurrentCountry
(type OID; entity Country)
GlobalParameter CurrentCountry
(type string; initialValue Italy)
```

set unit

```
<SetUnitDef>::= setUnit <SetUnitName>
     "(" parameter <GlobalParamName>":" <ParamName> ")"
<SetUnitName>::= <Name>
```

example:
```
setUnit SetCountry
(parameter CurrentCountry: CountryDataToSetCountry.?)
```

get unit

```
<GetUnitDef>::= getUnit <GetUnitName>
     "(" parameter <GlobalParamName> ")"
<GetUnitName>::= <Name>
```

example:
```
getUnit GetCountry
(parameter CurrentCountry)
```

login unit

```
<LoginUnitDef>::= login <LoginUnitName>
     "(" parameters UserName:=<ParamName> ","
```

```
                    Password:=<ParamName> ")"
<LoginUnitName>::= <Name>
```

example:
```
   login LoginUnit
   (parameters UserName:text, Password:text)
```

logout unit

```
<LogoutUnitDef>::= logout <LogoutUnitName>
<LogoutUnitName>::= <Name>
```

example:
```
   logout LogoutUnit
```

sendmail unit

```
<SendMailUnitDef>::=
     sendMail <SendMailUnitName>
    "(" parameters Sender:=<ParamName> ","
            Recipients:=<ParamName> ","
            Subject:=<ParamName> ","
            Body:=<ParamName>
            ["," Attachments:=<ParamName>] ")"
<SendMailUnitName>::= <Name>
```

example:
```
   sendMail SendReview
   (parameters Sender:text, Receiver:text, Subject:text,
     Body:text, Attach:text)
```

generic operation unit

```
<OpUnitDef>::=
  external <OpUnitName>
  ["("parameters [<OpParamName>:=<ParamName>
      {"," <OpParamName>:=<ParamName}] ")"]
<OpUnitName>::= <Name>
<OpParamName>::= <Name>
```

example:
```
   external ChargeCreditCard
   (parameters TotAmount integer, Shop text)
```

C

APPENDIX

OCL Syntax

```
oclFile                := ( "package" packageName
                             oclExpressions
                             "endpackage"
                         )+
packageName            := pathName
oclExpressions         := ( constraint )*
constraint             := contextDeclaration
                           ( ( "def" name? ":" letExpression*)
                             |
                             ( stereotype name? ":" oclExpression)
                           )+
contextDeclaration     := "context"
                           ( operationContext | classifierContext )
classifierContext      := ( name ":" name )
                           | name
operationContext       := name "::" operationName
                           "(" formalParameterList ")"
                           ( ":" returnType )?
stereotype             := ( "pre" | "post" | "inv" )
operationName          := name | "=" | "+" | "-" | "<" | "<=" |
                           ">=" | ">" | "/" | "*" | "<>" |
                           "implies" | "not" | "or" | "xor" | "and"
formalParameterList    := ( name ":" typeSpecifier
                                 ("," name ":" typeSpecifier )*
                             )?
typeSpecifier          := simpleTypeSpecifier
                           | collectionType
collectionType         := collectionKind
                           "(" simpleTypeSpecifier ")"
oclExpression          := (letExpression* "in")? expression
returnType             := typeSpecifier
expression             := logicalExpression
```

```
letExpression              := "let" name
                              ( "(" formalParameterList ")" )?
                              ( ":" typeSpecifier )?
                              "=" expression
ifExpression               := "if" expression
                              "then" expression
                              "else" expression
                              "endif"
logicalExpression          := relationalExpression
                              ( logicalOperator
                                relationalExpression
                              )*
relationalExpression       := additiveExpression
                              ( relationalOperator
                                additiveExpression
                              )?
additiveExpression         := multiplicativeExpression
                              ( addOperator
                                multiplicativeExpression
                              )*
multiplicativeExpression   := unaryExpression
                              ( multiplyOperator
                                unaryExpression
                              )*
unaryExpression            := ( unaryOperator
                                postfixExpression
                              )
                              | postfixExpression
postfixExpression          := primaryExpression
                              ( ("." | "->")propertyCall )*
primaryExpression          := literalCollection
                              | literal
                              | propertyCall
                              | "(" expression ")"
                              | ifExpression
propertyCallParameters     := "(" ( declarator )?
                              ( actualParameterList )? ")"
```

```
literal                   := string
                           | number
                           | enumLiteral
enumLiteral               := name "::" name( "::" name )*
simpleTypeSpecifier       := pathName
literalCollection         := collectionKind "{"
                             ( collectionIte m
                               ("," collectionItem )*
                             )?
                             "}"
collectionItem            := expression (".." expression )?
propertyCall              := pathName
                             ( timeExpression )?
                             ( qualifiers )?
                             ( propertyCallParameters )?
qualifiers                := "[" actualParameterList "]"
declarator                := name ( "," name )*
                             ( ":" simpleTypeSpecifier )?
                             ( ";" name ":" typeSpecifier "="
                               expression
                             )?
                             "|"
pathName                  := name ( "::" name )*
timeExpression            := "@" "pre"
actualParameterList       := expression ("," expression)*
logicalOperator           := "and" | "or" | "xor" | "implies"
collectionKind            := "Set" | "Bag" | "Sequence" | "Collection"
relationalOperator        := "=" | ">" | "<" | ">=" | "<=" | "<>"
addOperator               := "+" | "-"
multiplyOperator          := "*" | "/"
unaryOperator             := "-" | "not"
typeName                  := charForNameTop charForName*
name                      := charForNameTop charForName*
charForNameTop            := /* Characters except inhibitedChar
                             and ["0"-"9"]; the available
                             characters shall be determined by
                             the tool implementers ultimately.*/
```

```
charForName           := /* Characters except inhibitedChar; the
                         available characters shall be determined
                         by the tool implementers ultimately.*/
inhibitedChar         :=
                         "|"\"|"#"|"\"|"("|")"|"*"|"+"|","|
                         "|"."|"/"|":"|";"|"<"|"="|">"|"@"|
                         ["|"\\"|"]"|"{"|"|"|"}"
number                := ["0"-"9"] (["0"-"9"])*
                         ( "." ["0"-"9"] (["0"-"9"])* )?
                         ( ("e" | "E") ( "+" | "-" )? ["0"-"9"]
                         (["0"-"9"])*
                         )?
string                := " ' "
                         (( ~[" ","\\","\n","\r"] )
                           |("\\"
                             ( ["n","t","b","r","f","\\"," ' ","\" "]
                               | ["0"-"7"]
                                 ( ["0"-"7"] ( ["0"-"7"] )? )?
                             )
                           )
                         )*
                         " ' "
```

D

Summary of WebML Elements Implementation

WebML element	Database query	Implementation notes
AND pages	None	Each sub-page may be implemented as an independent file, representing a frame. A master file assembles all the page frames.
Areas/landmarks	None	All the non-contextual links represented by landmarks are made explicit and implemented as HTML anchors.
Connect unit	One-to-many relationship: UPDATE TargetEntity SET RelationshipColumn=NewValue [WHERE Selector] Many-to-many relationship: INSERT INTO BridgeTable(EntityAttributes) VALUES (ValuesList)	The operation is tentatively executed (e.g., inside a Java try-catch block) to trap possible execution errors. Based on operation result, control is forwarded to the destination page of the OK or KO link, passing also the possible output parameters (the OIDs of the connected objects, for the OK link, of the non-connected objects, for the KO link).
Contextual links	None	An anchor tag is created. Its href attribute contains a URL built from the name of the template implementing the page containing the destination unit (fixed part) and from the output parameters of the source unit (variable part). When the destination of the link is an operation some extra parameters may be carried by the link according to the rules explained in Section 12.4.7.

WebML element	Database query	Implementation notes
Contextual links from entry units	None	HTML form with an action attribute and a submit button. The action points to the destination page or operation. The form contains an INPUT tag for each field of the entry unit. When the destination of the link is an operation some extra hidden fields may be carried by the link according to the rules explained in Section 12.4.9.
Create unit Create	INSERT INTO TargetEntity (EntityAttributes) VALUES (InputParameters)	A unique identifier for the newly created object must be created. The operation is tentatively executed (e.g., inside a Java try-catch block) to trap possible execution errors. Based on operation result, the control is forwarded to the destination page of the OK or KO link, passing also the possible output parameters (the OIDs of the new object, for OK the link; no output, for the KO link).
Data unit Data unit	SELECT DisplayAttributes + OutputAttributes FROM TargetEntity WHERE Selector OutputAttributes represents the set of attributes carried by the output links of the unit	The values of the DisplayAttributes retrieved by the query are used to dynamically produce HTML content. The OutputAttributes are used for a) building the URL of the unit's manual output links or b) for passing parameters to other units of the page along automatic links.

WebML element	Database query	Implementation notes
Delete unit	DELETE FROM TargetEntity [WHERE Selector]	The operation is tentatively executed (e.g., inside a Java try-catch block) to trap possible execution errors. Based on operation result, control is forwarded to the destination page of the OK or KO link, passing also the possible output parameters (the OIDs of the non-deleted objects, for KO the link; no output, for the OK link).
Disconnect unit	One-to-many relationship: UPDATE TargetEntity SET RelationshipColumn=NULL [WHERE Selector] Many-to-many relationship: DELETE FROM BridgeEntity [WHERE Selector]	The operation is tentatively executed (e.g., inside a Java try-catch block) to trap possible execution errors. Based on operation result, control is forwarded to the destination page of the OK or KO link, passing also the possible output parameters (the OIDs of the disconnected objects, for the OK link, of the non-disconnected objects, for the KO link).
Entry unit	None	An HTML form is introduced, with an input tag for each field of the entry unit. The link exiting the entry unit is implemented using the action attribute and submit button of the HTML form.
Get unit	None	A value is retrieved from the session object (or from the HTTP request parameter) storing the global parameter.

WebML element	Database query	Implementation notes
Index unit	SELECT DisplayAttributes + OutputAttributes FROM TargetEntity [WHERE Selector] [ORDER BY SortAttributes]	The values of the DisplayAttributes are visualized in the HTML page by means of a loop, processing one row of the query result at a time. A link exiting the index unit is represented by an anchor for each row of the index. The href of the anchor is built from the OuputAttributes of each row of the query result.
Modify unit	UPDATE TargetEntity SET Attribute=Value {,Attribute=Value} [WHERE Selector]	The operation is tentatively executed (e.g., inside a Java try-catch block) to trap possible execution errors. Based on operation result, control is forwarded to the destination page of the OK or KO link, passing also the possible output parameters (the OIDs of the modified objects, for the OK link, of the non-modified objects for the KO link).
Multi-choice index unit	SELECT DisplayAttributes + OutputAttributes FROM TargetEntity [WHERE Selector] [ORDER BY SortAttributes]	The values of the DisplayAttributes are visualized inside an HTML form by means of a loop, processing one row of the query result at a time. Each element of the index is associated with a checkbox; all checkboxes have the same name and a value containing the OutputAttributes (typically the OID) of the current element of the query result. A link exiting the multi-choice index unit maps to the submit button of the form, which posts a multi-valued request parameter. The parameter is decoded in the page containing the destination unit of the link.

WebML element	Database query	Implementation notes
Multidata unit	SELECT DisplayAttributes + OutputAttributes FROM TargetEntity [WHERE Selector] [ORDER BY SortAttributes]	The values of the DisplayAttributes are visualized in the final page by means of a loop, processing one row table at a time. A link exiting the multidata index unit corresponds to a single anchor. The href of the anchor contains a single parameter whose value concatenates the OutputAttributes (typically the OID) of the selected entities. Such composite value is decoded in the page containing the destination unit of the link.
Non-contextual links	None	An anchor tag is created. Its href attribute contains a URL built from the name of the template implementing the destination page.
OR pages	None	The name of the currently displayed page is stored in an extra parameter associated to all the links accessing the page. Non-contextual links entering the page carry as parameter the name of the default page. Links entering an OR sub-page carry the name of the destination sub-page.
Scroller unit	SELECT OutputAttributes FROM TargetEntity [WHERE Selector] [ORDER BY SortAttributes]	A scroller has a single outgoing link implemented by a set of anchors (first, last, previous, next) whose URLs contain the OutputAttributes (typically the OID) of the appropriate object, determined by scanning the result set of the scroller unit's query. The current object is determined by the input value of the destination unit of the link.

WebML element	Database query	Implementation notes
Set unit	None	A new value is assigned to the session object storing the global parameter. Alternatively, URL rewriting can be used: the value of the global parameter must be passed as an extra parameter in all the links of the site view.
Selectors	The WHERE clause of the data retrieval query is built as a conjunctive expression of simple predicates over attributes or relationship roles. With *attribute predicate*s, the expression in the selector predicate maps into a SQL expression: Attribute Operator Value The IN clause, comparing a value with a set of values (e.g., OID IN {Value1, Value2, . . . ValueN}) is mapped into a disjunctive clause: (Attribute = Value1) OR (Attribute = Value2) OR . . . OR (Attribute = ValueN)	With a relationship *role predicate,* given the OID of the source entity of the relationship role (InputOID), two cases may arise: ■ One-to-many relationship: the predicated is expressed on the SourceOID column mapping the relationship: SELECT . . . FROM TargetEntity WHERE TargetEntity.SourceOID= InputOID ■ Many-to-many relationship: the predicated is expressed on the SourceOID column of the bridge table representing the relationship; the bridge table is joined with the table representing the unit's target entity as follows: SELECT . . . FROM TargetEntity T JOIN BridgeEntity B ON T. DestOID=B.DestOID WHERE BridgeEntity.SourceOID= InputOID

References

[Abbott83] R.J. Abbot. Program Design by Informal English Description. *Communications of the ACM*. 26(**11**), November 1983, pp. 882–894.

[ACM01] D. Alur, J. Crupi, D. Malks. *Core J2EE Patterns: Best Practices and Design Strategies.* Prentice Hall, 2001.

[ACPT99] P. Atzeni, S. Ceri, S. Paraboschi, R. Torlone. *Database Systems—Concepts, Languages and Architectures.* McGraw-Hill, 1999.

[AMM97] P. Atzeni, G. Mecca, P. Merialdo. To Weave the Web. VLDB 1997, pp. 206–215.

[AMMMS98] P. Atzeni, G. Mecca, P. Merialdo, A. Masci, G. Sindoni. The Araneus Web-Base Management System. SIGMOD Conference 1998, pp. 544–546.

[AMM98a] P. Atzeni, G. Mecca, P. Merialdo. Design and Maintenance of Data-Intensive Web Sites. EDBT 1998, pp. 436–450.

[Bales01] D. Bales. *Java Programming with Oracle JDBC.* O'Reilly & Associates, 2001.

[BC86] J. Biskup, B. Convent. A Formal View Integration Method. SIGMOD conference 1986, pp. 398–407.

[BCN92] C. Batini, S. Ceri, S.B. Navathe. *Conceptual Database Design–An Entity-Relationship Approach.* Benjamin Cummings, 1992.

[BLN86] C. Batini, M. Lenzerini, S.B. Navathe. A Comparative Analysis of Methodologies for Database Schema Integration. *ACM Computing Surveys,* 18(**4**), December 1986, pp. 323–364.

[Bergsten00] H. Bergsten. *Java Server Pages.* O'Reilley, 2000.

[BG96] H. Barnes, M. Gwyer. Designer/2000, Web Enabling Your Applications. Oracle Corporation white paper. March 1996.

[BJR98] G. Booch, I. Jacobson, J. Rumbaugh. *The Unified Modeling Language User Guide.* Addison Wesley (Object Technology Series), 1998.

[BLCLNS94] T. Berners-Lee, R. Cailliau, A. Luotonen, H. Frystyk Nielsen, A. Secret. The World-Wide Web. *Communication of ACM,* 37(**8**), August 1994, pp. 76–82.

[BLN86] C. Batini, M. Lenzerini, S.B. Navathe. A Comparative Analysis of Methodologies for Database Schema Integration. *ACM Computing Surveys,* 18(**4**), April 1986, pp. 323–364.

[BM93] E. Bertino, L. Martino. *Object-Oriented Database Systems: Concepts and Architecture.* Addison Wesley, 1993.

[Boehm88] B. Boehm. A Spiral Model of Software Development and Enhancement. *IEEE Computer,* 21(**5**), May 1988, pp. 61–72.

[Booch94] G. Booch. *Object Oriented Analysis and Design with Applications*. Second Edition. Benjamin Cummings, 1994.

[Bourke01] T. Bourke. *Server Load Balancing* (second edition). O'Reilly & Associates, 2001.

[Brodie81] M.L. Brodie. On Modelling Behavioural Semantics of Databases. VLDB 1981, pp. 32–42.

[BR82] M.L. Brodie, D. Ridjanovic. On the Design and Specification of Database Transactions. Proc. of On Conceptual Modelling (Intervale), 1982, pp. 277–312.

[Brusilovsky02] P. Brusilovsky, M.T. Maybury. From Adaptive Hypermedia to the Adaptive Web. *Communication of ACM,* 45(**5**), May 2002, pp. 30–33.

[BVGM92] A.P. Buchmann, M. Tamer Vzsu, D. Georgakopoulos, F. Manola. A Transaction Model for Active Distributed Object Systems. In [Elmagarmid 92], 1992, pp. 123–158.

[CF97] S. Ceri, P. Fraternali. *Designing Database Applications with Objects and Rules—The IDEA Methodology.* Addison Wesley (Database Systems and Applications Series), 1997.

[CF01] S. Comai, P. Fraternali. A semantic model for specifying hypermedia applications using WebML. Proc. of Int. Semantic Web Workshop, Infrastructure and Applications for the Semantic Web, July 2001, pp. 566–585.

[CFM01] S. Ceri, P. Fraternali, M. Matera. WebML Application Frameworks: A Conceptual Tool for Enhancing Design Reuse. Proc. of WWW10 Int. Workshop Web Engineering, May 2001.

[CFM02] S. Ceri, P. Fraternali, M. Matera. Conceptual Modeling of Data-intensive Web Applications. *IEEE Internet Computing,* 6(**4**), July–August 2002, pp. 20–30.

[CFMM01] S. Ceri, P. Fraternali, M. Matera, A. Maurino. Designing Multi-Role, Collaborative Web Sites with WebML: A Conference Management System Case Study. In [Pastor01], 2001 pp. 130–152.

[CFP99] S. Ceri, P. Fraternali, S. Paraboschi. Design Principles for Data-Intensive Web Sites. *SIGMOD Record,* 28(**1**) March 1999, pp. 84–89.

[Chen76]. P.P. Chen. The Entity-Relationship Model—Toward a Unified View of Data. *ACM TODS,* 1(**1**), March 1976, pp. 9–36.

[CKLMR97] L.S. Colby, A. Kawaguchi, D.F. Lieuwen, I.S. Mumick, K.A. Ross. Supporting Multiple View Maintenance Policies. SIGMOD Conference 1997, pp. 405–416.

[Conallen99] J. Conallen. Modeling Web Application Architectures with UML. *Communications of the ACM,* 42(**10**), October 1999, pp. 63–70.

[Conallen00] J. Conallen. *Building Web Applications with UML.* Addison Wesley (Object Technology Series), 2000.

[CPB80] S. Ceri, G. Pelagatti, G. Bracchi. Integrated Specification of Static and Dynamic Requirements of Database Applications: The Transaction Definition Language. IFIP Congress, October 1980, pp. 499–504.

[CP84] S. Ceri, G. Pelagatti. *Distributed Databases: Principles and Systems.* McGraw-Hill, 1984.

[CW02] T. Clark, J. Warmer (eds). *Object Modeling with the OCL: The Rationale Behind the Object Constraint Language.* Lecture Notes in Computer Science (LNCS) 2263, Springer Verlag, 2002.

[CY90] P. Caod, E. Yourdon. *Object-Oriented Design*. Prentice Hall International, 1990.

[Date95] C. Date. *An Introduction to Database Systems*. Vol. 1, Ed. 6. Addison Wesley, 1995.

[DFAB98] A. Dix, J. Finlay, G. Abowd, R. Beale. *Human-Computer Interaction* (second edition). Prentice Hall, 1998.

[Dickman95] A. Dickman. Two-Tier Versus Three-Tier Apps. *Information Week* 553. November 13, 1995, pp. 74–80.

[DKMRST01] S. Dill, R. Kumar, K. McCurley, S. Rajagopalan, D. Sivakumar, A. Tomkins. Self-similarity in the Web. VLDB, September 2001, pp. 69–78.

[DTL98] O. De Troyer, C.J. Leune. WSDM: A User Centered Design Method for Web Sites. *Computer Networks,* 30(**1-7**), 1998, pp. 85–94.

[Elmagarmid92] A.K. Elmagarmid (Ed.). *Database Transaction Models for Advanced Applications*. Morgan Kaufmann, 1992.

[ELMB92] A.K. Elmagarmid, Y. Leu, J.G. Mullen, O.A. Bukhres. Introduction to Advanced Transaction Models. In [Elmagarmid 92], 1992, pp. 33–52.

[EN94] R. El-Masri, S.B. Navathe. *Fundamentals of Database Systems* (second edition). Benjamin Cummings, 1994.

[EP00] H.E. Eriksson, M. Penker. *Business Modeling with UML—Business Patterns at Work*. John Wiley and Sons, 2000.

[Estefan00] J.A. Estefan. Exploring Open Software Standards for Enterprise e-business Computing. **IBM RedPaper,** REDP0043, August 2000.

[EW95] W.W. Eckerson. Three Tier Client/Server Architecture: Achieving Scalability, Performance, and Efficiency in Client Server Applications. *Open Information Systems,* 10(**1**), January 1995.

[FFKLS98] M.F. Fernandez, D. Florescu, J. Kang, A.Y. Levy, D. Suciu. Overview of Strudel—A Web-Site Management System. *Networking and Information Systems,* 1(**1**), 1998, pp. 115–140.

[FFL98] M.F. Fernandez, D. Florescu, A.Y. Levy, D. Suciu. Catching the Boat with Strudel: Experiences with a Web-Site Management System. SIGMOD Conference 1998, pp. 414–425.

[Fraternali99] P. Fraternali. Tools and Approaches for Developing Data-Intensive Web Applications: A Survey. *ACM Computing Surveys,* 31(**3**), September 1999, pp. 227–263.

[FTM01] M.C. Ferreira De Oliveira, M.A.S. Turine, P.C. Masiero. A Statechart-based Model for Modeling Hypermedia Applications. *ACM TOIS,* 19(**1**), January 2001, pp. 28–52.

[FVYI00] D. Florescu, P. Valduriez, K. Yagoub, V. Issarny. Caching Strategies for Data-intensive Web Sites. VLDB, September 2000, pp. 188–199.

[GBM86] S.J. Greenspan, A. Borgida, J. Mylopoulos. A Requirements Modeling Language and Its Logic. *Information Systems,* 11(**1**), 1986, pp. 9–23.

[GHJV95] E. Gamma, R. Helm, R. Johnson, J. Vlissedes. *Design Patterns—Elements of Reusable Object Oriented Software*. Addison Wesley, 1995.

[GJM96] A. Gupta, H.V. Jagadish, I.S. Mumick. Data Integration Using Self-Maintainable Views. EDBT 1996, pp. 140–144.

[GM01] A. Ginige, S. Murugesan (eds.). Web Engineering. An Introduction. Introduction to the Special Issue "Web Engineering," *IEEE MultiMedia,* vol 8(**1**), January–March 2001, pp. 16–18.

[GMP93] F. Garzotto, L. Mainetti, P. Paolini. HDM2: Extending the E-R Approach to Hypermedia Application Design. ER, December 1993, pp. 178–189.

[GMP95] F. Garzotto, L. Mainetti, P. Paolini. Hypermedia Design, Analysis and Evaluation Issues. *Communications of the ACM,* 38(**8**), August 1995, pp. 74–86.

[GP99] P. Gulutzan, T. Pelzer. *SQL-99 Complete, Really.* R&D Books, 1999.

[GPS91] F. Garzotto, P. Paolini, D. Schwabe. HDM, A Model for the Design of Hypertext Applications. ACM HT, 1991, pp. 313–328.

[GPS93] F. Garzotto, P. Paolini, D. Schwabe. HDM—A Model-based Approach to Hypertext Application Design. *ACM Transactions on Information Systems,* 11(**1**), January 1993, pp. 1–26.

[GR93] J. Gray, A. Reuter. *Transaction Processing: Concepts and Techniques.* Morgan Kaufmann, 1993.

[GVBA99] P.W.P.J. Grefen, J. Vonk, E. Boertjes, P.M.G. Apers. Semantics and Architecture of Global Transaction Support in Workflow Environments. CoopIS, September 1999, pp. 348–359.

[Gwyer96] M. Gwyer. Oracle Designer/2000, WebServer Generator Technical Overview (version 1.3.2). Oracle Corporation Technical Report, September 1996.

[Hall00] M. Hall. *Core Servlets and Java Server Pages.* Sun Microsystems Press/Prentice Hall PTR, May 2000.

[Harold01]. E.R. Harold. *XML Bible.* Hungry Minds Inc., 2001.

[HBR94] L. Hardman, D. Bulterman, G. Van Rossum. The Amsterdam Hypermedia Model: Adding Time and Context to the Dexter Model. *Communications of the ACM* 37(**2**) February 1994, pp. 50–62.

[HIM98] Hyperwave Information Management. Hyperwave User's Guide, Version 4.0. Munich, Germany: Hyperwave Information Management, 1998.

[HH97] M. Hauben, R. Hauben. *Netizens: On the History and Impact of Usenet and the Internet.* IEEE Computer Society, 1997.

[Hoven97] I.V. Hoven, 1997. Deploying Developer/2000 Applications on the Web. Oracle Corporation, White Paper, February 1997.

[HV00] M.J. Hernandez, J.L. Viescas. *SQL Queries for Mere Mortals: A Hands-On Guide to Data Manipulation in SQL.* Addison Wesley, 2000.

[ISB95] T. Isakowitz, E.A. Sthor, P. Balasubranian. RMM: A Methodology for Structured Hypermedia Design. *Communications of the ACM,* 38(**8**), August 1995, pp. 34–44.

[Jacobson94] I. Jacobson. *Object-Oriented Software Engineering: A Use Case Driven Approach.* Addison Wesley, 1994.

[JBR99] I. Jacobson, G. Booch, J. Rumbaugh. *The Unified Software Development Process.* Addison Wesley, 1999.

[Kimball96] R. Kimball. *The Data Warehouse Toolkit.* John Wiley and Sons, 1996.

[KL88] W. Kim, F.H. Lochovsky (eds.) *Object-Oriented Concepts, Databases, and Applications.* ACM Press/Addison Wesley, 1988.

[Kobsa01] A. Kobsa. Generic User Modeling Systems. *User Modeling and User-Adapted Interaction.* Vol. 11, 2001, pp. 49–63.

[Kopparapu02] C. Kopparapu. *Load Balancing Servers, Firewalls, and Caches.* John Wiley and Sons, 2002.

[Kruchten99] P. Kruchten. *The Rational Unified Process: An Introduction.* Addison Wesley, 1999.

[Laurent01] S. St. Laurent. *XML: A Primer.* Hungry Minds Inc., 2001.

[Loomis95] M.E.S. Loomis. *Object Databases: The Essentials.* Addison Wesley, 1995.

[MA01] D.A. Menasce, V.A.F. Almeida. *Scaling for E-Business: Technologies, Models, Performance, and Capacity Planning.* Prentice Hall, 2001.

[MBW80] J. Mylopoulos, P.A. Bernstein, H.K.T. Wong. A Language Facility for Designing Database-Intensive Applications. *Transactions on Database Systems,* 5(**2**), June 1980, pp. 185–207.

[Meyer88] B. Meyer. *Object-Oriented Software Construction.* Prentice Hall International, 1988.

[MR92] H. Mannila, K.J. Räihä. *The Design of Relational Databases.* Addison Wesley, 1992.

[MS01] D. Mack, D. Seven. *Programming Data Driven Web Applications with ASP.NET.* Sams, 2001.

[MSL99] R. Mohan, J. Smith, C. Li. Adapting Multimedia Internet Content for Universal Access. *IEEE Transactions on Multimedia,* 1(**1**), March 1999, pp. 104–114.

[NFS79] E.J. Neuhold, A. Furtado, & C.S. dosSantos. A Data Type Approach to the Entity-Relationship Model. In *The Entity-Relationship Approach to Systems Analysis and Design.* North-Holland, 1979.

[Nielsen93] J. Nielsen. *Usability Engineering.* Academic Press, 1993.

[Nielsen00] J. Nielsen. *Web Usability.* New Riders, 2000.

[NM01] E.J. Naiburg, R.A. Maximchuck. *UML for Database Design.* Addison Wesley (Object Technology Series), 2001.

[OV99] M.T. Özsu, P. Valduriez. *Principles of Distributed Database System* (second edition). Prentice Hall, 1999.

[Pastor01] O. Pastor (ed.). Proc. of the First International Workshop on Web-Oriented Software Technologies (IWWOST'01), June 2001.

[PR97] D. Peppers, M. Rogers. *Enterprise One to One: Tools for Competing in the Interactive Age.* Currency–Doubleday, 1997.

[PRSBHC94] J. Preece, Y. Rogers, H. Sharp, D. Benyon, S. Holland, T. Carey. 1994. *Human-Computer Interaction.* Addison Wesley, 1994.

[Pressman01] R.S. Pressman. What a Tangled Web We Weave. *IEEE Software,* 18(**1**), January–February 2001, pp. 18–21.

[Pressman98] R.S. Pressman. Can Internet-Based Applications Be Engineered? *IEEE Software,* 15(**5**), September–October 1998, pp. 104–110.

[RAJ01] E. Roman, S. Ambler, T. Jewell. *Mastering Enterprise JavaBeans* (Second edition). John Wiley and Sons, 2001.

[RB00] A. Rangone, R. Balocco. A Performance Measurement System for Planning and Controlling a B-to-C E-commerce Strategy. *Electronic Markets,* 10(**2**), May 2000.

[RBPEL91] J. Rumbaugh, M. Blaha, W. Premerlani, F. Eddy, W. Lorenson. *Object-Oriented Modeling and Design*. Prentice Hall, 1991.

[RHDS99] F. Reynolds, J. Hjelm, S. Dawkins, S. Singhal. Composite Capability/Preference Profiles (CC/PP): A User Side Framework for Content Negotiation. *W3C Note,* 1999.

[RS95] A. Reuter, F. Schwenkreis. ConTracts—A Low-Level Mechanism for Building General-Purpose Workflow Management Systems. *Data Engineering Bulletin,* 18(**1**), March 1995, pp. 4–10.

[RS02] M. Rabinovich, O. Spatscheck. *Web Caching and Replication*. Addison Wesley, 2002.

[Sano96] D. Sano. *Designing Large Scale Web Sites: A Visual Design Methodology*. John Wiley and Sons, 1996.

[SF89] P. Stotts, R. Furuta. Petri-Net-Based Hypertext: Document Structure with Browsing Semantics. ACM *TOIS,* 7(**1**), January 1989, pp. 3–29.

[Shackel91] B. Shackel. Usability—Context, Framework, Definition, Design and Evaluation. In *Human Factors for Informatics Usability,* B. Shackel and S. Richardson (eds.) Cambridge University Press, 1991, pp. 21–38.

[Shasha92] D. Shasha. *Database Tuning: A Principled Approach*. Prentice Hall, 1992.

[SM88] S. Schlaer, S. Mellor. *Object Oriented System Analysis: Modeling the World in Data*. Yourdon Press, 1988.

[SR95] D. Schwabe, G. Rossi. The Object-Oriented Hypermedia Design Model. *Communication of ACM,* 38(**8**), August 1995, pp. 45–46.

[SSW80] P. Scheuermann, G. Schiffner, H. Weber. *Abstraction Capabilities and Invariant Properties Modeling within the Entity-Relationship Approach*. North-Holland Publishing Company, 1980, pp. 121–140.

[SWJ98] G. Schneider, J.P. Winters, I. Jacobson. *Applying Use Cases: A Practical Guide*. Addison Wesley, 1998.

[Tanenbaum96] A.S. Tanenbaum. *Computer Networks*. Prentice Hall, 1996.

[Timmers99] P. Timmers. *Electronic Commerce: Strategies and Models for Business-to-Business Trading*. John Wiley and Sons, 1999.

[Ullman88] J. Ullman. *Principles of Database and Knowledge-Base Systems*. Vols. 1–2, Computer Science Press, 1988.

[UnwiredPlanet97] Unwired Planet Inc. Handheld Device Markup Language (HDML) Specification, April 1997.

[Uusitalo99] M.K. Uusitalo. Specification of Tools User Interface. Technical report, W3I3 Esprit Project n. 28771, February 1999.

[VT02] M. Van Steen, A.S. Tanenbaum. *Distributed Systems: Principles and Paradigms*. Prentice Hall, 2002.

[WebEng00] S. Murugesan, Y. Deshpande (eds.), Web Engineering, Software Engineering and Web Application Development. LNCS 2016, Springer Verlag, 2001.

[WebEng98] Proc. First Int'l Workshop on Web Engineering (WWW7 Conf.), Univ. of Western Sydney, Australia, April 1998, *fistserv.macarthur.uws.edu.au/san/WebE98*.

[WebEng99] Proc. Second Int'l Workshop on Web Engineering (WWW8 Conf.), Univ. of Wollongong, Wollongong, Australia, May 1999, *budhi.uow.edu.au/web-engineering99/web_engineering.html*.

[Wessel01] D. Wessels. *Web Caching.* O'Reilly & Associates (Internet Series), 2001.

[WFCHH99] S. White, M. Fisher, R. Cattell, G. Hamilton, M. Hapner. *JDBCTM API Tutorial and Reference (second edition) Universal Data Access for the Java 2 Platform.* Addison Wesley, 1999.

[WR92] H. Wachter, A. Reuter. The ConTract Model. In [Elmagarmid92], 1992, pp. 219–263.

[WS92] G. Weikum, H. Schek. Concepts and Applications of Multilevel Transactions and Open Nested Transactions. In [Elmagarmid92], 1992, pp. 515–553.

[ZP92] Y. Zheng, M. Pong. Using Statecharts to Model Hypertext. *ECHT*, December 1992, pp. 242–250.

Online References

[Allaire] Allaire Inc. Cold Fusion. *www.allaire.com/products/ColdFusion*

[Apache] Apache. Cocoon. *xml.apache.org/cocoon/*

[ASPNG] C. Carroll. ASP.net Tutorials. *www.aspng.com*

[ASC] Ascential DataStage XE. *www.ascentialsoftware.com*

[ATG] Art Technology Group. Dynamo. *www.atg.com*

[BLFF] T. Berners-Lee, R. Fielding, H. Frystyk. Request for Comment 1945: Hypertext Transfer Protocol—HTTP1.0. *www.ietf.org/rfc/rfc1945.txt*

[BLC] T. Berners-Lee, D. Connolly. Hypertext Markup Language—2.0, September 1995, MIT/W3C. *www.w3.org/MarkUp/html-spec/html-spec_toc.html*

[Bluestone] BlueStone. Sapphire/Web. *www.bluestone.com*

[BroadVision] BroadVision. One-to-One. *www.broadvision.com/*

[CGI] CGI. *hoohoo.ncsa.uiuc.edu/cgi/*

[CodeCharge] CodeCharge. *www.codecharge.com*

[Davis] M. Davis. Struts, an open-source MVC implementation. February 2001. *www-106.ibm.com/developerworks/library/j-struts/?n-j-2151*

[Engage] Engage. ProfileServer. *www.engage.com/*

[Fusion] NetObjects Inc. Fusion. *www.netobjects.com/html/nof.html*

[Hppm] HP Process Manager. White paper. *www.hp.com/go/hpprocessmanager*

[IETF] Internet Engineering Task Force home page. *www.ietf.org*

[ILux] iLux. Suite 2000. *www.ilux.com/*

[InterDev] Microsoft. Visual InterDev. *www.microsoft.com/vinterdev*

[JavasoftA] JavaApplets. *www.javasoft.com/applets/index.html*

[JavasoftB] JDBC. *www.javasoft.com/products/jdbc/index.html*

[Kassem01] N. Kassem, Enterprise Team. *Designing Enterprise Applications with the Java 2 Platform, Enterprise Edition* (second edition). Sun BluePrints, 2001. *java.sun.com/blueprints/ guidelines/designing_enterprise_applications/*

[LCC] B.M. Leiner, V.G. Cerf, D.D. Clark, R.E. Kahn, L. Kleinrock, D.C. Lynch, J. Postel, L.G. Roberts, S. Wolff. A Brief History of the Internet. *www.isoc.org/internet-history/brief.html*

[Microsofta] Microsoft. ASP. *msdn.microsoft.com/workshop/server/asp/asptutorial.asp*

[Microsoftb] Microsoft. ASP and IIS. *www.microsoft.com/iis/LearnAboutIIS/ActiveSevers/default.asp*

[Microsoftc] Microsoft. ActiveX. *www.microsoft.com/workshop/components*

[Microsoftd] Microsoft. VBScript & JScript. *www.microsoft.com/workshop/languages*

[Microsofte] Microsoft. Data Transformation Service in SQL Server 2000. msdn. *microsoft.com*

[OpenMarket] Divine Open Market. *www.openmarket.com/*

[Oraclea] Oracle Corporation. Designer 2000. *www.oracle.com/products/tools/des2k/collateral/wwwgen.pdf*

[Oracleb] Oracle Corporation. Developer 2000. *www.oracle.com/products/tools/dev2k/index.html*

[Oraclec] Oracle Corporation. Oracle9i Designer: Technical Overview. *www.oracle.com*

[Rugget] D. Rugget. HTML 3.2 Reference Specification, W3C Recommendation 14-Jan-1997. *www.w3.org/TR/REC-html32.html*

[Schussel] G. Schussel. Client/Server: Past, Present, and Future. *news.dci.com/geos/dbsejava.htm*

[Sun] Sun Microsystems. Java 2 Enterprise Edition. *java.sun.com/j2ee/*

[Suna] Sun Microsystems. JSP. *java.sun.com/products/jsp/index.html*

[Sunb] Sun Microsystems Java Servlet. *java.sun.com/products/servlet/index.html*

[SyBase] SyBase. PowerDesigner. *www.sybase.com/products/enterprisemodeling/powerdesigner*

[Terminals]. @Terminals. *www.esi.es/@Terminals*

[W3C] WWW Consortium home page. *www.w3.org*

[W3Ca] HTML 4.0 Specification, W3C Recommendation 24-Apr-1998. *www.w3.org/TR/REC-html40/*

[W3Cb] D. Raggett. Adding a touch of style, 1998. *www.w3.org/MarkUp/Guide/style.html*

[W3Cc] Extensible Markup Language (XML) 1.0 Specification, W3C Recommendation, October 2000. *www.w3.org/TR/REC-xml.html*

[W3Cd] Extensible Style Language (XSL). *www.w3.org/TR/1998/WD-xsl*

[W3Ce] HTTP1.1. Internet Draft <draft-ietf-http-v11-spec-rev-06> (November, 1998). *www.w3.org/Protocols/History.html#HTTP11*

[W3Cf] A Little History of the World Wide Web. *www.w3.org/History.html*

[W3S] W3 Schools HTML tutorial. *www.w3schools.com/html/default.asp*

[WDG] Web Design Group. HTML 4.0 Reference Manual. *www.htmlhelp.com/reference/html40/*

[WebRatio] WebRatio Site Development Studio. *www.webratio.com*

[WWW02] The Eleventh International World Wide Web Conference. *www2002.org*

[XML] XML. *www.xml.com*

Index

About the Authors

Stefano Ceri is full professor of Database Systems at the Politecnico di Milano; he was visiting professor in the computer science department at Stanford University from 1983 to 1990. His research interests are focused on extending database technology to incorporate data distribution, deductive and active rules, and object-orientation, and on semantic models and design methods for data-intensive Web sites. He is a member of the VLDB Endowment and of the EDBT Foundation. He was associate editor of ACM-Transactions on Database Systems and is currently an associate editor of several international journals, including *IEEE-Transactions on Software Engineering.* He is the author of numerous articles in international journals and conference proceedings, and is also the author of several books in English, including introductory-level textbooks on general computer science and database systems, as well as research-oriented books on distributed databases, logic programming and databases, conceptual database design, and active databases. He won the VLDB Ten Years Award in 2000 (VLDB in Cairo) and was the Coordinating Program Chair of VLDB 2001 in Rome.

Piero Fraternali is full professor of software engineering at the Politecnico di Milano. His research interests are focused on active rules, object-orientation, design methods for data-intensive Web sites, CASE tools for automatic Web site production, and wireless applications. He is the author of numerous articles in international journals and conference proceedings, and is also the author, with Stefano Ceri, of the book *Designing Database Applications with Objects and Rules: The IDEA Methodology* (Addison Wesley, 1997). He was the technical manager of the W3I3 Project: "Web-Based Intelligent Information Infrastructures" (1998–2000).

Aldo Bongio graduated from the Politecnico di Milano in 1999. His research interests include XML, Web modeling languages, and Web design patterns. He is the chief architect of WebRatio Site Development Studio.

Marco Brambilla graduated from the Politecnico di Milano in 2001 and is presently working on a Ph.D. in Computer and Automation Engineering at the Politecnico di Milano. His research interests include Web modeling methodologies, Web design patterns, and conceptual design of data-intensive Web applications. He has collaborated as an application analyst in several industrial projects with the WebRatio team.

Sara Comai has a Ph.D. in Computer and Automation Engineering and is currently an assistant professor in the dipartimento di elettronica e informazione at the Politecnico di Milano, where she teaches computer graphics (multimedia applications) and computer science fundamentals. Her main research interests include active databases, graphical languages for querying and restructuring XML and semi-structured data, and semantic models for data-intensive Web sites.

Maristella Matera has a Ph.D. in Computer and Automation Engineering and is currently assistant professor in the dipartimento di elettronica e informazione at the Politecnico di Milano, where she teaches databases and computer science fundamentals. She has been awarded several fellowships supporting her research work at Italian and foreign institutions; in particular, she has been visiting researcher at the Graphics, Visualization, and Usability Center at the Georgia Institute of Technology, Atlanta. Her research interests span design methods for Web and hypermedia applications, Web and hypermedia usability, and formal specification of interactive systems.